Cannibal Modernities

New World Studies

A. James Arnold, *Editor*

J. Michael Dash, David T. Haberly,
and Roberto Márquez,
Associate Editors

Antonio Benítez-Rojo, Joan Dayan,
Dell H. Hymes, Vera M. Kutzinski,
Candace Slater, and Iris M. Zavala,
Advisory Editors

Cannibal Modernities

POSTCOLONIALITY AND
THE AVANT-GARDE IN CARIBBEAN
AND BRAZILIAN LITERATURE

Luís Madureira

New World Studies

A. James Arnold, editor

University of Virginia Press
Charlottesville and London

University of Virginia Press
© 2005 by the Rector and Visitors of the University of Virginia
All rights reserved
Printed in the United States of America on acid-free paper
First published 2005

9 8 7 6 5 4 3 2 1

Library of Congress Cataloging-in-Publication Data

Madureira, Luís, 1960–
  Cannibal modernities : postcoloniality and the avant-garde in Caribbean and Brazilian literature / Luís Madureira.
      p.   cm. — (New World studies)
  Includes bibliographical references and index.
  ISBN 0-8139-2375-1 (cloth : alk. paper) — ISBN 0-8139-2376-X (pbk. : alk. paper)
  1. Caribbean literature—20th century—History and criticism. 2. Brazilian literature—20th century—History and criticism. I. Title. II. Series.
PN849.C3M333 2005
860.09'98—dc22

2005007876

Ao Luiz e à Francelina, a quem devo tudo o que hoje sou

Contents

Acknowledgments — ix

Introduction — 1

1 Lapses in Taste: *Antropofagia* as the Primitive Aesthetic of Underdeveloped Brazil — 21

2 In the Land of the Great Serpent: The Poetics of National Development and the Sublime Topography of the Amazon — 52

3 God in the Machine: Primitivism, National Identity, and the Question of Technology in Mário de Andrade's *Macunaíma* — 86

4 Cannibal Allegories: Cinema Novo and the "Myth" of Popular Cinema — 111

5 The Shadow Cast by the Enlightenment: The Haitian Revolution and the Naming of Modernity's Other — 131

6 The Marvelous Royalty of Henri Christophe's Kingdom: Cultural Difference and the Temporality of Underdevelopment — 164

7 "Something New in a Decaying World": Alejo Carpentier's
El siglo de las luces, or, The Signs of Progress on the
Margins of History 192

Conclusion 214

Notes 217

Bibliography 233

Index 249

Acknowledgments

THIS STUDY has been a long time in the making. Lengthy as it surely is in its current form, it was actually nearly twice as long in its initial iteration. In the course of about six years, what began as a single and, to my mind, flawed work was slowly and painstakingly transformed into two separate book manuscripts. This protracted task entailed not so much a revision as a radical reworking of the original, a process that has followed, like a persistent shadow, some of the most crucial and trying phases of my recent personal and professional life. The debts of gratitude I have accumulated in the process are therefore considerable.

I am grateful, first of all, to the generosity and intellectual support of my colleagues at the University of Wisconsin–Madison and my teachers at the University of California at San Diego. I will never forget and will never be able adequately to repay the debt I owe Carlos Blanco-Aguinaga, Jaime Concha, Masao Miyioshi, Lisa Lowe, Robert Cancel, Rosaura Sánchez, Richard Terdiman, Don Wayne, Andrew Wright, William Tay, Jean-Luc Nancy, and so many others at UCSD for their mentorship and inspiration. Severino de Albuquerque provided me with invaluable intellectual assistance and, above all, the gift of his friendship during the crucial incubation stages and throughout the writing of this work. Jane Tylus and my friend Jan Plug never stopped believing in me and in the promise of my work. Jan invariably succeeded in delivering exactly the sheltering word I needed in order to persevere with this project. To them I am deeply grateful. My friend Joseba Gabilondo always challenged me intellectually and aided me both in formulating and refining the core ideas expressed here. Much of this project began taking shape in classroom dialogue. My graduate and undergraduate students at the University of Wisconsin have continually assisted me both as sounding boards and spirited interlocutors. To them and many others who must regrettably remain unnamed this book owes whatever virtues it possesses. Its flaws, to repeat the hackneyed truism, are of course attributable solely to its author.

The University of Wisconsin's Graduate School partly supported research for this project with summer stipends and a sabbatical leave. My thanks to everyone at the University of Virginia Press who helped bring this book to light, in particular Cathie Brettschneider, for her assistance and guidance as well as her patience during the acquisitions process. K. David Jackson and the other "unknown" reader provided crucial and insightful commentary on the manuscript. And Jane Curran was an expert and thoughtful editor. Finally, I would not have been able to complete this project were it not for the support and encouragement of my family, especially my parents, Luiz and Francelina, and my peerless and beloved sisters Paula, Isabel, and Emilia. I have been fortunate as well to enjoy the love and support of my wife Sarah and my stepchildren Jasmina and Michael.

Chapter 1 appears in slightly different form in *Luso-Brazilian Review* 42 (1) 2005, and is included here by kind permission of the University of Wisconsin Press. Portions of chapters 3 and 4 appeared in abridged form in *Cannibalism, Colonialism and the Colonial World,* edited by Frances Barker, Peter Hulme, and Margaret Iverson (Cambridge University Press, 1998) and are reprinted here by permission of Cambridge University Press.

Cannibal Modernities

Introduction

> Apart from a few professors of philosophy, who receive a salary for it, there is only one type of person who really knows in its entirety the literature of Europe: the colonial.
> —Roberto Fernández Retámar, *Calibán*

> God knows the strength of an adjective, above all in young, hot countries.
> —Machado de Assis, *Posthumous Memoirs of Brás Cubas*

> I am only interested in what is not mine.
> —Oswald de Andrade, "Manifesto antropófago"

IN "Signature Event Context," Jacques Derrida makes several important claims about the theoretical insufficiency of the received idea of context whose consequences for the study of New World literatures and cultures are both provocative and far-reaching (307–30). The core argument of Derrida's seminal essay provides the point of departure for the present study. The latter's title, *Cannibal Modernities,* seeks precisely to call attention to the varied and complex implications that Derrida's revised notion of context has for a full-fledged analysis of the problem of origins and originality in the "peripheral" modernisms I am examining. The starting place for my inquiry is therefore the proposition that early-twentieth-century Caribbean and Latin American literary and cultural production, while replicating some of western modernity's central plotlines, ends up displacing, if not overturning, this now commonplace narrative. In this specific sense, then, my thesis arises out of Derrida's assertion that "a context is never absolutely determinable" (310). If, as the French critic proposes, every sign "carries with it a force of breaking with its context" (317); if every utterance is marked by this structural possibility of severing itself from its context, and thus repeating or resignifying itself "in the absence not only of its referent . . . but of a determined signified or current intention of signification" (318), then the presuppositions underwriting a number of influential readings of nonwestern modernisms ought to be submitted to a thoroughgoing reevaluation.

We would need to put to question, for instance, the wonted and virtually paradigmatic readings of New World avant-garde movements in terms of what Julio Ramos has called "the unequal modernization [*modernización desigual*] of Latin American literature at the time of its emergence" (*Desencuentros de la modernidad* 12). In a broader sense, we should query Marshall Berman's suggestion that "the anguish of backwardness and underdevelopment," which supposedly marked nineteenth- and early-twentieth-century Russian politics and culture, represents "an archetype of the emerging 20th-century Third World" (*All That Is Solid* 175). It would behoove us as well to interrogate Perry Anderson's affirmation that political and economic conditions in the "Third World" amount to "a kind of shadow configuration of what once prevailed in the first" ("Modernity and Revolution" 329). It is the conceptual order that governs this "hierarchical" temporality that I attempt to displace by sketching out, within "peripheral" retellings of the *grand récit* of modernity, a modality of repeating "that which does not repeat itself . . . the repetition of difference" (Derrida, *Writing and Difference* 250).

In this particular respect, my central argument follows Homi Bhabha's suggestion that we regard "ex-centric" reiterations of discourses of modernity precisely in a performative light: "each repetition of the sign of modernity is different, specific to its historical and cultural conditions of enunciation" (*Location of Culture* 247). For anyone even partially acquainted with the debates around Latin American imitations of hegemonic cultural models, Bhabha's contention should have a familiar ring. The putatively differential relationship between Latin American cultural production and metropolitan "originals" has figured at the center of its discourses on culture at least since Cuban anthropologist Fernando Ortiz coined the term *transculturación* (in 1947) to account for what Angel Rama, in his own formulation of the concept, designates as the capacity of New World cultures to appropriate in creative and original ways borrowed or inherited "traditions" and cultural practices. Indeed, Antonio Benítez Rojo, in a recent and important theoretical work on the Caribbean (*La isla que se repite*), stresses that the word *repeat* (*repite*)—within a context of cultural diversity and indeterminacy—ought to be grasped exactly in "the somewhat paradoxical sense" that every repetition necessarily entails a difference (iv).

As Fernando Ortiz famously defines it, "transculturation"—a notion that he regards as "indispensable to the understanding of the whole of

America"—means that alongside inevitable processes of deracination and destruction occurs "the creation of new cultural phenomena" (*Contrapunteo cubano* 260). Likewise, for Rama, transculturation constitutes a "force" (or "creative energy") that acts as much "upon [Latin America's] particular legacy" as "upon contributions from abroad," hence rendering contemporary Latin American culture crucially "distinct from a mere aggregate of [imported] norms, forms of behavior, beliefs and cultural objects" (*Transculturación narrativa* 34). Transculturation, in short, is the ability to translate "imitation" into "cultural authenticity" (*La crítica de la cultura* 93).

Clearly, what defines this fundamental concept is the drive to shift the dominant perspective on "the cultural exchange process between the metropolis and the periphery" by proposing to view it from the subordinate's standpoint (Alonso, *Burden of Modernity* 28). The same desire continues to characterize recent critical appraisals of Latin American variations on the prevalent theme of modernity. Alfonso de Toro, for instance, points to the specific case of Jorge Luis Borges to reach a familiar general conclusion. According to Toro, then, Borges was among the first Latin American writers to have shown "the way to follow" by producing texts that provide "an exemplary definition" of postcoloniality, that is, "an appropriation of the discourses of the center which are introduced in a recodified form through inclusion in a new context and historical paradigm" ("Epistemological Foundations" 47, 36). In a similar fashion, Carlos Rincón identifies "what is different in Borges's fiction [as] a historical (and political) dimension that goes beyond the strategies of the modern: the fact that the primacy of the original and the hierarchy of metropolis and periphery, model and copy, have been overcome" ("Peripheral Center of Postmodernism" 229). My aim in the chapters that follow is, in large measure, to persevere in the revisionist spirit sketched out here. In my own analyses of what García Canclini describes as "the utopian reflections and . . . practices of [early twentieth-century Brazilian] artists and intellectuals" in the first three chapters of the book, I therefore seek to ascertain the extent to which the former adumbrate the processes of "decollecting, deterritorialization, and hybridity" that the Argentinian sociologist associates with the postmodern epoch (*Hybrid Cultures* 243).

By the same token, my inquiry into early twentieth-century Caribbean representations of the Haitian Revolution in the last three chapters is informed by Paul Gilroy's conception of a diasporic or "non-traditional" (*Black Atlantic*) culture (defined by rhizomorphism or routedness rather than rootedness). My theoretical orientation thus accords to a substantial degree with Gilroy's own counter-hegemonic critical project: "the inversion of the relationship between margin and centre as it has appeared within the master discourses of the master race" (45), with his effort to reconstruct "the primal history of modernity . . . from the slaves' point of view" (55). Equally crucial to my reading of Caribbean literature is Édouard Glissant's notion of Diversity (le Divers), the effort toward "a cross-cultural relationship [*une relation transversale*], without universalist transcendence" (*Caribbean Discourse* 98). This idea of cultural "transversality" subtends what Glissant calls "the implosion [*l'irruption à elle-même*] of Caribbean history," a "subterranean convergence" of historical itineraries that "has roared around the rim of the Caribbean" and that ultimately does away with (*nous débarasse de*) "the linear, hierarchical vision of a single History that would run its unique course" (66). More recently, Glissant has proposed the experience and "thought" of Relation as one that defines not only Antillean culture but that "holds true, in many different ways, throughout the Americas" (*Poetics of Relation* 34). By "Relation" Glissant means "a mode of [cultural] encounter and connivance . . . linked not to a creation of the world but to the conscious and contradictory experience of contacts among cultures . . . a new and original dimension allowing each person to be there and elsewhere, rooted and open . . . in harmony and errantry" (33, 144, 34). It is to this sense of cultural and linguistic relatedness and heterogeneity that I seek to attend in my own readings of Caribbean modernisms.

At the same time, however, I am reluctant to affirm, as does J. Michael Dash, that "elements of the postmodern have been apparent from the earliest stages of the Caribbean's 'lived modernity'" (*Other America* 19). I also hesitate to go along with Nelly Richard's proposition that postmodernist reassessments of the relationship between copy and original enable not only a radical inversion of conventional definitions of Latin America as "dependent and imitative" but that they allow us to posit it as a "precursor of the postmodernist simulacrum." For Richard, in effect, Latin American culture "reverses the first World hierarchy of the model of imitation" for "the copy is now the adulterated hypothesis that the periphery theatricalizes in order to ridicule the dominant European belief in the integrity of the model" ("Cultural Peripheries" 220). Nor would I necessarily concur with Daniel Castillo-Durante's proposition that "Brazilian Modernism appears as a movement in cultural criticism, the first in Latin America, oriented to a 'deconstruction' *avant la lettre* both of the centre's hegemonic cultural tendencies and the politics of marginalization derived from its canons" ("From Postmodernity" 66). As Carlos Alonso shrewdly notes, the structural requirement for such instantiations of a "peripheral" yet premonitory postmodern configuration is that modernity in Latin America be always and inevitably registered and experienced in degraded and inchoate form.

As Alonso suggests, to reinterpret this purported insufficiency or "dependency" as an ironic rejection of absolutist paradigms of western knowledge is to engage in a rhetoric of "lack and compensation," since this interpretation has the attractiveness of turning into a virtue what was previously a defect (*Burden of Modernity* 154–55). As my prefatory remarks on the contingency of context should indicate, my own approach is incompatible with Alonso's call (which he advances as an alternative to such compensatory readings) for a reconsideration of Latin American modernity in terms of an "adequation" or "organic" link between its discourses and the historical circumstances in which they are produced. I agree nevertheless with his earlier and seemingly paradoxical suggestion that New World attempts to undermine the authority of adopted European models, which characterize the concept of transculturation, for example, fail to reckon with "the plurivocal, self-contradictory, and open-ended dimension of metropolitan discourse" (28).

As Glissant appositely observes, these "counter-discursive" strategies neglect to take into account the fact that "the West is not monolithic," and that invariably it has "itself produced the variables to contradict its impressive trajectory" (*Poetics of Relation* 191). In my endeavor to trace the complex and contradictory entanglement between metropolitan and American modernities, I have thus sought to pay particular heed to this heteroglossic dimension of metropolitan discourses. If this desire at times leads me close to betraying what Fernández Retámar regards as the colonial's characteristic compensatory desire to flaunt his familiarity with the "literature" of Europe, I hope that my sustained engagement with these magisterial European texts will be understood primarily as an effort to undo their alleged cohesion, consistency, and authority.

Although I am certainly not proposing that Brazilian and Caribbean modernisms prefigure the plurivocity and indeterminacy that putatively define the postmodern epoch, I would insist nevertheless that to argue that they are "centered on an organicist dream of the union between man and nature—an 'existentialist' bonding . . . that [is] monologic, lyrical, and [celebrates] the primacy of the transcendental subject" (Dash, *Other America* 61) is to read perhaps too hastily. I should like to suggest instead that the relation between Aimé Césaire's radical poetics from the 1930s and Walcott's recent poetic production, for instance, is underwritten not by an "epistemological break" (99) but by a latticework of uneven and subtle continuities. Only by deliberately slowing down the pace of our reading, I would contend, can we forestall the admittedly seductive conclusion that writers like Walcott and Glissant evince "a decisive break with the preoccupation with *enracinement,* filiation, and a foundational poetics that have dominated Caribbean thought for the better part of this century," that they have achieved this salutary rupture precisely because they have moved "away from the temptation of new beginnings, of pastoral plenitude" allegedly imbuing Césairean poetics (99), and because they have thus come to recognize the Caribbean "experience [as a] complex and relational" one (151).

By contrast, in my view, the rapport between modernist and postmodernist poetics, rather than being marked by a radical discontinuity, might instead reveal the kind of perplexity that Roberto Schwartz identifies in the narrative discourse of Machado de Assis. If one proposes the vision of the Caribbean as "threshold—as liminal space, the confluence of innumerable conjunctions and disjunctions" (*Other America* 163) as the correlate to "the historical position of reason" in late-nineteenth-century Brazil, then this vision of the Caribbean could likewise be "seen simultaneously as having been overtaken and as not yet having been reached" (Schwarz, *Master on the Periphery* 24) in the early-twentieth-century Caribbean avant-garde, for instance. To the two alternatives supposedly confronting the critic of peripheral modernisms—on the one hand to read them as either degraded or disruptive parodies of the metropolitan original, on the other hand to reconsider their status as "proper" to their own cultural and geographical locations—one should therefore add a third and arguably aporetic one. From this indeterminate position, those contextual and conjunctural elements that, "in their obvious aspect," we ought to define as "backward" could be grasped in a more disturbing light, that is, in terms of their "affinity" with tendencies that are just beginning to emerge in the "center" and have yet to manifest themselves in the "periphery" (123). To reread the center-periphery disjunction in this new "dialectical" sense is also perhaps to gauge the critical potential that "peripheral modernisms" may contain. Thus, while it is true, for example, that the *négritude* discourses I examine in chapter 5 militate for the entrance into History (the same History that Glissant regards as defined by a "linear, hierarchical vision" [*Caribbean Discourse* 66]) of the peoples once deemed to be without history, it is crucial to adduce, I argue, that their emergent and discontinuous sense of historical becoming already begins to undo this universalizing and homogenizing conception of history.

Broadly speaking, then, my critical objective approximates what Gayatri Spivak, alluding to the Derridean essay I reference above, provisionally designates "postcoloniality as agency": the possibility of indicating "that the alternative to Europe's long story—generally translated as 'great narratives'—is not only short tales (*petits récits*) but tampering with the authority of storylines. In all beginning, repetition, signature" (*Outside in the Teaching Machine* 65). Acknowledging that both my own critical enterprise and the body of texts under study here are inevitably determined by "the magisterial texts" of the western philosophical tradition, I endeavor likewise to ascertain whether these very texts can now be turned into "our servants, as the new magisterium constructs itself in the name of the Other" (Spivak, *Critique of Postcolonial Reason* 7). To a certain extent, therefore, this book exemplifies the general tendency in postcolonial criticism to "provincialize the west."[1] One of the key additions it brings to this familiar project, however, is a sustained investigation of the Brazilian experiences of "postcoloniality," which, along with those of Latin America as a whole, still remain largely unconsidered in postcolonial studies. I have a bit more to say about my particular "supplementation" to this critical field below. Nonetheless, before turning to a description of the book's contents, I should like to look more closely into both the critical trend it purports to represent as well as some of its more powerful critiques.

A little more than a decade ago, Fredric Jameson suggested that many of the critical interrogations of hegemonic and homogenizing constructions of identity, and the concomitant linkage of enunciations of "cultural difference" with practices of resistance, amount to little more than "liberal tolerance, a position ... which at least has the merit of raising the embarrassing historical question of whether the tolerance of difference, as a social fact, is not the result of social homogenization and standardization and the obliteration of genuine social difference in the first place" (*Postmodernism* 341). Jameson's better-known intervention into what was then a still emerging field is, of course, his notion of third-world narrative fiction as "national allegories." In a scathing retort to Jameson's 1986 essay, Aijaz Ahmad takes the Marxist critic to task for encapsulating the "experience" of the "third world" within Hegel's master-slave allegory (*In Theory* 109). Jameson's main point, however, is not to ascribe to the literary production of the "third world" a cultural "backwardness" that supposedly echoes the west's outmoded stages. His conclusion is rather the opposite. Just as for Hegel the slave's situation constitutes "the beginning of wisdom," so does Jameson's third-world novelist supercede the "epistemologically crippling" view of the "masters of the world" (that is, their inability to grasp "the social totality") ("Third World Literature" 85–86). By virtue of her subordinate place in the world system, the third-world writer is thus able to narrate a collective story that appears both to adumbrate and antecede the "aesthetic of cognitive mapping" that Jameson will later propose as "a pedagogic political culture" aimed at endowing the postmodern "individual subject with some new heightened sense of its place in the global system" (*Postmodernism* 54). It is exactly the ability to chart its position in this new global space that, according to Jameson, the postmodern subject "constitutively" lacks.

The same inability, Jameson argues, is registered in poststructuralist theoretical approaches that ultimately "can yield no experimental information as to the shape of the [global] system and its boundaries, the specific social and historical fashion in which an outside is unattainable and we are turned back in on ourselves" (*Postmodernism* 208–9). Elsewhere, Jameson asserts that the "loss of history" is one of the major symptoms of the postmodern condition, not the disappearance of images of history, but rather the cultural production of "simulacra, and pastiches of the past [that] are effectively a way of satisfying a chemical craving for historicity, using a product that substitutes for and blocks it" (Stephanson, "Regarding Postmodernism" 18).

It is to the status of an ideological substitution that Arlif Dirlik reduces postcolonial criticism as well ("Postcolonial Aura" 328–56). What the latter fails to do, Dirlik declares, is exactly "to retain a sense of structure and totality in the confrontation of fragmentation and locality, the alternative to which may be complicity in the consolidation of hegemony in the very process of questioning it" (347–48). Not only does its privileging of heterogeneity fail to come to grips with the globalization crisis, Dirlik continues, but it may in effect turn out to be a "superstructural" expression of the current stage of capitalist expansion (353).

The Marxist critique of the postcolonial imperative to shift beyond "a profoundly parochial" celebration of the collapse of "the 'grand narratives' of postenlightenment rationalism" (Bhabha, *Location of Culture* 4) seems at once uncompromising and stark.[2] In accordance with this postcolonial ethic, the "space clearing gesture" signified by the prefix post (Appiah, *In My Father's House* 145) can "only embody [the latter's] restless and revisionary energy if [it] transforms the present into an expanded and ex-centric site of experience," if it is tempered by "the awareness that the epistemological 'limits' of those ethnocentric ideas are also the enunciative boundaries of a range of other dissonant, even dissident histories and voices" (Bhabha, *Location of Culture* 4–5). In other (perhaps overly reductive) terms, the metanarrative about the end of metanarratives ought to be recognized as the condition of possibility for the presencing of multiple narratives of postcolonial emancipation. On the other hand, Marxist theoretical models call for critical vigilance before this turn to the different and heterogeneous, precisely in light of capitalism's capacity to reconfigure the local in global terms, to incorporate, disassemble, and remake different cultures "in accordance with the requirements of production and consumption" (Dirlik, "Postcolonial Aura" 351). Whereas theories of postcoloniality posit local sites of resistance as broaching the possibility of new forms of agency, the more systematic of the "globalizing" approaches seek "to collect these isolated concepts, [and] articulate them.... drawing the logically necessary conclusions" (Larsen, "Postmodernism" 134).

This confrontation between what are essentially two incompatible formulations of historical agency thus assumes the character of an aporia: on one side an interrogation of "the onto-theo- but also archeo-teleological concept of history.... Not in order to oppose it with an end of history or antihistoricity, but, on the contrary, in order to show that this onto-theo-archeo-teleology locks up, and finally cancels historicity, [in order] to open up access to an affirmative thinking of the messianic and emancipatory as promise: as promise and not as onto-theological or teleo-eschatological program or design" (Derrida, *Specters of Marx* 74–75). On the other side lies a designation of this kind of deconstructive procedure (or political "practice," as Homi Bhabha, for example, will insist on calling it) as no more than "a politics of spontaneity and myth.... the tacit abandonment of conscious and scientific revolutionary strategy and organization" (Larsen, "Postmodernism" 129). The former puts into question the very speculative and universalizing operations to which the latter has recourse as both the ground and the telos of any thorough understanding and transformation of the world in which we live. Jameson's proposed resolution of this theoretical dilemma provides a keen sense of the incommensurability between these two theoretical approaches, for the sublatory move he advocates belongs exactly to the conceptual order that "postcoloniality" endeavors to overturn.

In the conclusion to his book on postmodernism, Jameson argues that the ideological supremacy of the postmodern aesthetic of information over "classical" ideology resides in its capacity to organize reality "schizophrenically," that is, to defuse knowledges and information "which can only be activated locally or contextually ('nominalistically') in distinct moments of time and by various unrelated subject positions" (*Postmodernism* 375), and which, despite their incompatibility, succeed in 'coexisting' with each other. Postmodernism's critics must therefore grapple with the conundrum that "as an ideology which is also a reality, the 'postmodern' cannot be disproved insofar as its fundamental feature is the radical separation of all the levels and voices whose recombination in their totality could alone disprove it" (376). To try to determine whether local or "subaltern" instances of resistance are, in effect, generated by capitalism itself ("in its interminable inner self-differentiation and self-reproduction"), or whether they are examples of new and 'oppositional' historical agencies (forcing the system "against the direction of its own internal logic into new reforms and internal modifications" [326]) is thus, both from the standpoint of theory and political praxis, a sterile endeavor: "this is precisely a false opposition about which it would be just as satisfactory to say that both positions are right."

The "crucial issue," Jameson determines, is the dilemma reproduced in both theoretical stances of an apparent "explanatory choice" between "the alternatives of system and agency" (*Postmodernism* 326), an aporia that, again, can be sublated only by means of a dialectical (or teleological) shift in perspective to "the very ends of time." The relevance of this philosophical solution is that it cancels out the need to make a "sterile choice" between two absolutely incompatible alternatives by providing "the simultaneous possibility of active political commitment along with disabused systemic realism and contemplation" (330). For a productive politics to be elaborated, Jameson continues, the local and global must be articulated. To uncouple the two levels and circumscribe the ground of politics to an interminable series of local issues invested "with the willed euphoria of some metaphysical permanent revolution" is, in the end, to compensate for a situation in which "genuine (or 'totalizing') politics is no longer possible" (330). What this euphoric local politics cannot challenge, or indeed even theorize, is, of course, the economic or systemic, that is, the mode of production (330). This effacement of the global dimension, the resistance to the concepts of totality and history are thus in the last instance ideological "symptoms" of the postmodern—a belated and radically homogenizing capitalist stage "from which many of the hitherto surviving enclaves of socioeconomic difference have been effaced (by way of their colonization and absorption by the commodity form)"; "where everything is henceforth systemic the very notion of a system seems to lose its reason for being" (405).

It is no accident, therefore, that the collective "non-centered subject" Jameson posits as the third or sublatory term, which at one and the same time cancels and preserves the old centered and inner-directed (Hegelian) subject and the "new non-subject of the fragmented or schizophrenic self" (*Postmodernism* 345), is predicated on class identification. "Class consciousness . . . masters the interpellative process in a new way (different from the usual reactive mode), such that it becomes, however momentarily, capable of interpellating itself and dictating the terms of its own speculative image" (345–46). In sum, one can "see down through class categories to the rocky bottom of the stream" (346). Just as unsurprisingly, Homi Bhabha describes this mode of identification as "narcissistic," "caught in an autotelic disavowal of [its] own discursive and epistemic limits," an instantiation of theoretical sovereignty that is simultaneously "an act of surveillance" (*Location of Culture* 222).

I am not proposing here, or in the chapters that follow, to surmount this impasse. Indeed I lack both the training and erudition to undertake such a task. My aim is rather more modest. I should like to chart the boundaries of my own approach. By outlining the important critical terrain with which my analyses will intersect only tangentially, I hope concomitantly to illumine the theoretical dilemma at the heart of this study. Thus, while I take very seriously the Marxian imperative to articulate the local with the global, I cannot but consider just as fundamental the postcolonial interrogation of the (epistemic) violence associated with such totalizing (critical) projects. I remain nonetheless reluctant to follow Homi Bhabha's lead in his influential readings of mimicry, and postulate as he does, for instance, that the essential iterability of modernity's long story (that is, its "de-contextualized" replication in Brazilian and Caribbean literary discourse) provides "a political space to articulate and negotiate . . . culturally hybrid social identities," or that it "produces a subversive strategy of subaltern agency that negotiates its own authority" (*Location of Culture* 250, 185).

To begin with, what remains un- (or under-) theorized in Bhabha's notion of difference as resistance, it seems to me, are the modes of articulation between the rhetorical and the political. Not only are the specific social and political conditions enabling the emergence of such hybrid or contestatory identities inchoately defined, but the particular character and extent of their political efficacy is never satisfactorily explained. Whether, for example, the local collapse of developmentalism within those texts that seek to reproduce the western program of modernization in Brazil leads to such a social or political opening remains a rather vexed (and ultimately undecidable) question for me. For Bhabha, however, it all seems to happen as if the undecidable "outcome" of the citationality of discourses of modernity can simply be interrupted on the signification of political empowerment. It is as though the political and aesthetic (or philosophical) senses of representation are confused.

In a polemical and influential reading of Marx's *Eighteenth Brumaire*, Gayatri Spivak has in effect stressed that these two meanings of representation—"within state formation and the law, on the one hand, and in subject-predication, on the other—are related but irreducibly discontinuous" (*Critique of Postcolonial Reason* 257). If she dwells extensively on the doubling of this fundamental concept, it is to foreground, first, the potential "complicity" of the intellectual in "the constitution of the Other as the Self's shadow" (266). Second, she wishes to underscore the irreducibility of the economic factor in "reinscrib[ing] the social text," while simultaneously indicating its erasure when it is posited, as in Jameson and Dirlik, as "the last instance" (266). Just as teleological concepts of history imprison or cancel historicity, according to Derrida, so do appeals to the "mode of production" as the final (narrative or interpretive) horizon substitute a rhetorical construction for economic reality. Spivak uses the name *subaltern* to designate a dimension of experience that is rendered invisible (or ineluctably "scriptural") by "class categories." "If, as Jameson suggests, the mode of production narrative is the final reference, [subaltern] women are insufficiently represented or representable in that narration" (244). The subaltern not only "mark the points of fadeout in the writing of disciplinary history" (244), but they also illuminate an important discontinuity between Spivak's and Bhabha's articulations of postcoloniality, between the former's "subalternity" and the latter's "hybridity."

As Spivak herself has recently suggested, the two notions run on parallel courses. "The postcolonial informant has rather little to say about the oppressed minorities in the decolonized nation as such.... The more stellar level [of postcolonial scholarship confines] the destabilization of the metropole merely to the changes in the ethnic composition of the population.... Both the racial underclass and the subaltern South step back into the penumbra" (*Critique* 360).

I would therefore insist, along with Spivak, that if the powerful and vexed exchange between Latin America and Europe ought to be included in any full-fledged articulation of postcoloniality, this reconsideration will be postcolonial only insofar as it takes up the question of the subaltern. In her formulation, postcolonial critical discourse must entail, by ethical necessity, an acknowledgment of both the theoretical impossibility of knowing the 'true' subaltern and the imperative not simply to turn away from representing it. It is this double bind that I endeavor to foreground both in the Brazilian and Caribbean texts I examine below and in my own readings. In contrast to Bhabha's "mimic men," Spivak's subaltern marks the site of a "displacement of the colonization-decolonization reversal" (*Outside in the Teaching Machine* 49).

As I argue elsewhere,[3] to circumscribe one's account of the subaltern to this logic of inversion is inevitably to stay caught within what she designates as the "ethnocentric and reverse-ethnocentric benevolent double bind (that is, considering the 'native' as object for enthusiastic information-retrieval and thus denying its own 'worlding')" (*Critique of Postcolonial Reason* 118). It is largely within this benign oscillation between a profound ethnocentrism and what Derrida has memorably called "an ethnocentrism thinking itself as an anti-ethnocentrism, an ethnocentrism in the consciousness of a liberating progressivism" (*Of Grammatology* 120), that the Brazilian works I analyze remain confined as well.

At the same time, the image of the subaltern, or the "primitive," often operates in these texts as both the source of a fundamental cultural "secret" and the site of an untranscendable epistemological horizon. For the adherents of the 1928–29 *antropofagia* movement, for instance, it is in the recovery and resignification of the most emblematic and infamous ritual associated with the Tupi—the "first peoples" of Brazil—that the possibility of reclaiming a genuine national culture resides. Yet, having been effectively eradicated by the early seventeenth century, these "original Brazilians" had long been tragically unavailable as "native informants." They linger only as distorted and unreliable traces in the very colonial archive in which their utter destruction is not only recorded but all too often justified, even celebrated. *Antropofagia*'s metaphoric return to Brazil's authentic "cannibalistic" roots, then, cannot but assume the form of a treacherous detour through inauthentic and unstable textual regions.

This is precisely the contradiction I explore in the opening chapter of *Cannibal Modernities*—where I study the movement in the broader context of European and Latin American modernisms. Thus, on the one hand, its reclamation of the "anthropophagus" is invariably reduced to the structures (and strictures) of speculative reason—in other words, the future *antropofagia* sets out to construct adheres in large measure to the familiar contours of western discourses of emancipation. One the other hand, however, *antropofagia*'s attempt to convert the Tupi's alleged craving for the heterogeneous[4] into an ethical and political imperative seems to indicate a new historical direction: a future that is at least imaginatively distinct from the one enforced by European models of modernization. In this sense, Oswald de Andrade's renowned "Manifesto Anthropófago" (1928) anticipates the inversion between margin and center that Paul Gilroy (in *Black Atlantic*) proposes as the point of departure for a rewriting (from the margins) of the history of modernity. By the same token, *antropofagia*'s refiguration of the very "dull savages" that Hegel excises from universal History as universal subjects appears to adumbrate a postcolonial critique of the enlightenment that posits the latter's foreclosure and excision of "the savage" as precisely the condition of possibility for the investiture of the European Subject as universal.

If *antropofagia* construes itself as "vengefully" opposed to the cultural and epistemological legacy of the west, the contemporaneous *modernista* literary production I examine in chapter 2 seeks instead to establish a relatively seamless continuity between not just European and Brazilian models of modernization, but between the latter and the colonial project of conquest and territorial expansion. The two poetic works I analyze in this chapter—Raul Bopp's *Cobra Norato* and Cassiano Ricardo's *Martim Cererê* both composed around 1928—have thus far received little or no critical attention outside Luso-Brazilian studies. As they both focus on the cultures and space of the Amazon, I study them in relation to a body of roughly contemporaneous and better-known Latin American narratives that treat the rain forest as a site of irreducible "barbarism" (among them, José Eustacio Rivera's *Vorágine* [1925] and Rómulo Gallegos's *Canaima* [1935]). In the two Brazilian texts, the Tupi serves as the key figure in a "eugenic" romance of miscegenation (between male European migrants and native Brazilian women). While ascribing to noble autochthons a "spiritual" (i.e., figural) agency, this rhetorical appropriation ultimately reinforces prevalent racist theories, relegating blacks, for instance, to the margins of the narrative of the modern nation.

Hence, although Oswald de Andrade (*antropofagia*'s self-appointed leader) deemed Bopp's *Cobra Norato* as quintessentially *antropofágico*, my close analysis of the poem suggests that this "modernist epic" oscillates between a recognizably *antropofagista* reclamation of Tupi culture and a program for the technological supercession, and indeed suppression, of the primitive. This program has closer affinities with the right-wing triumphalism of the nationalistic *verde-amarelismo* movement (with which Bopp was also briefly linked) than with the more radical *antropofagia*. In the idiom of the long-standing debate between civilization and barbarism, which undergirds much of Latin America's nineteenth- and early-twentieth-century literary and cultural production, *Cobra Norato* remains ambivalently and precariously positioned between these two irreconcilable terms. The poem never fully overcomes this contradiction, leaving it instead suspended as an aporia, which can aspire only to a figural resolution.

By contrast, Ricardo's 1928 epic *Martim Cererê* reimagines the westward itinerary of colonial expeditions (undertaken from the late sixteenth-century by the São Paulo–based adventurer-explorers known as *bandeirantes*) as the urtext for a modernized Brazil. It presents as the telos and destination of these voyages of "spatial conquest" São Paulo's urbanscape—supposedly the embodiment and culmination of a national development project. Nevertheless, the poem's effort to convert the urban-rural divide into a dialectic in which the latter (as the "weaker term") would be sublated in an ultramodern, skyscraping topography is finally undone. Its attempt to figure rural Brazil as the negative or vestigial term is undercut by a subterranean "counter-narrative" that surreptitiously renders the rural as the "term" that both enables and sustains Brazil's urban modernity.

Moreover, as the site of a monoculture economy whose specific character as well as rate and modality of exchange are decided elsewhere, the "backward" Brazilian countryside not only overdetermines its modern (urban) counterpart but finally emerges as a figure of the impossibility of development. Its overt developmentalism notwithstanding, the figuration of rural space in Ricardo's poem ultimately discloses (in Octavio Paz's memorable words) that "the kingdom of progress is not of this world: the paradise it promises us lies in the future, in an untouchable, unreachable, perpetual future."[5] One of the chapter's closing sections consists, in fact, of a comparative analysis of the critique of the idea of progress in Alejo Carpentier's autotelic representation of the Amazon forest in his 1953 novel *Lost Steps* (*Los pasos perdidos*). Even as they subscribe uncritically to the logic of developmentalism, I conclude, both *Cobra Norato* and *Martim Cererê* "unconsciously" disclose the limits of a modernization model predicated on the "peripheral" replication of Europe's metanarrative of progress.

It is nonetheless in Mário de Andrade's *Macunaíma* (1928)—which, after a cursory reading, one would be tempted to classify as an exemplary primitivist text—that the developmentalist project as well as primitivism itself are most consistently undermined. As I argue in chapter 3, *Macunaíma* develops all the familiar *modernista* themes: the idea of racial democracy, the attempted recovery of a genuine national culture "in the depths" of the rain forest, as well as the search for a new idiom capable of expressing a hybrid national identity. The narrative aims at a unique fusion between self-regarding formal experimentation and the Amerindian oral tradition. Conventional readings of the novel—bolstered by the author's own repeated pronouncements on the matter—have tended to interpret its eponymous protagonist as a national symbol.

Yet, as *Macunaíma*'s ironic subtitle itself suggests (*O herói sem nenhum caráter* [the hero without any character]), the main character's identity resides in his difference. (Indeed, equally convincing cases can be made for his white, black, and "Indian" identifications.) Thus, as the characterless "symbol" of a nation bereft of character, *Macunaíma* is at once (and discontinuously) an alien and a native. Far from figuring the unconscious of the nation, he interrupts figuration itself by foregrounding his scriptural provenance. *Macunaíma,* in short, stands for the insistent and troubling remembrance of a memory of genocide that *modernista* primitivisms, by laying claim to the authority to "modernize" or "nationalize" Brazil's "original story," either repress or sublimate. The novel's self-referentiality can in effect be construed as self-consciously undoing this appropriation of narrative control. In this way, then, *Macunaíma* seeks to preserve, while attempting neither to negate nor supercede, the irreducible heterogeneity of the marginalized peoples and cultures of Brazil. Its modernprimitive protagonist emerges as a trace of the suppressions and exclusions that enable both the developmentalist program and *modernista* efforts to hyphenate the nation's genuine character with obliterated, enslaved, or disappearing "primitives."

The fourth chapter focuses on two cinematic adaptations of seminal modernista texts: Joaquim Pedro de Andrade's *Macunaíma* (1969) and Nelson Pereira dos Santos's *Como era gostoso o meu francês* (*How Tasty Was My Little Frenchman,* 1971), which engage directly with anthropophagist polemics. Made by two of the main exponents of Cinema Novo during the most repressive phase of Brazil's military dictatorship, both films propose that the terms of the national debate around modernity and modernization animating 1920s artists and intellectuals still retain their centrality four decades later. In the grips of an authoritarian state whose developmentalist policies aimed at securing massive foreign investment as the vehicle for rapid modernization, the country seemed as dependent on the whims of international capital and as distant from that elusive modernizing goal as it was at the height of *antropofagia,* or indeed during the colonial era. Yet if "cannibalism" operates as the core metaphor in the two films, its meanings are distinct.

Whereas in *How Tasty Was My Little Frenchman* anthropophagy, as in the movement that inspired it, functions as a rhetorical alternative to enforced unequal exchange and foreign consumption, in *Macunaíma* it serves as an index of capital's "cannibalistic" drive. Not only has capitalism in Pedro de Andrade's film "devoured" the few surviving residues of cultural difference that, for the 1928 anthropophagists, for example, embodied the potential to resist its metastasis in the social "body," but this devouring logic has been adopted wholesale by those very primitive remnants (that is, Macunaíma himself). In *Macunaíma*, in other words, the agent of anthropophagy turns out to be global capital, not a reinvigorated and recalcitrant nation. And the only active role reserved for the "natives" is to accelerate this homogenizing process via self-consumption.

On the other hand, while *How Tasty Was My Little Frenchman* ostensibly subscribes to the *antropofagista* recuperation of the anthropophagic act as a strategy of cultural and economic resistance, it ultimately exposes the "rhetoricity" of this allegorical solution to the dilemma of development. This turn inward (into diegetic space), which is also staged by *Macunaíma*, points to the widening gulf separating the self-professed makers of a popular cinema from their popular audience, a gap that, although politically enforced, is, I suggest, just as much a product of the movement's poetics. At the same time, the film's autotelism also constitutes an acknowledgment that the symbolic lesson imparted by the Brazilian primitive cannot but remain confined to the archival sources where the filmmaker has deciphered it, for, in the last instance, the effacement of Brazil's "original inhabitants," their violent reduction to rhetorical tropes is the nation's very condition of possibility.

The task of the last three chapters of the book is, in effect, to analyze the ways in which a corpus of Caribbean texts discloses the limitations inherent in similar returns to primitive or nativist cultural sources as part of a general program to rewrite modernity. Chapter 5, which is divided into two major sections, opens with a comparative analysis of C. L. R. James's *Black Jacobins* (1938) and Aimé Césaire's *Toussaint Louverture* (1961). Similarly to *antropofagia*, these two histories of the Haitian Revolution and war of independence attempt to displace linear and hierarchical notions of history, which locate in Europe modernity's principal impetus and point of departure. Both Haiti's liberation struggle and the figure of its most remarkable leader, Toussaint Louverture, are operationalized as the grounding for a reorientation of a largely Hegelian historiographic paradigm.

Haiti's rebellious slaves, in other words, demonstrate not only that Africans can "make history," but that the historical project they undertake is a radically modern as well as universal one. As I point out in my analysis, while these efforts to revise Hegel are finally and inevitably determined by Hegel, they should not for that reason be dismissed as proof of the ineluctable failure of such revisionary projects. Indeed, Paul Gilroy has argued in *Black Atlantic* that "marginal" critiques of modernity are necessarily located both inside and outside the very enlightenment tradition whose "operational principles" they seek simultaneously to put into question. James and Césaire's critiques of Hegel, then, ultimately reaffirm the concept of historical becoming that they contest, for the very terms of their contestations are sustained and indeed determined by the discourses they endeavor to displace. Just as I argue in the first chapter in relation to *antropofagia,* I propose that both Césaire and James, their "epistemic" determination notwithstanding, may also adumbrate the "alternative to Europe's long story" that Spivak has posited as a key index of postcoloniality.

The second section of chapter 5 begins with a close reading of the intricate ways in which this ambivalent relationship with Europe's familiar metanarrative is staged in Césaire's 1939 work *Cahier d'un retour au pays natal (Notebook of a Return to My Native Land).* In the closing pages of the chapter, I turn to a reassessment of the *négritude* movement in light of this contradictory rewriting of western modernity. I draw a sharp distinction between Césaire's own conception of this polemical idea and the one elaborated by the movement's other founder, the late poet-laureate and former president of Senegal, Léopold Senghor (a distinction that I sought to establish as well between *antropofagia* and contemporaneous Brazilian *modernismos*) in terms of their engagement with dominant discourses of modernity. While Senghorian *négritude,* not unlike Brazil's *verde-amarelismo,* internalizes a hierarchical and "provincial" idea of progress, Césaire's variation on the concept, like C. L. R. James's contrapuntal historiography and *antropofagia* itself, constitutes an "addition" to the enlightenment grand narrative that, in keeping with the logic of supplementarity, ultimately displaces the latter's authority and calls into question its claim to originality.

The crucial paradox that occupies me in chapter 6 is thus not entirely dissimilar from the one that both Cassiano Ricardo's and Raul Bopp's poetic texts disclose (at the same time that they conceal) in chapter 2, that is, the impossibility of replicating "on the margins" the enlightenment project of development. The first of the chapter's three sections concentrates on *La tragédie du roi Christophe* (1964), Césaire's representation of Henri Christophe's ruthless attempt in 1806 to establish Haiti's—and indeed the New World's—first monarchy (modeled on France's ancien régime).

This sanguinary and ephemeral political experiment by Toussaint's former general can therefore be posited as an early instantiation of the enforced and arrested modernization that would become the bane of the

Caribbean and Latin America throughout the twentieth century. Given the self-crowned monarch's unquestioning adoption of a Hegelian conception of history that relegates the African to prehistory, however, his brutal project of development appears, by his own admission (in Césaire's play), destined to remain "quelque chose d'impossible" (something impossible)—rendered impracticable by the very developmentalist logic that governs it. It is a "double negative," as it were: the attempted supercession of a historical void (the African's absence of History) for the sake of a historicity ineluctably defined by a temporal lack (a future that will always-already reflect a European past).

Section two examines another well-known Caribbean literary account of Christophe's monarchic regime, Carpentier's 1949 work *El reino de este mundo* (*The Kingdom of This World*). I also endeavor to reread "the marvelous real" (*lo real maravilloso*), the concept that the Cuban novelist first introduces in a preface to the original edition of the novel, and that he defines as the indelible "inscription" in the history of the continent. Going slightly against the grain of several critiques of this notion of a marvelous (American) reality as either Romantic or exoticizing, I seek to analyze Carpentier's "master concept" in the context of other influential Caribbean articulations of Antillean cultural difference, namely those of Guyana's Wilson Harris and Martinique's Edouard Glissant. In this sense, *lo real maravilloso* constitutes an effort to register the unrepeatable difference in Caribbean (or Latin American) repetitions of European epistemological paradigms. Not only does this difference signify the reinsertion of African and American peoples into "universal history," but it shares with the Brazilian and Caribbean discourses analyzed in preceding chapters the attempt to retell—wholly to refigure, in fact—that very history from the margins.

The book's seventh and final chapter treats Carpentier's project to chart the differences (or *differend*) produced by the reiterations of French revolutionary phrases in the Caribbean and Latin America in his 1962 novel *El siglo de las luces* (*Explosion in a Cathedral*). Significantly, *El siglo* returns precisely to the same historical period as the one that *Kingdom of This World* chronicles. Just as importantly, the historical events that lie at the center of his 1949 novel are pushed to the narrative edges in the later text. If then *El siglo* seeks, like its predecessor, to narrativize the complex and contradictory modes in which enlightenment discourses are "de-territorialized" in the New World—that is, the historical and cultural differences in Caribbean repetitions of European discourses of emancipation—in contrast to *Kingdom of This World,* it eschews the narrative presentation of the Antillean reversals and undoings of "a linear and hierarchical History."

In its studied reluctance to represent these supposedly "minor" struggles and uprisings—including the Haitian Revolution itself—Carpentier's *El siglo* thus appears to reproduce that "grand narrative's" placement of such events outside the historical. At the same time, the novel suggests, even if obliquely, that these heterogenous histories not only elude the grasp of that discursive tradition but return in its margins to undo and rewrite the major historical plot that *El siglo* repeats . . . with a difference.

1 Lapses in Taste
Antropofagia as the Primitive Aesthetic of Underdeveloped Brazil

> The sixteenth-century consciousness was lacking in an element more important than knowledge: a quality indispensable to scientific thought. The men of that time were not sensitive to the harmonious arrangement of the universe. . . . The mermaids and sheep tree constitute something different from, and more than, just objective mistakes; on the intellectual level, they are to be considered rather as *lapses in taste*.
> —Claude Lévi-Strauss, *Tristes Tropiques*

> There . . . they began to mock me, and king [Cunhambebe's] son bound my legs in three places, and I was forced to hop through the huts on both feet, at which they [laughed, and called out]: 'Here comes our food hopping toward us.'
> —Hans Staden, *The True History of His Captivity*

IN THE BEGINNING there was a banquet, for these were the Banquet Years of São Paulo.[1] The restaurant where this inaugural symposium took place was renowned for its specialty: frogs' legs. As a tray brimming over with the delicacy was being brought to the table, Oswald de Andrade—whom Blaise Cendrars was to anoint "le prophète du modernisme à São Paulo" (White, *Les années vingt au Brésil* 40)—rose to toast not love but the batrachian. He then embarked on a parodic exposition of the theory of evolution, his main argument being that the frog (the same frog that the symposiasts were, at that very moment, tasting between measured sips of chilled Chablis) was man's evolutionary ancestor. Oswald's demonstration drew from such apocryphal authorities as the Dutch "ovoists," the "homunculus" theorists, and the "spermatists." The cohost, painter Tarsila do Amaral, cut into her husband's peroration, remarking that the logical conclusion to his premise was that the banqueters were "quasi-anthropophagi." At the end of the ensuing playful analysis of the idea of Anthropophagy came the clincher, the quote from Hans Staden's 1557 captive narrative—a "classic" of the genre: "Here comes our food hopping toward us." It was reportedly at this point that Oswald limberly executed his famous verbal sleight of hand, "Tupi or not Tupi, that is the question."

Several days later, at her salon, Tarsila unveiled the painting, which Oswald is said to have christened Abaropu (the Tupi term for "anthropophagus"). Out of a series of subsequent meetings emerged the *Revista de Antropofagia* (Review of Anthropophagy), in whose first issue appeared Oswald's "Manifesto Antropófago" (May 1928). Plans for the First World Conference on Anthropophagy, to be held on October 11, the eve of Columbus's landfall in the Bahamas, and thus a commemoration of a "de-Vespucci-ated and de-Columbus-ed America," of its "last day of freedom," were in the offing.[2] But the movement's organ did not survive beyond its second volume, or "dentition" (*dentição*). (Its last issue was published as a supplement to the *Diário de São Paulo* on August 1, 1929.) The inner circle was dissolved by "Libido's stealthy entrance into the Anthropophagist paradise" (Bopp, *Vida e morte* 53). Oswald and Tarsila separated, and before the end of 1929, "Anthropophagy on a grand scale, whose sheer force had threatened to pull down classical structures, had come to nought . . . probably destined to be recorded in the obituary of an era" (Bopp, *Movimentos modernistas no Brasil* 94. And thus, according to one of its chroniclers, did Brazil's *antropofagia* movement rise and fall (Bopp, *Vida e morte* 40–54).

The character and significance of the movement obviously exceed any merely anecdotal account. This inaugural meal serves nonetheless as a convenient metaphor for the cluster of problems I wish to broach in what follows. Like its ancient model—the Platonic Symposium—this banquet, too, was deeply concerned with etiologies: the origins of a genuine national culture. Yet, as with the symposium, these original sources can be retrieved only in simulacral form, only as protean, unreliable traces from which the authenticity of the original Brazilians (a profoundly inauthentic expression) must be purged of the distortions imposed by Renaissance Europe's alleged lack of taste for the cruel integrity of the savage. (Of course, the quest for "natural man" informs those early modern texts as well.)

The symposial setting is itself unoriginal, moreover, not only because it follows the classical model but also because it belongs to the series of "inaugural" colloquia, dinners, and salons that literary histories customarily link with literary modernity. The banquet also points to a class and cultural privilege, which, in a country where the illiteracy rate exceeded

75 percent in 1929, inevitably renders the poetic turn to the popular at once exoticizing and parochial. These contradictions are obviously not unique to Anthropophagy. They recur in most modernist or avant-garde movements. In any event, the presence of this poetic privilege has led at least one prominent Brazilian critic to dismiss *antropofagia* as a nationalist abstraction, an empty analogy that "throws absolutely no light on the politics and aesthetics of contemporary cultural life" (Schwarz, *Misplaced Ideas* 9).

The dual task of this chapter is in effect to elucidate and examine the proposition that the aesthetic and political claims advanced by Anthropophagy are either empty or ultimately "self-referential." I should like first to ascertain whether the limitations supposedly specific to its project might not in effect be intrinsic to modernist aesthetics in general. In other words, can the lapses in taste and politics *antropofagia* allegedly discloses ever be supplanted by the correct hermeneutics, as Roberto Schwarz's reading seems to promise? Or are they rather constitutive of the very idea of modernity underpinning the movement? In the final section of the chapter, I pose the question whether, despite its undeniable reliance on the very European tradition it seeks to displace, Anthropophagy may nevertheless put into question the authority of Europe's 'long story' of modernity. In short, I ask whether Anthropophagy broaches a shift beyond a "sectarian" idea of modernity "founding [itself] on universal, exclusive truths" (Freire, *Pedagogy of Hope* 50). What I begin to posit, then, is the possibility that *antropofagia* anticipates what Paulo Freire has called a "postmodern" alternative to the west's narrative of emancipation: the repudiation of a "modernist" politics calling for a "'pragmatic' accommodation to the facts, as if the facts had turned immutable" (50–51). Before addressing these questions, however, it behooves me to provide a brief historical overview of the movement.

Futurism inside a Theater, or, the Inevitable Dead End of a Peripheral Modernism?

The collapse of Anthropophagy closes the avant-garde cycle initiated by the Semana de Arte Moderna (Week of Modern Art) held at São Paulo's Municipal Theater in the second week of February 1922—an event that, according to the Uruguayan critic Angel Rama, marks the formal opening of the modernist epoch in Latin America (Schwartz, *Vanguardas Latino-Americanas* 32). For Raul Bopp—one of the founders of the movement—the demise of Anthropophagy in 1929 coincides *grosso modo* with "the end of an era." In the following year, Oswald, now romantically involved with the militant artist Patrícia Galvão, founds *Homem do Povo* (Man of the People), a Communist Party (PCB) periodical. Abandoning, and indeed violently rejecting, his previous "experimental" work, he turns instead to social realism. As Jorge Schwartz observes, Oswald's "plunge" into political militancy follows a general reorientation among Latin American modernists of the period toward concerns of a more "ideological order" (*Vanguardas* 33).

This about-face occurs in an international context of economic collapse (the 1929 stock market crash leads to Oswald's personal bankruptcy, for instance), and a political shift to the right, signaled not only by the rise of European fascisms but a series of Latin American military coups "whose consequences would be devastating in the cultural sector" (Schwartz, *Vanguardas* 33). In Brazil, where the Great Depression touches off a calamitous drop in the sales of its main export, coffee, Getúlio Vargas's October 1930 'revolution' is emblematic of the latter political trend. Vargas's 'revolution' overthrows the First Republic and paves the way for the authoritarian or corporatist Estado Novo (New State) of 1937–1945, instituted after his November 1937 coup. Mário de Andrade, alluding to the militancy of several *modernistas* in the political struggles of 1930, claims that Modernismo prepared the ground for the ensuing "destructive social movement" ("O movimento modernista" 241–42).

With the end of the old seigneurial politics of *café com leite* (that is, the alternation of political power between the state of São Paulo's coffee-producing barons and the dairy oligarchy of Minas Gerais), modernism and modernization (i.e., a program to increase the country's level of industrialization) became the state ideology of Vargas's "progressive" provisional government (1930–37), and even, one could argue, of the autarkic Estado Novo he was to establish. Modernismo appears, in this sense, to have met the fate that, according to Raymond Williams, is reserved for modernisms as a whole: "a comfortable integration into the new international capitalism" (*Politics of Modernism* 35). And *antropofagia* was the most iconoclastic of the *modernista* onslaughts against the academicism of a stolid Tradition, the last and perhaps most strident in a series of declarations of aesthetic freedom (1922 marked the first centenary of Brazil's independence).

Anthropophagy rode the crest of a wave of "isms" that was supposedly destined to wash over the "cradle of a racial, industrial, and economic futurism" that was allegedly São Paulo in the early 1920s (Menotti del Picchia, *O Gedeão do modernismo* 317).[3] Or else it was one of several "fashions ... directly imported from Europe [by] a tiny group of São Paulo intellectuals" (M. de Andrade, "O movimento modernista" 232, 236). Both of these accounts attest to the emergence in Brazil's second major city (the point of destination of over half the European immigrants entering Brazil at the time) of a metropolitan culture whose complexity and miscellaneity Williams regards as "the key cultural factor in the modernist shift," as "a definition of modernity itself" (Williams, *Politics of Modernism* 45, 79). Whether this metropolitan immigration exerted the same influence on formal innovation and linguistic experimentation in Brazil (and other areas of the continent) that Williams perceives in Europe's modernisms and avant-gardes (45–47, 77–80) is an open question. Nevertheless, in the 1920s, the effort "to think a new language . . . to renew existing languages . . . and assert an idiom different from the one bequeathed by the discovering countries" remained one of the defining utopian dimensions of Latin American modernisms, especially in the southern cone and Peru (Schwartz, *Vanguardas* 45).

As Angel Rama puts it, during the period between the two world wars, language, for the intellectual elites, was at once "the defensive redoubt" (*el reducto defensivo*) and "a demonstration of independence" (*una prueba de independencia*) (*Transculturación narrativa* 40). To borrow Jorge Schwartz's felicitous phrase, the new was Modernismo's registered trademark (*Vanguardas* 40). In the lecture that inaugurated the Week of Modern Art, for example, Graça Aranha, the "veteran" of the *modernista* group and a member of the Academia Brasileira, declared that "academicism . . . kills the profound and tumultuous originality of our forest of words, phrases and ideas at its birth" (*Obra completa* 743).[4] Two years later, in a speech delivered before the academy in July 1924, he was to pronounce the celebrated epigram, "se a Academia não se renova, morra a Academia" (754) [if the Academy does not renew itself, let the Academy die]. (In October of the same year he resigned.)

Jean Franco has aptly described this attitude as an uncompromising refusal on the part of the "sophisticated urbanites" who filled the ranks of Brazil's avant-garde movement to look to the past: "the past must be ruthlessly destroyed . . . so that a new and creative literature could arise" (*Modern Culture* 94, 96). Even a quick glance at a few of the *modernista* journals cropping up in various parts of Brazil in the 1920s confirms Mário de Andrade's assertion that Modernismo saw itself as the embodiment of "a new art, a new spirit" ("O movimento modernista" 232). Thus, invoking the sense of absolute modernity promised by the title of the opening poem of Rimbaud's *Illuminations*—"Après le déluge"— Oswaldo Costa, in the first issue of the *Revista de Antropofagia,* adopts, as the model for the Anthropophagist tabula rasa, the Biblical Flood: "God erased everything in order to begin anew. . . . But he had a weakness: he spared Noah. Anthropophagy—the most remarkable movement since the Flood—comes about in order to eat Noah" ("Revisão necessária" 8). Modernismo would thus presumably be imbued with that lassitude with the ancient world that Apollinaire famously expresses in the opening lines of "Zone."[5]

As an outright repudiation of "old-fashioned conventions and academicism" and "the servile imitation of European models" noted by Jean Franco (*Modern Culture* 96), it would also exhibit the rage against reigning aesthetic taste, which Perry Anderson identifies as one of the three "decisive coordinates" enabling the emergence of European modernisms.[6] For Mário de Andrade, the movement's "true and specific meaning" lay precisely in this "destructive spirit" ("O movimento modernista" 240), in its effort to construct itself as a terminus, to stop history dead, as Raymond Williams puts it (*Politics of Modernism* 34–35). Like other literary vanguards in Latin America, then, Modernismo seeks to overcome what Angel Rama terms the "diglossia" marking Latin American societies at least since the colonial period, that is, the discursive gulf between a public, formalized and largely scriptural language, on one hand, and popular, private and spoken expression, on the other (*La ciudad letrada* 43).

Notwithstanding what Jorge Schwartz calls the semantic ambiguity of Mário's "winds of destruction, [which,] during a time of festivity and the immoderate cult of pleasure, swept over a whole generation" (M. de Andrade, "O movimento modernista" 241), the "destructive attitude" that pervades Mário's retrospective look at the movement (Schwartz, *Vanguardas* 62) echoes Nietzsche's call for the "destruction and dissolution" of what came before, for the a posteriori invention of "a past in which one would like to originate [as opposed] to that in which one did originate" ("On the Uses and Disadvantages" 75, 76). It is in this "desire to wipe out whatever came earlier, in the hope of reaching at last a point that could be called the true present, a point of origin that marks a new departure," in "this combined interplay of deliberate forgetting with an action that is also a new origin," that Paul De Man discerns "the idea of modernity" in its full power (*Blindness and Insight,* 148).

Yet, as Mário de Andrade's allusion to the movement's wholesale importation of European trends suggests, Modernismo was apparently never more a copy than in its effort to be original. The quest for the Adamic innocence of language, for a return to the inarticulate(d) promise of infancy (in-fons) is, as the first line of Rimbaud's second "Illumination"

("Enfance") indicates, something like the "idol" of modernity.[7] It marks a search for a "new world" that has always-already been discovered, whose iterability seems, in the last instance, to reaffirm modernism's modal character. In "Enfance's" penultimate line, for instance, the poet declares himself "the master of silence": "Je suis maître du silence" (Rimbaud, *Collected Poems* 240).

Yet "silence" is precisely not the poem's last word; its immediacy and finality are, in effect, put into question by an echo: an illuminated "appearance" (that is, an idol or re-presentation: "Pourquoi une apparence de soupirail blêmirait-elle au coin de la voûte?" (240) ["Why should [the appearance] of a skylight pale at the corner of the vault?"; 240]). The citationality of the new language supposedly emerging from a silenced tradition ("demandons au poète du nouveau," as Rimbaud's famous injunction goes [*Collected Poems* 14]) is then already "reflected" in the poem. The "appearance" of the last phrase replicates the "idol" of the first, the latter's uniqueness or lack of affiliation (*sans parents*) mirroring phonetically the closing after-image (*apparence*). The "beaches" of the first sentence reflect the "vault" of the last, and so on. *Soupirail* (skylight), etymologically linked to *soupir* (sigh; from the Latin *suspiriu*), invokes the celestial and vaulted "breath," the *pneuma* or Spirit of infancy, only apparently, only in a pallid, repeatable reflection.

The Idea of modernity—"l'idée du Déluge" (the idea of the flood) that opens the collection (Rimbaud, *Collected Poems* 233)—is thus reduced, or fragmented, to an endlessly reproducible idol. It is, nonetheless, exactly a poetics of discovery that the *modernista* Paulo Prado stresses in his preface to Oswald's poetry collection *Poesia Pau-Brasil* (1925), by designating the latter an "egg of Columbus" (O. de Andrade, *Do 'Pau-Brasil'* 5).

In his first *modernista* manifesto ("Manifesto da poesia pau-brasil" [Manifesto of Brazilwood Poetry]) in 1924, Oswald calls for a "naïve and nimble poetry [,] like a child," for a "Language without archaisms, without erudition. Natural and neological . . . As we speak. As we are . . . Invention / Surprise / A new perspective / A new scale . . . To see with free eyes" (*Do 'Pau-Brasil'* 6, 8, 9). What distinguishes *pau-brasil* from the multiple avant-gardes that precede it, though, is its radical turn toward the national, for *pau-brasil* opens Modernismo's second or nationalist phase (1924–30), the generalized search for the pleonastic originality of a "Brazilian Brazil." In a retrospective evaluation of his early phase, Oswald argues that the Pau-Brasil Manifesto's call for the production of "export poetry" (*poesia de exportação*) was "a rallying cry against import poetry," a defense of the "the nation's wealth" (*divisas nacionais*);

hence the appeal to "our first export product": brazilwood (O. de Andrade, *Estética e política*, 129).

Thus, in an effort to capture "the amazement of the first chroniclers before the [new] land" (128), the collection's "History of Brazil" section opens with an ironic rewriting of these early modern texts. Indeed, the movement's core metaphor may well have been borrowed from Jean de Léry's *Histoire d'un voyage fait en la terre du Brésil* (1578), which the celebrated "proto-ethnographer" claims to have reconstructed from his "memoirs. . . . written with brazilwood ink, and in America itself" ("les memoires que j'avois . . . escrits d'ancre de Bresil, et en l'Amerique mesme" [*History of a Voyage*, xlv; *Histoire d'un voyage*, 61).

Oswald would later call this ostensibly "natural" label (brazilwood) "a factory brand" (*uma marca de fábrica*), "a patent of invention" (*Estética e política* 128), perhaps suggesting that in its very desire to "write the world anew," the collection inevitably reiterates not only the very fifteenth- and sixteenth-century "discovery" claims whose historical primacy it seeks to displace, but colonial extraction itself. Michel de Certeau's remarks about Léry's text could therefore apply to Oswald's *pau-brasil* poetry itself: it is "a raw material doubly drawn from the tropics, since the very characters that bring the primitive object into the textual web are made from a red ink extracted from the *pau-brasil*, a wood that is one of the principal imports to sixteenth-century Europe" (*Writing of History*, 218).

In a posthumously published set of critical notes, Mário de Andrade identifies a comparable paradox in Oswald's preambular "speech" (*falação*, an abbreviated version of the "Brazilwood Manifesto") to the *Pau-Brasil* collection: "The *falação* exemplifies what it so justifiably rails against: the writing of someone steeped in erudition. For this return to popular material, to the errors of the people, is the most erudite of desires" ("Oswald de Andrade," 230). As Jean Franco remarks, "the primitivism fashionable in contemporary Europe was not entirely absent from Brazilian Modernismo" (*Modern Culture* 97). Modernismo, Franco adduces, thus combines elements of the avant-garde, including "a vision of an integrated and modern Brazil, whose distinctive form of civilization and culture" would be São Paulo (the 'city of the future'), "with the search for roots among the most primitive elements of the population and in primitive nature" (98, 268).

The search for a point of origin, for a new departure, was in this sense the catalyst for most of the offshoots of Modernismo's second phase. As Mário de Andrade has observed, the question of nationalism was central to this quest ("O movimento modernista" 243). Brazilian critic Renato Ortiz, summing up his own evaluation of the movement, also argues that the "common territory" shared by *modernistas* of every political stripe during this second nationalist period was an effort to build a conceptual bridge between the "will to modernity" and "the construction of national identity" (*A moderna cultura*, 35).

It is therefore important to recognize, Ortiz continues, that over and above their substantial political disagreements, the *modernistas*' "principal collective cry" (M. de Andrade, "O movimento modernista" 231) remained the same. Only insofar as they accommodated themselves to the native soil, as Mário de Andrade puts it (243), only inasmuch as they were national, could they become modern (Ortiz, *A moderna cultura* 35). After 1924, the claims to modernity are increasingly formulated in terms of cultural authenticity and national rebirth, or, more specifically, in terms of an emblematically European reclamation of the creative power of the primitive, of the culture and language of Brazil's "original" decimated inhabitants, the Tupi—the Anta people—who come to figure something like the nation's Unconscious.

Thus, for example, Menotti del Picchia,[8] repeating Oswald's procedure in the "History of Brazil" section of *Pau-Brasil,* invokes America's "violent morning / announced by the caravels" in the opening strophes of a 1928 poetry collection (*República dos Estados Unidos do Brasil* 120):

> When I was a child
> I would trace with a colored pencil
> upon the faded blue of the Atlantic
> the map of the two continents,
> which the daring entrepreneur of worlds, Christopher Columbus
> opened up like a motion-picture theater
> in the darkness of the Sea of Night.[9]

The collection's "Inauguration" poem depicts the "discoverer" of Brazil, Pedro Álvares Cabral, "inaugurating the future Republic . . . at the invitation of Universal History" (*República* 129). Raul Bopp, in an effort to reproduce the genesial innocence of a Tupi creation myth, re-creates the Brazilian dawn in a poem appropriately titled "Princípio" (Beginning): "In the beginning there was sun . . . sun . . . sun . . . / The Amazon river was not yet ready. / The belated waters / overran the jungle pell-mell" (*Cobra Norato e outros poemas,* 73).

The first stanza of another nationalist epic by the *verde-amarelista* Cassiano Ricardo (*Martim Cererê,* which was also published in 1928) retells the same Tupi myth: "At first in the world / there was only sun nothing else / night did not exist" (Ricardo, *Poesias completas,* 85). Plínio Salgado—the future leader of the fascist Integralista movement in the 1930s, and cofounder with Raul Bopp of the 1927 Anta (tapir) school (at the time the "left-wing" of the ultra-nationalist *verde-amarelismo* movement)—provides a Spenglerian variation on this inaugural motif in a 1926 lecture on the meaning of the Anta symbol: "A night is falling agonizingly upon the world. I believe the New Day will arise in Latin America, and especially in Brazil" (*Despertemos a Nação!* 34). "It is day-break [*madrugada*] here [Salgado proclaims], with locomotives and automobiles piercing the virgin forest, ploughs gnawing at the inviolate earth, axes tearing forth echoes from the back lands [*sertão*]" (35).[10]

This quest for a national childhood, combined with the anti-academicist effort "to renew existing languages . . . and assert an idiom different from the one bequeathed" by metropolitan culture (Schwartz, *Vanguardas* 45), leads several *modernistas* to an intensive study of the Tupi language. Plínio Salgado describes Tupi as "a language almost in its nascent stage, directly linked to nature" ("A língua Tupy" 6). For the future Integralista, "Anta is the wild spirit of America. . . . It is the burning of libraries. The virginal innocence and dumb violence of new-born beings acting on will alone [em função de querer]."[11] In the *verde-amarelista* manifesto ("Nhengaçú verde amarelo"),[12] co-authored by Salgado, the authentic meaning of Brazil's national character is said to reside in the unyielding and savage will of the Anta people, as expressed in their precolonial descent into the Atlantic coast from the continental plateau (the "epic itinerary of their plumed canoes"), advancing inexorably, with tapir-like single-mindedness, across the Amazon, finally to expel the shore-dwelling Tapuias (Salgado, *Despertemos a nação!* 37):

> All forms of Jacobinism in America [which "means isolation, hence disintegration"] are Tapuia. Sound nationalism, with great historical purpose and a human predestination, is perforce Tupi. . . . The Tupi signifies the absence of prejudices. The Tapuia is prejudice itself fleeing into the back lands [*sertão*].[13] . . . The Tapuia isolated himself in the jungle in order to survive; and was killed off by the muskets and arrows of the enemy. The Tupi became social, fearless of death; and was immortalized in the blood of our race. The Tapuia is dead, the Tupi alive . . . Tupi philosophy must necessarily be the 'non-philosophy.' . . . Any philosophical systematization amongst us will be Tapuia (destined to disappear besieged by so many other doctrines). (Salgado, Menotti del Picchia, and Ricardo, "Nhengaçú verde amarelo," 234, 235, 237)

To borrow Peter Hulme's assessment of the opposition between peaceful Arawaks and warlike Caribs operationalized in European histories and anthropologies of the Caribbean, Salgado's account "seems to belong to some nineteenth-century discourse of racial destinies" (Hulme, *Colonial Encounters*, 48). Lévi-Strauss conjectures that the Tupi diaspora was fueled by "the belief that they might, somewhere, find a land free from both death and evil" (*Tristes Tropiques*, 252 [1992 translation]). Alejo Carpentier advances a similar hypothesis in his own account of the Carib migration in *El siglo de las luces* (*Explosion in a Cathedral*), positing, as the impetus for the Caribs' northward march, their ancestral desire to reach a mythic Empire, "a Land-in-Waiting, where the Chosen People would necessarily settle one day, once a celestial sign should have come for them to depart" (242).

As Carpentier's protagonist retells it, the arrival of Columbus's ghostly ships—"strange, unrecognized shapes, with hollows in their sides, and trees growing on top of them, bearing [panels of cloth] which billowed and fluttered, [displaying] unknown symbols" (*Explosion* 244)—irremediably checks the Caribs' advance: "Two irreconcilable historical periods confronted one another in this struggle where no truce was possible. Totemic Man was opposed to Theological Man. . . . The Caribs would never reach the empire of the Mayas, but would remain a frustrated people who had been dealt a death wound just as their age-old design reached its climax" (244). This account subscribes to what Peter Hulme has called "an old argument which sees an analogy between Caribs and Spaniards as colonists: the Caribs were beginning to colonize the islands but were defeated by the more powerful European colonists against whom they turned their outward thrust, resentful of the Europeans' superior strength" (*Colonial Encounters* 86).

For the *verde-amarelistas*, neither the original motivation for the Tupi migration nor the consequences of their fateful confrontation with European "discoverers" is as significant as the analogy that can putatively be drawn between the two. The historical meaning of the Tupi odyssey is accordingly rethought as a prefiguration of "the nostalgia for the West which . . . still points out the nation's ordained path" (Salgado, *Despertemos a nação!* 37), that is, the epic westward expansion undertaken in the sixteenth and seventeenth centuries by Portuguese explorers known as *bandeirantes*[14]—"a cross between hero and geographer, between daring and civilizing spirit" (Vasconcelos, *La raza cósmica* 108). As early as 1638, the *bandeirantes* had reportedly established the boundaries of present-day Brazil. For *verde-amarelismo*, the twentieth-century heir to their expansionist legacy is the European immigrant, the modern artisan of a cosmopolitan nation: "We are a country of immigrants, and will remain the refuge of humanity for geographic and economic reasons that are all too well-known" (Salgado, Menotti del Picchia, and Ricardo, "Nhengaçú verde amarelo" 236).

The antagonism between the Tupi and the Tapuias is thus refigured as a nationalist "equation" in which the Tupi variable yields the solution to the problem of national identity. The postgenocidal lesson of the Anta people, then, resides precisely in their absence, in their eradication: "What is Anta?"—Salgado asks, and promptly answers: "Nothing . . . The totem of a vanished race" ("O significado da Anta" 287). The Tupis' destiny—Salgado continues—was "to be absorbed. To dissolve themselves in the blood of the new folk" ("Nhengaçú verde amarelo" 233), and thereby achieve a peculiar spiritual victory[15]: "The Portuguese thought the Tupi had ceased to exist; yet the Portuguese had been changed, and emerged with the features of a new nation formed in opposition to the metropolis: because the Tupi were victorious in the blood and soul of the Portuguese" (234). The Tupi "lives on subjectively, and will live on always as a harmonizing element within all those who, before landing in the port of Santos, threw overboard, like Zarathustra's corpse, the philosophies and prejudices of origin" (237–38). Within *verde-amarelista* iconography, the Tupi, in the last instance, signify precisely nothing.

Transubstantiated "in a Eucharist of blood from every origin" (Salgado, *Despertemos a nação!* 40), consumed in a sublimated reversal of their reported anthropophagous rite of revengeful incorporation, the Tupi subsist only as an "absence of prejudices," a 'non-philosophy,' a spiritual presence, a "centripetal force" (Salgado, "Nhengaçú verde amarelo" 235–36), as the palimpsestic trace, the cultural degree zero out of which a "common Fatherland, integrating all our ethnic, social, religious and political expressions," can be erected (236). That this rhetorical transubstantiation effectively compensates for the incontrovertible historical fact that, "for all their heroic adventures, [the *bandeirantes*] were merely rediscovering the old tracks and rivers the Indians already used with their canoes" goes almost without saying (Braudel, *Structures of Everyday Life*, 62).

The formula for national rebirth outlined in the Nhengaçú closely follows the trajectory of the German spirit's return to itself (its "blissful self-rediscovery"), which Nietzsche charts toward the end of *The Birth of Tragedy*: the adumbration of a "Dyonisiac wisdom," "a new mode of existence" (*eine neue Daseinform*)," in the course of which Germany would experience "the great epochs of Hellenism in reverse order" and finally return to "the original source of its being . . . freed from the apron-strings of Romance civilization" (95–96). The obliteration of the Tupi is thus itself allegedly undertaken at the "invitation of universal history." It lays the ground for the future creation of "the cosmic race" (Mexican sociologist José Vasconcelos's celebrated *idée fixe*).

As the authors of the *verde-amarelista* Manifesto observe (236), for Vasconcelos, Brazil is the eugenic "promised land" (*La raza cósmica* 31): "it is in the Amazon and La Plata basins that [Vasconcelos's] 'fifth race' will emerge, the 'cosmic race' that will fulfill the universal concord because it will be the child of the sorrows and hopes of all of humanity" (Salgado, "Nhengaçú verde amarelo" 236). Vasconcelos defines the advent of *la raza cósmica* in his eponymous essay (1925) as America's "predestination," a response to "the design of forming the cradle of a race . . . which will be the fusion of all peoples, and will replace the four races that have been independently forging History" (*La raza cósmica* 24–25). This pan-American project for the creation of what Salgado, in a 1927 article, calls "the harmonious race": "a future human type which will become indisputably one of the most superior and intelligent" (*Despertemos a nação!* 58–59), may echo the Nietzschean desire to produce "international racial unions whose task will be to rear a master race, the future 'masters of the earth'" (Nietzsche, *Will to Power* 504). As if that "tremendous aristocracy" foretold by Nietzsche will indeed have begun "to work as artists upon 'man' himself" (504), in this "third period" of racial evolution (as Vasconcelos designates it), "the mysterious eugenics of aesthetic taste will prevail over scientific eugenics": "The very ugly will not procreate, will not wish to procreate; what difference will it make then that every race will be mixed, if the unattractive will be allowed no progeny?" (Vasconcelos, *La raza cósmica* 38).

In light of the dominant role they accord to the European immigrant in the development of this racial utopia, it is not surprising that the *verde-amarelistas* attempt to establish a seamless historical progression from the conquest and settlement of the "province of Santa Cruz" to early twentieth-century waves of European migration.[16] The occidental character of the future nation is in their eyes predestined as well. In this sense, the proponents of *verde-amarelismo* disclose "the demagogic zeal" that Angel Rama ascribes to "Latin American letters" as a whole, namely, the reiterated rhetorical use of the Indian as "a pretext" for the *criollo*'s own political and cultural claims (*Transculturación narrativa* 11–12). Upon this point, however, *verde-amarelismo* diverges from *anthropofagia*, whose adherents insist, by contrast, upon the accidental nature of occidental Brazil. As Oswaldo Costa quips, "westernized Brazil is . . . a case of historical pseudomorphism" ("Revisão necessária," 6).

Raymond Williams has noted that modernist and avant-garde appropriations of the primitive and the popular follow disparate political orientations as they develop: either toward "socialist and other radical and revolutionary tendencies [or] very strong national and eventually nationalist identifications, of the kind heavily drawn upon in both Italian and German Fascism" (*Politics of Modernism* 58). One could similarly distinguish between the *verde-amarelista* "desire for the doublet and moral slavery, the colonization by the arrogant and idiotic European," in the partisan words of one of the *Revista de Antropofagia*'s editorials ("Uma adesão," 10), and a broadly "leftist" insistence on the "discovery's" aleatory nature: *o acaso dos Brasis* (the fortuitousness of Brazil's [discovery]), to build on Oswald's line.[17] Mário de Andrade expresses a similar sentiment in a 1931 article: "accidental Cabral [*o acaso dos Cabrais*], having by probable chance [*acaso*] discovered Brazil for the probable first time, ended up claiming Brazil for Portugal" (*Macunaíma* (1988 ed.) 427).

This polemic persists and is obviously not peculiar to Brazil. It lies at the core of modernist efforts to redefine the cultural identity of America. It resonates, for instance, in the conflicting readings of Columbus's arrival in the Caribbean by McCaslin Edmonds and Isaac McCaslin in Faulkner's "The Bear." The former considers it no more than "an accidental egg [that] discovered . . . a new hemisphere." While the latter, apparently glossing Columbus's own belief that Eden lay somewhere below the Gulf of Paria, regards the same event as a sign of divine intervention, as the promise of a civilizational point of departure: "[God] used a simple egg to discover to [humanity] a new world where a nation of people could be founded in humility and pity and sufferance and pride of one to another" (Faulkner, *Go Down, Moses* 247).

But while Anthropophagy's descent into "genuine and still pristine sources" also sought to "garner the seeds of renewal [and reach an] authentic cultural synthesis with a deeper national consciousness" (Bopp, *Vida e morte* 41), its attempt to recover "the other Brazil: subjacent, still unknown, yet to be discovered" (Bopp, *Movimentos modernistas* 64), was carried out under the sign of an irredentist barbarism. The Anthropophagists present themselves as Nietzsche's "new barbarians" (*Will to Power* 478). They reject outright any attempt to subsume Brazil's national culture under a Judeo-Christian ethos.

"Manifesto Antropofágico": A Cannibal Recipe to Turn a Dessert Country into the Main Course

Along with other *modernista* primitivisms, Anthropophagy thus sets out to "solve the problem of the formation of the Brazilian language and of a Brazilian Brazil, [of] the great Brazilian nation." Unlike them, however, it wishes to distinguish between "the élite, European, and the people, Brazilian, to side with the latter against . . . western culture" ("Algumas notas sobre" n.p.). The Indian extolled by the *verde-amarelistas,* charges another of the pieces published in the *Revista de Antropofagia,* is the Romantic, commonplace Guarani created by the nineteenth-century novelist José de Alencar. "The 'Anthropophagus' [on the other hand] is no bottle-label Indian" [*"o 'antropófago' não é índio de rótulo de garrafa"*] (O. de Andrade, "Uma adesão" 10).

One of the *Revista*'s editorials faults Modernismo for having "limited itself to an aesthetic revolution . . . when its function was to create the new Brazilian thought [o novo pensamento brasileiro]"; it charges the movement with having remained "enslaved to [a] European culture . . . agonizing" in a Spenglerian twilight, with having failed to recognize "the rift separating . . . the deep layers of nationality from the thick, moth-infested rind enveloping it" (Oswald de Andrade, "Moquém" 6). Finally and probably retorting to the *verde-amarelistas,* the same editorial declares that *modernistas* never "realized the painful consequences of the 'spiritual conquest' of the Tupi nation," concluding: "Down with spiritual domination. What counts now is mastication" ["Para o canto as ditaduras espirituais. O que vale agora são as dentaduras"] (6). As Oswald's pun on "Hamlet's crude question" ("Tupi or not Tupi"; Sommer, *Foundational Fictions* 138)—and, indeed, the movement's name—indicate, it is the Tupi as well who holds the answer to this Anthropophagist interrogation of identity.

Like Diotima in Plato's *Symposium,* the Tupi is exhumed to deliver a critical and posthumous—postprandial—lesson for the present. He is the absent presence of Anthropophagy, the phantasmal agent of "the Carib Revolution" ("greater than the French Revolution"), for which the "Manifesto Antropófago" calls.[18] Apparently heeding Nietzsche's demand to "open one's eyes and take a new look at cruelty or "learn cruelty anew" ["Man soll über die Grausamkeit umlernen und die Augen aufmachen"], (Nietzsche, *Beyond Good and Evil* 159; *Jenseits von Gut und Böse* 171), Anthropophagy seeks to resolve the "problem" articulated in *The Will to Power*—"where are the barbarians of the twentieth century?" And it proposes to accomplish this by unloosing "the most powerful and most dangerous passions of man" (*Will to Power* 465). As one of the contributors to the *Revista de Antropofagia* (presumably Oswald himself) declares, "Anthropophagy is the journey toward (not the return to) natural man" (O. de Andrade, "Uma adesão" 10).

In his introduction to the Anthropophagy volume of Oswald's complete works, Benedito Nunes writes that Oswald's master concept is defined by a "circular dialectical movement" (*Do 'Pau-Brasil'* xlvi).[19] The philosophical foundation of Anthropophagy, by Oswald's own admission, is the "dialectical method," the notion that human development proceeds by contradictions, as well as the insistence, taken from Hegel as well as Marx, that the dialectic has both a "conservative" and a negative component (*Do 'Pau-Brasil'* 28; *Estética e política* 103, 286). As a full-fledged philosophical concept (its final incarnation), Anthropophagy becomes a figure for Hegel's *Aufhebung*. More specifically, it attempts a dialectical supersession of Nietzsche's notion of eternal recurrence.

Thus, in "A crise da filosofia messiânica" (The Crisis of Messianic Philosophy)—a thesis presented in 1950 as part of his candidacy to a philosophy professorship at the University of São Paulo—Oswald describes Anthrophagy as a "metaphysical operation," a weltanschauung or "mode of thought" linked to a "primitive phase of the whole of humanity" (*Do 'Pau-Brasil'* 77). The essay develops and systematizes the Manifesto's lapidary formulas, whose conceptual debts to Marx, Nietzsche, and Freud are already pronounced.[20] While the Manifesto's underlying ethos is a sort of radical humanism—Perry Anderson's "imagined revolution"[21]—both the ground of its aphoristic reversal of (western) axiologies and of its reclamation of a primitive "Dyonisian" past derive considerably from Nietzsche's vitalism and critique of values.

Perhaps one of the most recognizable features of the Manifesto is its emphasis on the concrete, on carnality and the corporeal:

> We are concretists. Ideas take charge, react, have people burned in public squares.[22] Let us suppress ideas and other paralyses. . . . Down with Father Vieira. . . . The permanent transformation of Taboo into Totem. . . . Down with antagonistic sublimations. Brought over in caravels. . . . The absorption of the sacral enemy. In order to turn him into a totem. . . . Reality without complexes, without insanity, without prostitutions and without penitentiaries, in the matriarchate of Pindorama.[23] (*Do 'Pau-Brasil'* 15, 17, 18, 19)

Given the obvious references to Freud's seminal work, this "concretism" has usually been read as a call to shatter mechanisms of repression and sublimation. In his famous myth of the origin of human culture, Freud sees in the totemic animal a substitute for the slain patriarch (*Totem and Taboo*, 176). The totem contains a recent and concrete memory trace of the killing and devouring of the father, of the end of patriarchal rule. It is the rule of the Father, which Freud's sociological writings in particular relate to the rise of civilization, or *Kultur*, that is supposedly consolidated and internalized in the transition from totem to taboo. If totemism is "a product of the conditions involved in the Oedipus complex," if it is symptomatic of the childhood of cultures, and occurs invariably among "the most backward and miserable of savages," the taboo, on the other hand, is the sign of a "higher" stage of civilization, of an ethics that "is not so remote from us" (164, 4, 29).

In advocating the "transfiguration" of taboo into totem, the Manifesto thus calls for the destruction of western systems of morality and religion ("the clothed and oppressive reality recorded by Freud" [*Do 'Pau-Brasil'* 19]). It aims at a transvaluation of established ethical and social norms. Only in this limited and specific sense, I would stress, can the "mechanisms" of cultural criticism and self-criticism it utilizes, as well as the subversion of "Western reason," or "carnivalization of the centre" it arguably achieves, be designated "a 'deconstruction' *avant la lettre*" (Castillo-Durante, "From Postmodernity to the Rubbish Heap" 66). By the same token—although the injunction to reverse taboo into totem can certainly be regarded as "an epistemological tool for the Latin American problematic" of modernity (68)—its implications are cultural and political just as much as they are ethical and epistemological.

As Benedito Nunes observes in his analysis of "A crise da filosofia messiânica," a geographic division between north and south (in broad terms, between the developed, or colonizing world, and the colonized world) underlies Oswald's conception of human evolution. World history is accordingly subordinated to a transhistorical dialectical antagonism between primitive and civilized man, which in turn generates an asynchronous and imbricated series of binaries: a humanistic cultivation of leisure [*otium*] negated by the capitalist or Protestant work ethic [*nec-otium*] (*ócio* versus *negócio* [trade or commerce] in Portuguese), and a matriarchal or "natural" culture opposed to (and by) patriarchal civilization.

The latter stage constitutes the second or negative moment of the dialectic (*Do 'Pau-Brasil'* 79). Anthropophagy is hence posited as the third or sublatory term, the "synthesis" of natural and civilized man: "Keyserling's technicized barbarian" (14) in the "Manifesto," "technicized natural man," or, "the technicized restoration of an anthropophagic culture" in

"A crise da filosofia messiânica" (79, 129). Despite the obvious overlap between the essay and the Manifesto, the former is no mere recapitulation and expansion of the latter, however. It is precisely in terms of concretism that the difference between the two ought to be grasped.

Aside from its Freudian inflections, the Manifesto's emphasis on the concrete contains at least a faint echo of the dialectical materialist insistence that "it is not the consciousness of men that determines their [being,] but their social [being] that determines their consciousness" (Marx, *Contribution to the Critique* 21). In this sense, Anthropophagy subscribes to the principle that "the history of humanity is no more than [an] abstract universal becoming concrete," to borrow C. L. R. James's elegant formulation.[24] By declaring in the essay that "there is a chronology of ideas which supersedes the chronology of dates" (*Do 'Pau-Brasil'* 79), Oswald effectively refutes the Manifesto's focus on the concrete. To coin the Marxian metaphor, he descends from heaven to earth.

While the essay retains the Manifesto's "third-worldism," its teleological framing of Anthropophagy operates a (German) Idealist turn that negates the "concretism," the suppression of ideas and descent into prelogic, which anchors the Manifesto. In this way, the "digestive sublation" effected by the ritualistic act of anthropophagy, that is, the consumption and vindictive incorporation of the enemy's power and strength, is replicated, in the realm of Ideas, by a dialectic of the human Spirit, an inversion "of the limit and negation into a favorable element" (*Do 'Pau-Brasil'* 77–8; *Estética e política* 104).

This sublation of the cruel savage into a "technicized natural man" projects onto the world historical stage the reconciliation or "mysterious marriage" between the Dyonisian and the Apollinian impulses that, according to Nietzsche, Attic tragedy alone is able to achieve (*Birth of Tragedy* 27). Anthropophagy thus restores what Nietzsche would later call *The Birth of Tragedy*'s offensive Hegelian smell (*Genealogy of Morals* 270) to its own appropriation of the German philosopher's reclamation of "the innocent conscience of the beast of prey [die Unschuld des Raubtier-Gewissens]" (40). It circumscribes to a teleology of progress the inextricable link between the desire to know [*Erkennen-Wollen*] and the will to power articulated in *Beyond Good and Evil,* for example.[25]

Nietzsche's rejection of rationalism abrogates the possibility of reaching transcendental truth. It imposes an unsurpassable limit on the cognitive process, asserting the inevitably asymptotic apperception of the Real and ultimately fragmenting the fictive unity of the knowing subject. By contrast, Anthropophagy's rehabilitation of the instinctual and paralogical is rationalized in its philosophical incarnation, unified under a "spiritual" totality that places "'modernity' in the perspective of the metaphor of nourishment and digestion" (Nietzsche, *Will to Power* 47).

As a philosophical notion, Anthropophagy names and affixes "the hopes that as yet have no names," with which *Beyond Good and Evil* closes (216). It assigns a point of destination to the voyage into the unknown that is Nietzsche's metaphor for his desire for the new: "We do not yet know the 'wither' toward which we are driven once we have detached ourselves from our old soil" (*Will to Power* 219). Against the current of the Manifesto's renunciation of "spiritual dictatorships," against its promise to see with new eyes the 'spiritual conquest' of the Tupi nation, "philosophical" Anthropophagy becomes a voyage of (re)discovery and conquest. Its programmatic effort to supplant the story of human progress borne across the Atlantic by the 'caravels of Christ' ultimately duplicates the latter's plot, its very destination and epistemological claims: "Utopias begin with the discovery of natural man and his torrid paradise in the sixteenth century" (*Do 'Pau-Brasil'* 223); "it was Vespucci who defined natural man" (213).

The primitive sources from which "natural man" is to be retrieved are revealed as inevitably scriptural, artificed by what Michel de Certeau has famously called the "writing that conquers, [that] will use the New World as if it were a blank, 'savage' page on which Western desire will be written" (*Writing of History* xxv):

> Despite all the coercion and wantonness of the white folk, the best that remained of the natural state of the Americas was not destroyed. *Its* culture resisted from the depth of the forests, in the refusal of every enslaving force. Decimated, killed off, perverted, *they* subsisted unscathed in the documents of the conquest itself. All that literature, the missionary included, which in the sixteenth century filled the world with novelty, survived here to the scandal of the clothed and manacled world that was being brought to *us*. (O. de Andrade, *Estética e política* 284; my italics)

The pronominal shift from the savage *they* to the first-person plural inserting itself in the place of the "native witness" at the end of the fragment reproduces the very cultural erasure that Oswald censures. In thus displacing the "agency" of the "Carib Revolution," he may, in effect, be alluding to "the tenacity of Brazil's 'Indian' identity [persisting] even though the country was founded on Indian removal" (Sommer, *Foundational Fictions* 139). But the slippage ultimately calls into question the very 'Indianness' of the identity Anthropophagy seeks to uncover. In this respect, the (Tupi) meaning of the term "Carib" (Caraíba) becomes productively ambiguous. It designates not only the "warlike tribes" of Amazonia and the Antilles, but a shaman or "prophet" endowed with supernatural powers.

According to sixteenth-century European chroniclers, the word *Caraíba*, like the word *Maíra*, was the generic name for Tupi founding heroes. After 1500, however, Caraíba, as well as Maíra, becomes the common designation for the European newcomers.[26] Significantly, the alleged supernatural powers attributed to the Europeans are usually associated with writing, with the production of the very texts in which the delatory figure of the Anthropophagus endures as a lesson to be gleaned by the most radical of Brazil's Modernismos.[27] In this sense, never does the European appear more a Caraíba than when he reveals himself as the master of the written sign, when he wields the familiar arbitrary power to script the newness of an ancient world and thereby assert his absolute modernity: "ce que je vous ay bien voulu icy representer [est] chose non encore veuë, ny descrite par aucun des anciens ny modernes" (Thevet 94) [what I have resolved to represent for you here (is) something never before seen or described by either ancient or modern].

As Certeau puts it, "with writing the Westerner has a sword in his hand which will extend its gesture but never modify its subject. . . . The power that writing's expansionism leaves intact is colonial in principle. It is extended without being changed. It is tautological, immunized against both any alterity that might transform it and whatever dares to resist it" (*Writing of History* 216). In this way the long shadow of European "inauthenticity," of early modern "productions of the Tupi primitive, casts itself over the Anthropophagist project to rediscover their "natural" and naked truth.

If the Anthropophagus is a figure for the radical forgetting of "the histories of man that begin at Cape Finisterre," for a renewed "contact with Caraíba Brasil," the hearkening of the voice of "natural man" (*Do 'Pau-Brasil'* 16, 14); if the *Caraíba* Revolution signifies the reorientation of Brazil's cultural "itineraries," the stripping of an alien cultural garb that alone can renovate the nation, then the habit of Tradition seems ultimately to re-cover its conceptual nudity.[28] Its emancipatory desire reproduces the positive and utopian valuation of the "cannibal" in early modern texts. The negativity that conventionally attaches itself to these inaugural representations of primitive cultures becomes transitive in Oswald's philosophical reformulation, indeed agential, albeit in an idealist sense.

"Savagery" is no longer written as a blank page awaiting the imprint of Christian civilization, but as an active negation and ethical condemnation of the latter (*Do 'Pau-Brasil'* 165, 189, 190; *Estética e política* 251, 254). Vespucci, More, and Montaigne figure prominently among the humanist "team" (*Do 'Pau-Brasil'* 166) whose affirmation of a naked humanity existing "beyond good and evil" Oswald regards as an opening of the horizons of Utopia, as the first leg in the long and tortuous march toward the emancipation of humankind (*Do 'Pau-Brasil'* 187, 213; *Estética e política* 253). In this fashion, the philosophical systematization of *antropofagia* reproduces a contradiction that Paul de Man identifies in Nietzsche's early work. It employs "epistemologically rigorous methods as the only possible means to reflect on the limitations of these methods" (*Allegories of Reading* 86). Anthropophagy, in brief, ends up retelling one of modernity's most enduring grand narratives.

De Man's suspension of the dialectical play between literary modernity and literary history seems pertinent in this context as well: "the claim . . . to a new beginning turns out to be the repetition of a claim that has always already been made" (*Blindness and Insight* 161). In other words, modernity—the moment of radical rupture with history—at once cancels and preserves that which it negates. For de Man, however, the process does not unfold in a diachronic sequence. There is neither progression nor ascension in a temporal sense. The motions of this dialectic "cannot be located, dated and represented as if they were places in a geography of events in a genetic history" (163).

They occur, as it were, simultaneously, "as a synchronic juxtaposition" within the "space" of literature, in an ontological mode whose very essence is to be, forever and ineluctably, at odds with itself (*Blindness and Insight* 163–64). On the other hand, this radical troping of temporality renders ultimately untenable any endeavor to extend de Man's reading of modernity to a "peripheral" modernism that emerges both as a result and a response to the "time lag" between north and south. What de Man's "deconstruction" of the historical fails to take into account is the possibility that Anthropophagy's repetition of European epistemological paradigms may not result in their consolidation but rather their displacement.

In contrast to Perry Anderson's and Raymond Williams's formulations of modernism's "insurgency" against tradition, for example, de Man's account of literary modernity eschews periodization. It arrests itself before the articulation of this enduring antagonism with materialist coordinates. Yet, in the last analysis, de Man's spatialization of the modernity/history dialectic renounces, rather than invalidates, an extension of the analysis into the social and economic fields, the very fields that, according to Williams and Anderson, condition the emergence of modernism. For the view that "the bases for historical knowledge are not empirical facts but written texts, even if these texts masquerade in the guise of wars and revolutions" (*Blindness and Insight* 165) need not entail the following correlate: to propose that history cannot be reduced to the tropological, that it is a kind of insurmountable limit to critical reading itself, is inevitably to confuse linguistic with natural reality.

To put it another way, the proposition that reference is a trope does not, and indeed should not, foreclose the possibility of thinking the historical, or even the promise of emancipation. My aim here is not to uphold the epistemological primacy of historical materialism against an approach that asserts the irreducible rhetoricity of the Real. Rather, what I am trying to call to notice is de Man's theoretically unwarranted circumscription of the space within which the dialectic between modernity and history plays itself out to that of written texts (in the narrow sense), to literature, whose distinctness from all other discourses de Man appears at times simply to take for granted.

I began this account of the rise of *antropofagia* with a passing reference to its historical coincidence with specific economic and political conditions (as well as its direct engagement with the question of nationalism) not to signify that these are linked in a direct causal relationship, but in an effort to broach the complexity of the discursive cluster within which the movement operates. As Raymond Williams notes, one of the crucial differences between the conceptions of invention of early-twentieth-century avant-gardes and those of Romanticism, for instance, is the emphasis placed by the former on "creative engineering, [the] construction of a future" (*Politics of Modernism* 53). The opening *a linea* of the "Manifesto Antropófago" alludes aphoristically to this project of social transformation: "Only Anthropophagy unites us. Socially. Economically. Philosophically" (O. de Andrade, *Do 'Pau-Brasil'* 13).

In order fully to understand it, then, one needs to look closely into the extension of the idea of Anthropophagy into these "extra-literary" fields. Perry Anderson's approach thus allows for a more ecumenical reading of Anthropophagy, not necessarily because it yields a "truer picture" of it, but because it relies precisely on the model of "expressive causality" that subtends Anthropophagy as well. For Anderson, Modernisms are the "superstructural" expression of a political and socioeconomic totality that, as Althusser remarks, can always "be reducible to an inner essence" (Althusser and Balibar, *Reading Capital* 187). It is a version of this Hegelian model of causality that governs Anthropophagy's sociological analysis as well.

Antropofagia posits the parousia (or revengeful second coming) of the Wild Man: the symbol of "the ahistorical peoples whose aim is simply to live, without setting themselves up as conquerors, as owners of the world and makers of empires" (O. de Andrade, *Do 'Pau-Brasil'* 189). It sets out, in this sense, to make whole again the fractured and unrealized Carib epic that, in Carpentier's account of the "discovery," the sudden advent of Christian time in the Caribbean archipelago irremediably shatters (*Explosion in a Cathedral* 242–45). It seeks to reverse, precisely in Hegelian terms, Hegel's apparently irreversible expunction of America's "dull savages" from History (*Philosophy of Mind,* 45). Against the Eurocentric civilizational itinerary that Hegel famously lays out in *The Philosophy of History, antropofagia* intimates that Europe's hegemony may not have been the result of its superiority of mind, culture, or environment, but something of a historical "accident." It thus establishes a correlation between the Tupi's relation to the evolution of European thought and that of Brazil's raw materials to the development of (European) industry: "Without us Europe would not even have its poor declaration of the rights of man" (*Do 'Pau-Brasil'* 14). "Here in Brazil, we were forced to sweat upon the earth, both slaves and settlers, in order to provide resources to Europe, whose Industrial Revolution was feeding off the vein of our precious metals" (O. de Andrade, *Estética e política* 283). To borrow Raul Bopp's prandial metaphor, Anthropophagy attempts to replace the prevalent menus (*Movimentos modernistas* 71).

It is a "counter-meal" (*almoçar contra*), "not just a matter of gastronomy, but a battle formation" (*Estética e política* 133). It aims at reorienting Brazil toward the "main course," as it were: "We are a dessert country.[29] With sugar, coffee and tobacco we can be listed only at the bottom of imperialist menus. . . . When our main customers, out of greed or lack of funds, cut dessert, we plunge into the most desperate and unpredictable of crises. . . . If we knew how to exploit our El Dorados, which are no legends. . . . Develop our heavy industries. Back our paper currency with our gold! . . . We could wreck London or New York" (167).

This industrial potential, Oswald later asserts, is "the Sleeping Beauty whom [no one] is able to awaken" (*Estética e Política* 178). The Portuguese term for dessert, *sobremesa* (literally: "upon the table"), functions as an appropriate figure for the serving up of Brazil's agricultural products on the "tables" of developed Capital: "Nature / upon the table" ("Natureza / sobre a mesa"), to quote from one of Oswald's early poems (*Pau Brasil*, 46). It also suggests an inversion of the relation between base and superstructure (i.e., a *sobre/mesa* country, or "a country with an imported superstructure"[30]). According to Renato Ortiz, this reversal defines underdeveloped projects of modernization (*A moderna cultura* 35–36). *Antropofagia,* in its politico-economic variant, is thus a recipe for self-development.

For many of its critics, the terms and social positions from which this prescription for overcoming backwardness is articulated point to a crucial social contradiction. They indicate a class privilege symptomatic of the "brutal forms of inequality" produced in peripheral societies (Schwarz, *Misplaced Ideas* 15). Nevertheless, to argue that "the innocence cultivated by Oswald [rides] on the wave of prosperity brought by coffee" (120), or that *modernista* projects in general are linked to the dominant classes (Ortiz, *A moderna cultura* 32), is to repeat a *modernista* self-critique.[31]

By the same token, the Anthropophagists' class interest reinscribes itself as a symbolic (that is, ideological) resolution of the contradiction between its modernizing aspirations and the context of "dependency" and "underdevelopment" within which it putatively emerges. In Roberto Schwarz's terms, the movement "aimed at leaping a whole stage" of development (*Mispaced Ideas* 8). Similarly for Renato Ortiz, modernism in Brazil cannot but be a "misplaced idea" (*uma idéia fora do lugar*) (*A moderna cultura* 35). It can only be a movement which—in contrast to "developed" modernisms—arises out of a "peripheral" asynchrony [descompasso] between a base (lacking the ["modernized"] economic structures from which full-blown European modernisms are "directly derived" [33]) and a superstructure that can only permit the expression of modernity as a wish-fantasy (32–34).

Antropofagistas—to cite the passage from Marshall Berman's discussion of the nineteenth-century Russian experience of modernity upon which Ortiz grounds his analysis—could only apprehend modernization "as something that was not happening; or else as something that was happening far away, in realms . . . experienced more as fantastic anti-worlds than as social actualities" (*All That Is Solid,* 175). Hence, like the German idealists derided by the early Marx, the Brazilian modernists have apparently "thought what ['advanced nations'] have done. . . . The abstraction and presumption of [their intellectual production] was in step with the partial and stunted character of their reality" (Tucker, *Marx-Engels Reader* 59). It is an open question, however, whether the movement's elitism can be ascribed exclusively to infrastructural lack of development. For modernisms, as Raymond Williams points out, "have never involved, as producers or as publics, more than minorities; often very small minorities" (*Politics of*

Modernism 77). The latter, moreover, invariably comprise "the authentic avant-garde" of the bourgeoisie itself (56).

As it turns out, these Brazilian critiques' emphasis on the elitism and referential emptiness of Anthropophagy subscribes to the very developmentalist logic that governs the movement—a logic that inevitably renders it at once anachronistic and parachronistic. From the standpoint of this developmental narrative, then, Anthropophagy is an aesthetics rooted in the backwardness of Brazil, a kind of longing expressed before its time. It can serve only as a compensation for the condition of underdevelopment. It is either the expression of the dominant classes' "wish to be recognized [as modern, or] an effort to carve a self-portrait of Brazil consistent with the civilized imaginary" (Ortiz, *A moderna cultura* 32).

In this light, the negation, the blank into which the Anthropophagus is usually converted in sixteenth-century descriptions of Brazil finds its twentieth-century correlate in the *antropofagista* perception of modernity as a negative. Modernity, in this sense, turns out to be nothing but the spatio-temporal gap (the "not-yet" and the "elsewhere") to which development narratives tend to reduce the history of the "underdeveloped" world.

Lévi-Strauss remarks, for example, that "the tropics are less exotic than out of date" (*Tristes Tropiques* 87). In the urban centers of Brazil in the 1930s he encounters "a social evolution which had occurred in Paris in the nineteenth century and which São Paulo (and Rio de Janeiro) were then reliving" (102). Perry Anderson reiterates and extends this historical logic: "in the Third World generally, a kind of shadow configuration of what once prevailed in the First World does exist today" ("Modernity and Revolution" 329). It is this implacable temporal mechanism that Octavio Paz describes ironically as "the strait-jacket of development" in a 1969 Postdate to his polemical analysis of Mexico's identity crisis: "something is ending in the developed world: precisely that which amongst us is just beginning. What is sunrise in Mexico is sunset over there and what it is dawn over there is still *nothing* in Mexico" (*El laberinto,* 288, 276; my translation and italics).

This perdurable dilemma has frequently taken the troubling form of an unswerving faith in the positive values of modernization and civilization. For Raymond Williams, it has all too often given rise to "a major distortion in the history of communism," that is, the untold damage wrought upon rural populations by "revolutionary" development projects (*Country and the City* 303). In Octavio Paz's more abstract formulation, this blind faith in the necessity of modernization has the potential to unleash in underdeveloped countries the "disaster" that "all the development models we know, whether they originate from the West or the East," have hitherto produced (*El laberinto* 273). In addition, the fact that "the 'rural idiots' and the 'barbarians and semi-barbarians' have been [at least since the beginning of the period of national and social liberation struggles] the main revolutionary force in the world" ultimately reveals the blind spot of this developmentalist logic (Williams, *Country and the City* 304).

In this way, Anthropophagy follows the spirit of Frantz Fanon's assertion that Marx's postulation of the European proletariat as the driving force of the revolution needs to be "slightly extended" (*légèrement distendu*) in the context of Africa and other colonial regions (Fanon, *Les damnés de la terre* 33). Indeed, as Édouard Glissant has noted, Marxism has since undertaken the very revision Fanon called for: "The facts have imposed upon Marxist thought the idea that it is neither in the more technically advanced countries, nor through more organized proletariats that the revolution first triumphs" (*Le discours antillais* 132; my translation). C. L. R. James has summed up the central theme of Aimé Césaire's *Notebook of a Return to My Native Land* (1939) along similar lines: "Africa and Africans will move towards an integrated humanity . . . no longer from external stimulus but from their own self-generated and independent being and motion" (*C. L. R. James Reader* 304). This is essentially what *antropofagia* proposes for Brazil and Brazilians.

Granted, Anthropophagy's proposed rupture with the past ends up largely replicating the very epistemic violence it seeks to negate, reinserting itself into the same scriptural order it sets out to revise, if not undo. It may perhaps be this reinscription that its critics then transcode as an "an uncritical [i.e., "peripheral"] vision of the modern world" (Ortiz, *A moderna cultura* 36). But to maintain that Anthropophagy arises in the wrong place at the wrong time is, in the last instance, to construe the problem of underdevelopment in Anthropophagist (or *modernista*) terms, since Anthropophagy's point of departure is precisely the recognition of this temporal *décalage*. What it proposes is nothing less than the supersession of history as repetition. It imagines a future where Brazil's present would be something other than a shadow cast by the First World's past, where modernity would come to be experienced as fulfillment rather than absence.

Paradoxically, it is this absent of history—apparently compelled prima facie to return eternally—that, in contemporary analyses of the movement, comes back to determine Anthropophagy's lack of historical relevance and referentiality. As Paul de Man's examination of the dialectic between literary history and literary modernity indicates, however, there is likewise nothing uniquely underdeveloped about this reintegration. Modernity, in its modal sense, whether it is developed or not, is always "elsewhere," both "not yet" and "always-already" in place.

Perry Anderson himself suggests as much when he argues that modernisms, at the same time that they define themselves in opposition to "academicism," utilize the latter's established, "partially aristocratic" canons as an axiological foundation from which the cultural and social depredations of market capitalism ("the commercial spirit of the age") can be resisted and condemned ("Modernity and Revolution" 325).[32] In Anderson's view, the absence, which developmental narratives tend to translate into a sign of backwardness or dependency, ultimately resides within the notion of modernism itself. "Modernism is the emptiest of all cultural categories," he concludes, "it designates no object in its own right at all: it is completely lacking in positive content... a portmanteau concept whose only referent is the blank passage of time" (332). Raymond Williams alludes also to the ultimate lack of specificity of this 'modern absolute.' "the defined universality of a human condition which is effectively permanent" (*Politics of Modernism* 38).

Like Marx's bourgeois revolution—which stands opposed to a "socialist revolution" that putatively draws its poetry from the future and will finally abolish modernity (Anderson, "Modernity and Revolution" 333)—modernism for both Anderson and Williams is therefore "the phrase that goes beyond the content" (Marx, *Eighteenth Brumaire* 18). In this manner, Anthropophagy's gap (or referential emptiness) registers not so much an asynchrony between core and peripheral modernisms but a historically determined discontinuity between modernism's figural appeal to the new and the historical content of a revolutionary future. It discloses the insuperable restrictions that ideology imposes upon modernism's utopian desire, whether the latter originates in the core or the periphery. In this light, Ortiz's and Schwarz's critiques of the movement's irrelevance neglect to take into consideration what Carlos Alonso designates "the plurivocal, self-contradictory, and open-ended dimension" of the metropolitan discourses which *antropofagia* seeks to rewrite (*Burden of Modernity* 28).

Anthropophagy's critics stop short of considering the possibility that the movement's political and aesthetic "recipe" for the future may arise precisely from a tacit recognition that the model of modernity it seeks to reproduce ultimately puts to question this "reproducibility" itself. They fail to account for the fact that "the West," as Édouard Glissant argues, "is not monolithic"; indeed, it has "itself produced the variables to contradict its impressive trajectory every time" (*Poetics of Relation* 191). If then there is a hollow at the core of Anthropophagy, its explanation must be sought elsewhere.

Pierre Macherey's notion of textual silence can, I believe, serve as the groundwork for such an elucidation. For Macherey, "the gap [*le creux*] inside which the text unfolds," the hollow where "nothing is said" and which nonetheless no phrase can ever fulfill—becomes the condition of the literary work's possibility: an "unconscious" that overflows textual limits finally to intersect with History (*Pour une théorie* 101–16). The absence within modernist projects may be said to mark a similar "unconscious." Fredric Jameson postulates, in fact, that, in the final instance, what (western) modernisms repress is the globalization of Capital. In an early formulation of this thesis, Jameson links the modernist rejection of realist modes of representation to the emergence of late monopoly capitalism and its attendant "subjectivization and fragmentation of our social life, and of our very existences" ("Beyond the Cave" 132). Just as the nineteenth-century "ideology of realism" is inseparable from that stage of capitalism during which the market system rationalizes "the older hierarchical . . . feudal or magical environment," a phase in which the bourgeoisie still conceives of itself as a vital, cohesive social group, the rise of modernism will coincide with the decay of the bourgeoisie as a class, with "a world of social anomie and fragmentation" (122).

Modernist texts, then, are "simply cancelled realistic ones" (129), the sites of a literary "self-reflection" that manifests itself as "an increasing (structural) incapacity to generalize or universalize private or lived experience" (131). They reject the mimetic model and turn inward into "so private a speech that it is henceforth bereft of any public consequences or resonances" (131). Jameson's reading thus attempts to chart a dialectical-materialist geography of modernism's absent content, a sociology of "the consolation and pleasure" that, according to Lyotard, modernist literature offers the reader. As I hope to illustrate in what follows, it is in its 'global reach' that Jameson's analysis may ultimately throw a provocative light on the utopian dimension of Anthropophagy.

In a later article, Jameson argues that radical formalisms as a whole are "a compensation and a substitution for precisely those more basic realities of the colonial situation and the native population, which . . . have been systematically repressed and excluded in the strict Freudian sense of neurotic denial or Verneinung (the Lacanian *dénégation*)" ("Modernism and Its Repressed" 174). He now formulates the absent of modernism as the metropole's irrecuperable other ("colonial life, colonial suffering, and exploitation"), conceiving it as a narrative and epistemological inability to include the unimaginable alterity of that significant segment of metropolitan existence whose meaning lies elsewhere, beyond the imperial center ("Modernism and Imperialism" 51, 50).

As with Macherey's hollow in the text, no restitution can ever be made for this void. It is a sense of deprivation "comparable to another dimension, an outside like the other face of a mirror, which [the modernist text] constitutively lacks, and which can never be made up or made good" ("Modernism and Imperialism" 51). For Jameson, then, this is the dilemma, the "formal contradiction" that modernist writing attempts to resolve. The problem is not just specific to, but generative of, modernism, for "it is only that new kind of art which reflexively perceives this problem and lives this formal dilemma that can be called modernism in the first place" (51). The modernist reflex—writing's folding back upon the space of writing itself: 'style'—"now becomes the marker and the substitute (the 'tenant-lieu,' or place-holding, in Lacanian language) of the [colonial system's] unrepresentable totality" (58).

Antropofagia would thus seem to originate precisely in that other dimension, that other side of the looking glass, which metropolitan modernisms can "figure" only as an empty place. This in essence is the claim Jameson makes for Joyce's *Ulysses,* whose sweeping transformation of "the modernist formal project" turns out to be a reflection of the "radically different kind of space" that is Ireland under British rule: "a space ... marked as marginal and ex-centric after the fashion of the colonized areas of the imperial system" ("Modernism and Imperialism" 60). Joyce's then is a "Third World modernism [that] slyly [turns] the imperial relationship inside out" (64). It is a modernist projection whose ex-centricity, rather than manifest itself as a temporal lag, becomes, in effect, proleptic: "As with revolutionary modes of production, Joyce leaps over the stage of the modern into full postmodernism" (62). While I would stop short of reproducing uncritically Jameson's "modes of production" narrative, I should like nevertheless to propose, in closing, a reading of Anthropophagy's attempt to "leap a whole stage" in terms of a similar futural promise, in terms of what Lyotard calls "the paradox of the future (post) anterior (modo)" (*Postmodern Explained* 15).

I am certainly not asserting that Oswald "prophesies" postmodernism, as Blaise Cendrars might have phrased it; or that *antropofagia* embodies a revolutionary potential yet to be unveiled. I am indicating, though, that, notwithstanding its reliance on the logic of development, *antropofagia* is ultimately something more complex and indeterminate than the expression of an anachronistic desire to be developed. Totalizing as it sometimes purports to be, it nonetheless evokes, if only inchoately, the terror of totalizing projects. That its ambivalent engagement with the magisterial philosophical texts that narrate the west's long story of emancipation can all too easily be dismissed as no more than scattershot should not exclude the possibility that *antropofagia* represents an early skirmish in the now familiar war on totality.

Even more cogently, however, Anthropophagy aims at inverting "the relationship between margin and centre as it has appeared within the master discourses of the master race" (Gilroy, *Black Atlantic* 45). It seeks to reconstruct "the primal history of modernity . . . from the [others'] point of view" (55). As García Canclini proposes, *antropofagia* may constitute one of the modernist "antecedents" to the processes of "decollecting and deterritorialization" [*descollección y desterritorialización*] that he identifies with the postmodern epoch (*Hybrid Cultures* 243).

To borrow the terms of Roberto Schwarz's magisterial study of Machado de Assis's narrative fiction, the counter-hegemonic practices broadly ascribed to postmodernist poetics are neither entirely absent from nor necessarily manifested *avant la lettre* in the heterogenous and often self-contradictory discourse of *antropofagia*. Rather, like "the historical position of reason" in the narrative discourse of Machado de Assis, "postmodernity" can be "seen simultaneously as having been overtaken and as not yet having been reached" by the Anthropophagists (*Master on the Periphery* 24).

From this aporetic stance, any aspect that might ordinarily be designated as "backward" could also be understood in terms of its "affinity" with trends that are just beginning to materialize in the "center" and have yet to become visible in the "periphery" (Schwartz, *Master in the Periphery* 123). Hence, the Manifesto's shibboleth regarding the inscription of the American indigene in Europe's discourses of republicanism ("Without us Europe would not even have its poor declaration of the rights of man")—as much as it subscribes to the Hegelian logic of *antropofagia*'s effort to reverse Hegel's "course of history"—can also be reread in a performative sense, as a "repetition of the sign of modernity [that] is different, specific to its historical and cultural conditions of enunciation" (Bhabha, *Location of Culture* 247).

One could posit it therefore as an adumbration of Gayatri Spivak's proposition that western philosophy at once forecloses and excises the figure of the primitive (or "native informant") in order to establish the

"Northwestern European" Subject as universal (*Critique of Postcolonial Reason*, 1–111). Indebted to and embedded as it is in the very cultural and philosophical tradition it seeks to displace, *antropofagia* cannot but tacitly (and tactically) acknowledge the extent of its determination by the "magisterial texts" of the west. By this same token, however, it also broaches the possibility that those same texts can now be turned into "our servants, as the new magisterium constructs itself in the name of the Other" (7). As we shall see in the chapter that follows, *antropofagia*'s critical stance toward the west in general, and the colonial archive in particular, stands in sharp contrast to that assumed by the Brazilian literary and cultural production of the same period.

2 In the Land of the Great Serpent
The Poetics of National Development and the Sublime Topography of the Amazon

> Exploring about the interior one day with twenty men, we saw a snake, or serpent, some eight braccia long, and the width of my waist: it frightened us very much, and at the sight of it we returned to the sea.
> —Amerigo Vespucci, *Letters from a New World*

> Children of the sun, mother of the living. Discovered and ferociously loved, with all the hypocrisy of longing, by the immigrants, the trafficked and the *touristes*. In the land of the Great Snake.
> —Oswald de Andrade, "Manifesto Antropófago"

ONE OF the grand projects of Anthropophagy that eventually "came to naught" was the creation of a Little Anthropophagist Library (Bibliotequinha antropofágica) in which Mário de Andrade's *Macunaíma* (1928) and Raul Bopp's *Cobra Norato* were to figure prominently (Bopp, *Movimentos modernistas* 94, 82). Written at the height of the movement (1927–28), but published in its entirety only in 1931 (though fragments of it appeared in the *Revista de Antropofagia*), Bopp's narrative poem, perhaps even more than Mário's hybrid text, is usually regarded as the consummate expression of the *antropofagista* aesthetic. Despite Mário's insistent objections,[1] Oswald insisted that the two texts were distinctively Anthropophagic: "Whatever the outcome of the movement—he was to comment years later—it can pride itself on having given *Macunaíma* and *Cobra Norato* to Brazil" (*Estética e política* 19). *Cobra Norato*, like many of the poetic works produced during Modernismo's nationalist phase, and arguably *Macunaíma* itself, is not entirely bereft of "the primitivism fashionable in contemporary Europe" (Franco, *Modern Culture* 97).

In keeping with the "search for roots among the most primitive elements of the population and in primitive nature" (Franco, *Modern Culture* 268), which characterizes the literary production of this period, the plot of Bopp's poem is based on a Tupi legend treated in several other works written at the time.[2] It narrates the eponymous hero's Orphic quest for a young woman held captive in the forest underworld by Cobra Grande (Great Serpent). At first glance, Cobra Grande emerges as the Amazonian counterpart to the Minotaur, or indeed any of several reptilian nemeses of chivalric heroes, including inevitably the dragon slain by Saint George, Portugal's patron saint. *Cobra Norato* thus evinces "the tension" that Jean Franco identifies "between the need for roots and the urge for modernity" at the same time that it aims at "a combination of the avant-garde and the search for [primitive] roots" (267–68). In this manner, the poem comes to us exegetically "prescribed" as "a penetration into the dark and oneirical world of the forest, [into] a universe of myths and unconscious forces" (Averbuck, *Cobra Norato* 125), as an excavation of "primitive roots, [and] the depths of the Brazilian past" (163).

The late Lígia Averbuck, perhaps one of the most thoughtful readers of Bopp's *modernista* epic, defines its thematics as a series of "syntheses": (1) the translation of the natural, hallucinatory "voice" of the Amazon into poetic technique (Averbuck, *Cobra Norato* 83, 87, 113), (2) the "complete fusion" of a "cultivated poetic language" with "popular expression" (193), (3) a "perfect symbiosis between signifier and signified" (215) (that is, Saussure's classic definition of the linguistic sign), (4) the union of subject and object (219), (5) a thematic or "metaphoric" coalescence between the savage and the technological worlds (170–71), (6) between the rural and the urban (172), and finally, (7) "a model of signification . . . and promise for the future," since the syntheses it projects at the aesthetic level—a reconciliation of antinomies (or "supersession of contradictions") (210)—can only be fully grasped *now*: namely, in the reader's present and the poem's future, a prospective time when "the contradictions of an emergent [Brazilian] culture" that the poem seeks to resolve are "gradually becoming understood" (221).

Bopp himself endorses this "synthetic" interpretation, defining the poem as a "descent" into an "obscure pre-history . . . [into] immense, atavistic depths, [and] the geographic stew . . . stirring within anthropophagic frontiers: the forest in all its brutality, generating worlds of magic" (Bopp, *Vida e morte da Antropofagia* 69–70). Like the oneirical geography, "the sources of poetic imagination" indicated by Surrealism's "arrow" (Breton, *Manifestes du surréalisme* 29), Bopp's Amazon figures the (national) unconscious. Plotting the telluric course to which "the Anthropophagic arrow points" (*Movimentos modernistas* 71), *Cobra Norato*, according to both Bopp and Oswald, participates in a programmatic effort to fashion "a Brazil in our likeness" (64). In my own reading of *Cobra Norato*,

I attempt, in an initial moment, to utilize Averbuck's hypothesis as a point of departure for an understanding of what could be called Bopp's "rain forest" poetics. Ultimately, however, I wish to test the limits of this synthetic model and ascertain the extent to which the opposing terms that structure *Cobra*'s plot are indeed reconciled in the last instance, that is, superseded into a higher form embodied by the poem itself.

González Echevarría has argued that Latin America's so-called *novelas de la tierra*—"a tag that can most productively be translated as novels about the earth and novels of the earth" (*Voice of the Masters* 44), such as Rómulo Gallegos's *Doña Bárbara* (Venezuela, 1929) and José Eustacio Rivera's *La vorágine* (Colombia, 1925)—utilize the "ground" [*la tierra*] "as an outside referent whose own difference will make Latin American literature distinct and original. The ground is both origin and difference ... a metaphor of culture [and] the source of authority. It informs the text, giving it referential validity and endowing it with the power to articulate the truth" (*Voice of the Masters* 45). The Amazonian "ground" functions in a similar manner in *Cobra Norato*.

The hero's very name suggests an incorporation into and domination of chthonic forces. Subscribing to the ancestral Tupi custom of acquiring the names of defeated and devoured enemies, Cobra Norato earns the name and attributes of his vanquished adversary, the serpent, a synecdoche of the jungle itself.[3] Upon entering the seething chiaroscuro of the Amazon, in fact, he proclaims "the forest ... the enemy of man" (*Cobra Norato* [1994] 10). Moreover, Norato's inaugural feat is itself a *literalization* of this onomastic conquest: he strangles a snake and slips into its "silk elastic skin" (3). He will remain enveloped by it until the end of his epic journey.

As a trope, the voyage into a hostile, antediluvian nature has a lengthy genealogy in western literature. Among modernist texts, Conrad's paradigmatic travel narrative comes unavoidably to mind. Not unexpectedly, however, *Cobra Norato*'s tropology reveals a much closer affinity with the Latin American *novelas de la tierra* examined by González Echevarría. Eustacio Rivera's *La vorágine*, for instance, presents the Amazon as both inimical and inhuman: "an anthropophagous abyss ... gaping before the soul like a mouth swallowing up men whom hunger and dejection deposit in its jaws" (223, 236). Rómulo Gallegos writes in similar terms of "the man-devouring wilderness" [la barbarie devoradora de hombres] (*Doña Bárbara*, 221, 262). In his 1935 "jungle novel" *Canaima*, Gallegos depicts the tropical forest as "abyssal [and] inhuman," an "outdated, [and] unfinished world ... a disquieting landscape over which the primeval awe of the world's first morning still seemed to reign"; those who dare to cross its boundaries, Gallegos cautions us, are bound to become "either something more or something less than men" (119, 4). As in these emblematic narratives, in *Cobra Norato* both the threat and the unruly fecundity of the jungle are gendered feminine:

> I blend into the jungle's womb. (3)
>
> This is the forest . . . breeding serpents
> . . . .
> with pregnant trees sitting in the dark. (9, 12)
>
> I'm bogged in a swampy matrix. (14)
>
> Forest wombs cry out: 'Fill me!' The pond is wrinkled
> like a tired ovary
> . . . .
> The water has the smooth silkiness of a young girl's leg. (20–21)
>
> I was a single river
> . . . . . .
> but the jungle clogged me up.
> Now my womb is aching ow ow. (24)

This gendering of the tropical forest, its conversion into "an unredeemed feminine space that infuriated men with its flirtatious proliferation of identities, a gushing, overwhelming womb that refused patronymic interventions" (Sommer, *Foundational Fictions* 263), is a recurring feature in *modernista* representations of the Amazon jungle.

In Menotti del Picchia's *República dos Estados Unidos do Brasil* (1928), a "nationalist epic" by the fellow *verde-amarelista*, the Brazilian landscape becomes a "feminine" disposition to cultural insemination. The "Inaugural Canto" invokes "the millenary wealth and extraordinary beauty of [the poet's] native land," whose "virginal, mestizo body," fragrant and recumbent "like [that of] a Creole woman bathed in morning dew," is "stiffened by the muscles of its minerals[,] rich in wood and pastures / erupting in a plethora of vegetational health . . . full of gold and diamonds . . . / of long, nocturnal, underground veins / of coal and of iron" (125). According to the positivist framework that generally governs these figurations, only the rule of development can subdue this "feminine" exuberance. This theme is particularly salient in the work of Gallegos, for whom, as Carlos Fuentes remarks, the philosophy of progress is something of a "weakness" (*punto flaco*) (qtd. in *Canaima* xv).

At "the doctrinal level" (i.e., of "the meaning inscribed in the text itself," not the one "extracted by the reader" [González Echevarría, *Voice of the Masters* 47]), *Doña Bárbara* is an allegory of the conflict between barbarism and civilization: a morality play pitting the "holy light" [*santa luz*] of modern civilization (hence the symbolism of the protagonist's name: Santos Luzardo) against "the archaic darkness of barbarous black magic" (Sommer, *Foundational Fictions* 278).[4] By the same token, "the drama of the virgin forest" staged in *Canaima*, the calamities of a "region withdrawn from progress and abandoned to the satanic rule of violence, [partake] of the nature of Biblical curses" (Gallegos, *Canaima* 44–45). In the final instance, though, what the Caroní River falls—whose waters shudder "in the vast surrounding silence with the enraged clamor of their massive squandered power" (45)—seem to signify more than anything is a waste of industrial potential: "Imagine what the harnessing of these waterfalls would mean to [the city of] Guayana and perhaps the country as a whole ... the incalculable horse-power which is being wasted in these cascades" (45).

Its poetics of authenticity notwithstanding, one could place *Cobra Norato* squarely within this positivist tradition as well. This "masterpiece" of Anthropophagy is, in this sense, also an allegory of development, (pre)figuring the capitalist penetration and rationalization of the rain forest's unharnessed power. Despite its ostensible primitivism, in other words, and as Jean Franco has asserted, Bopp's nationalism, like that of the Modernistas as a whole, "was very much associated with a vision of an integrated and modern Brazil" (*Modern Culture* 98). Nowhere is this poetic economy better illuminated than in Bopp's so-called Anthropophagist aesthetics.

For Bopp, the Amazon first manifests itself to the imagination as a formless mass, inevitably exceeding the confines of inherited poetic forms:

> The romance of the Amazon, with its fabular poetic substance, a wilderness filled with sounds, mingled with the pulse of insomniac forests, could not fit within the perimeter of measured compositions. The fractional metric molds served to express the stuff of a classical universe. But they either deformed or fell short of reflecting with sensitivity a mysterious and obscure world defined by pre-logical modes of existence. (*Samburá* 21)

To translate this problem of representation into Kantian terms, the Amazon embodies nature's sublime precisely in its formlessness, "in its chaos or in its wildest and most irregular disorder and desolation" (Kant, *Critique of Judgment* 84). As Bopp's remarks above make clear, however, his Anthropophagist aesthetics has little in common with an aesthetic of the sublime. *Cobra Norato,* in other words, does not invoke the unpresentable in presentation itself. Rather, it seeks an appropriate poetic form. In this sense, the poem exemplifies what Lyotard calls a modern aesthetics, which "allows the unpresentable to be put forward only as the missing contents; but the form, because of its recognizable consistency, continues to offer to the reader or viewer matter for solace and pleasure" (*Postmodern Condition,* 81).

Nevertheless, whatever difficulties the poet may face in attempting to represent the Amazon are to be surmounted at the end of a successful search for the correspondence between the incommensurability of the Amazon and a "freer" mode of expression, a quest for the correct form, the naive and natural language that Oswald de Andrade proposes in the *Pau Brasil* Manifesto as the only genuine expression of "a Brazilian Brazil." "It became necessary, Bopp argues concurrently, to break with these [formal] limitations; to try something in a loose language [em linguagem solta], in different rhythmic molds" (*Movimentos modernistas* 110).

One of the forms that this formal emancipation will take in *Cobra Norato* will be the paradigmatic effort to assert a new language, one radically distinct from that bequeathed by the metropole; hence, for instance, the proliferation of popular idioms in the poem. This desired coincidence between form and content is indicated even in the poem's division into thirty-three sections—a number at once cabalistic and Genesial: its sum a possible allusion to the six days of Creation, its doubleness and indivisibility potentially opening up a repetition ad infinitum, a numerical index of the forest's endless, inchoate topography. In this respect, the series of productive and rationalistic metaphors should only be regarded as a synthesis of the natural and technological realms (as Averbuck avers) if one understands "synthesis" in the Hegelian sense, as a violent technological negation and overcoming of the unruly natural forces of the Amazon:

Now begins the ciphered forest. (5)

[A] school of trees . . . studying geometry.[5] (10)

They are soldering sawing sawing
As if earth was being manufactured

. . . .

Convoys of *matupás* [fluvial grasses] are coming slowly upriver for the construction of new islands
in a silent engineering. (30)

Nickel-plated trees

. . . . . .

playing at being a city (31, 44)

One tree telegraphed another

. . . .

What you're seeing is no vessel. It's Cobra Grande.[6] (49)

If one sees this geometric and industrial reduction of the Amazon as a metaphor for literary technique itself, that is, the "consumption" and regulation of the jungle's "inimical" and unproductive engendering (in both senses) by the poem's formal project, then the tropological antagonism between industrial production and excessive, uncontrolled germination would finally be reined in by *Cobra Norato*'s structure itself. The poem's structure, or *technè* in more general terms, suggests itself as the aesthetic analogue to the "grand-scale plan" that Bopp recommends for the 'occupation' of the Amazon basin and "the development of its economic potential" (*Putirum* 220).

It would be the force lending measure and purpose to "the ungoverned embryos" [*embriões desgovernados*] proliferating superfluously in fathomless thickets (Bopp, *Samburá* 22). Poetic creation (recapitulating one of its avatars, the scriptural *logos,* as well as the biblical conquest of nature perfected or brought up to date by modern technology) is thus itself an image of the telos completing what Bopp calls a "geography of the unfinished . . . forests without end" (21). *Poeisis* would in this sense be a figure for the project of development. This is a correlation that the poem's plot appears to bear out.

After Norato's rescue of Queen Luzia's daughter, who awaits his arrival "naked as a flower" (52), Cobra Grande pursues them, enraged, flattening the horizon, and causing the wind to "bite the tip of its own tail" (53). The Serpent finally dies with its head "stuck" under the feet of the Virgin Mary's statue inside the cathedral of Belém ("Cobra Grande . . . / Entrou no cano da Sé / e ficou com a cabeça enfiada debaixo dos pés de Nossa Senhora" [54]). The image of the defeated Cobra Grande loops back to the beginning of the poem, to the strangulation of the snake whose integument Norato slips into before he embarks upon his quest. As the repetition—with a graphemic difference—of the first and last lines indicates ("One day / I will yet go live in the lands Without-end" [3] [Um dia / ainda eu hei de morar nas *terras* do Sem-fim]; "I'll be waiting for you / behind the ranges Without-end" [57] [Fico lê esperando / atrás das *serras* do Sem-fim]), the poem, like Cobra Grande, bites its own tail.

It traces an archetypal circumference that iterates on the one hand the formulaic metamorphosis of the Serpent, or Boiúna, into the lunar disk in Tupi cosmogony, and the unbound (rather than "metric") structure of the poem on the other. This recoiling movement may also signal a kind of limit that technology imposes upon the obscure, pre-logical world of the forest, upon its "ungoverned" sublimity. Confronted with an overpowering *technè*, nature coils back upon itself in surrender. Cobra Grande's incorporation into a Christian icon—which revises or "updates" Tupi oral tradition— embodies the syncretism or "synthesis" that purportedly defines Brazilian national culture.

At the same time, however, Cobra Grande's transmutation into the biblical serpent, crushed beneath the Virgin's feet, replicates a conversion plot common to the European narrative of conquest and discovery. In this respect, the poem retells what Doris Sommer has called the foundational romance between the proverbially beautiful native girl, one of the "magnificent and wanton Eves," and "the white *caraíba*" (Ricardo, *Marcha para Oeste*, 1: 109). In this respect, the serpentine loop might signify the wedding band, the nuptials announced at the end of the poem between Cobra Norato, the white *caraíba* or civilizational hero, and the naked Eve he snatches from the jaws of the autochthonous snake.

As Gilberto Freyre, the eminent sociologist (and author of a 1926 "Regionalist Manifesto"), indicates in his account of the "discovery," this interracial romance harks back to Brazil's "historical beginnings": "the atmosphere in which Brazilian life began was one of near sexual intoxication, the European leapt ashore only to slide into naked Indian woman" (*Casa grande* 60). The inaugural coupling of white men and Amerindian women was, of course, seminal to Modernismo's "cosmic race" narratives, but its employment as "a natural foundation for Brazil's future" (Sommer, *Foundational Fictions* 144) predates the movement by more than a century. Not only does it pervade the fiction of nineteenth-century Romantic writer José de Alencar—the most apposite example being the union between the "virginal" and anagrammatic Iracema (i.e., America) and a Portuguese warrior appropriately named Martim[7]—but it governs the plot of a 1781 epic (*O Caramurú*) by the Augustinian friar Santa Rita Durão, for instance.

This poem, whose form and diction is largely derivative of Camões's *Lusíadas* (1572), was a frequent target of *modernista* attacks on literary archaism.[8] *Caramurú* is supposedly the demiurgic title ("the son of Thunder" [Durão, *Caramurú* 1: 1]) bestowed upon the half-Promethean, half-Robinsonian hero by a horde of prostrate cannibals terrified by the "thunder and lightening" his musket discharges (2: 44–46). To cite Oswald's mordant but succinct summary, Durão's epic is "a laughable panegyric of paternal legitimacy in which a Portuguese warrior leads his bride, the Indian Paraguaçu, in a long caravel raid to the land of France, where, intact and virginal, she will marry the future originator of an untouchable colonial genealogy" (*Estética e política* 244–45).[9] The matron of honor is none other than Catherine of Médici, whose name (Catarina) Paraguaçu receives upon her baptism (*Caramurú* 7: 19).

During their return voyage, and after the fashion of Camões's soothsaying nymph, who in the last two cantos of the *Lusíadas* enumerates the future glories of the Portuguese eastern empire, Paraguaçu narrates a prophetic history of Brazil that closes with a familiar vision of the Virgin Mary: "At the feet of our merciful mother can be seen, vanquished, the treacherous serpent of old, whose head raised in blame is crushed by the glorious and virginal sole" (Durão *Caramurú* 10: 11). Later in the poem, the image reappears in an icon, recovered from a Carijó Indian, as he is attempting to smuggle it out of the ship's bilge. It is subsequently proclaimed "by divine invocation" as Our Lady of Grace, to be thenceforth worshiped as the patroness of Bahia, the alleged site of Brazil's "original church" (10: 47). The icon symbolizes both Paraguaçu's deliverance from paganism and the future Evangelization of heathen Brazil, of which her own conversion is no doubt intended to be metonymic.

Cobra Norato therefore provides a modern variation on this Christian motif. By shifting the Lady of the Serpent's site to Belém (named after the biblical Bethlehem[10]) on the delta (or "head") of the serpentine Amazon, the poem rewrites the *origin* that the trodden serpent symbolizes in *Caramurú*: "The Amazon river is the key to our penetration into the interior. . . . The region remains practically unchanged, with its vast spaces still unexploited. If the Amazonian world had an appropriate economic development, the city of Belém, on the delta, would have the exceptional conditions to become, in the future, the Buenos Aires of the North" (Bopp, *Putirum* 219). No longer the biblical symbol of evil, Cobra Grande is converted in Bopp's epic into a synecdoche of the immense telluric energy that only a technological subjugation will be able to harness.

To borrow Conrad's almost iconic description of the river Congo, the Amazon River is likewise figured here as "an immense snake uncoiled, with its head in the sea, its body at rest curving afar over a vast country, and its tail lost in the depths of the land" (*Heart of Darkness* 22). Like José Vasconcelos, and most of his fellow Modernistas, Bopp emphasizes the necessity of maintaining this industrial development under strict *national* (i.e., "indigenous") control. It is this autonomy that his protagonist allegedly symbolizes. Bopp cautions us against the rapacity of industrialized countries for the vast wealth of the Amazon and offers, as the most effective means of precluding "any attempt at territorial appropriation," an officially sponsored settlement of the region, an "expansion of its human frontier" (*Putirum* 219–20).[11]

To read the Holy Mother's trampling of the serpent in the light of this project of modernization is to reinterpret it as an allegory of development, of the taming of nature and insemination of the virgin forest with the spirit of progress and modernity. In the end, this rhetorical procedure reproduces with a crucial (technological) difference the paradox of the virgin mother, for, like Mary, the Amazon forest is also simultaneously virginal and penetrated: at once sublimely chaotic and reined in by *order and progress*. The conundrum is extended into the figuration of technology as a penetrating virgin. Belém, the holy site of an immaculate birth that marks both the origin of the Gospel and the dawn of a new era, is recoded in its New World location into the bridgehead of a modern expansion into the interior.

The source of the gospel of modernization, Belém becomes the outpost of a capitalist penetration and insemination of the Amazon basin to which the sexual union between Norato and "the autochthonous Eve" serves as a fitting counterpart. It is the link between this inaugural interracial romance—which the *verde-amarelista* sociologist Alfredo Ellis regards as a "eugenic sexual selection" (*Raça de gigantes*, 69)—and Brazil's process of modernization that the poem's marriage plot reinforces. Before resuming my analysis of this aspect of Bopp's poem, I should like to consider in greater detail the treatment of this miscegenation romance, the program for racial improvement sometimes designated as "Aryanization," by Brazil's Modernistas.

Apparently predestined by the beauty of the Amerindian women as well as the polygamous ardor of the Iberian colonizer (*Raça de gigantes* 69; Ricardo, *Marcha para Oeste* 1: 109), this "sublime union" (Ellis, *A madrugada paulista* 26) was to produce "the eugenic exponents of the race": a "race of giants" (*Raça de gigantes* 134), to use the phrase Ellis borrows from the early nineteenth-century French traveler Auguste de Saint-Hilaire.[12] The label refers to the mestizo *bandeirantes* whose unquenchable yearning for the west supposedly forged the borders of present-day Brazil. As Fernand Braudel memorably puts it, "the real issue [for the *bandeirantes*] was not conquest of men (they were annihilated) but of space" (*Structures of Everyday Life* 98). Cobra Norato's Odyssean quest, his so-called Orphic descent, though ostensibly *antropofágico* in its politics and aesthetics, owes at least the structure of its plot, to say nothing for now of its politics, to the miscegenation romance and the nationalist myth of the *bandeira* (or, sixteenth-century territorial exploration).

Ellis, for instance, regards the *bandeira* as the "outpost of nationhood" (*Raça de gigantes* 249). In a historical study originally published in 1940 and substantially revised in 1970, which Oswald de Andrade includes, along with Euclides da Cunha's *Os Sertões* (1902) and Gilberto Freyre's *Casa-grande e Senzala*, in a privileged selection of "totemic books" (*Estética e política* 217), Cassiano Ricardo, another prominent *verde-amarelista*, defines this territorial expansion as "the modern world's greatest geographic revolution": "When the first *bandeira* goes into the jungle, the history of Portugal ends and that of Brazil begins" (*Marcha para Oeste* 1: 68, 229).

This nationalist refiguration of the *bandeiras*—whose pronounced mythic character may be gauged if we contrast it to Braudel's account of the "famous expeditions of the *Paulistas* across the wastes of South America in the sixteenth century [as] voyages neither of conquest nor of colonization [which] left no more trace behind them than a ship does in the sea" (*Perspective of the World*, 388)—have as their foundation a familiar *verde-amarelista* hypothesis. This hypothesis, which also underpins Ricardo's 1928 epic *Martim Cererê*, posits the "Tupi spirit" as central to the *bandeirantes*' "second discovery" of Brazil: "Only the *bandeirante* realizes [the potential of "our savage"], taking advantage of his nomadism, [of] 'his psychological specialization for displacement', and transferring it onto a new social and human order to which he would accede because of his specific qualities" (*Marcha para Oeste* 1: 270).

Though the explorers "hunted savages," the latter were already waging a "fierce struggle against each other," Ricardo explains, reiterating a familiar topos in colonialist discourse (*Marcha para Oeste* 1: 270). The *bandeirante*, whose "technique" consists in "regressing as far as he can to the primitive state; in adopting indigenous cultural patterns; in crossing himself with the aborigine [and] perpetuating the Indian (whose expansionist impetus he adopted)," simply utilizes the existing rivalry to his advantage, "allying himself with the Tupis against the Tapuias" (1: 270). These historical and poetic transformations of the *bandeira* obviously leave intact the prevailing class and racial hierarchies. They ultimately expose the porosity of *verde-amarelismo* (and its precursors) in relation to state-sponsored ideologies of nationalism.

When, for example, in 1920 the Brazilian government commissions the sculptor Victor Brecheret to produce a sculpture commemorating the upcoming centennial of Brazil's independence, it is to the *bandeirante* epic that the artist turns for an expression of "the glory of our race and the spirit of independence of our people" (Menotti del Picchia, O *Gedeão do modernismo* 69).[13] The sculptor himself describes the monument's mockup as a sort of allegory of colonization: "a phalanx [*teoria*] of Herculean men" advances "on its way to the conquered Land, the fertile and immortal Brazilian motherland" (Brecheret, "Monumento das Bandeiras," 54–55). In his own description of the projected sculpture, Mário de Andrade, in a characteristic feminization of national (and natural) space, refers to the latter as "a fecund sleeping woman" ("De São Paulo" 56).

In his avowedly nationalist 1928 epic *Martim Cererê*, Cassiano Ricardo seeks similarly to combine the racial and the expansionist aspects of the country's history to fashion "the myth of infant-Brazil" [*o mito do Brasil-menino*] (*"Martim Cererê"* 103, 105). The poem, according to Ricardo's own reading, addresses the "color problem" directly and endeavors to represent "our people's ethnic synthesis" (103). The title itself, for example, is intended to signify "a reconciliation of the three races" that collaborated "in our early formation" (105). As Ricardo elucidates, *Martim Cererê* preserves the evolution undergone by the "indigenous name" of the striped cuckoo (*Saci-Pererê*): the African-influenced shift from *Pererê* to *Cererê*, and the Portuguese introduction of *Martintapereira* (*Poesias completas* 81). Martim, moreover, as I have already indicated above, is the conventional name for the conventional sixteenth-century Portuguese warrior.

Martim Afonso, with whom Ricardo associates the title's Martim (*22 e a poesia de hoje* 20), is a probable allusion to the Captain-Governor of Brazil, who in 1531–32 ordered the first inland expeditions from Rio de Janeiro and São Vicente—purportedly the harbingers of the *bandeiras* of the following century. In addition, the name Martim Cererê, as Ricardo observes as well, reproduces the Tupi's onomastic incorporations and their practice of taking on European names, of giving indigenous names to the white man (*"Caramurú*, for example"). Conversely, the appellation signifies the white man's custom of ascribing to himself indigenous names, a self-christening that Ricardo reads as a sign of "the native struggle against the kingdom-born [*reinol*]" (*"Martim Cererê"* 105).

The protagonist of Ricardo's epic thus embodies the prototype of the Brazilian New Man, the *bandeirante*, as he appears in the *verde-amarelista* Manifesto: "The Portuguese thought the Tupi had ceased to exist; yet the Portuguese had been changed, and emerged with the features of a new nation opposed to the metropolis: because the Tupi were victorious in the blood and soul of the Portuguese" (Salgado, Menotti de Picchia, and Ricardo, "Nhengaçú verde amarelo" 234). The *bandeira,* in sum, contains "the seeds of our political democracy" (Ricardo, *Marcha para Oeste* 1: 190). Though it was never formally proclaimed, it endures as "the first and most original" of Brazil's republics (1: 196). For *verde-amarelismo,* in other words, the *bandeira* is something like the organic passage from colony to nation. It is metonymic not only of a future independent and "racially democratic" Brazil, but of an "indigenous" developmentalism that will turn this future Brazil into a beacon of Latin American nations.

The celebration of "the victorious experiences of [this] new civilization" in Menotti del Picchia's *República dos Estados Unidos do Brasil* (120) thus privileges the obligatory *bandeirante,* "son of the scholar and [Rita Durão's] Paraguaçu" (121). In *República,* the latter's mapping "of the greatest American motherland" is invested with Messianic value. Apparently appropriating Plínio Salgado's metaphor of a racial Eucharist, Menotti describes the Magi arriving before the new land—a sort of baby Jesus of nations bearing "the firstlings of all the races / and, like the host made of wheat from every granary, / a strong and free people communed in the consciousness / of the New Motherland" (121). In another poem from the collection titled "Língua brasileira" (Brazilian Language), the Christ parallel is reinforced, as "the infant people . . . [await] the Christmas gifts" of language and culture brought over by successive migratory waves: "the King of the West" gave it, among other literary gifts, "the epic of Camões"; the "jet-black" Melchior's "magical and guttural" offerings were "the cabala's monosyllables"; and "the Cosmopolitan King" of European migrations presented it with "the regal gift . . . of universal articulations" (Menotti del Picchia, *República* 135).

The outcome is "the mixed language of Babel and America" (*República* 136). The effort to renew the national, "popular" idiom, to affirm its difference from the language of the metropolis (or prove its "independence," as Angel Rama phrases it [*Transculturación* 40]) is evident here, as it is in Ricardo's etymological explanation of the title of his *modernista* epic. In spite of their ostensible nativism, however, and as the following analysis seeks to indicate, these projects continue to be governed by a colonialist perspective.

Consistent with the *verde-amarelista* myth contriving a historical and cultural continuity between the *bandeirantes* and the Tupi, Ricardo's epic, *Martim Cererê,* interlaces the *bandeirante* saga with Tupi cosmogony. As the poem opens, for example, Uiara, "a strange-looking woman" whose "green hair [and] golden eyes" (Ricardo, *Poesias completas* 88) repeat the colors of the national flag, asks a Tapuia suitor to bring her the Night (since in her homeland "only morning existed") before she will consent to marry him (85). The Tapuia, whom the "Nhengaçú verde amarelo" defines as "prejudice itself fleeing into the *sertão*" (235), predictably fails in his quest. He is promptly supplanted by a Lusitanian mariner who has sailed across "seas no one had sailed before" (*Poesias completas* 107).[14]

In direct contrast to Carpentier's account of an implacable struggle between Totemic and Theological Man, the fateful encounter between the modern Argonauts ("following the path of the Sun, / in search of a treasure / called the Sun of the Earth / (a new Golden Fleece)") and the Tupis (emerging from the hinterland "in search of Night / as if they were able to divine, / by strange magic, / that a Sea of Night existed" [106]) produces an ambivalent cultural fusion. It prefigures the marriage between "the most beautiful woman in the world" (127) and Martim, the Portuguese "sea-wolf" (131).

To Uiara's ineffable joy, Martim succeeds in enclosing a racial Night in the holds of slave ships (119), bearing it across the Atlantic to Brazil: "coal destined for the workshop of the races" (*Poesias completas* 121). After her marriage, performed by the official founder of São Paulo, the Jesuit Father José de Anchieta, Uiara offers the two European founding heroes a glimpse into "the green night" of the *sertão:* "the end of the world, / where the 'endless' horizon ['sem-fim'] was trilling, / league upon sleeping league / and which no one so much as budged" (132), the mythic territory holding "all the virginal treasure of the Earth" (134). The penetration of "the open space to be conquered by human settlement," which, in the words of Fernand Braudel, loomed "forever on the horizon of American history" (*Perspective of the World* 388), inevitably follows. The conquest of the *sertão* thus doubles the insemination of Uiara by the European *caraíba*.

The teratological progeny that their union will produce is something like the cross between Ellis's eugenic colossi and the antediluvian giants, the offspring of the daughters of men and the sons of God (or, of Amerindian Eves and European demigods, in the New World variation of the etiological story from the Book of Genesis): "No sooner had the Portuguese sailor married Uiara than the Giants in Boots [*Gigantes de Botas*] were born" (136). *Gigantes de Botas* is Ricardo's phrase for the "geographic heroes," modeled on historical *bandeirantes,* "who will cross the land of a mysterious, as-yet concealed America in every direction" (*Poesias completas* 136), and whose legendary exploits provide the epic with much of its plot.

Auguste de Saint-Hilaire compares the *bandeirantes* to the ancient Greeks, because, like them, they faced countless perils, fought gallant battles, but "left nothing in writing" (*Viagem à província* 36). Alfredo Ellis also faults the explorers for not having bequeathed "a single artistic vestige" to posterity (*Raça de gigantes* 198). It is presumably no accident, then, that Ricardo's epic repeatedly converts their feats of geographic exploration into poetry (a compensatory rhetorical gesture that is a commonplace in Portugal's sixteenth-century discourses about maritime expansion). Thus, one of the "Giants" is described as a "bush poet," the leader of a "troop of poets, among whom would march / some half-breed Orpheus [*Orfeu caboclo*], lyre in hand," his blunderbuss "loaded with more poetry than lead" (*Poesias completas* 162). With "a poem in each leg" (164), the epic wanderers shape Brazil in "the form of a harp" (197, 216), an image borrowed from a sixteenth-century chronicle of the "province."[15]

Their Odyssean effort is, in effect, antithetical to intellectual or aesthetic production, as Ricardo will later argue, since "the absence of intellectualism was initially a condition for the success of an enterprise which allows only for the attributes of daring and heroism" (*Marcha para Oeste* 1: 183). At the same time, however, both the poetic and the heroic "attitudes" are conflated in the crafting of the *bandeirante* epic, as the poet proclaims himself "an obscure *bandeirante* / born with [his] back to the sea" (*Poesias completas* 211), labeling Brazil his "infant poem" (216). This metaphoric extension, borrowed perhaps from Menotti's partisan réportages on the aesthetic feats of the "futurist *bandeira*" in 1921–22 (*O Gedeão do modernismo* 266, 319, 373), operates a symbolic fusion between the lyre and the (territorial) harp, between poetry and geographic expansion.

Just as Camões proffers his *Lusíadas* as an overdue commemoration of the inadequately celebrated feats of early Portuguese imperialism, *Martim Cererê* stands forth as the poetic compensation for the *bandeira*'s discursive lack. Concurrently, the *bandeirante*'s westward progress, like the logic of industrialization governing *Cobra Norato*, symbolizes poetic form. As in Gallegos's description of the fencing of the Venezuelan plain, the imprints made by the expeditions across the infant body of Brazil retrace the "straight line" that man imposes upon "the curved line of nature," a single, direct path pointing "toward the future" (*Doña Bárbara* 97).

In the same way that "the boundaries marked off by barbed wire fences redeem the plain from nature's incoherence, from the total absence of signs" (González Echevarría, *Voice of the Masters* 48), the paths of the *bandeirantes* await, like so many taut strings traversing the territory of the harp nation, the gifted hand that shall pluck from them a teleological melody:

> In the midst of disparate, unyielding racial elements, rebellious against every disciplining and organizing power, the *bandeira* acts as the living geometry which frames and rectifies it all. Within it, the shreds and edges of humanity discarded by miscegenation, relegated to lawlessness by the metropolis, dispersed by conflicts with a tropical environment, hurled aside like so much debris by the large estates [*latifúndios*], take on a useful meaning. (Ricardo, *Marcha para Oeste* 2: 355)

The poet-*bandeirante* thus comes to resemble Aimé Césaire's Prospero, who, in the Martinican playwright's adaptation of Shakespeare's *Tempest*, functions as the prototype of the European colonizer, as the "composer" who alone is capable of drawing music from the sound and fury of the wilderness, "the conductor of an immense score . . . organizing out of the confusion / the single intelligible line" (Césaire, *Tempest* 90). Similarly, for Ricardo, the *bandeira* is at once the essential expression of Brazil's national character and a "genuinely Brazilian" model of development, simultaneously the trope and the blueprint for order, progress, and national identity.

This national symphony is nonetheless performed on a rigidly hierarchical scale, which assigns "each color . . . its role and function[:] upon departure, it is the white man who is the organizer; as [the *bandeira*] gets under way, it is the Indian who opens the way, who serves as the scout; in the end, the Negro miner replaces the indigenous hand" (*Marcha para Oeste* 1: 324). The metonymic reduction of the African to a laboring "hand" ([*braço*] is consistent with the negligible nation-building role ascribed to him in the majority of *modernista* writings until 1930. The "'Negro moment' of the *bandeira*" seems entirely reducible to his manual labor: "to till the land around the gold mines [*os descobertos*]. There the African fits like a cog in a wheel [*como a peça de uma engrenagem*] [or like coal in 'the workshop of the races'], because the Cabinda and the Bakongo were born to cultivate the land" (1: 328). The black's menial place in Brazil's "racial democracy" had already been assigned by Alfredo Ellis and Menotti del Picchia.

In *Juca Mulato* (1917), for example, one of Menotti's early narrative poems about a "mulatto" farmhand's impossible love for the daughter of a white estate owner, the protagonist is told by a wise shaman that he is "like a toad in love with a star" (73). In the end, Juca persuades himself to forget his unrequited passion, "to return to the soil, / and search for his love in a sister soul," for though his own soul was prone to dream, his "arm was born to till the earth" (85). In Menotti's *República,* the offspring of racial crossings with the African (*o mulato, o cafuzo, o caboclo, o bujamé*[16]) are branded "the failed monsters of our racial type" (179). Similarly, for Alfredo Ellis, miscegenation with the "Negro" brings about "a bastardization of the eugenic element" (*Raça de gigantes* 185)—a value judgment determined in a sense by the etymology of the term *mulatto* (i.e., "mule-like") itself. "The substitution of the Negro hand with the Italian and Spanish settler" therefore constitutes an ethnic advantage for the nation because it ensures the perseverance of "the old Iberian-American stock which is our pride and the basis of our greatness" (192).

In a similar vein, in *Leite Criôlo* [Creole Milk], a *modernista* publication that appeared throughout 1929 as a supplement to a Belo Horizonte newspaper, and that Jorge Schwartz rates as "a pioneering journal in the context of *Modernismo,* insofar as it deals exclusively with black Brazilian themes, although the manner in which it treats these questions is callow, not to say racist" (*Vanguardas* 248), miscegenation is proposed precisely as the solution to Brazil's "Negro problem" (that is, "the century-old laziness of the Brazilian character" [qtd. in *Vanguardas* 249]). One of the journal's editorials thus declares "Eugenics is just the thing . . . to awaken the national character, frozen [as a result of] living in the Negro's shadow: the smudge on our ["civilized"] human face . . . Eugenics for the Brazilian soul. To *eugenicize.* Against the Negro [who] annuls himself by his own doing through racial mixture [*mestiçagem*]. . . . [We must] select the types which will improve our race" (qtd. in *Vanguardas* 250).

Ricardo develops an analogous eugenic theme in his monumental monograph on the *bandeiras,* asserting that "the *bandeirante*'s most recent kin is the immigrant" (*Marcha para Oeste* 2: 642). As we see above, however, by emphasizing the role of black labor in the *bandeira,* he endeavors to dispel the racist myth of the lazy black. Nevertheless, in reclaiming the *bandeira* as both a point of departure and blueprint for modern national development, in founding on eugenics Brazil's "racial democracy" (or "chromocracy")—"the admirable sum" of the three races (*Marcha para Oeste* 1: 326–27)—his treatment of the "Negro question" in *Martim Cererê* seems, in the end, to be just as "callow, not to say racist."

To resume my discussion of Raul Bopp's poem, within the context outlined above, the thematic centrality of the nostalgia for the infinite (*Sem-fim*) in *Cobra Norato* would thus appear clearly to point to an affiliation between the poem's protagonist and the *bandeirante*—Bopp's preferred hero type[17]—between Cobra Norato's quest and the national epic of territorial expansion. The poem in this restricted sense responds to Oswald de Andrade's call in the *Pau Brasil* Manifesto to recover "the whole of *bandeirante* history[18] as well as the commercial history of Brazil" (O. de Andrade *Do 'Pau-Brasil'* 5).

The fulfillment of Cobra Norato's desire to settle in the "land Without-End [and] marry the daughter [of Queen Luzia]" (*Cobra Norato* 3), his wish to marry a daughter of the Amazon and colonize its territory, the conversion of his initial nomadic "hope" into a sedentary "waiting," all these reproduce *verde-amarelismo*'s signature conflation of the expansionist and eugenic narratives: "One day / I will yet go and live in the land Without-End [*terras do Sem-fim*] / I am walking trekking trekking" (3) (*vou andando caminhando caminhando*); "I'll be waiting [*esperando*] for you / behind the ranges Without-End [*serras do Sem-fim*]" (57) (*esperar* means both "to wait" and "to hope" in Portuguese).

In the gerund's shift from an index of geographic displacement ("walking, trekking") to a sign of settlement ("waiting") resides the (nationalistic) meaning of Cobra Norato's journey across the Amazon. The sense of infinity invoked in the poem's opening lines ("One day / I will yet go and live in the land Without-End") is thus apparently superseded at the end of the poem. The limitless territory [*terras do Sem-fim*] is limned by a configuration of *serras,* or the saw-like formation of the Andes whose dentiform outline suggests a sort of "consumption" of infinity: the Serpent's autophagic circle. The felicitous homophony between *serras* ("mountain ranges") and *cerras* (present indicative form of the verb *cerrar,* "to close") becomes significant in this respect, as do the reiterated images of enclosed or "devoured" horizons: "the shadow is slowly eating up the swollen horizons" (*Cobra Norato* 12), "Squatting monsters / plug up thick-lipped horizons" (13), "Horizons are sinking / in a delayed shipwreck" (23), "the horizon was flattened" (53).

It is difficult not to see in this devouring of distances a trope for the *bandeiras*' stretching "of Brazil's latitudes, [its] pot-bellied growth toward the West" (Bopp, *Movimentos modernistas* 82), as the straight line of technology cutting across and redeeming the unyielding curvature of nature. To be sure, for both Ricardo and Bopp, the purposive linearity of the road—"the courageous heroism" that President Juscelino Kubitschek's administration (1956–60) purportedly demonstrated in "tearing open hundreds of kilometers of roadway inside the virgin forest" (220), or the visionary construction of the "Trans-Amazonian" highway carried out under the auspices of the military dictatorship—marks the latest phase of "Brazil's definitive conquest of itself" (Ricardo, *Marcha para Oeste* 2: 646).

In Ricardo's historical monograph, the *bandeira* operates as the paradigm for a series of disparate modes of "modernization," including the "warlike geometric battalions" of coffee plantations and other "agricultural *bandeiras*" (*Marcha* 2: 558) as well as the "vertical *bandeirismo*" of São Paulo's skyline (2: 560). In fact, both *Martim Cererê* and Menotti's *República* close with odes to the skyscraper (Ricardo, *Poesias completas* 201), the "tower of Babel" or "*bandeirante* of the clouds" (*República* 193, 196)—that is, the *concrete* copy of Bopp's Andean original, as it were. Jean Franco's important reminder that, despite its ostensible primitivism, the nationalism of the Modernistas was closely linked with "a vision of an integrated and modern Brazil whose distinctive form of civilization and culture would not be a mere regional folk culture" (*Modern Culture* 98) becomes once again pertinent.

The closing stanzas of these nationalist epics, then, metaphorically cross the horizontal line of territorial expansion with the dazzling upward flight of the modern metropolis, the much augured 'city of the future'. In the intersection of these two "itineraries of progress" resides the transcendental meaning of the nation's destiny. Menotti, whose Messianic tropology has already been referenced, foregrounds the Christian symbolism of this Cross-ing with a final invocation of the divine Word (*a voz de Deus*), proclaiming the glory of the poet's city, state, and republic (*República* 206). In a procedure that, during his "concrete phase," he was to interpret as an anticipation of concrete poetry (*22 e a poesia de hoje* 30), Ricardo eulogizes the neon "inscription" of the word *Jacy* (the Tupi term for Moon and the name of the poet's wife) flashing against São Paulo's night sky.[19] Not only does this image repeat "electrically" Menotti's invocation of the Logos, but it also doubles the troping of the stars (of the nationally symbolic Southern Cross?) "into commercial signs" in the opening lines of *República*'s "Tower of Babel" section (195).

This technical (i.e., "poetic") as well as technological simulation of God's *handiwork*, as "the firmament" is described in Psalm 19, secularizes to an extent the Christian telos. It joins together—as origin and destination of a single historical trajectory—the sixteenth-century evangelization of Santa Cruz ("the Land of the Holy Cross") and early twentieth-century industrialism. São Paulo's urban grid—its breathtaking architectural élan, in other words—constitutes the most advanced form of order and progress, a cosmopolitan signpost indicating the nation's path to the future.

In "Tower of Babel," for example, Menotti contrasts the skyscraper's "rigorous geometry" with the dilapidated shack, "uglier than a termitarium" [*mais feia do que a toca do cupim*], of Jéca Tatú (202). Created by Monteiro Lobato, Jéca Tatú is the parody of the backward and lazy *sertão* dweller, the embodiment of what one of the contributors to *Leite Criôlo* calls "the century-old laziness [*preguiça secular*] of the Brazilian character . . . the stewed soul of Brazil [*a alma encachaçada do Brasil*]" (qtd. in Schwartz, *Vanguardas* 249). In "Urupês," the title piece of a short-story collection (1918), which, according to one of Oswald de Andrade's more conciliatory retrospectives, marks "the true degree zero" (*o verdadeiro Marco Zero*[20]) of his *Pau Brasil* poetics (*Ponta de lança* 4), Lobato compares his *caboclo* stereotype (Jéca Tatú) to a rotting human fungus, an agaric (i.e., *urupê*) festering amid the frothing "Dyonisian life" of Brazilian nature (*Urupês* 291–92).

Jéca is depicted as a "squatting, vegetating [individual], incapable of evolution, impenetrable to progress" (*Urupês* 279), the faithful follower of the "Great Rule of the Least Effort" (283). His mud and grass house "brings a smile to burrowing animals and peals of laughter to the ovenbird" (281). Menotti's gloss of Lobato's satirical sketch, entitled "Jéca," appears as the last in a series of odes to the cultural heroes of Brazil. In it Lobato's character becomes the epitome of the debased *bandeirante* ("bravery degenerated / into mystical laziness" [*República* 178]). In Menotti's piece, Jéca Tatú takes on the added role of a feudalistic progenitor of the "failed monsters of our racial type" (179), relegated to the "side of the [civilizational] road," rendered "useless, contemplative, documental" (180). Jéca Tatú is, in this sense, the obverse of Cassiano Ricardo's human "debris" recuperated by the salvational thrust of the *bandeira*.

By contrast, Jéca's life ebbs away in the slow, immemorial tempo of Brazil's irredemptive backwardness. He is development's negative term: "Amazonian man . . . fills himself with superstitions [and] becomes therefore imprisoned by his own codes of obedience, [maintaining] an ancestral respect for totemic forces" (Bopp, *Samburá* 24); "[Brazil's] rural physiognomy remains the same, with low-yield lands. The sauba ant has taken over the fields. Resigned populations get used to letting things be" in "a sort of philosophical laziness, of Brazilian slackness [*mussangulá*] . . . opposed to all that is coherent, syllogistic, geometric, Cartesian" (Bopp, *Movimentos modernistas* 87, 84). Ironically, though, it is exactly with this mood of degeneration and temporal stagnation that *Cobra Norato* closes.

The protagonist's vision of his future, which takes up the poem's penultimate section, remains caught in the squalid and slothful atemporality that Jéca Tatú allegedly incarnates:

> I want to take my bride away
> tarry sweetly by her side [*Quero estarzinho com ela*]
> . . . .
> [I want] to sit in the bush's shade
> . . . .
> [and] lazily stretch out [*se espreguiçar*]
> . . . .
> And while we lie around waiting [*à espera*]
> for night to come back again
> I'm going to tell her stories
> to write names upon the sand
> which in fun the wind will wipe away [*brincar de apagar*]. (56)

Cobra Norato's temporal trajectory is thus circular in the broader context of Modernismo's nationalist poetry. The point of destination of the hero's journey is precisely the topos that in Ricardo's and Menotti's writings represents the historical point of departure, the term to be negated and superseded by the developmental project: a shabby, forlorn settlement (i.e., "a house where we can dwell with a wee door painted blue" [56]) lying at the end of a journey whose grandiose destiny only the metropolis can fulfill. In this manner, *Cobra Norato* is perched ambivalently between Anthropophagy's revindication of the "savage" and *verde-amarelismo*'s project for overcoming primitivism (the *conditio sine qua non* of development).

To put it in somewhat schematic terms, the poem totters on the cusp of a "modern" rejection of "anthropophagic primitivisms" [*Nunca primitivismos antropofágicos*]—to quote from the inaugural issue of an anti-*Antropofagia* journal (*Arco e Flexa* [Bow and Arrow]) that emerges in Bahia during Modernismo's final stages (qtd. in Schwartz, *Vanguardas* 247)—and a post-Modernista (or *antropofagista*) attempt to reevaluate the philosophical and cultural presuppositions of the Modernista program to supersede "barbarism." As the poem closes, Norato's body seems indeed to stretch out lazily "in the *mapamundi* of Brazil," as the line from Oswald's Manifesto has it (*Do 'Pau-Brasil'* 14).

By the same token, what *Cobra Norato* lacks is precisely the "violence and clangor" that *Arco e Flexa* finds so disturbing in Anthropophagy (qtd. in Schwartz, *Vanguardas* 247). As against the *antropofagista* desire to repudiate the cultural legacy of the occident, *Cobra Norato* adopts the more moderate stance laid out by one of *Arco e Flexa*'s editors: "We don't want cruelly to dismiss the past" (247). The poem's ambiguous attitude toward western "tradition" has already been indicated. It is borne out in the excerpt—ostensibly a paean to "uncivilized" existence—quoted earlier in this paragraph.

Norato's sand writing, for example ("I'm going . . . to write names upon the sand which . . . the wind will wipe away [*brincar de apagar*]"), alludes more than likely to a "scriptural instance" that Cassiano Ricardo regards as the original model for concrete poetry (*22 e a poesia de hoje* 37, 82): the ode to the Virgin that Father José Anchieta writes upon the strand of São Vicente, supposedly as a vow of chastity in the face of constant temptation from native women, while he was being held captive by the Tamoio Indians. In *verde-amarelista* iconography, Anchieta is the far-sighted Renaissance man who both blesses and foretells "the grand civilizational task" that the union between the indigenous and ultramarine "races" will accomplish (Ellis, *A Madrugada paulista* 27).

From Oswald's Anthropophagist perspective, however, Anchieta imports to the New World an "aggressive institution of monogamy" (the patriarchal rule codified by the apostle after whom the city of São Paulo is named) that is absolutely antithetical to the amoral "matriarchate" that Anthropophagy aspires to restore (*Do 'Pau-Brasil'* 97). As the "Manifesto Antropófago" declares, "Down with Anchieta singing of the eleven thousand virgins of Heaven in the land of Iracema" (19). On the other hand, the fact that it is Anchieta who celebrates the marriage between Martim and Uiara in Cassiano Ricardo's *Martim Cererê* is consonant with the foundational role accorded to him by *verde-amarelismo*. So is the repeated invocation of his name in Menotti's collection—in conventional *Ubi Sunt* formulas ("Onde estás meu seráfico Anchieta" [Menotti del Picchia, *República* 196, 201] [Where are you my seraphic Anchieta]). For Menotti, the missionary is the founder of "the seedling-house [*casa-semente*: the Colégio de São Paulo] whence [the *bandeirante* capital] sprouted" (201). Anchieta's patriarchal code cannot but proscribe as illegitimate the prolific progeny of the likes of João Ramalho, the "illicit father" of São Paulo who settled amid the Guayaná Indians several years prior to the city's founding by the Jesuits in 1554.

Ramalho, who fathered a brood of biracial children and led the Tamoios' resistance against the missionaries, is fittingly pitted in the Anthropophagist Manifesto against Anchieta: "Down with Anchieta. . . . The patriarch João Ramalho, founder of São Paulo" (*Do 'Pau-Brasil'* 19). By contrast, then, the association between Anchieta's sand poem (inextricably linked with Norato's vision of connubial bliss), along with the image of the Virgin crushing the Serpent's head as well as Norato's *Caramurú*-like refusal to accept the sexual favors of another woman (*Cobra Norato* [1994] 37), suggests that a Christian ethos ultimately governs the union between Norato and the autochthonous princess. Norato's subjection to "the truth of missionary peoples" (*Do 'Pau-Brasil'* 17) imposes precisely the moral discipline and "sublimation" of an unruly yet "natural" sex drive that, according to the Manifesto Antropófago, produces "all the [catechist] ills identified by Freud" (*Do 'Pau-Brasil'* 18–19): "We are tired of all the suspicious Catholic husbands figured in dramas. . . . The paterfamilias and the creation of the Morality of the Stork: Real ignorance of things + lack of imagination + a sense of authority before curious descendants" (13, 17).

More than curbing a "characteristically Iberian" polygamous ardor, though, Cobra Norato's marriage plans ultimately interrupt the very transcendental coitus from which the nation's multiethnic character purportedly originates. In contradistinction to the culturally significant miscegenation constituting the teleology of Ricardo's epic, Norato's conjugal future is apparently consigned to an excessive consumption of "intoxicating mixtures (*Cobra Norato* [1956] 69)" [*misturas de embebedar*], to quote a line expunged from *Cobra*'s later editions—a "stewing (or, *en-cachaçamento*) of the soul" that is entirely consistent with the lazy mood [*preguiça secular*] evoked in the poem's penultimate section. It as though, by the end of the poem, the Judeo-Christian telos incarnated by Anchieta (or the religious legitimation of miscegenation) is irremediably sundered from the carnality of the procreative act.

Norato's marriage remains a deferred, utopian wish, unconsummated, un-conjugated (so to speak). It remains an infinitive: "I'm going to get married [*me casar*]" (*Cobra Norato* [1994] 57). If then Anchieta's famous sand poem mirrors its future in print, whereas Anchieta's "lunar poem [written] by a star shining across the *sertão*" (Menotti de Picchia, *República* 165) subsequently becomes a part of that lyrical colonial archive that one cannot touch "without staining one's hands with poetry" (Ricardo, *Marcha para Oeste* 2: 402); if the patriarch's ode is a sort of literal inscription of or on national soil and will continue to be memorialized in the hallowed pages of National History, the names Norato inscribes on the sand refer to nothing at all. They compose only an ephemeral, repeatedly effaced sand script.

Apagar ("to erase") is in effect the final word of this section of the poem. As the main verb in the last verbal locution formed with the future auxiliary *haver*, the last verb to which this future form points (*hei de . . . apagar* [I will . . . erase]), *apagar* (with a slight alteration of the original syntax) can be turned into the ultimate expression of Norato's desire. Earlier editions of the poem include, following the line "I'm going to tell her stories," the parenthetical phrase "stories that say-nothing-at-all [*Histórias de não-dizer-nada*]" (*Cobra Norato* [1956] 68), hinting possibly at an attendant yearning for meaninglessness, that is, [*não*] *querer dizer nada* (to mean [literally: "to want to say"] nothing).

To wipe out everything that precedes it in order to begin anew is, of course, one of *antropofagia*'s signature demands. But when *apagar* is coupled with the poem's final non-place, or *u-topos* (*apagar . . . sem-fim*), whatever dialectic of progress the poem may outline, whatever foundation for a "creative engineering" or construction of the future (Williams, *Politics of Modernism* 53) it may propose, seems to be reduced to the ever effaceable geography of a dream. Progress (allegedly the purpose and destination of Norato's odyssey) appears as unreachable (as unreadable) as the line of the equator, that geographic abstraction that, in one of Bopp's later writings, is made to coincide with the main street of a sleepy Amazonian town.

During a visit to the town of Macapá, Bopp recollects, he encouraged the mayor to extend its "urban axis" far into the jungle, so that Macapá could boast of having "the longest street of Brazil. But these practical plans and calculations were lost in talk and draughts of hard liquor [*jucarina*]" (*Samburá* 25). They dissipated into a familiar laziness [*preguiça secular*] and a "stewing up" of the Brazilian soul, in other words. And thus, like García Márquez's Macondo, Macapá would seem destined to be tossed "into the corner where towns that have stopped being of any service to creation are kept" (*Leafstorm and Other Stories* 93). It is with a similar and ceaseless erasure (*apagar sem-fim*), a re-flexive recoiling of the arrow of development, that *Cobra Norato* closes . . . only to open again. The doubled *Sem-fins*, the indefinite waiting or hope (*à espera* [56], *esperando* [57]) with which Norato's journey ends, suggest an eternal recurrence of the Same that is incommensurate with *verde-amarelismo*'s narrative of progress.

The serpentine circle is left un-squared, as it were. The contradiction between primitivism and technological advancement subtending, with crucial differences, both Oswald's philosophical systematization of Anthropophagy and *verde-amarelismo* is never sublated in *Cobra Norato*. It is frozen as an unresolved antagonism between the chaos of the jungle and the geometry of development. The enclosure of the infinite in the final strophe of the poem remains therefore a mere figure—a trope, moreover, that in the last instance self-destructs. For it is the essence of infinity always to lie beyond a receding horizon, to be forever the sign of an interminable, unfulfilled yearning, an unbroken asyndeton of infinitives.

In his analysis of E. M. Forster's *Howards End,* Fredric Jameson reads the trope of infinity in the novel as a formal compensation for a systemically determined incompleteness of metropolitan representations of imperial space: "The other pole of the [colonial] relationship . . . remains structurally occluded [as a result of] the way in which internal national or metropolitan daily life is absolutely sundered from this other world henceforth in thrall to it" ("Modernism and Imperialism" 58). A comparable compensatory mechanism may be at work both in *Cobra Norato* and *Martim Cererê.* Infinity, in these two instances, figures not so much imperial extension as an incipiently global capitalist reach. *Martim Cererê,* as I have suggested, seeks to make the space of global capitalism coterminous with the geometric "*bandeira* of the coffee plantation" (Ricardo, *Marcha para Oeste* 2: 559).

In "Café-Expresso,"[21] the site of this conjunction is an espresso cup's "liquid and aromatic night," in which the speaker discovers the Proustian "summary of everything [seen] in the plantation" (Ricardo, *Poesias completas* 203): "an oxcart striking the road gates . . . men / carrying multicolored panniers / filled with coffee grains / on their backs . . . a little moon-colored house" (203–4). The contradiction between this recollected pastoral tranquility and the dizzying pace of his present urban existence ("An up-and-down of people going to factories. / A to-and-fro of automobiles. Klaxons. Signs" [204]) is subsequently telescoped into the opposition between "the velvet eyes of a cunning half-breed girl [*cabocla*]" hailing from the poet's rural past and the "red-haired river-nymph [*uiara*]" that is the city of São Paulo (204).

Like the whole of the rural atmosphere depicted in the poem, the barefoot *cabocla,* whose troubling dark gaze the poet reencounters in the bottom of his coffee cup, belongs to a persistent "past" that both in personal and national terms is supplanted by a productive and feminized metropolis: the enchantress figure or *uiara* of Tupi mythology ("our own sort of fluvial siren" [Ricardo, *Marcha para Oeste* 2: 393]). What motivates the poet's final turn away from a remembrance of the rural past to the irresistible immediacy of the urban setting is the city's all-consuming modernity itself, its breathless rhythm of existence: "I have no time to think about these things! / I'm in a hurry. A big hurry!" (204). This substitution of the *cabocla* (Uiara's twentieth-century daughter) with the metropolitan enchantress is nevertheless considerably more contradictory and ambivalent than a mere election of modernity over tradition would suggest.[22]

The description of São Paulo as a mythological figure, for example, may be read in several different ways. On the one hand it sublimates the modern poet's unfulfilled and retrospective desire for the dark-eyed *cabocla*, his yearning for a carnal knowledge (promised by the "cunning" [*malícia*] in her eyes) that he was never able to acquire. On the other hand it tropes the union between the primitive and the technological, a figural closure of the temporal and spatial gap severing São Paulo from the coffee plantation. Yet the discontinuity between rural "timelessness" and urban technological progress (whose metonym in "Café-Expresso" is the espresso machine) returns in the form of a longing, a persisting antinomy between the *cabocla*'s cunning eyes ("two big coffee drops" poured into the poet's soul [204]) and the soulless dripping of the espresso machine (203). Albeit an attempt to reconcile rhetorically the city and the country (or the wilderness), the figuration of São Paulo as a *uiara*, a sort of "ghost in the machine," never quite transcends its two opposing terms, the mythic and the technological. The *uiara* retains at least an affiliation with the *mãe-d'água* of *bandeirante* legend, the lethal "water mother," whose beguiling treachery is described earlier in the epic (Ricardo, *Poesias completas* 147), and which, in the *bandeirante* saga, serves as a conventional representation of a mythic or pre-industrial obstruction to the pioneer's progress (Ricardo, *Marcha para Oeste* 392).

In Victor Brecheret's allegorical Monument of the *Bandeiras*, for instance, the *mãe-d'água* is one of the Perfidies (Insídias) ("enigmatic and serpent-like women as beautiful as all that promises and lies" ["Monumento das Bandeiras" 55]), flanking the central column of marching heroes and luring them away from their single-minded objective. She symbolizes the resistance of a duplicitous Brazilian Land: "a compassionate and virtuous mother, but also a cruel and merciless killer" (55). She is, in this sense, the specular image of the fecund Uiara. For while the latter functions as the passive term of a racial synthesis, the "fluvial siren" necessarily interrupts the figural fusion between the wilderness and civilization. She marks the site of an impasse and makes a redoubtable affirmative reply to the rhetorical question ("Is that the face of the other?" [206]) about racial harmony posed in the last line of "A Hora Futura" (The Hour of the Future, the poem that follows "Café-Expresso" in the collection).

Even refigured as the symbol of a modern metropolis, the *uiara* inevitably preserves some of this telluric menace. The path ascending ineluctably toward cosmopolitan time (São Paulo is "the city of the earliest risers in the world" [204]), which *Martim* ostensibly traces—the itinerary leading to the civilizational "Hour of the Future" stamped by God himself upon the faces of newly arrived Levantine and Baltic immigrants (206)—hence folds back upon itself in the face of that irreducible Other whom the discourse of modernity will never completely know or fully supersede. The figural synthesis between the primitive and the urban/industrial is thus breached to reveal the fundamental contradiction, the enduring unequal relationship between the city and the countryside, a contradiction that is one of the more familiar indexes of "underdevelopment." In the last instance, the antagonism between the two remains insuperable for the backwardness of the coffee plantation, of rural Brazil as a whole, is the condition of possibility of São Paulo's modernity. The urban *uiara* points precisely to this antinomy, to the rural "ghost" lurking beneath São Paulo's dazzling modernity.

As Ricardo points out, around the time of *Martim*'s publication, the State of São Paulo, "produce[d] more coffee than the entire world combined" (*Marcha para Oeste* 2: 559). Coffee accounted for over 70 percent of Brazil's export earnings. At the same time, however, the economic crisis unleashed by the sharp drop in coffee prices following the 1929 stock-market crash exposed the precariousness of this wealth. Far from constituting a measure of Brazil's (economic) power, the phalanxes of coffee trees stretching ad infinitum in the countryside around São Paulo indicated rather its impotence, or what Oswald de Andrade calls its "dessert country" status. The coffee monoculture, in short, is a sign not of development but of economic "dependency" and marginality.

Brazil's nearly exclusive reliance on coffee for its export earnings serves as an uncomfortable reminder that Brazilians dwell "on the suburbs of history," that they are "the uninvited commensals who have slipped in through the West's back door, the intruders who arrived at modernity's function just as the lights were about to go out" (Paz, *El laberinto de la soledad* 237). Compared with western metropolises, then, São Paulo remains ineluctably an earlier model. It is, in the words of Lévi-Strauss, a "Paris of the nineteenth century," defined by an "increased rate of differentiation between town and country, with the former developing at the expense of the latter, so that the newly urbanized community was anxious to have no truck with rustic naïvety" (*Tristes Tropiques* 102).

This persisting (economic, cultural) inequality is registered obliquely in the curious Parisian setting of a poem from the same section of Ricardo's *Martim*, "Moça Tomando Café" (Girl Having a Coffee). As with "Café-Expresso," the European metropolis functions in this poem as a *lieu de mémoire.* Yet, in direct contrast to the Proustian invocation of farm life in "Café-Expresso," the memory of the plantation is recalled not by the title's "fortunate girl," sipping coffee in a Parisian café, but interjected by the poet himself as a site that is unknown to the Parisian girl, which can be evoked only from *this* side of the Atlantic:

> But the girl does not know
> . . . .
> that there is a blue sea before her coffee cup
> a long ship before the blue sea
> . . . .
> before [that] a southern [seaport]
> . . . .
> and before the seaport an early-rising train
> . . . .
> And before that . . . sprawls the coffee plantation.
> And before that plantation, finally, the man
> who cleared the wild forest by himself. (208)

This allusion to a characteristically European ignorance of South America in a national epic is no doubt intended as an implicit assertion of aesthetic autonomy, of Modernismo's fundamental *national* distinction from the prevalent European variants. Significantly, the poetic journey to the source, to the *before*-time of a monocultural economy, duplicates the itinerary of the *bandeira* and of early modern colonization. It is in this sense a mode of time travel that reaffirms the disjunctive temporality of the southern (underdeveloped) land.

In "Moça Tomando Café," the whole of Brazil relates to the European capital in the manner that the plantation does to São Paulo in "Café-Expresso." Yet, unlike the latter poem's "indigenous" persona, the coffee-sipping *moça* knows absolutely nothing about the trajectory from the tropical plantation to the Parisian coffee shop. The intricate infrastructure that the poem sketches out remains for her an absent cause. Nevertheless, the sustenance and "solvency" of this complex socioeconomic "base" depends entirely upon an uninterrupted series of similarly oblivious European acts of consumption, upon the developed world's enduring taste for dessert, as Oswald de Andrade might have put it.

The capriciousness and immensity of the influence that this external market exerts upon the nation's economic fortunes is what the poem leaves unsaid, what it registers only periphrastically. Nonetheless, the power of the European consumer reappears in the form of another feminized trope:

Fortune, the coffee farmer's "bride... who promises and fails unwillingly" (209), who can at any moment be suddenly wrenched from his hands (209) and leave him a poor man (208). Fortune seems an all too obvious metaphor for the "thoughtless" inconstancy of the global market, for its potential to unleash sudden and total ruin on *this* side of the Atlantic, in a territory that, from the *other* side, is but a remote, exotic land, metonymically reduced to the contents of a coffee cup consumed in blissful ignorance by a pretty gray-eyed girl.

It is precisely away from the peril and uncertainty of this global conjuncture that Ricardo's epic veers in the end. *Martim Cererê* closes with a return to the interior, a reaffirmation of the ethic of *bandeirismo:* "I'm a lowly *bandeirante* / born with my back to the sea. / There's much treachery in these isles... / My wife is *terra firma*... / and the sirens are at sea" (211). But, like Cobra Norato's betrothal to the autochthonous princess, Martim's "marriage" to the *sertão*—the final in a series of exchanges of metaphoric spouses and objects of desire in the poem—interrupts the narrative of progress that begins to unfold in *Martim*'s urban section. His telluric wedlock stakes an epilogic claim of *national* ownership and domination.

It is a symbolic "de-linkage" from the capitalist exchange circuit that is annulled by the distant and intractable market forces whose seductive "siren-song" not only sets cargo ships to sail across the vast blue sea, but determines, in the last instance, both the extent and the configuration which that proprietary hold takes. The space of global exchange that the sirens come to occupy at the end of the poem thus exerts its irresistible pull, despite Martim's "chthonic" deafness to their song, to render *im*proper his final claim to the national soil.

In both *Cobra Norato* and *Martim,* infinity figures the horizon of progress, an "elsewhere" or "other side" that will always remain beyond reach. It is this paradox, which Ricardo's epic only adumbrates, that the cyclical structure of *Cobra Norato* foregrounds with singular force. For the temporal stagnation, the "laziness" and rejection of all that is geometric and Cartesian in which Norato's journey culminates, is, like *Martim*'s anachronistic coffee plantation, at once the obverse and the enabling condition of Brazil's "peripheral" modernity. Locked into a structure of repetition, its terminus always-already in place elsewhere, the "road to development" in both narrative poems turns out to be a parabolic return to a state of "backwardness."

The ineluctably *prior* emplacement of this idea of the future renders the stage of "underdevelopment" insurmountable, indeed necessary to the developmentalist (or systemic) logic underpinning the idea of development itself. As Octavio Paz wryly observes, "the kingdom of progress is not of this world: the paradise it promises us lies in the future, in an untouchable, unreachable, perpetual future" (*El laberinto de soledad* 244; my translation). In this manner, the 'developed world' becomes analogous to the realm of Platonic Ideas, to that original state that 'developing' peoples can never directly behold, or, as in Plato's cave, can only glimpse as "a shadow configuration."

Read against the grain of the overtly developmentalist ethos informing their poetics, both *Cobra Norato* and *Martim Cererê* can be seen to gesture inchoately toward an interrogation of the logic of progress. Through the fissures in the emancipatory narrative (to which both *Martim Cererê* and *Cobra Norato* generally subscribe), we are occasionally afforded a glimpse of something like Nietzsche's radical perspectivism, an incipient relativism that suggests that the teleological organization of the world is nothing more than a necessarily *particular* exertion of power, and progress consequently no more than a local and *interested* fiction. Albeit in a periphrastic and tentative mode, the two poems disclose a doubt in the attainability, or *calculability*, of development *in this world*. As I propose in the analysis of Alejo Carpentier's 1953 novel *Los pasos perdidos* (*The Lost Steps*) that follows, in this restricted sense, both texts participate in the modernist variation on (or adumbration of) a contemporary (or postmodern) suspicion of universalisms. It is this incredulity in the west's long story of progress that the two poems at times share in common with Carpentier's novel.

There are, to be sure, significant distinctions between *Los pasos perdidos* and the two Modernista "epics" I have been examining. For, if it is not necessarily exemplary of "a deconstructive force," as J. Michael Dash would have it, Carpentier's novel, in marked contrast to *Martim Cererê* and *Cobra Norato*, "consistently mocks the idea of new beginnings and the dream of absolute mastery of nature" that largely defines the two Brazilian texts (Dash, *Other America* 84). In Jean Franco's more straightforward terms, *Los pasos* "makes the point that, while the artist can and should trace lost steps to his own cultural roots, [he or she] must not stay in the past . . . [for] indigenous peoples and the telluric force of nature are only, after all, aspects of a vastly complex Latin American reality" (*Modern Culture* 132). To cite González Echeverría's seminal analysis of the Cuban novelist's fictional production, while it retraces the itinerary of a Romantic search for the absolute (the quest exemplified by the Bildungsreise), *The Lost Steps* proposes that the culmination of the protagonist's "educational journey" entails "recognizing the necessity of subverting that [Romantic] tradition," that "restitution, reintegration is impossible," in the final analysis (*Alejo Carpentier* 164).

In a well-known reading of Lévi-Strauss's "Writing Lesson," which seeks to deconstruct the opposition between natural and technological man, that is, "the myth of a speech originally good, and of a [scriptural] violence which would come to pounce upon it as a fatal accident" of history (*Of Grammatology* 135), Derrida ascribes the Swiss ethnologist's defense of "natural man" and his concomitant indictment of writing to "an ethnocentrism *thinking itself* as anti-ethnocentrism, an ethnocentrism in the consciousness of a liberating progressivism" (120). It is a similar "ethnocentrism"—which, to paraphrase Derrida, severs primitivism from civilization with an ax—that provides the brittle ethico-political foundation for the Brazilian nativisms I have been discussing. The latter's cohesion, as I have attempted to demonstrate, tends finally to fracture, revealing not only the rhetoricity of the antinomies that structure their accounts of national history, but also the very ground of the emancipatory discourses that govern the latter.

In *The Lost Steps*, Alejo Carpentier turns this process of decomposition into a self-conscious and reiterated procedure, in which the narrator-protagonist's paradigmatic journey into the heart of the Amazon becomes interchangeable with the act of reading itself:

> I had spent long hours looking at the banks, without taking my eyes for too long from the narration of Fray Servando de Castillejos, who had brought his sandals here three centuries ago. His quaint prose was still valid. Where the author mentioned a rock . . . there it was, high on the right bank. Where the chronicler spoke with amazement of seeing gigantic trees, I had seen gigantic trees, descendants of his trees. (*Lost Steps* 110–11)

The difference between the "natural" referent of the protagonist's narrative discourse and that narrative (or genre) itself is blurred here, as Carpentier's protagonist discovers that the primitive, "original" language that is the object of his obsessive quest is always-already *denatured*, textualized. In González Echevarría's words, he confronts the "road to paradise littered with texts that form an unpliable and dense memory from which he can find no release" (*Alejo Carpentier* 174).

The "real jungle" [*la selva verdadera*] is no sooner "announced" by the guide or Adelantado who leads Carpentier's protagonist into the "heart of the Amazon," than it reveals itself to be nothing more than a "jungle made of books."[23] Its truth is camouflaged, displaced by a succession of tropes (trees with "the air of boats at anchor," which "seemed more marble than wood, [and] stood out like the towering obelisks of a drowned city" [*Lost Steps* 164]), by "the inexhaustible mimetism of virgin nature" (165). "*The* source of the novel does not exist as such. The novel falls within such a vast literary and paraliterary tradition of travel journals and novels that listing one or many books is as futile as the protagonist's quest" (*Alejo Carpentier* 177).

The paradoxically reproductive potential of "virgin nature" erases the distinction between copy and original, reality and representation: "everything seemed something else, thus creating a world of appearances that concealed reality, censuring [*poniendo en entredicho*] many truths" (*Lost Steps* 165). "There are, in fact, no geneses in the novel, only repetitions, rediscoveries, and falsifications" (*Alejo Carpentier* 167). At the very moment of its deictic designation ('There is the entrance!' [*Lost Steps* 159] ['¡Ahí está la puerta!' (*Los pasos* 222)]) the "real jungle" begins its slippage into a "world of deceit, subterfuge, duplicity," where everything "is disguise, stratagem, [play of appearances], metamorphosis" (*Lost Steps* 166). Rather than the primeval substratum beneath a palimpsest of textual layers, nature is in effect constituted by that imbricated textuality. As the sign posted at "the gate" of the 'real' jungle indicates, nature's "original speech" is always unoriginal and citational. Carved on a tree trunk, into the very "skin" of the forest, this sign ("three V's, one fitting vertically into another in a design that might have been repeated ad infinitum, but which here was multiplied only in the reflection of the waters" [159]) places the rain forest within a series of embedded, and inverted, quotation marks, guillemets (»«), which remain nonetheless open, repeatable, returning in the last sentence of the novel.[24]

The V's, as González Echeverría remarks, initiate "a kind of composition *en abîme*—a series of infinitely repeated and receding sequences" (*Alejo Carpentier* 183). It is as if this inscription serves to indicate on the forest's very surface a "buried similitude," the visible mark for the invisible analogy between the Amazon and its textual representations, the *signature* on the Amazon's skin without which, as Foucault writes in a different context, resemblance is not possible: "the world of similarity can only be a world of signs" [*Order of Things* 26] (le monde du similaire ne peut être qu'un monde marqué).

These arboreal citation marks are echoed in turn by the mood of performativity or "representation" with which the narrative begins (the inauthenticity purportedly attaching itself to urban living and hence opposed to the genuine reality of the jungle). As the last capitalized Word—

the Logos itself?—this Sign takes on the symbolic force of an exergue. It is an inscription of the iterability of the novel's discourse on nature, a "natural language" that, like the narrator's thwarted attempt to return to the jungle at the end of the novel—to replicate a Same that was always-already sundered from itself—will never coincide with the original.

Although far from approaching the sustained self-reflexivity of Carpentier's narration, Bopp's *Cobra Norato* at times approximates its "artificing" of the natural in its representation of the Amazon. One of the more notable indexes of this "denaturation" is, contradictorily enough, the "elastic" snake skin with which Cobra Norato "clothes himself" just before his "penetration into the dark and oneirical world of the forest," supposedly the realm of the unconscious (Averbuck 125). Even though it allegedly signifies the connective tissue between the civilizational hero and the "womb" of the wilderness, the skin actually serves a protective function, for once Norato converts it into a prophylactic, he has obviously wrenched it from the natural world. The skin thus belongs to the industrial tropology that marks the poem's description of the Amazon.

The metaphor that Fernand Braudel uses to describe "the way in which the New World, after 1492, was gradually drawn—body and soul, past, present and future—into the European sphere of action and thought" provides a somewhat disparate though cogent indication of what I am trying to get at here. The Americas, Braudel remarks, were "Europe's 'periphery', its 'outer skin'" (*Perspective of the World* 387). Correlatively, the snake skin becomes an especially inappropriate metaphor for the unconscious, since, in accordance with Freud's topographic model of the human mind, "consciousness is the *surface* of the mental apparatus; [it] is spatially the first one reached from the external world" (*Ego and the Id* 11).

For Freud, the Id (which, as is known, is not coterminous with the Unconscious but may serve here as a convenient trope of "wildness") is the older "province" of the mind: "the Ego has developed out of it through the influence of the outer world as the bark develops around a tree" (*Interpretation of Dreams* 123). Rather than the national "id": Brazil's "obscure Pre-history, [its] immense and atavistic depths, [its] origins, the roots of the race" (Bopp, *Movimentos modernistas* 97), the snake skin would more properly figure the poetic "ego"—the poem proper as well as the poetic "I's" proper name—or even the palimpsestic "tegument" upon which they are both inscribed.

As I indicate above, the antagonistic Cobra Grande, the poem's central trope, operates both as a synecdoche of nature and the metaphor for poetic self-reflexivity, a recoiling before an original referent that—like the 'real' Brazil—looms perennially "just ahead" of the poem: "In the land-that-has-no-end" (Bopp, *Movimentos modernistas* 97). It is this parabolic re-flex, in the form of the trodden *Cobra Grande*—its head crushed beneath the Virgin's feet—that the camouflaged protagonist appears to symbolize. In a figural sense, the latter is the verso of the former—a specular repetition that the use of the Portuguese verb *enfiar* for both "slip into" and "stick under" (*"me enfio nessa pele"* [3] [I slip myself into that skin], "Cobra Grande . . . ficou com a cabeça *enfiada*" [54] [Cobra Grande . . . got its head stuck under]) apparently reinforces. *Cobra Norato*'s referent splits into the poet's "instrument" or "alter ego" (Cobra Norato) and the metonym for the rain forest (Cobra Grande), vacillating between an elusive "natural" referent and the space of writing itself.

In the last instance, the Serpent functions as the Sign of this undecidability, of a spiraling, iterable and iterated script that remains inadequate to its example. The inability to express the reality of the Amazon, the characteristically sublime agitation between the pain of unpresentability and the double pleasure arising on the one hand from the negative assertion of the strength of an imagination striving to figure even that which cannot be figured and the immense power of rationality on the other (Lyotard, *Inhuman* 98), the inward collapse of the teleology of progress, all these may be read as so many invocations of the unpresentable, as the unthought of "modernizing" projects.

As I shall propose in my analysis of Mário de Andrade's *Macunaíma* in the next chapter, this aporia may also elicit a dehiscent breach onto a "future which can only be anticipated in the form of an absolute danger, which breaks absolutely with constituted normality and can only be proclaimed, *presented,* as a sort of monstrosity" (Derrida, *Of Grammatology* 5), as an opening onto that future anterior for which, as Derrida concludes (or begins), "there is as yet no exergue" (5).

3   God in the Machine

Primitivism, National Identity, and the Question of Technology in Mário de Andrade's *Macunaíma*

> A poet is a light and winged thing, and holy, and never able to compose until he has become inspired, and is beside himself, and reason is no longer in him. . . . And you rhapsodists interpret the utterances of the poets. . . . You are interpreters of interpreters.
>
> —Plato, *Ion*

As EARLY AS 1926, in an unpublished preface to *Macunaíma*—perhaps the most renowned of Modernismo's primitivist texts—Mário de Andrade defines the "style" of his novel as rhapsodic (*Macunaíma* [1988] 354). Not until 1937, however (nine years after the novel first appeared), did Mário "courageously," that is, in the title page of the novel's second edition, identify the novel's genre as a rhapsody (Ancona Lopez, in M. de Andrade, *Macunaíma* [1988], 268. In light of sustained Modernista efforts to align the originality of their literary production with that of Brazil's original cultures, the question I explore in this chapter concerns exactly the originality of Mário's rhapsodic primitivism. Let me broach it by turning to the writer himself:

> What amazes me and what I regard as sublime goodwill on the part of my detractors is that they forget everything they know, restricting my plagiarism [*cópia*] to Koch-Grünberg, when I copied everyone. . . . I confess that I copied, sometimes verbatim. . . . Not only did I copy the ethnographers and Amerindian texts, [but] I included entire sentences . . . from Portuguese colonial chroniclers. . . . Finally . . . I copied Brazil, at least insofar as I was interested in satirizing Brazil through Brazil itself [*por meio dele mesmo*]. But not even the idea of satire is my own. . . . The only [original] thing left to me then is the accidental [Pedro Àlvares] Cabral [*só me resta pois o acaso dos Cabrais*], who, having by probable chance discovered Brazil for the probable first time, ended up claiming

Brazil for Portugal. My name is on the cover of *Macunaíma* and nobody can take that away from me. (*Macunaíma* [1988] 427)

This open admission of plagiarism—a famous 1931 response to Raimundo Moraes's rejection of prevailing assertions that Mário's book owed more than a substantial debt to a collection of Amerindian oral narratives edited by the German ethnographer Theodor Koch-Grünberg (*Vom Roraima zum Orinoco* [1917])—clearly goes against the grain of contemporaneous Modernista calls for the creation of an original national culture. It foregrounds the novel's iterable and iterated textuality at a moment when the authenticity of an oral or "natural" language was the privileged mode and referent of literary expression.

Were *Macunaíma* to assume its pride of place on the bookshelves of that Little Anthropophagist Library (Bibliotequinha antropofágica) envisioned by Oswald, in other words, it would turn into just another volume in a Babelic archive encompassing "all that is able to be expressed" (Borges, *Collected Fictions* 115). The genuine 'primitiveness' of the novel's hero would vanish before the "certainty that everything [about him] has already been written," before an all-pervasive Logos that finally nullifies him or makes of him no more than a phantom, a sign (118). "Macunaíma is at bottom nothing at all," writes Augusto Meyer in a brief review (*critiquinha*) (qtd. in *Macunaíma* [1978], 347–48), which Mário deemed "more clear-sighted than any other, an admirable synthesis chock-full of truths" (*Macunaíma* [1988] 411). The novel's main character "tends toward dispersion," Meyer continues; what prevails after an attentive reading is "a void, a sense of failure" (*Macunaíma* [1978] 348). The national or psychological "lack of character," which the novel's subtitle ("The Hero without Any Character") underscores, would be the titular indication of the referential emptiness to which Meyer alludes. The closing reference to the novel's lack of reference would in this sense be the recollection of Macunaíma's words and deeds by a "green parrot with a golden beak" (168),[1] who then parrots them to the rhapsode, who will in turn parrot them to the reader.

It is therefore not surprising that Mário should regard as "nonsense" (*bobice*) a September 1928 review of the novel that declares its language "so much 'our own' that it ceases to be ours," its "reality so 'real' that we no longer recognize ourselves in it" (Tristão de Athayde, qtd. in *Macunaíma* [1978] 338). In Mário's view, since *Macunaíma*'s "artificial, artistic language"—which he contrasts with "basic, spoken language"— ultimately resembles writing rather than speech, that is, the literary work itself, Athayde's intended rebuke turns out to be "truly a compliment" (*redunda em verdadeiro elogio*) (*Macunaíma* [1988] 407–8).

Augusto Meyer is similarly careful to distinguish the psychological void, the novel's purported sense of ethical failure, from its status as a work of art, since, as Meyer asserts, it is only insofar as it willfully detaches itself from its social milieu that the literary work attains aesthetic value (qtd. in *Macunaíma* [1978] 348). On this point, then, Meyer would concur with Mário: *Macunaíma* "is the only truly artistic, that is to say, disinterested, work of art that I have ever produced" (*Macunaíma* [1988] 400). This disinterested aestheticism contrasts directly with the programmatic "social primitivism" of Oswald de Andrade's *Pau Brasil* poetry, for instance. It has no place in Modernismo's "phase of social construction." It would be as incongruous in such a context "as a pebble inside a shoe" (M. de Andrade, *Ensaio sôbre* 18).

This artistic autonomy would seem to be symbolized in the novel by the formulaic transformation of several of its characters into a starry alphabet:[2] "the beautiful but useless shine of yet another constellation" (*o brilho bonito mas inútil de mais uma constelação*) (*Macunaíma* [1988] 165), which is "the fate of all beings" (*o destino fatal dos seres*) (397). Macunaíma's metamorphosis into Ursa Major (166) at the end of the novel—an anthropomorphic constellation "brooding alone in the vast expanse of the heavens" (*banzando solitário no campo vasto do céu*) (166) —ultimately expresses, in Mário's words, "a second [presumably formalist] intention" (412). Its professed rootedness in Amerindian "tradition" notwithstanding, the procedure—which Haroldo de Campos calls the novel's "astronomic code" (*Morfologia do Macunaíma* 266–69)—is a characteristically Modernista conceit. It is replicated, for instance, in the "stars enclosed in photographic negatives" that Oswald associates with a new perspective in *Pau Brasil*'s opening poem (15), in the stars that in Menotti del Picchia's *República* are converted "into commercial signs" (195), as well as in Cassiano Ricardo's neon inscription of his lover's name across São Paulo's night sky in *Martim Cererê*.

As the examples to follow suggest, moreover, the novel's carefully constructed 'astronomic' imagery tends to intersect with what Barthes would designate the "literary code"—those sites where it self-consciously refuses to enter into a referential relationship with the 'world'—be it traditional or modern—where it participates fully in a stereotypically modernist tautology and aspires to signify only itself. Thus, for example, Macunaíma's beloved, the Amazon or *icamiaba* Ci, Mother of the Jungle, ascends to the sky in mourning for the death by poisoning of their only son. There she becomes Beta Centauri, one of the principal stars of Centaurus, a constellation in the Hercules family. The other member of this constellation family is the Southern Cross, the "national constellation," into which a "patriarchal" figure—Pauí Pódole, Father of the Crested Curassow[3]—is transformed.

The final destination of Macunaíma's two brothers, Jiguê and Maanape, is an inverted image of the Southern Cross's avian outline: the leprous shadow-head of Father or King Vulture (*urubu-rei, o Pai do Urubu*; the allusion to Alfred Jarry's dramatic trilogy seems obvious enough). In a fanciful etiology of the *boi-bumbá* or *bumba-meu-boi* popular dance (whose main feature is the parading of a bull (*boi*) made of wood and cloth), Jiguê's ghostly shadow perches predatorily upon the flank of "a Malabar bull called Espácio" (154).[4] The shadow-Jiguê figures the "dark side" of the Pleiades, which is the shoulder of the Bull in the morphology of the Taurus constellation (the "Seven Sisters" is the celestial shape adopted at the end of the preceding chapter by Iriqui, the last in Macunaíma's long list of lovers). Finally, two secondary female characters, the youngest daughter of Macunaíma's antagonist and Jiguê's bride, are transformed into appropriately "minor" celestial objects: a comet and a meteorite (or a "falling star"), respectively.

This elaborate system of interlinked tropes indicates that the novel's 'astronomic code' is something other than an anthropological datum. Its function is "poetic," in Roman Jakobson's sense. It figures a reversal, or turning inside out, of the space of writing. In this sense, Macunaíma's blackness[5] would constitute an allusion to his scriptural provenance, of which his final sidereal destination becomes the inverted image: an autotelic project "reinforced and corroborated [*roborado e corroborado*], like an immense chiasmus, from the inaugural silence of its first page to the augural silence of the last" (Campos, *Morfologia do Macunaíma* 275): "There was a moment when the silence was so great listening to the whispering of the river Uraricoera" (5); "an immense silence was slumbering on the banks of the Uraricoera" (167). The hero-constellation, then, signifies the muting of the tribe's speech, the literary sublation of a vanished oral tradition whose final term is the space of literature itself: the shining telos of a literary production about the production of literature itself.

The conversation between Mário and Mallarmé ("another 'name beginning with Ma'" [*Morfologia do Macunaíma* 292]) that Haroldo de Campos intercepts "within the text's erasures and sutures" (291), despite the former's "clamoring rejection" of Mallarméan poetics (279), apparently continues to resonate in the following line from "Action restreinte" (which Campos does not cite): "on n'écrit pas, lumineusement, sur champ obscur, l'alphabet des astres, seul, ainsi s'indique, ébauche ou interromp; l'homme poursuit noir sur blanc" (Mallarmé, *Oeuvres* 284) ("one doesn't write luminously, upon a dark surface, only the alphabet of the stars is thus indicated, sketched out or broken; man pursues in black on white").

As Paul de Man observes, for Mallarmé, the star figures the literary work itself, "the timeless project of the universal Book, the literary paradigm that Mallarmé, half-ironically, half-prophetically, keeps announcing as the *telos* of his and of all literary enterprise" (*Blindness and Insight* 180). To borrow Haroldo de Campos's gloss of the lapidary phrase from "Le Livre, Instrument Spirituel," the world of Andrade's hero seems indeed to exist only in order to end up as a book (Campos, *Morfologia do Macunaíma* 271). One could evidently introduce other participants into Campos's symposium of the dead and listen for an echo of Macunaíma's transformation in the "star-infused" poetic persona of Rimbaud's "Drunken Boat" (*Oeuvres complètes* 294). Or, one could see in the magical cleansing of Macunaíma's *négritude* (*pretume*)—his emergence from an enchanted pond as "white, blond and blue-eyed" (34)—a possible inversion of the trajectory of the "I" in Rimbaud's "Mauvais Sang," which moves from an identification with the Gauls in the opening line: "J'ai de mes ancêtres gaulois l'oeil bleu blanc" (412) (I inherit from my Gaulish ancestors my whitish-blue eye), to an appropriation, toward the end of the poem, of a radical "racial" alterity: "Je suis une bête, un nègre" (308) (I am an animal, a nigger[6] [(*Oeuvres complètes* 417]).

Yet, to interpret the novel's metaphors of race and light as indexes of a formalist negation of its mimetic function is merely to replace an external referent with an immanent one, to remain caught within "a representational poetics that remains fundamentally mimetic throughout" (de Man, *Blindness and Insight* 182). It is also to accept uncritically what Fredric Jameson has called "the formalist stereotype of the modern": "its apolitical character, its turn inward and away from the social materials associated with realism, its increased subjectification and introspective psychologization . . . its aestheticism and its ideological commitment to the supreme value of a now autonomous Art" ("Modernism and Imperialism" 45). Only by moving beyond a formalist reading of the novel, I would submit, can we come to grips with its complexities and contradictions.

Mário himself calls *Macunaíma*'s supposed artistic autonomy into question when he insists that the book is a social satire (*Macunaíma* [1988] 407), even "a perverse [social] satire" (403), that it fuses "the fantastic and the real ["symbol, satire, and fantasy"] in the same plane" (416). To take this other—contradictory—authorial cue, then, is to move beyond the subtle pleasures of a formalistic squaring of the circle and to begin, however indistinctly, to glimpse in *Macunaíma*'s absences "the informing presence of the extraliterary, of the political and the economic" (Jameson, "Modernism and Imperialism" 45). The void that Augusto Meyer identifies at the center of *Macunaíma* would therefore constitute not so much the locus of the novel's folding back upon itself as that of an intersection with the extraliterary.

Somewhat like Macherey's "hollow" in the text, *Macunaíma*'s consistent negation of referentiality becomes the textual edge beyond which the social and the historical (the obverse of what is written, in Macherey's formulation) begin to unfold (*Pour une théorie* 115). At first glance, the novel's (and the protagonist's) absence of character foregrounds the irreducible rhetoricity of Modernista quests for "a Brazilian Brazil," of nativist attempts to retrieve from the absents of history (precolonial cultures) the symbolic solutions to the vexed questions of national identity and economic development. What for *verde-amarelismo,* the Anta school, and *antropofagia* stands forth as the sociocultural reference point—the authentic source of an authentic national character—is in *Macunaíma* emptied into the "practical nullity" to which Mário, in an ethnomusicological study also published in 1928, reduces "the Amerindian element in Brazilian popular culture" (*Ensaio sôbre* 16).

As I point out in chapter 1, for the Anta school, the Tupi ultimately signifies nothing as well. He is a blank, articulated as a positivity, which nevertheless manifests itself only as an absence: "What is *Anta*? Nothing . . . The totem of a vanished race" (Salgado, Menotti del Picchia, and Ricardo, "Nhengaçú verde amarelo" 287). The Anta school's Tupi is thus the absent yet common topos of national identity, a free-floating "common denominator" that "every foreign race" must acquire upon arrival if it is to rise to homogenous Brazilian-ness (Salgado, *Despertemos a nação* 38). Yet this trace turns out to be as preterit and as intuited as that of the implausible urban tapir (*anta*) that Macunaíma deceives a motley crowd of "businessmen, wholesalers, stock jobbers, fat cats, hucksters, canvassers, peddlers, prostitutes, and Hungarians" (*Macunaíma* [1988] 97) into tracking on the sidewalk of São Paulo's Commodity Exchange. Thus, in the end, and notwithstanding Oswald de Andrade's evocation of "Montaigne's natural man" in the "Manifesto Antropófago" (*Do 'Pau-Brasil'* 14), the textual place of Mário's savage hero seems, much more than that of the Anthropophagus, as "emptied . . . vacant and distant" (Certeau, *Heterologies* 73) as that of the "cannibals" in Montaigne's essay.

Oswald's Anthropophagus, as the embodiment of a Hegelian theodicy, requires a symbolic consistency that Macunaíma repeatedly shatters. For the latter contains no design for the future of the nation. He "is not a symbol of the Brazilian," and his "character is precisely to be without a character," to evoke "discontinuously" a set of discrete ethnic characteristics and ethical values (*Macunaíma* [1988] 398). In this respect, the characterization of Macunaíma resonates with Brecht's theatrical procedure (in a play whose original version dates back to 1926) of having "a man reassembled [*unmontiert*] like a car / Leaving all his individual components just as they are" (*Man Equals Man* 38).

So, if this story of a "hero of our people" (*Macunaíma* [1988] 168) born in "the depths of the virgin forest" (5) is intended as a narration of the nation, a copy of Brazil proper, then it can only be a blank copy, since Brazil is inevitably at variance with itself. As Mário asserts, Brazil is always already improper (*impróprio*), its identity an absent term:

> What undoubtedly interested me in Macunaíma [Mário writes in the 1926 preface] was my ongoing preoccupation with working through and discovering all I can about the national identity of Brazilians.... The Brazilian has no character. And by character I do not simply mean a moral reality... [but rather] a permanent psychic identity, manifesting itself in everything, in the mores, in outward actions, in emotions, in language, in History... in good as well as in evil. The Brazilian has no character because he has neither a civilization of his own [*civilização própria*] nor a traditional consciousness. (351–52)

In light of this hollowing out of Brazilian-ness, the national symbolism conventionally ascribed to the "green parrot with a golden beak," which remains to tell Macunaíma's story at the end of the novel, becomes untenable. Perched upon the national bard's head, the macaw appears indeed to figure something like the "crown" or blazon of narratorial legitimation, to be the light and winged autochthon authorizing the singer of tales to recount the narrative of "the hero of our people" (*herói de nossa gente*) in an "impure language" (*Macunaíma* [1988] 168). But which people is Macunaíma a hero of?

By posing the question I am not merely suggesting that, because the novel's symbolic structure inheres in an analogical link between two empty places (a characterless hero and a nation without a character), the site of the national in the novel is ultimately emptied out. What I am asking, rather, is whether, given Macunaíma's heterogenous and agonistic identifications, he can ever be so unequivocally related to "the people" (*a gente*), whether "the people" whose hero he purportedly is and in whose name the story is written—the source of narrative authority that the parrot would embody in the last instance—is not in effect the emptiest of the novel's empty places.

"Everything in the last chapters was written in great agitation and sorrow. . . . The two or three times I reread that finale . . . I was overwhelmed by the same sadness, the same loving desire that it had not been so," Mário writes in a 1942 letter (*Macunaíma* [1988] 417). It all happens as if the condition of possibility of Macunaíma's emergence as a *literary* character is the "death of speech" (Certeau, *Heterologies* 78), the "ruin" of the Cannibals that Montaigne supposes "far advanced already" (Montaigne, *Les Essais* 118), the dual silencing of an "original" narrative and of its "original" narrators that, according to Certeau's reading, enables Montaigne's representation of the Tupi as well. It is in effect this "absent presence" that the parrot supplements.

The parrot is the sole vestige of an annihilated culture (the last of a canopy of macaws that, in "those far-off times when Macunaíma had been the Great Emperor" of the Amazons (*Macunaíma* [1988] (168), hovered above the hero's head like an avian crown). It is the only remaining shard of a pre-European "marvelous reality" catalogued in the documents of the "discovery": "[hay] manadas de los papagayos que ascureçen el sol, y aves y paxaritos de tantas maneras y tan diversas . . . que es maravilla" (Colón, *Los cuatro viajes* 77) ([there are] flocks of parrots darkening the sun and so many different varieties of large and small birds . . . that it is a marvel"); "there [were] so many parrots, of such diverse kinds, that it was a marvel" (Vespucci, *Letters from a New World* 5).

In the end, Macunaíma's retinue of birds flies off in search of maize to "the land of the English" (Guyana) (*Macunaíma* [1988] 158), and the parrot/narrator itself "spread[s] its wings bound for Lisbon" (168), just before "the man" takes up the story. The "national" bird is the residue, the resonating fragment of Macunaíma's ruined (narratorial) authority. Whatever legitimacy derives from its autochthony dissipates in its final flight to Lisbon, for the parrot's body becomes "literally" metaphoric, a body in transit or trans-lation, in aporetic suspension between "the depths of the virgin forest"—which for Raul Bopp represent the national substratum indicated by "the Anthropophagic arrow" (*Movimentos modernistas* 71)—and the old colonial metropolis, the very topos of identitarian inauthenticity, the most antipodean of sites in the "authentic" geography of the nation.

Like Macunaíma himself—who, by the time of his final transformation, had, of course, long been a blond and blue-eyed alien—the parrot is an estranged autochthon. The forest has ceased to be his homeland: "At that time Macunaíma no longer saw anything worth living for on this earth [*não achou mais graça nesta terra*]. . . . At least he would be like all those relatives of his, all the forebears of earthly beings . . . who now live on in the useless shine of the stars" (164–65). No longer the privileged place of the nation's unconscious, the forest in the novel is relegated anew to the status of a pagan outland (or, the *pagus*, which, as Lyotard points out, is etymologically linked to *país* [country] [*Instructions païennes* 43]). It becomes the periphery, the unknown region, a site of "non-centrality, non-finality, and untruth" (Lyotard, *Rudiments païens* 230), against which the former colonial power appears once again on the verge of reaffirming itself as the center. Not only is the pagan (the "native" and the "natural") turned as a result into an artifice of writing, but it is effectively made strange, incompatible with the identity of the nation.

The "arrow" described by the parrot's flight is finally that of the novel's language itself: "the impure speech" into which the human narrator translates the parrot's treacherous, intoxicating and "completely new tongue" (168), and which appears to counter Mallarmé's memorable account of Edgar Allan Poe's poetic project: *donner un sens plus pur aux mots de la tribu*. Thus, at the very moment that it seeks to coincide with its "virginal" referent ("In the depths of the virgin forest, Macunaíma, the hero of our people, was born" [5]), the novel's writing begins to differ from and defer its object, to curve back—parabolically—toward the "inauthentic" site whence the masters' voice (in González-Echevarría's phrase) originates. The parrot becomes, in this manner, the herald or insignia of *Macunaíma*'s technicity, a phantasmal trace. It is an echo of the genocidal silence that enables the novel's writing and for which that writing—indeed, the proper name "Macunaíma"—can only serve as a supplement. It is a proxy, "a place assigned in [its] structure by the mark of an emptiness" (Derrida, *Of Grammatology* 145), a "hollow in the text" reverberating mockingly, sorrowfully, in the very last sentence of the novel.

Tem mais não, Andrade's version of the pleonastic, formulaic ending of Tupi oral narratives, is the colloquial (or "popular") form of the grammatically correct *não tem mais* (there is no more). As Mário's own reading of the novel suggests, *Macunaíma*'s last phrase expresses a regret, an impossible desire for presence. The sentence begins as an affirmative (*tem mais:* there is more) and closes as a negative. The surplus (*mais*) is ostensibly crossed out by the final particle (*não*). Yet it remains indelibly inscribed in that negation itself, for *não* is at once the doubling of and a supplement to an omitted particle: [*não*] *tem mais, não*. Replicating the novel's invocation of a cultural presence that is always-already absent, this final word is at once an addition and an erasure: a supplement to a virginal world that never was, or to a world whose virginity is produced by its very dissolution.

In the 1942 letter I quote above, Mário remarks that the Modernistas of his generation saw *Macunaíma* as "'the lyrical projection of Brazilian feeling, the virginal and unknown soul of Brazil!' Virginal! Unknown! [he protests] Not in the least! My God! A Nazi dog would be a lot more virginal!" (*Macunaíma* [1988] 417). In effect, the novel's last word erases the nativist hyphenations of national identity with the virginity of natural Brazil. *Não* repeats the expunction of the narrative's "original" referent enacted by the winged cross that is the parrot in flight. A scriptural echo of this cross of feathers, *não* abrogates the autochthonous narration, its very signifying structure, plunging it *in an abyss* (*en abîme*: originally a term of heraldry whose approximate meaning is "placement at the center" of a coat of arms).

The closing phrase is thus an impure translation (a substitution) of the silenced tribal tongue, remitting us back not just to the heraldic parrot in translation, but to a hero translated into a stellar alphabet, to all the dismembered and reconfigured Macunaímas: "an infinite chain, ineluctably multiplying the supplementary mediations that produce the sense of the very thing they defer: the image of the thing itself, of immediate presence, of originary perception" (Derrida, *Of Grammatology* 157). In this way, *tem mais não* stages a kind of negative dialectics: a suspension of Modernista presentations of "natural man" as a surplus to modernity, to nationality, as a ghostly (*geistige*) positive term to be recuperated, sublated (*aufgehoben*) in Anthropophagy's dialectic of the Spirit, or transubstantiated in a *verde-amarelista* "Eucharist of blood from every origin" (Salgado, *Despertemos a nação* 40). It places finality itself under erasure.

Andrade's macaw can therefore evoke a *verde-amarelista* national spirit only parodically. Its fitting counterpart is the worm-eaten, stuffed parrot that in Flaubert's "A Simple Heart" is memorably and idolatrously conflated with the Holy Ghost. The hollowness of Félicité's Loulou is duplicated in the conspicuous absence of history in Flaubert's *Tale*. In contrast to the surfeit of historical detail in the collection's two other pieces ("The Legend of St Julian Hospitator" and "Herodias"), history in "A Simple Heart" is reduced to a series of necrological dates in the most obscure and mediocre of lives.

The events that would provide the historical background of the Tale are, in fact, the gap in Flaubert's text, as though mimesis could only lapse into mechanical reproducibility, as though thenceforward modern history will occur exclusively under the sign of repetition—"the first time as tragedy, the second as farce," to coin a famous phrase—as a succession of derisory *parousias* (or second comings) of monarchies, republics, and empires. Just as the identification of the stuffed parrot with the Holy Spirit appropriately metaphorizes the emptying of the teleological in nineteenth-century French history—what Nietzsche calls the transformation of "the romantic faith in love and the future ... into the desire for the nothing" in Flaubert (*Will to Power* 66)—Andrade's parrot/narrator also performs, as I have indicated, a crossing out of the justifications of God (or a racial, cultural, and indeed technological *Geist*) in History that are routinely mobilized by various Modernista currents.

At the same time, however, Andrade's parrot is itself a sort of minor god, at least according to the following definition of divinity: "un dieu païen, c'est par exemple un narrateur efficace" (Lyotard, *Instructions païennes* 46) (a pagan god is, for example, an efficient narrator). The point where the story of "our hero" is transmitted in the novel is simultaneously the moment when God (or the Geist) splits into a multiplicity of narrator-gods, of pagan deities who can never guarantee "the conformity between the narrative and its object" because their "speech isn't any more truthful than human speech" (45), divinities who refuse "to attribute to any discourse even a modestly epistemological authority which would be established once and for all above all others" (Lyotard, *Rudiments païens* 246).

For if Macunaíma is yet another of the many names of God, its meaning must reside beyond good and evil. He is both an absence and a surfeit of the sacred, at once a "yearning for the divine" and a "contempt for the tiresome notion of God" (*Macunaíma* [1988] 412). His is the name of an unbearable memory of genocide—actively forgotten, or repressed by Modernista primitivisms—witnessed and mourned in *absentia*, the name of a narratorial authorization that, like the one insistently solicited in Montaigne's famous essay, is always and irrevocably lost in translation.[7] "God and the cannibal, equally elusive, are assigned by the text the role of the Word in whose name its writing takes place—but also the role of a place constantly altered by the inaccessible (t)exterior [*hors-texte*] which authorizes that writing" (Certeau, *Heterologies* 69).

Thus, Macunaíma's ascension to heaven at the end of the novel figures not a telos but its fragmentation. It splinters the dialectic equilibrium between "the starry heavens above me and the moral law within me" ("the two things [that] fill the mind with ever new and increasing wonder and awe") with which Kant's *Critique of Practical Reason* closes (169).

For Kant, the infinity of the heavens annihilates, in a first moment, the importance of the individual as an animal creature "which must give back to the planet (a mere speck in the universe) the matter from which it came" (169). At the same time, the self's faculty to grasp the vastness of the universe

> infinitely raises my worth as that of an *intelligence* . . . in which the moral law reveals a life independent of all animality and even of the whole world of sense—at least so far as it may be inferred from the final destination assigned to my existence by this law, a destination which is not restricted to the conditions and boundaries of this life but reaches into the infinite. (169)

To read Macunaíma's dispersal into an astral script as literature's inward turn is in a sense to transpose into aesthetic terms this consolatory inner infinity. It is also to avert one's gaze from the void, from "the vast expanse of the heavens" (*Macunaíma* [1988] 166), which is a sort of spatialization of the lingering, genocidal silence repeated (or echoed) in the novel's epilogue. The reading of *Macunaíma*'s star-script toward which I am gesturing here may perhaps be illumined by the following section from Nietzsche's *Beyond Good and Evil:* "It is to be *inferred* that there exist countless dark bodies close to the sun—such as we shall never see. This is, between ourselves, a parable; and a moral psychologist reads the whole starry script only as a parable and sign-language by means of which many things can be kept secret" (118).

The section's opening or revelatory movement (*Erschließung*), its expression of an epistemological desire to pry into the solar core itself, pierces —dialectically—all the way through the sun of enlightenment and out its other, dark side. It bends asymptotically back upon itself, or into an *Abschluß,* a closing down, a cloaking. Unlike Kant's inference of an inner, moral infinity from an outer one, Nietzsche's "parable" does not allow for an ethically redemptive reading of the "starry heavens." It leads chiasmically from an opening (*erschließen*) to an epistemic outer rim, a threshold watched (over) by an exegete (a moral psychologist) whose function, akin to that of a gatekeeper or *Schließer,* is to guard the secret (the silence) of the stars, their parabolic obscurity, rather than to interpret and elucidate.

The sidereal Macunaíma is just as much a sign of occlusion, of the "other side" of narration and hermeneutics, the topos of the unknowable and the untold, of the parabolic and tropological in the Nietzschean sense. Whatever ethical (national, aesthetic) consciousness lies "behind" *Macunaíma*'s stellar script is thus either dismembered into "too many things" or dissolved into "practically nothing," into "something provisional... of the order of astronomy" (Niestzsche, *Beyond Good and Evil* 63, 64), as provisional and aleatory, in fact, as the legendry of constellations. As with the spatial analysis of the human body hypothesized by Nietzsche (by means of which "we gain precisely the same image of it as we have of the stellar system"), the hero-constellation collapses "the distinction between the organic and inorganic" (*Will to Power* 357), the corporeal and the spiritual. And the contingent celestial geometry of the Great Bear "reflects" back upon the written page precisely the annihilation, the fragmentation of a "paganism" that returns to shake the very ground of a Kantian universal ethics—of the enlightenment project itself.

If there is one thing that sets Mário apart from his fellow Modernistas, it is precisely the reluctance to retell the west's master narrative of progress, a hesitancy, perhaps even an anxiety, that seems to grip him just before that epistemological threshold where the futural promise offered up by the available teleologies of social and technological progress begins to unfold:

> In times of social transition such as the present one, it is hard to make a commitment to what is to come, to what no one knows anything about [he confesses in another unpublished preface (of 1928)] ... I don't wish for the return of the past, and for that reason I can no longer glean from it a normative fable. The Jeremiah mode seems on the other hand just as ineffectual to me. The present is a dense and misty cloud [*O presente é uma neblina vasta*]. To hesitate is a sign of weakness, I know. But it's not a matter of hesitation in my case. It is a true inability—the worst one—to know even the name of the unknown. (*Macunaíma* [1988] 375–76)

This kind of cautiousness is uncommon among Mário's fellow Modernistas. It contrasts sharply with the sentiment expressed in the closing poem of Menotti del Picchia's *República dos Estados Unidos do Brasil,* where the divine Word rises triumphantly out of the Machine in order to sanction industrial progress itself: the fusion of "man's energy ... with the forces of the earth" (206). It is a similarly overriding rule by the goddess Machine (*Máquina* is a feminine noun in Portuguese) that Macunaíma encounters upon arriving in the city. The hero's "pagan imagination" typically converts technology into a powerful fetish. He recodes it as an urban counterpart of the Forest Mother: a technological correlate to the *Mãe-d'água* (or "water mother") of *bandeirante* legend, whom he regards with a mixture of envy and respect, and desires above all to dominate sexually: "He decided to fool around [*brincar*] with the Machine in order to make himself emperor of the children of manioc [the whites]" (40), just as he had become emperor of the *icamiabas* (or "Amazons") by raping their empress, the Forest Mother Ci. Nevertheless, as a trio of metropolitan prostitutes informs him, "the machine was no god [*A máquina não era deus não*] . . . it worked by electricity, by fire, by wind, by steam, men taking advantage of the forces of nature" (41).

Although *deus* seems here to be unquestionably "ex-ed" out of the *máquina*, the hero remains unconvinced. After prolonged "machinations" (*maquinando*) on the matter, he surmises that "the machine must be a god which men didn't truly own because they had not been able to turn her into an explainable *Iara*[8] but only into a worldly reality" (41). Interestingly, Macunaíma's line of reasoning here approximates that of Alfred Jarry on the origins of the automobile, whose idea the French playwright traces back to the ancient Greeks. In a piece published in *La Plume* (15 June 1903), Jarry asserts that "it is the machine alone which performs god's work. *Deus ex machina,* God is extracted from the machine. The machine thoroughly replaces God. It has progressed higher than God because man has made it not in his own image but endowed it with unexpected power" (*Oeuvres complètes* 462, 463).

Macunaíma concludes less apocalyptically that the struggle between man and machine has ended in a draw (*empate*) (41), or at least a chiasmus, an *x:* "it's the men who are the machines and the machines who are men" (41). Deriving "a mother of satisfactions" (*uma satisfa mãe*) from this sally, the hero promptly turns one of his brothers into a telephone and orders up some lobsters and an assortment of prostitutes (41–42). Even a cursory summary such as this provides a sense of the contradictoriness inherent in what is apparently a simple animist reduction of technology to what Heidegger might have called a mythological abstraction.

Macunaíma's fetishization of technology subscribes to a structure of inversion set in motion by his voyage to the coast. While reproducing the itinerary of the Tupis' precolonial descent into the Atlantic, his move from the jungle to the city reverses the expansionist westward trajectory of Brazil's geographic heroes, the *bandeirantes,* which, in Ricardo's *Martim Cererê,* Menotti's *República,* and Bopp's *Cobra Norato,* represents the inaugural stage of the nation's epic journey toward modernity. In line with this reversal, Macunaíma's sexual desire for the Machine would enact a figural revenge of the wilderness against a civilizational order that converts nature into "a fecund, slumbering woman," to borrow one of Mário's own metaphors ("De São Paulo" 58), a "virginal, mestizo body" recumbent and available to prosthetic penetration, a body "stiffened by the muscles of its minerals, rich in woods and pastures . . . full of gold and diamonds . . . / of long, nocturnal, underground veins / of iron and of coal" (Menotti del Picchia, *República* 125).

Poetic unveiling, or *poiesis* (the bringing forth of what presences into appearance, in Heidegger's jargon), is in Menotti's poem substituted by a technological mode of revealing that in the *Question Concerning Technology* Heidegger designates *Ge-stell* or "Enframing." Menotti's presentation of the land is suffused, in short, with that "monstrousness" that Heidegger regards as the essence of technology:

> The revealing that rules throughout modern technology has the character of a setting-upon, in the sense of a challenging-forth. That challenging happens in that the energy concealed in nature is unlocked, what is unlocked is transformed, what is transformed is stored up, what is stored up is, in turn, distributed, and what is distributed is switched about ever anew. . . . That revealing concerns nature, above all, as the chief storehouse of the standing energy reserve . . . [a] way of representing [that] pursues and entraps nature as a calculable coherence of forces. (16, 21)

It as though Macunaíma's gendering of the Machine originates from the wild side of this technological mode of representation. It affords a primal revealing, a glimpse of the *pagus:* "those borderlands where matter offers itself up in a raw state before being tamed," the forest: "FORIS, outside. Beyond the pale, beyond the cultivated land, beyond the realm of form" (Lyotard, *Inhuman* 186). Yet the hero's technology fetishism is reproduced in Menotti's already cited invocation of God (or the Spirit of Modernity) in the Machine, as well as in Cassiano Ricardo's figural synthesis of primitive cosmogony and the urban-industrial scape in his description of São Paulo as a "red-haired *uiara*" (*Poesias completas* 204).

It is also echoed in the "Futurist" enthusiasm for the Machine expressed by one of the heteronyms of Portuguese modernist poet Fernando Pessoa (Álvaro de Campos) in his "Ode Triunfal" (Triumphant Ode), published for the first time in 1915 in the journal *Orfeu:* "Tanks, canons, machine-guns, submarines, airplanes! / I love you all . . . like a savage beast . . . The new metallic and dynamic Revelation of God [*Nova Revelação metálica e dinâmica de Deus*]!" (Campos, *Poesias de Álvaro de Campos* 148–49). In other words, Macunaíma is never more a technological man than when he attempts to "naturalize" the Machine.

It is the Light of Reason itself ("an immense light shone upon his brain" [69]), in fact, which apparently guides the hero, when, "waving his arms above the fatherland" (69), he delivers the solemn dictum that becomes one of the novel's two principal refrains: "Too little health and too many ants are the evils of Brazil" (Pouca saúde e muita saúva, os males do Brasil são) (69). This motto is probably a gloss of the improving axioms proffered by Jéca Tatú at the end of a didactic postscript to Monteiro Lobato's famous 1918 caricature of the lazy *sertão* dweller. What brings about Jéca's "Resurrection" (the piece's subtitle) or transformation from a rotting human fungus (*urupê*), inhabiting an ant-infested hovel, into a harbinger of progress is his recovery from malaria and attendant realization that the virus is at the root of his chronic laziness. Jéca's journey toward "improvement, progress and American things" culminates unsurprisingly with the mechanization of agriculture (*Urupês* 337):

> Everything [in the plantation] was [now] carried out by means of the radio and electricity.... [Jéca] would press a button and the pigs' trough was automatically filled with well-apportioned rations. He would press another, and a jet of corn would attract the whole of chickendom [*galinhada*]!... His ranches were connected by telephone ... and by means of a telescope [he could] see everything that took place in the plantation. (338–39)

Just as panoptic is the direct correspondence between development and the general improvement of the rural population's health that Jéca establishes at the end of the piece: "I will employ my whole fortune toward this universal health care project. This is the measure of my patriotism. My motto: To heal people. Down with the germs devouring the Brazilian people" (*Urupês* 339). In keeping with this program, Brazil's unproductive populace is presented as a vast unexploited national resource, as a "storehouse of the standing energy reserve" (Heidegger, *Question Concerning Technology* 21). The logic underpinning this instrumentalization of humanity dates back at least to Aristotle's *Politics* (Book I, Ch. 4). It is this "point where [man] himself will have to be taken as standing-reserve" or *Bestand*, that Heidegger calls "the very brink of a precipitous fall" (*Question Concerning Technology* 27). And this is precisely the edge that Macunaíma approaches as well, as he begins to pose the question concerning technology, so to speak.

The rationalist, Modernista answer to this question in the novel is iterated by three women whose bodies have been effectively instrumentalized.[9] By the time of his symbolic reversal of the industrial taming of the land (his attempted sexual subjugation of the Machine) Macunaíma has, of course, been thoroughly integrated into the commodity exchange circuit within which the prostitutes circulate. Indeed, by "technologizing" one of his brothers and commodifying the sexual act, he seems to operate entirely in accordance with his stated premise that men are machines and machine are men.

He apparently subscribes entirely to the developmentalist logic of conquest and domination that already subtends his rape of the slumbering Ci (she has to be held down by his two brothers while he performs the act that will render him lord emperor of the virgin forest). Ci's violent repulsion of Macunaíma's initial advances renders her as much a symbol of telluric resistance as the *mãe-d'água* in Victor Brecheret's Bandeiras Monument. The latter, according to the sculptor himself, signifies, as we have seen, a Land that is at once "a compassionate and virtuous mother [and] a cruel and merciless killer" ("Monumento das Bandeiras" 55). Unlike the epic march of the Bandeiras in Modernista narrations of the nation, however, Macunaíma's jungle empire is an ephemeral one. It is of little or no national consequence. *Emperor* is an empty ceremonial title whose single external sign is the retinue of macaws. Andrade's hero remains obdurately underdeveloped, in other words.

Like the etymologically related Canaima of Rómulo Gallegos's eponymous novel, he seems to be the very negation of progress: the savage spirit of the Amazon jungle (*el mal de la selva*) that, in Gallegos's *Canaima*, takes possession of a protagonist who refuses to "cultivate himself, to civilize the barbarous force dwelling within him" (170), and finally ("tragically") chooses to go native. Macunaíma, then, is a dedicated follower of the "Great Rule of the Least Effort" (Lobato, *Urupês* 283). He is stuck on the "side of the [civilizational] road," wallowing in a "mystical laziness," irremediably "useless, contemplative, documental" (Menotti del Picchia, *República* 178, 180). As Augusto Meyer writes, what rules him is "the imperative of sloth, of moral indifference, the tendency toward dispersion . . . a Jéca-Tatú-like inertia" (M. de Andrade, *Macunaíma* [1978] 348).

He is governed by a "slackness [*mussangulá*] [which is] opposed to all that is coherent, syllogistic, geometric, Cartesian," which Raul Bopp presents as the essence of the rural Brazilian (*Movimentos modernistas* 84), and into which, in the end, Cobra Norato appears to sink as well. It is this inactivity, this immeasurable lack of productivity that the first phrase uttered by Macunaíma expresses: "Ai! que preguiça!" (5) (I feel so lazy!—literally, What laziness!), which is the novel's second major refrain. Though juxtaposed throughout this rhapsodic text like theme and counterpoint, the two refrains (technology and the primitive) never coalesce into a single melody.[10] There is no dialectic bridging them, no communication across their discrete referential universes. They remain incommensurable, as if signified in different idioms. Between them lies a silence, an abyss: "the unstable state and instant of language wherein something which must be able to be put into phrases cannot yet be," the "heterogeneity of phrase regimens and of genres of discourse," which Lyotard names the *differend* (*Differend* 13, 181). Like Macunaíma himself, the linking of these two phrases engenders nothing, yields no result.

The same "barrenness" underlies Macunaíma's prodigious sex drive, the novel's "disorganized pornography," as Mário designates it in the 1926 preface, and which he justifies as an adequate reflection either of the "obscenity" of the Amerindian tales themselves or of the "everyday life of the nation" (*Macunaíma* [1988] 354). Haroldo de Campos reads *Macunaíma*'s exuberant eroticism as "a good-humored portrait of Brazilian sensuality" (*Morfologia do Macunaíma* 192), echoing Mário's own interpretation of the book's "immorality" in the 1928 preface as a complacent mockery of what he designates "a Brazilian constant" (*Macunaíma* [1988] 372). Nonetheless, what is striking about Macunaíma's frenzied sexual activity is precisely that—in contrast to the foundational romance between Amerindian mother figures and Lusitanian patriarchs—it is not "re-productive."

Macunaíma's only son, the unnamed "red-skinned" product of his union with Ci, dies in infancy upon suckling his mother's poisoned breast. Once she is transformed into Beta Centauri, Ci becomes as sterile as the Machine: a negative image of her maternal, reproductive self, for whom Macunaíma will simultaneously yearn and substitute with an endless succession of "daughters of manioc," or white women. Macunaíma's racial cleansing, his reemergence as a blond and blue-eyed "Aryan" from a pond formed by the giant footprint of the apostle Saint Thomas (or Sumé) is in a sense his only offspring. In its aftermath, Mani ("whiteness," Ci's inverted image) becomes the name of Macunaíma's desire, literally a *satisfa mãe*: a "satisfaction" or desire that is self-sustaining, self-engendering, that is its own mother, as it were, or whose object is the other of a split subject: a projection of the ideal European that the hero embodies and yet will never become.

In the novel's last chapter, in a scene that harks back to that of Macunaíma's racial transformation, a treacherous white beauty, a *mãe d'água* or Uiara (the name of the fertile autochthonous mother in Cassiano Ricardo's *Martim Cererê*, it will be recalled) beckons the hero seductively from the bottom of an appropriately specular lagoon. When he crawls out of the water, he is "bleeding, his body bitten all over, his right leg was missing, as were the toes on his left, his Bahia-coconuts, his ears, his nose, and all of his treasures" (163). The Uiara is the last emblem of Macunaíma's desire for whiteness, and she turns out to be the most sterile and destructive of the novel's barren mothers.

To read Macunaíma's final "Aryanization" (his dismemberment and subsequent transformation into a stellar or mirror image of his black *tapanhuma* self) allegorically, and against the backdrop of *verde-amarelismo*'s accounts of the formation of a "harmonious race," is to posit the Uiara (or Mani) as a kind of ideological matrix for such narratives of racial destiny: as "the recommendable *Eugénia*" (Eugenics is a feminine noun in Portuguese), whom Macunaíma, in a parodic epistle to his "Amazon," or Icamiaba subjects, confesses never to have met in person (*Macunaíma* [1988] 81). Macunaíma's double "whitening" is thus the figural equivalent of what the *verde-amarelistas* called the Tupi's "spiritual" triumph. His residual presence can similarly be recoded as "a harmonizing element" (Salgado, Menotti del Picchia, and Ricardo, "Nhengaçú verde amarelo" 234, 238), a "common denominator" (Salgado, *Despertemos a nação* 38), enduring only "in the blood and soul" of those newly arrived immigrants upon whose faces Cassiano Ricardo has God himself imprint the Hour of the Future (*Poesias completas* 206).

By the same token, Macunaíma's inability to engender seems to be one of the "constants" of his (or the Brazilian) "character" (*Macunaíma* [1988] 372). The question I broach above about the identity of Macunaíma's "people" (*a nossa gente*) must thus be posed once again. Rather than a symbol of racial or national unity, Macunaíma appears to be a *degree zero* of ethnicity (*gentis*). To see, for example, in the "rainbow trio" made up by the hero and his two brothers ("one blond, another red, and the other black" [38], as they step out of the magical pond) "a transparent symbol of [multiracial] Brazil" (Athayde in *Macunaíma* [1978] 336) comparable to the three magi of the races (the "Western," the "Cosmopolitan," and "Melchior of the slave quarter" [*mocambo*]) from Menotti's *República* (135), or the red, white, and black Kings of Cassiano's epic (*Poesias completas* 143), is, I think, to read a little too hastily. Not only does such a reading gloss over the inconvenient fact that, as Macunaíma's immediate adoption of a racist attitude indicates, the three skin tones compose not a harmonic but an ascending scale—with the blond and blue-eyed hero unquestionably at the top—but it takes for granted the enigmatic presence of a "black" brother amid the original Amerindian trio.

The blackness, which was once Macunaíma's own, superimposes upon the putative Amerindian referent of *tapanhuma* (the name of Macunaíma's tribe) another "incompatible" meaning (Ricardo, *Marcha para Oeste* 1: 288): a runaway slave living in a jungle redoubt, or *quilombo*.[11] This referential shift is at least adumbrated by the ascription of the title *Rei Nagô* to the tribal leader in the beginning of the novel. Rei Nagô is the legendary West African King of the Nagos, whose spirit is summoned up during a macumba ceremony in a later chapter. In addition, Mário chooses to use a term of African (Kimbundu) origin, *mucambo,* to designate the hero's family dwelling place. Macunaíma's original ethnic identity thus becomes itself undecidable, a site of slippage and indeterminacy. And if *tapanhuma* indeed points to the hero's African origin, it would signify another of the absents of the eugenic narrations of Brazil.

To recall the words of the *verde-amarelista* sociologist Alfredo Ellis, "Only two elements weighed in the formation of the [São Paulo] population [from the sixteenth to the mid-eighteenth century]: the red American race and the one from overseas. . . . The Negro was absent and almost unknown" (*Raça de gigantes* 89). For Ellis, unions with the African could only produce "a bastardization of the eugenic element" (185), or what Menotti del Picchia designates "the failed monsters of our racial type" (*República* 179). Not surprisingly, Ellis considers that the zenith of São Paulo's "eugenic potential" is reached in the second half of the nineteenth century with the substitution of the "Negro hand with the Italian and Spanish settler" (*Raça de gigantes* 191–92). The association between the African "element" and Brazil's underdevelopment is, in fact, a common topos in the writings of Mário's "Aryanist" contemporaries. Raul Bopp, for example, bemoans, in an early poem, the rejection of a German immigrant's application for residence in Brazil by Immigration Services bureaucrats who allege shortsightedly that the foreign "European" migrant's technical skill and experience would give him an unfair advantage over the domestic labor force. And "poor Brazil," the poet concludes,

> remains padlocked
> dripping with second-class Jews
> dripping with Portuguese bumpkins
> who immediately shack up with the mulatta.
> The distant West with its open spaces
> full of unexploited forces
> awaits the human hand
> which will come one day to raise up the nation
> to its uttermost limits.
> (*Cobra Norato* 120–21)

Even Cassiano Ricardo, who criticizes Ellis's exclusion of the African from the *Bandeiras* (*Marcha para Oeste* 1: 284–321), defines the latter's contribution only in terms of an instrumental metaphorics, as "a cog in a wheel" (1: 328), or "black coal for the workshop of the races" (*Poesias completas* 121). From such a standpoint, the *quilombo* stands as an obstacle to the nation's "ethnic democracy," "the greatest threat to the future civilization of Brazil" (*Marcha para Oeste* 453, 460).

If Macunaíma's black complexion in effect discloses what Ellis describes as "the stigmas of the ebony race" (*Raça de gigantes* 91), then his "Aryanization" represents not only the subsumption of a "native spirit" by successive European migrants, but a eugenically requisite substitution of the black by a "more advanced" racial type. In this sense, the hero remains ineluctably split between his "outer" and "inner" ethnic identification: white on the outside, black/Indian on the inside: "without a character," evoking randomly and "discontinuously ethnic or circumstantial racial values" (*Macunaíma* [1988] 398). His birthplace—the symbolic "depths of the virgin forest" (5)—reveals itself once again as something other than the original referent of the original story of Brazil. It is rather an obstruction, a suspension of the nation's narration emerging from another of its forgotten corners.

It is this aporia that *Macunaíma*'s human narrator signifies in the last instance. The rhapsode situates himself "simultaneously" in two opposite narrative poles—at the beginning of the novel, where the birth of "the hero of our people" is recounted, and at the end, the place of his tautological self-identification ("the man is myself, my people" [168] [*o homem sou eu, minha gente*]). These are the two poles where the storyteller, like the Cashinahua informant from whom Koch-Grünberg might have collected some of the stories retold in the novel, is at once the addressee of the narrative and its referent or subject matter.

Lyotard calls this narrative situation the "essential feature of paganism [and] probably what has been the most eradicated in Western thought" (Lyotard and Thébaud, *Just Gaming* 33). Unlike the Cashinahua informant, however, the novel's narrator cannot speak "in the place of the referent" (41). His narration comes after the disappearance of Macunaíma's people. It is *epilogic*, a supplement to the vanished speech of the tribe preserved by the parrot-narrator whose final flight figures precisely this referential absence and indeterminacy.

Between the story's subject matter—*a gente*—and its listener-storyteller—the "popular" narrator—another insurmountable rift opens up. It is within that gap that "the people" dwell in *Macunaíma*. The novel's narration, in other words, consistently refuses to perform that work of forgetfulness that Nietzsche posits as the condition of possibility for the rise of the new, the sustenance of "life" itself ("On the Uses and Disadvantages" 76). It negates the forgetting (*l'oubli*) of the brutality and deeds of violence at the origin of every political formation, which Ernest Renan, in his famous essay on nationalism, defines as "un facteur essentiel de la création d'une nation" (*Qu'est-ce qu'une nation?* 41). *Macunaíma* emerges in this sense as an anamnestic negation of nationalism itself.

In an influential discussion of western nationalisms, Homi Bhabha ascribes the narratorial paganism, which Lyotard uncovers in the Cashinahua tradition and defines as the repressed of Platonic and Kantian thought, to the "people in the diaspora" who inhabit "the nation's edge" (*Location of Culture* 139, 170). Once the people "turn pagan" or "bipolar" in this narratorial sense, Bhabha argues, "any supremacist, or nationalist claims to cultural mastery [become untenable], for the position of narrative control is neither monocular nor monological" (150). For Bhabha, it is from within a rift akin to the one I identify above in *Macunaíma*'s narration, and which he regards as a dehiscence splitting apart dominant nationalisms, that diasporic peoples are able to gather their dissonant voices and unsettle the myth of a national homogeneity. According to Bhabha, this disjunction (or "splitting of the people") arises from two asynchronous moments in the narrative address of the nation—the "pedagogical" and "the performative":

> the nation's people must be thought in a double-time; the people are the historical 'objects' of a nationalist pedagogy, giving the discourse an authority that is based on a pre-given or constituted historical origin *in the past;* the people are also the 'subjects' of a process of signification that must erase any prior or originary presence of the nation-people to demonstrate the prodigious, living principles of the people as a contemporaneity: as that sign of the *present* through which national life is redeemed and iterated as a reproductive process.... In the production of the nation as narration there is a split between the continuist, accumulative temporality of the pedagogical, and the repetitious, recursive strategy of the performative. (145)

The national narrative is consequently disjointed, split between tradition and invention, as it were, and finally becomes "a liminal signifying space that is *internally* marked by the discourses of minorities, the heterogenous histories of contending peoples, antagonistic authorities and tense locations of cultural difference" (*Location of Culture* 148). As the national 'subject's' time-space of intervention, Bhabha argues, the performative allows for the possibility of minoritarian agencies, providing "both a theoretical position and a narrative authority for marginal voices" (150)—even for the establishment of political solidarity (157).

This notion of minoritarian intervention resonates with the models of political resistance elaborated by Ernesto Laclau and Chantal Mouffe. Hence, according to the former, the fact that the open-endedness of political argument and discourse enables the very construction of social reality becomes a "source of a greater activism and a more radical libertarianism": "Humankind, having always bowed to external forces—God, Nature, the necessary laws of History—can now, at the threshold of postmodernity, consider itself for the first time the creator and constructor of its own history" (Mouffe, "Radical Democracy" 39–40).

Elsewhere Mouffe asserts that one of the necessary conditions for the emergence of political struggle or "antagonism" is a "contradictory interpellation": "a situation in which subjects constructed in subordination by a set of discourses are, at the same time, interpellated as equal by other discourses" ("Hegemony and New Political Subjects" 95). She provides as an example the suffragist movement, which arises at the end of the "democratic revolution," when "as citizens women are equal, or at least interpellated as equal, but that equality is negated by their being women" (95). Bhabha's blueprint for the distension of western national traditions seems at least "inspired" by Laclau's and Mouffe's anti-foundationalism and "deconstruction" of the referential function of political discourse as well as by their privileging of moments of disjunctive interpellation.

His own contribution is to make the split in narrations of nationalism essentially, even *necessarily,* productive in political terms: an inevitable opening onto the edges of the nation. Nevertheless, what remain unarticulated in Bhabha's theoretical model are the conditions enabling the emergence of these contestatory "strategies" and "practices." The closest he comes to such an articulation is to compare the coming into being of a "non-pluralistic politics of difference" to the introduction of a supplementary question in the British Parliament: "Coming 'after' the original, or in 'addition to' it, gives the supplementary question the advantage of introducing a sense of 'secondariness' or belatedness into the structure of the original demand. The supplementary suggests that adding 'to' need not 'add up' but may disturb the calculation" (*Location of Culture* 155).

This disturbance will nonetheless remain ineluctably contained within the space of ritualized political debate. In other words, the parliamentary metaphor suggests that the struggle's future time must be known a priori, that the political agonistics will be played out necessarily in accordance with pre-established rules of order. Since the split to which an emancipatory potential is so readily assigned may just as well produce a contraction, a closing down or limiting of political debate, the shift from the identification of a fissure in the narration of the nation to its instantiation as the site of a political opening can be effected only by means of a disavowed appeal to speculative logic, only by means of a dialectic of the Spirit that posits as the *Aufhebung,* the moment of minoritarian intervention. In order to articulate this model of resistance, the theorist must occupy at one and the same time two distinct and discontinuous poles of narration: the present of his writing, and the time after the end, a future whose secret signs he must be able to decode.

It is the discontinuity between these two poles that I have attempted to pay heed to in my own analysis. Unlike Homi Bhabha, I read the rift separating *Macunaíma*'s "people" from its "popular" storyteller not as an opening, but as an impasse: the site of "a memory [that] flashes up at a moment of danger" (Benjamin, *Illuminations* 255). What the novel's fissuring of nationalist narratives adumbrates, I believe, is the differend that Lyotard identifies in the republican discourse of legitimation. Here, as with the discourses of nationalism, the first-person plural pronoun (as in *We, the French people*) operates as the linchpin of republican authorization. Yet this homogenous *we* masks "a double heterogeneity": the discontinuity in the positions occupied by the *we* in the "normative" and the "prescriptive" instances ("The normative phrase is *We, the French people, decree as a norm that,* etc.; the prescriptive phrase is *We, the French people, ought to carry out act α*" [Lyotard, *Differend* 98]). In the first (normative) instance, the *we* is the addressor of the norm; in the second or prescriptive instance, it is the addressee of the obligation. The *we* is thus split between a declarative *I* ("the instance that prescribes") and a *you* that is the addressee of the obligation (i.e., *You ought to* . . .). "One may make the law and submit to it, but not 'in the same place,' that is, not in the same phrase" (98).

Thus, the rift between the two instances can be bridged only by an "illegitimate" and 'illusory' ("in the Kantian sense of transcendental illusion") positing of a subject-substance (the *we*) that would be both a 'subject of the uttering' (even though it is not the addressor in the prescriptive) and the permanence of a self (even though from one phrase to the next it shifts from one instance to another). 'Auschwitz' is for Lyotard the sign of the fracturing of this transcendental illusion, of the abyss that opens up between the obligee and the legislator when, in the name of progress or national redemption, a segment of the people is designated as useless, superfluous, targeted for destruction.

Whether the void that the *gentis* comes to occupy in *Macunaíma* can ever provide "a theoretical position and a narrative authority for marginal voices" (Bhabha, *Location of Culture* 150) must remain an open question. Nonetheless, what the novel's refusal to repress or actively forget the genocide at the origin of Brazil underwrites is that nationalism's work of forgetting not only reiterates that original violence but also retains the potential to reproduce it. It seems to signal that the "anonym" that constitutes for Lyotard the model for a negative dialectics (and that in Mário's novel identifies "the most primitive elements of the population" [Franco, *Modern Culture* 268])—the figure for that which will always return to negate sublation itself, to cancel out the progress of the mind—may yet emerge as one of the names of what is to come. It would thus seem to be a similar reading of these "primitive elements" that is suggested by the return of the "savage" as part and parcel of a renewed interrogation of discourses of modernity in the films I examine in the following chapter.

4 Cannibal Allegories
Cinema Novo and the "Myth" of Popular Cinema

> The film-maker trying to make a popular cinema has . . . an impossible, almost mythical task! . . . Our cinema is supported by a vehicle for capitalism, a state enterprise. The contradiction is obvious. . . . But that is precisely the situation of the Brazilian film-maker who has no other source of capital and tries of justify certain films, allegorical, elitist, and almost masturbatory in their form of expression, in an attempt to reconcile this contradiction.
> —Ruy Guerra, "Popular Cinema and the State"

> At this point history took such a strange turn that I am surprised no novelist or scenario-writer has as yet made use of it. *What a film it would make!* A handful of Frenchmen . . . [who] now found themselves alone on a continent as unfamiliar as a different planet, knowing nothing of the geographical circumstances or the natives, incapable of growing food to keep themselves alive, stricken with sickness and disease and depending for all their needs on an extremely hostile community whose language they could not understand . . . were caught in a trap of their own making.
> —Claude Lévi-Strauss, *Tristes Tropiques*

THE RELEASE of Joaquim Pedro de Andrade's cinematic adaptation of Mário de Andrade's novel *Macunaíma* in 1969 has been hailed as a watershed moment in the cultural debates around modernity and national culture taking place in Brazil in the 1960s. As the political and cultural "crisis" unleashed by the 1964 military coup was once again forcing the problems of modernity and modernization back to the forefront of "national life," Cinema Novo (New Cinema) cineasts, who had hitherto looked to the social realist or "regionalist" fiction of the 1930s for their literary sources, began, during this "cannibal-tropicalist phase" of the movement (1968–1971)—partly as a result of heightened political censorship—to return to such Modernista currents as *antropofagia* for answers to the "slippery question" of Brazilian identity (Ramos, *Cinema, estado* 79).

Faced with the veritable reign of terror unleashed against leftist intellectuals and student groups by the military regime after the 1968 "coup within the coup," they resorted increasingly to allegory as their mode of artistic and political expression. What their cinema allegorized, to paraphrase the title of a recent study of the movement, was underdevelopment itself. Thus, in Pedro de Andrade's *Macunaíma,* modernity, which for so many of the Modernistas had supposedly loomed like a shining promise just beyond the temporal horizon, lapses into the preterit tense: "Colonization, economic expansion, migrations, ore extraction, renewed conflicts between intruders and aborigines, miscegenation; everything has already happened and these processes have left traces in the land where the hero is born as well as in the make-up of his family" (Xavier, *Alegorias* 141). As we saw in the preceding chapter, however, whether Modernista texts as a whole do indeed figure technology as the promise of a modern utopia remains an open question.

On the face of it, Pedro de Andrade seems to have taken a cue from Oswald's reading of Mário's novel as distinctly Anthropophagic. Just as in the novel, the signifiers *primitive* and *modern* are set afloat in the film. They lose their referential moorings, as Progress becomes "an illusion, a bourgeois fabrication" (Xavier, *Alegorias* 150). Thus, for example, Macunaíma and his two brothers return to their forest home at the end of the film loaded with appliances and consumer goods. The utter uselessness of these gadgets (a television set, an electric guitar) in an already ravaged "traditional" setting functions as yet another sign of what Roberto Schwarz might call a "misplaced" consumerism. In the absence of a productive infrastructure that would sustain an unfettered consumption, that consumption turns inevitably inward. It becomes self-consumption: autophagy.

Consumerism, like the imported goods themselves, is a "foreign" idea that has gone native. It now permeates the nation down to its very "Anthropophagist" core. Antropofagia itself, wrested once and for all from its autochthonous referent, becomes the sign of a peripheral modernity, of the "Anthropophagic" social relations defining a "savage" or dependent capitalism (Ramos, *Cinema, estado* 82; Xavier, *Alegorias* 150). This is the indiscriminate or "cannibalistic" accumulation and consumption to which Antropofagia "on a grand scale" (Bopp, *Movimentos modernistas* 94) has been reduced. The distinction that the Anthropophagists wished to draw between "the deep layers of nationality [and] the thick, moth-infested rind enveloping it," "the new Brazilian thought" (*o novo pensamento brasileiro*) rooted in "the other Brazil: subjacent, still unknown, yet to be discovered" (Bopp, *Movimentos modernistas* 64), the distinction between a truly "national culture" and a servile adherence to "a European culture ... agonizing" in a Spenglerian twilight (O. de Andrade, "Moquém" 6), this difference has, in fact, already been obliterated in the opening sequence of the film.

Its erasure seems to be obliquely suggested by the cineast himself, who, in an introduction to the film's release by Globo Video, informs the audience that what motivated Mário de Andrade's writing of the novel was his Bakhtinian insight that Brazilian "popular culture"—"always irreverent, humorous and indeed subversive in relation to hypocritical moral paradigms dominant in different periods of our history"—"retained the spirit, stories, and even characters created by our own Indians centuries ago." After the scrolling of the opening credits—superimposed upon the backdrop of an "impressionistic" pictorial composition combining the three "national" colors (green, yellow, and blue)—to the accompaniment of a nationalist march by Mário de Andrade's good friend and fellow traveler Heitor Villa-Lobos (*Desfile aos heróis do Brasil*), the screen turns completely red. The voice-over narration of the birth of Macunaíma, "in the depths of the virgin forest" (the first lines of Mário's novel), then begins, only to be abruptly interrupted by the piercing diegetic scream of Macunaíma's mother (portrayed by the same actor who will play the "white" Macunaíma) in the throes of what turns out nonetheless to be a rather perfunctory parturition. As the infant Macunaíma, played by the definitely overgrown black comic actor Grande Otelo, drops head first to the ground, the "Tapanhuma Indian woman" announces matter-of-factly: "Pronto. Nasceu." (All right. He's been born.) The bawling man-child's two older brothers promptly proclaim him "the hero of our people," thus inserting him in a mock-epic register into the "parade" (*desfile*) of national heroes extolled in Villa-Lobos's march.

The film then briefly reverts again to nondiegetic sound, as the off-camera narrator resumes his story (with a sentence adapted from Mário's novel): "And so it was that in the place called Pai da Tocandeira, Brazil, Macunaíma, the hero of our people, was born." In the space of about four minutes, there have been at least five sustained and utterly conventional visual and auditory cues stressing Macunaíma's Brazilian-ness. The narrative has barely got underway, and already Macunaíma's national identity has become commonplace, redundant, parodically hyperbolic. It overflows the frame of the story of his "adventures" before its cinematic telling has even commenced. Already then, rhetorical superfluity has attached itself to "the deep layers of nationality," which the film, mimicking what is already a consummately "mimetic" text, ostensibly sets out to uncover. By the time the "subjective" hand-held camera has led the spectator to the allegedly "pristine sources [of] the other [sylvan] Brazil: subjacent, still unknown, yet to be discovered," its primitive authenticity has been coated with a "thick and moth-infested [tropological] rind." The film's anthropophagist "journey toward (not the return to) natural man" (O. de Andrade, "Uma adesão" 10) cannot but take place under the twin signs of parody and pastiche.

As Macunaíma and his two brothers step off a truck converted into a public bus on the outskirts of the film's "metropolis," the truck driver proclaims: "Now it's everyone for himself, and God against all." The phrase seems intended as the motto for the "cannibalistic" social relations into which the hero and his brothers are about to enter. From this point onward, almost without exception, every interpersonal relationship depicted in the film will be driven by unmitigated self-interest. Characters, whose sole reason for being seems to be to satisfy their voracious appetite for food, sex, capital, and various kinds of luxury goods, literally and figuratively consume each other. While the film remains generally faithful to the novel's close and supposedly "traditional" association between the sexual act and the practice of Anthropophagy, in the former, the unproductive sexual relations do not appear to indicate an interruption of the nationalist figurations of miscegenation. Sexuality in the film becomes merely another facet of a consumerist "self-cannibalism." Its obsessive reproducibility, its lack of productivity and auto-consumptive drive, mirrors the logic of a "foreign" system that has now come to define the national character itself.

If Oswald de Andrade, for instance, reads *Macunaíma,* as he does his own sublated *Antropófago,* as an "unscathed" reminder that "the best that remained of the natural state of the Americas was not destroyed, [that] its culture resisted from the depth of the forests, in the rejection of every enslaving force, [and] survived ... to the scandal of the clothed and manacled world that was being brought to us" (*Estética e política* 284), Andrade the *cinemanovista,* on the other hand, would probably concur with Frederic Jameson: "the prodigious new expansion of multinational capital ... is a purer and more homogenous expression of classical capitalism, from which many of the hitherto surviving enclaves of socio-economic difference have been effaced (by way of colonization and absorption by the commodity form)" (*Postmodernism* 49, 405).

As a result, the "primitive communism" that one would expect to prevail in Macunaíma's tribal society has already been colonized. What governs the social relations among the members of the Tapanhuma tribe is in effect the same autophagic logic predominant in the urban setting. Almost from the moment he comes into existence, Macunaíma engages in a kind of primitive accumulation whose sole objective is the satisfaction of his own insatiable appetites and desires. Like the stereotypical capitalist, Macunaíma seeks to profit from the product of his fellows' labor. The "laziness" (*preguiça*), which the film's "national hero" borrows from the novel as one of his refrains, alludes in synoptic form to the paradoxical advocacy—on the part of Modernistas who were, broadly speaking, members of the leisure class—of social measures that would induce a rise in the productivity of the rural Brazilian. It also registers ironically not only the long-standing tradition of colonialist figurations of the "lazy native," but the generalized "dependency" that defines Brazilian capitalism.

What the film attempts to underscore, in short, is the "peripheral" asynchrony (*descompasso*) I discuss in chapter 1 between a base (lacking the economic and political ["modernized"] structures from which full-blown European modernisms are "directly derived") and a superstructure that can only permit the expression of modernity as a wish-fantasy (Ortiz, *A moderna cultura* 32–34). This contradiction underpins the caricaturesque figure of the Brazilian "champion of private enterprise," the urban counterpart to the "virgin forest's" man-eating giant: Venceslau Pietro Pietra, the conventional bourgeois philistine who is also the film's most conspicuous consumer. In his museum of a house he has assembled a heteroclite collection of primitive and contemporary art, pornography (both films "and the books on which they are based," Pietro Pietra adduces with a self-referential wink), as well as human beings. This same lack of "distinction" in taste extends to his sexual preference: upon discovering that the "French lady," whom he has aggressively been trying to woo, is in reality a *rapaz* (a "boy," that is, Macunaíma), he exclaims, without missing a beat, "No matter, I'm not prejudiced."

In another key scene, the Ubuesque Pietro Pietra, with a gaggle of sycophantic reporters at his heels, discusses the capital-accumulating virtues of a talisman he has purloined from Macunaíma's dead lover (the "raw material" at the source of his wealth, in a manner of speaking). Motioning majestically to the industrial wasteland around him, he trumpets in macaronic Portuguese: "This is all brand-new machinery. American. Secondhand." To paraphrase Octavio Paz, what is modern (or "brand-new") in Brazil is already last year's model ("secondhand") in the capitalist "core."

As I argue in my discussion of the novel, one of Mário's "aesthetic" aims in creating Macunaíma is "more or less to characterize... the Brazilian's lack of character" (*Macunaíma* [1988] 395), to produce a kind of typically modernist negative identification not dissimilar to the one that Jarry seeks to elicit from the bourgeois spectator of his *Ubu roi:* "Once the curtain was raised, I wanted the set to be like [a] fairytale mirror [where] the audience would behold with stupor the sight of its vile double [*à la vue de son double ignoble*], whom it had not yet confronted in its entirety" (*Tout Ubu* 153).

Not surprisingly, Pedro de Andrade's characterization of Brazil's "national hero" seems, by contrast, aimed at producing a much more "alienating" effect, in the Brechtian sense. As with Brecht's *Mother Courage,* for example, the lesson that the film seeks to impart is that Macunaíma's tactic of voluntarily and actively engaging in, as well as seeking to profit from, the capitalist game of exchange is both futile and self-destructive. Like Courage, Macunaíma is blind to the fact that, by strictly adhering to Capital's commodifying logic in his relations with fellow Brazilians, he simultaneously allows himself to be reduced to a commodity and participates in his own commodification. In this sense, Macunaíma's death allegorizes the dead end of the neoliberal economic model: the assimilation of a logic of capitalist accumulation that Brazil remains incapable of generating on its own (Xavier, *Alegorias* 155). To be modern, then, comes to signify the irreflexive reproduction of an imposed socioeconomic model, a mimetic—that is to say, "Macunaímic"—consumerist impulse shared by all social classes, which now defines the "national character."

Unlike the novel's hero, who is transformed into a constellation (a conversion that one critic reads as "a hopeful sign" [Ramos, *Cinema, estado* 81]), the film's protagonist is consumed by the *uiara* in a lagoon, to the accompaniment of the same Villa-Lobos march with which the film opens. According to different critics, this scene either points to the precariousness of the nationalist project (82) or satirizes the "nationalist myths appropriated by the military regime (summarized in the lyrics of Villa-Lobos's march): the glorification of nature, the cult of heroism, as well as the tropical paradise and great national destiny myths" (Xavier, *Alegorias* 155). By dint of what one might properly call asynchronous synchronization, the march's opening bars are made to coincide exactly with Macunaíma's final and fatal attempt to satisfy his consummerist drive: his plunge into the lagoon. The camera then cuts to the hero's green jacket floating up to the water's surface, and as the first verse of the *ufanista* (or ultra-nationalist) lyrics is sung ("Glória aos nobres que elevam a pátria, esta pátria querida que é o nosso Brasil" [Glory to the noble men who raise up the fatherland, this beloved fatherland that is our Brazil]), blood starts to spread upon the water's blue-green surface.

Before the final cut to the credits, the red stain has extended across almost the entire screen. The diegesis of Macunaíma's death loops self-referentially back to the initial sequence of the film. There, the finale of the Villa-Lobos anthem ("Glória aos homens, heróis desta pátria, da terra feliz do Cruzeiro do Sul" [Glory to the men, the heroes of the fatherland, of the joyful land of the Southern Cross]) matches the final opening credit: the director's name (Joaquim Pedro de Andrade's authorial signature in a sense). The birth of Macunaíma is subsequently narrated in voice-over against a red backdrop. The color of blood thus opens and closes the film, drawing an "autophagic" circle not unlike the one that Raul Bopp's *Cobra Norato* executes.

It is as though the parodic excess and tropological surfeit that mark the filmic reiteration of Macunaíma's nationality in the film's opening sequence now return thoroughly to "overflow" his figure. In the words of the director himself, the hero in the end is "devoured by Brazil" (J. P. de Andrade, "Cannibalism and Self-Cannibalism" 83). The rhetorical exorbitance associated from the outset with Macunaíma's national identity prefigures, or inscribes in exergue, the thematic of autophagic consumption. By dint of the "separation" (in the Brechtian sense) between the Villa-Lobos nationalist hymn and the iconography of the film's closing sequence (the asynchronization between image and music), the familiar national myths pastiched in the beginning of the film have been effectively de-familiarized by its end.

In a similar vein, the film's closing sequence echoes its last urban sequence: the Felliniesque wedding banquet for one of Pietro Pietra's daughters. This carnivalesque feast takes place around a large indoor pool filled with human remains, presumably the fare being served up to the guests. The bodies, as it turns out, are those of the guests themselves, who are periodically thrown into the pool whenever their names are drawn in a lottery. At the end of the scene, wearing a green and yellow tuxedo and blue socks, Macunaíma, who is forced by the grotesque entrepreneur to sway back and forth on a gigantic swing above the blood-spattered pool to the tune of Strauss's "Blue Danube," succeeds in tricking the giant into climbing on the swing. A "point of view shot" (high-angle long shot) shows the hero reaching for a bow and arrow, as the Rabelaisian financier swings helplessly to and fro. A medium shot follows, in which Macunaíma, donning on his forehead the precious talisman, or *muiraquitã,* that Pietro

Pietra had stolen from his Amazon lover Ci, wounds the giant with an arrow. As the cannibal-capitalist disappears beneath the bloodstained waters, the same high-angle long shot presents the hero standing, with both arms raised in victory, on a yellow and green dais at the edge of the pool.

This is undoubtedly Macunaíma's moment of triumph: the end of a purported Anthropophagist "journey toward (not the return to) natural man." In effect, one could read the medium shot that shows him shooting the (Anthropophagist) arrow, so to speak, as an almost iconic figuration of the "Manifesto Antropófago's" sublation of natural and civilized man: "Keyserling's technicized barbarian" (O. de Andrade, *Do 'Pau-Brasil'* 14), of "the technicized restoration of an anthropophagic culture" (129). He would be the embodiment of an authentic national culture, drawn from "the pristine sources [of] the other [primitive] Brazil," radically rejecting foreign capital and culture—the inauthenticity that Pietro Pietra's name and accented Portuguese as well as the Strauss waltz reinforce.

In keeping with this reading of the hero's moment of victory, Macunaíma would carry on the armed struggle of his revolutionary lover, who herself putatively embodies a "synthesis" between a modern urban guerrilla and a Tupi mythological figure. The scene thus enacts the *Aufhebung,* or "third term" forecast by the most radical of Brazil's Modernismos: "the Carib Revolution. Greater than the French Revolution. The unification of all effective revolts waged in name of humanity [*na direção do homem*]," for which the "Manifesto Antropófago" calls (O. de Andrade, *Do 'Pau-Brasil'* 14). As the hero, his latest female companion, and his brothers leave the city for their native land in the next sequence, he is described in voice-over as brimming over with "the immense satisfaction [*satisfa imensa*] which only a hero can feel."

The filmic representation of his departure from the city is in fact one of the film's "direct quotations" from the novel: "Waving his arms above the fatherland" (*Macunaíma* [1988] 69), Macunaíma, with his back to the camera, shouts the saying that functions as the novel's (and the film's) ironically developmentalist refrain: "Too little health and too many ants are the evils of Brazil" (*Pouca saúde e muita saúva, os males do Brasil são*). Along with the scene of his arrival in the city, where he is shot from a similar angle, standing, arm in arm with a different consort (who, unsurprisingly, soon becomes a prostitute), on a rise above the metropolis's squalid outskirts, the "farewell" scene punctuates, like a sort of "bookend," the urban section of the film. Whereas the area of the city he overlooks upon his arrival is a nebulous waste—suggesting either a garbage dump or the desolate edge of a sprawling *favela*—it is to a block of high-rises that he shouts his edifying slogan. Thus, both the latter's modernizing ethos and the modernity of the setting presumably accentuate the "synthesis," performed under the sign of national autonomy, of technology and primitivism. Only if this were the film's last scene, however, would the preceding be a valid reading.

The nature and circumstances of the hero's journey to Pai da Tocandeira —Bopp's "other Brazil"—mark the suspension rather than the supersession of what, in "A crise da filosofia messiânica," Oswald sees as a dialectical antagonism between north and south (between the developed or colonizing world and the colonized world, between primitive and civilized man). Upon his return to the Amazon, he lapses into a cultivation of leisure (*otium*)—*preguiça* (laziness), the first word Macunaíma ever utters, and part of his other contrapuntal refrain. Yet, as I suggest in my reading of Mário de Andrade's novel in the previous chapter, Macunaíma's *preguiça* has little of the cultural force with which Oswald wishes to invest his notion of *otium* (*ócio*), the defining character of a matriarchal or "natural" culture that the capitalist or Protestant work ethic (*nec-otium*) (*negócio* [business] in Portuguese), or patriarchal civilization negates.

In the film, Macunaíma's *preguiça* signifies Brazil's dependent status, a collective lack of initiative. *Ócio* has in effect become the national *negócio*. Indeed, the failure of the Modernista project has already been coded in the point of view from which Macunaíma's defeat of Pietro Pietra is shot. The high-angle shot imposes upon his "nationalist" victory a preferred reading. It is gazed upon from above, from the vantage point of almost forty years of history during which the "primitive" places and peoples of Brazil, who yielded the 1920s avant-gardes their source of inspiration and aesthetic raw material, now face ecological devastation and systematic proletarianization. If, by cinematic convention, the high-angle emphasizes Macunaíma's vulnerability as a symbol of a failed emancipatory politics, by that same convention the horizontal (90-degree) angle from which his plunge into the arms of the "perfidious, man-eating *uiara*" is shown constitutes an *objective* presentation of his final subjection to an insatiable appetite for (self-)consumption.

If, as I argue in chapter 2, in the *bandeirante* saga, the *uiara*, or *mãe-d'água*, represents a mythic or pre-industrial survival obstructing the single-minded progress of the heroic carvers of national territory (Ricardo, *Marcha para Oeste* 392), if she symbolizes the resistance of a duplicitous Brazilian Land: "a compassionate and virtuous mother, but also a cruel and merciless killer" (Brecheret, "Monumento" 55)—a kind of telluric *vagina dentata*—here she stands for the autophagic nation itself. Rather than an obstacle to development, she is the culmination of developmentalism itself. Along with her urban counterpart, the urban guerrilla fighter Ci (whose role I examine in greater detail below), the naked and "insidious" *uiara* is the only derisory vestige of the shining modernist utopia heralded by the last lines of Oswald's "Manifesto": "Down with the *clothed* and oppressive social reality recorded by Freud—reality without complexes, without madness and without penitentiaries, *in the matriarchate of Pindorama*" (Do *'Pau-Brasil'* 19; my italics).

But there is more. Even at the superficial level of nationalist iconography, an asynchrony remains between the Villa-Lobos march and the symbolism of the film's last sequence, for, while Villa-Lobos's *Desfile* ostensibly glorifies the *Brazilian* nation, the "national colors" (red and green) that simultaneously spread across the screen are those of the former colonial power: Portugal. Indeed, the second line of the anthem refers specifically to the scene of Brazil's "discovery": "Bem que fez o Cabral que esta terra chamou gloriosa num dia de Abril" (Cabral was right to call this land glorious on an April day). In this specific manner, the film's last sequence "quotes" the final scene of Mário's novel: the parrot's "inauthentic" flight to Lisbon. In light of the film's political pedagogics, this allusion to the colonial past functions as the symbol of Brazil's "dependency" on international capital, as the symbol of a historical vicious circle similar to the one that compels the characters of García Márquez's *Autumn of the Patriarch* to relive forever "that historical October Friday" when Columbus's three caravels moored in the Sea of Darkness (*El Otoño del patriarca* 44–46).

In Xavier's reading, Macunaíma's romance with Ci—the novel's traditional Amazon, or *Icamiaba* figure converted in the film into an urban guerrilla fighter—signifies exactly this dependency. According to Xavier, the film's Ci embodies not just modern technology, but the city itself. She is the imperious machine-"mother" whose vortical womb—figured by the elevator shaft where she and the hero first engage in violent sex (Xavier, *Alegorias* 144–49)—represents a "gentle uterine prison" (147). The urban Ci would thus be a prosopopoeia of the novel's Machine goddess, the powerful fetish into which the hero's savage mind converts the wonders of modern technology. Ci is the technicized counterpart to the *uiara* that destroys him in the end and whom he desires above all to dominate sexually. "I want you in the worst way, lady" (*tenho uma vontade danada da senhora*), Macunaíma tells a decidedly uninterested Ci in the film. At the same time, however, it remains undecidable whether Macunaíma's animist transformation of Ci into a mythological abstraction is merely a sign of his primitivism or a figural allusion to the Modernista cult of technological progress, the synthesis between "man's energy . . . [and] the forces of the earth" (Menotti del Picchia, *República* 206), whose impossibility the film seeks to underscore by dint of its reiterative representations of Brazil's condition of insurmountable underdevelopment.

Ci's emergence on the screen, wielding an obligatory AK-47, coincides with a series of gunshots and explosions. It occurs immediately after Macunaíma, overlooking the metropolitan night traffic, is said (in voice-over) to have reached his chiasmic insight about the essence of technology: "it's the men who are the machines and the machines who are men" (*Macunaíma* [1988] 41). In a scene that it is difficult not to see as an ironic citation of the slaughter of a cattleman's henchmen by António das Mortes (in the eponymous Glauber Rocha film), the woman warrior (*guerreira*) proceeds to gun down at least eight police agents. This fierce and bloody battle is punctuated with the pop beat of Roberto Carlos's hit "Papo firme"—a song about an ultra-modern girl (*garota*) who moves only at breakneck speed (*em disparada,* literally: "shooting" speed) and says to hell with everything (*manda tudo pró inferno*).

Roberto Carlos's *garota* could well be a 1960s update of the 'tropicalist' "garota de Ipanema." As the song lyrics insist, the context that defines the "assertive" (*de papo firme*) *garota* is *moderno;* "it exists today." The violent sex act that follows between Ci and the hero takes place entirely inside a parking structure elevator. In the final shot of the sequence, the two lovers—Ci expectedly straddling Macunaíma—are shot from a high angle as the elevator plunges downward. In contrast to the outcome of his rape of Ci in the novel, Macunaíma does not come out on top, as it were. He never becomes emperor of the *icamiabas,* and their ensuing conjugal arrangement is a complete reversal of conventional gender roles.

It is, in fact, Macunaíma's "domestication" that seems to be underscored in the next sequence, shot almost entirely indoors and hitherto the longest "domestic" sequence of the film. As the off-camera narration informs us, "Ci woke up very early each morning and went warring in the city. Macunaíma stayed home resting." Although at first glance this inverted relationship may suggest, albeit in restricted and burlesque form, the Anthropophagist "matriarchate of Pindorama," a closer examination reveals its patriarchal and paternalistic underpinnings. The inversion of patriarchy is, in other words, complete—so complete, in fact, that it sustains and perpetuates the very terms it attempts to subvert. Thus, Ci participates in the "prostitution" that, according to a long-standing Marxian critique of the family, defines the bourgeois institution of marriage. She forces Macunaíma "to work" for the money she brings him by satisfying her voracious sexual appetite.

When, after several "shifts," the hero falls asleep in the midst of the act, Ci, denouncing his "laziness," resorts to the slave owner's expedient by whipping him. Indeed, the link between her matriarchal rule and the slave regime had already been intimated by a shot of Ci's residence (the only outdoor shot in the sequence): a dilapidated plantation house (or *casa-grande*) complete with slave quarters (or *senzalas*). In this sense, Ci's relationship with Macunaíma replicates the elitism proper to most avant-gardes, both poetic and political. Their unequal union reproduces the privileged terms and social positions from which the enlightened vanguard's emancipatory programs are articulated, the class inequality symptomatic of the "brutal forms of inequality" produced in peripheral societies (Schwarz, *Misplaced Ideas* 15).

Like *modernismo* itself, which, as Mário de Andrade writes, was closely associated with São Paulo's "traditional [coffee] aristocracy" ("O movimento modernista" 236), the "post-Modernista" radical politics that Ci ambivalently espouses in the film originates among the dominant classes (Ortiz, *A moderna cultura* 32). Rather than supersede the contradictoriness and inauthenticity of the condition of underdevelopment, then, Ci's guerrilla struggle reproduces both the social inequality that it aims at eliminating and the unequal exchange, or "global rift," that its radical nationalism proposes to overcome. Yet, as I have argued in the preceding chapters, this critique is already incipient in much of Modernista literary production. Nowhere is it more prominent, in fact, than in Mário's hybrid novel.

One of the effects of the film's allegorical structure is to foreclose, to an extent, the novel's interrogation of modernity. As Joaquim Pedro de Andrade himself indicates, what motivates the *cinemanovistas*' return to Modernismo in the first place is not a critical reexamination of the movement's ostensibly *acritical* acceptance and reproduction of the ideology of modernism. The lessons of Modernismo lie elsewhere:

> The *modernistas* of 1922 . . . reject[ed] all imported values and techniques not relevant to our reality in favor of authentically Brazilian processes that would be, in principle, communicative and unalienating. The works produced by this movement, according to this rationale, should have had a greater degree of communication than they in fact had. Despite the good intentions of their program, the movement's complex intellectual processes and intellectual pretension made such communication impossible. We would do well to re-examine the movement of 1922 in terms of the present situation. ("Criticism and Self-Criticism" 74)

It is in terms of this disjuncture between the popular artist and the people, in terms of the collapse of the revolutionary politics or the popular-nationalist project of Cinema Novo itself, that I think the film needs to be read. What Augusto Boal has written of Brecht's epic theater, could be ascribed to Cinema Novo as well. It is a poetics "of the enlightened vanguard [*é a Poética da Conscientização*], [not] a poetics of the oppressed" (*Theatre of the Oppressed* 155). In an introduction to the film, written for the 1969 Venice Film Festival, *Macunaíma*'s director, pointing to Oswald de Andrade's 1928 "Manifesto Antropófago" as an important cultural reference point, asserts that the country's situation has not significantly changed since the 1920s, and that the same social inequality and brutal exploitation persist (J. P. de Andrade, "Cannibalism and Self-Cannibalism" 82).

The cinematic turn to Modernismo thus becomes itself allegorical. It marks not only the collapse of "modernization," but also the insertion of the modern into a structure of deferral and repetition in which the "new" or "what is to come" comes to mark the "non-place" (or *u-topos*) of an objectless desire for change. If the horizon of social transformation has been thus effaced, what then remains of the political pedagogics of Cinema Novo? Where have the potentially revolutionary classes that would constitute the object of that revolutionary education been relegated to?

For Glauber Rocha, one of the movement's principal theorists, "popular cinema" seeks to replace an "alienating" bourgeois aesthetic with an "aesthetic of hunger." Its objective is to "give back to the public a consciousness of its own misery" (qtd. in Ramos, *Cinema, estado* 76), to link up filmic production with a popular-revolutionary pedagogics that would ultimately liberate the nation from its dependent or "neo-colonialist" status: "The emergence of *auteur* as the name for a film-maker announces a new artist in our time. . . . The *auteur* is the one who is the most responsible for the truth: his aesthetics is an ethics, his *mise-en-scène* a politics. . . . If commercial cinema is tradition, the *auteur*'s cinema is revolution. The politics of a modern *auteur* is a revolutionary politics" (Rocha, *Revisão crítica* 13, 14).

In his influential analysis of the movement, Jean-Claude Bernardet (*Trajetória crítica*) argues that the aim of the cultural policies put into place by the military regime toward the end of the 1960s is to sever the *cinema-novistas* from the new public they had begun to interpellate. Until 1975, for example, the military regime imposed no restrictions upon Hollywood distribution chains, virtually ensuring that political or "art" films would reach only restricted audiences. Paradoxically, it was during its second and most repressive phase of the dictatorship that the state initiated a program of cultural nationalism that co-opted and broadly redefined some of the most recognizable components of the "national culture" project introduced by the Left in the early 1960s.

As José Ortiz Ramos observes, the nationalist dream, which the 1964 coup canceled so abruptly, resurfaced in the early 1970s as the ideology of the ultra-conservative, militarist state (*Cinema, estado* 94–95). In 1970, for example, the minister of education and culture (Jarbas Passarinho) makes the following pronouncement: "For me, the ideal culture would not alienate people, in the sense that it would not be dissociated from Brazilian reality, but would serve to validate the country itself in national terms.... I think [this culture] should underpin the belief in a national identity. It cannot be imported, it cannot take the form of the cultural colonialism which we have for so long experienced in this country" (92). State intervention in the film industry increased sharply after 1969, the year when a state film enterprise (Embrafilme) was founded with an ostensible mandate to promote the distribution of Brazilian films abroad.

What Embrafilme proceeded to do in effect was to exercise a much tighter control over the content of national (and nationalist) cinema. After the Ministry of Education and Culture issued a series of incentives for their production and distribution, historical films retelling the official story of the nation and geared toward popular consumption became the rage. Cut off from the "potentially revolutionary" classes, Cinema Novo turned inward in a social sense, that is, toward the intellectual elite from which most *cinema-novistas* originated. As Ruy Guerra suggests in the fragment that provides the epigraph for this section, the gulf between ethics and aesthetics that the *auteur* was to transcend returned with a vengeance.

It is in this context that the intersection between Ci's militancy in the film and the revolutionary pedagogics of Cinema Novo acquires particular relevance. In other words, Ci's presence registers the impossibility of producing a popular cinema. Whether she represents a critique of the "thoughtlessness" of the armed struggle (Ramos, *Cinema, estado* 82) or a "utopian reconciliation of opposites"—'alienation' and militancy, an archetypally "feminist" threat to patriarchy and an insertion into consumer culture (Xavier, *Alegorias* 148)—Ci is also the only oppositional figure in the film. And she is killed along with her infant son (played once again by the irrepressible Grande Otelo) by her own bomb at the end of the "domestic" sequence. Her "materialization" on the screen as well as her expunction ("the hero was unable to find anything he could bury") are thus marked by symmetrical explosions. She is in any event the only character who sacrifices her life for something other than the principle of material acquisition (however ambiguous her political commitment may be). To this extent, then, the political space she occupies intersects with Cinema Novo's political pedagogics.

The purposelessness of her armed struggle, its removal from an identifiable horizon of revolution or social change, seems to prefigure a radical postmodern politics from which truth, finality, or unity have been effectively eliminated. Her struggle includes no program of mobilization, no intended public or political pupils, its objective having apparently been reduced to the provisional disorganization of the enemy, to a retortion or retaliation (*rétorsion*): "the ruse or machination by means of which the little people, the 'weak,' become for an instant more powerful than the most powerful" (Lyotard, *Rudiments païens* 154). The radical micrology of Ci's political struggle reproduces the displacement of Cinema Novo's emancipatory aesthetics to the outer rim of national politics, the process at the end of which the "people" have become as removed from "popular cinema"—as much an empty place—as they are in Ci's "autotelic" revolutionary program.

This metaphorical erasure of the people also appears to inform Nelson Pereira dos Santos' 1971 cinematic recuperation of the rhetoric of *antropofagia,* titled *Como era gostoso o meu francês* (*How Tasty Was My Little Frenchman*). Pereira dos Santos has been called the consummate cinematic *auteur* (Rocha, *Revisão crítica* 82). The film was produced as the Ministry of Education and Culture began its active promotion of historical cinema. Indeed, Pereira dos Santos received substantial government funding for its production.[1] Following its temporary suppression in Brazil by military censors troubled by the (white) protagonist's frontal nudity, it became one of the biggest box office hits of 1972 (Ramos, *Cinema, estado* 62). The plot of *Como era gostoso* is largely based on one of the classics of *antropofagia*: Hans Staden's 1557 captive narrative. The ethnographic material derives from Thevet's *Cosmographie* and Léry's *Histoire d'un voyage*. Montaigne's famous essay, on the other hand, appears to provide the film's ethos.

The historical situation *Como era gostoso* reconstructs centers on the mid-sixteenth-century struggle for the possession of Guanabara Bay (present-day Rio de Janeiro) between French and Portuguese colonists. Since the Tupinambá group had allied itself with the French, and Staden was a German mercenary in the service of the Portuguese, his dilemma upon being captured by the Tupinambá is the same as that of the film's protagonist: to convince his captors of his Gallic ancestry in order to avoid being killed and eaten. The film changes the protagonist's nationality (as its title indicates) as well as some of the historical circumstances surrounding his capture.

As the title also makes explicit, there is no redemptive return to Christian Europe in store for the hapless Frenchman, as his journey ends presumably in his captors' digestive tract. The film's protagonist is a mercenary either executed (thrown in chains into the sea) or banished for allegedly plotting to assassinate the commander of Fort Coligny, a French settlement on the island of Guanabara (France antarctique), which prevailed for five years (1555–1560) under the ruthless command of its sometimes Catholic, sometimes Huguenot ruler, Villegagnon. The establishment of this island colony came at the end of a decades-long struggle for control of the coastal trade (pepper and brazilwood) between the French and the Portuguese.

As the film's alteration of the redemptive plot of Staden's narrative already indicates, the relationship between the film and its archival sources is not just documental but agonistic as well. At the same time that it anchors itself in this colonial archive, eliciting from it its claim of ethnographic and historical accuracy, the film seeks, at the diegetic level, to subvert the epistemological authority of those very documents. The most commonplace method of undermining the validity of this archive is to juxtapose (or contradict) it with the images portrayed on the screen. The voice-over narration of the accidental drowning of several of Fort Coligny's mutinous mercenaries, taken from a 1557 letter to John Calvin by Villegagnon and read in the mode of a newsreel feature ("the latest news from Terra Firma") in the film's preambular sequence, is belied by a simultaneous scene in which the chained protagonist, dragging a ball and chain, is hurled into the sea.[2]

As previous critics (Johnson, *Cinema Novo x 5*; Peña, *"How Tasty Was My Little Frenchman"* 191–99) of the film have observed, this juxtaposition of textual deception to cinematic *vérité* apparently places it firmly within the Anthropophagist "tradition" of reclaiming the cultural truth of natural man. In keeping with this reading, *Como era gostoso* would seek to fulfill the following laconic prophecy from Oswald's "Manifesto": "Let us reject clothed man. American cinema will inform us" (*Do 'Pau-Brasil'* 14).[3] The exuberant frontal nudity (male as well as female) displayed in the film would illustrate a similar thematics.

This supposed "Anthropophagic" validation of natural man is epitomized in what could be called the film's epigraph, as the protagonist, now in the service of the Portuguese, captured by the Tupinambá and ordered by the *cacique* to speak, recites the following fragment from a 1558 "Ode sur les singularitez de la France Antarctique d'André Thevet" by Étienne Jodelle: "Ces Barbares marchent tous nuds: / Et nous, nous marchons incogneus, / Fardés, masquez" (These barbarians walk naked, but we walk unknown, made up, masked).[4] By fragmenting its sources into nine title cards[5]—white script on a black screen—and interspersing them throughout the film, My Little Frenchman supposedly reenacts upon cinematic space the Tupi ethics of Anthropophagy, a sort of revenge of the exterminated primitive.

The film "cannibalizes" its colonial archive, in short. The latter loses its integrity and is "re-membered" as an assimilated part of a new (cinematic) whole. In this sense, Como era gostoso would seek to perform the same reversal of historical itineraries as *antropofagia*: "Down with all the histories of men that begin in Cape Finisterre" (O. de Andrade, Do 'Pau-Brasil' 16). Indeed, its very historical point of departure—a moment of conflict and undecidability as to the ultimate (colonial) identity of Brazil—suggests that the Catholic and Portuguese components of the Brazilian "character" are the result of an historical accident.

Nevertheless, in light of the "artificiality" of cinematic representation, this validation of nudity as truth is imbued with irony. It is ultimately the actors, in other words, the "Indians of Ipanema," to borrow the director's own expression, who go around naked.[6] Their elaborately adorned bodies function in this instance as the costumes or masks appropriate to their roles as naked savages. There is, in this specific sense, no difference between nudity and disguise. By dint of this "tropological" nakedness, the cinematic presentation of the primitive is reinscribed within the same rhetorical structure that registers the latter's eradication. It places it within a cycle of reproductions and re-presentations that inevitably calls into question Como era gostoso's claims of cultural authenticity and historical accuracy.

To put it in other terms, other than the writing that retains the trace of the people who hold the cultural secret the film sets out to recover, the film has no referent at all. It is this cultural death that is imprinted in the masked nudity of the "Indians from Ipanema" and, in the end, in Como era gostoso's historiographic project itself. Its complicity with the violence it seeks simultaneously to denounce and overturn is thus inscribed in the very "interstices" of filmic space. The return to an "original" colonial situation comes to be performed not under the sign of History but Allegory.

Unlike its model, which, as Oswald insists, constitutes a weltanschauung, Anthropophagy in the film plays a self-consciously "prescriptive" role. It ostensibly outlines a strategy for entering modernity on nationalist or local terms, for an aggressive or "revengeful" modernization radically opposed to the conservative or neoliberal model of development. *Antropofagia* allegorizes what Oswald once named the "third solution" (*Estética e política* 236), that is, an alternative model to the unequal exchange defining the economic and cultural relations between center and periphery. This would take the form of a de-linking from global capitalism, which is generally coterminous with the politics of national liberation underpinning Glauber Rocha's call for an "aesthetics of hunger."

This is nonetheless a political recipe whose rhetorical conceit is underscored in the scene of the Frenchman's capture by the Tupinambá. The Portuguese soldiers' response to the "linguistic test" to which the *cacique* Cunhambebe submits them is to recite culinary recipes—a speech act that reaffirms their national identity in folkloric or stereotypical terms (since it evinces the proverbial gluttony of the Portuguese), and simultaneously guarantees and foreshadows (that is, "prescribes") their eventual dismemberment and consumption. The black humor of the sequence is evident enough.

At the same time, the juxtaposition of these recipes to the Frenchman's ethical imperative (the fragment from Etienne Jodelle's Ode) bares the film's device, as it were. The sequence discloses the prescriptive aim or pedagogics of the film's political allegory, while establishing an ironic distance from that project. The irony arises not only from the necessarily inauthentic primitive world re-created in the film but also from the assertion of the inauthenticity (or autonomous aestheticism) of its "popular" aesthetics. In the final analysis, the Anthropophagy of *Como era gostoso* reveals not an ethics but an aesthetics. In a reversal of Glauber Rocha's formula, it returns to the "alienating" bourgeois aesthetics that, according to Rocha, the cinematic *auteur* should transcend.

In the end, the film's closest affinity with Modernismo is precisely—and ironically—this stereotypically modernist turn inward. Initially, this "defamiliarizing" procedure appears to follow the pedagogical objective of Brecht's *Verfremdungseffekt,* seeking similarly "to free socially-conditioned phenomena from that stamp of familiarity which protects them against our grasp . . . in order to unearth society's laws of motion" (Brecht, *Brecht on Theatre* 192, 193). Yet the mode of recognition enacted by this baring of the film's device does not move in the direction of an objective and politically empowering understanding of social phenomena. Instead, *Como era gostoso* is split between the presentation of a political allegory and an ironic acknowledgment of the latter's technicity, of the irreducible aestheticism of its revolutionary ethics.

An example of this irony is the sexual pun in the film's title. The figurative sense of "to eat" (*comer*) in Portuguese is "to copulate"; "tasty" (*gostoso*) has therefore a clearly erotic connotation. The phrase expresses both a symbolic Anthropophagic vengeance and the "native" woman's sexual desire. The two meanings are indissoluble, since the phrase is presumably enunciated from the perspective of Sebiopepe, the Tupi widow who takes the Frenchman as a consort before eventually devouring him or, more specifically (if one lends credence to Thevet's "ethnography"), before consuming his "shameful parts" (*Les français en Amerique* 203)— "my little neck," as she euphemistically refers to the organ in question in the film.

The title's invocation of what Michel de Certeau has called "the Western phantasm" of the *vagina dentata* (*Writing of History* 233) remits us to the original colonial encounter, to the voracious native woman whose exuberant and overpowering sexuality Vespucci finds at once menacing and fascinating. The Frenchman's native bride is the antithesis both of the "naked Eves" of Vaz de Caminha's 1500 Letter of Discovery and those of the eugenic narratives of the 1920s. She is the site of a primitive vengeance, the limit of European penetration—the title's *Was* (*era*) is crucial in this respect. Sebiopepe's, then, is a native body that refuses to yield to European attempts to recode it, a body that will (re)produce only on its own terms. In sequence after sequence, the protagonist is thus consistently thwarted in his efforts to present himself either as Sebiopepe's savior (in the tradition of Rita Durão's *Caramurú*, for example) or a *Caraíba* (a European version of the autochthonous technological hero). Significantly, the film's penultimate shot is a close-up of Sebiopepe consuming the unfortunate Frenchman.

By the same token, however, the phrase could be spoken by the implied spectator. It is either an aesthetic judgment or an expression of desire for a nude actor on the screen. The Anthropophagic politics of the film risks becoming a self-conscious joke, in other words, and the reconstruction of the primitive world is once again revealed as a masquerade. For the luminous writing of the title cards turns out to be the only space in the film where the primitive dwells: an ironic reference to the star-script that, to paraphrase Mário de Andrade, is the final sorrowful destination of the Tupi being.

The last title card, which functions as the film's epilogue, is a fragment from Governor Mem de Sá's 1560 letter to the Portuguese Regent describing the amassed bodies of the massacred "Tupiniquin [who, during the period portrayed in the film, had been Portugal's allies] covering more than five leagues of shoreline." The quote is both an historical beginning (1560, the year when the French were expelled from Guanabara, also marks the start of the process leading up to the consolidation of Portuguese colonial rule) and the last word, the epitaph to a Tupi culture reduced, in the last instance, to the "useless shine" of spectral Anthropophagi upon a silver screen. Whatever cultural and political lesson present-day Brazilians may be enjoined to glean from the vanished Tupi, only in bad faith can the former refuse to recognize that it is upon those spectral corpses that the modern nation has been erected.

Although it may be an overstatement to suggest that these two films write the final word on modernist nativisms, or that they mark the point of no return for primitivist aesthetics, both *Macunaíma* and *Como era gostoso* gesture ambivalently, and contradictorily, to the impossibility of their own projects of cultural recuperation. The task of the next two chapters will be precisely to examine the several modes in which the limitations inherent in similar primitivist or nativist returns are acknowledged and ultimately confronted in a body of Caribbean texts.

5 The Shadow Cast by the Enlightenment

The Haitian Revolution and the Naming of Modernity's Other

It is against the double claim of a History with a capital H and of a literature sacralized in the absoluteness of the written sign that the peoples who have hitherto inhabited the hidden face of the earth struggled, at the same time that they fought for food and freedom.
—Edouard Glissant, *Le discours antillais*

It was not Black Quashee, or those he represents, that made those West India Islands what they are. . . . Never by art of his could one pumpkin have grown there to solace any human throat; nothing but savagery and reeking putrefaction could have grown there. . . . Quashee, if he will not help in bringing-out the spices, will get himself made a slave again (which state will be a little less ugly than his present one), and with beneficent whip, since other methods avail not, will be compelled to work. Or, alas, let him look across to Haiti, and trace a far sterner prophecy! Let him, by his ugliness, idleness, rebellion, banish all White men from the West Indies, and make it all one Haiti,—with little or no sugar growing, black Peter exterminating black Paul, and where a garden of the Hesperides might be, nothing but a tropical dogkennel and pestiferous jungle.
—Thomas Carlyle, *Occasional Discourse on the Nigger Question*

The difficulty was that though one could trap them like animals, transport them in pens, work them alongside an ass or a horse and beat both with the same stick, stable them and starve them, they remained, despite their black skins and curly hair, quite invincibly human beings; with the intelligence and resentments of human beings.
—C. L. R. James, *The Black Jacobins*

Slavery as the Other (of) Modernity

In the preface to *The Black Jacobins,* his magisterial history of the Haitian Revolution, C. L. R. James calls "the transformation of slaves, trembling in hundreds before a single white man, into a people able to organise themselves and defeat the most powerful European nations of their day . . . one of the great epics of revolutionary struggle and achievement" (ix). For James, "the grand patriarch of contemporary West Indian culture" (Said, *Culture and Imperialism* 257) life under slavery—one of the three monstrosities (the other two being colonialism and Nazism) produced by the distinctively western fusion of the will to truth and the will to power, according to V. Y. Mudimbe (*Idea of Africa* 212)—"was in its essence a modern life" (James, *Black Jacobins* 392). When the 1791 slave revolt, which launched the long and harrowing march toward independence, erupted in what was then the plantation colony of San Domingo, the slaves, James argues, "were closer to a modern proletariat than any group of workers in existence at the time. The rising was therefore a thoroughly prepared and organised mass movement" (86).

Aimé Césaire reiterates this thesis in his biography of Toussaint Louverture. Not only does he identify in the Caribbean slave regime a prefiguration of the industrial proletariat, but he asserts that the Haitian revolution marks "one of the origins of current western civilization" (*Toussaint Louverture* 34, 21).[1] Both Césaire and James aim therefore to give the San Domingo slaves "their actual historical due," to redress "one of the great underestimations of the whole of historiography: the contribution of the slaves to the making of America as a civilization" (James, *Future in the Present* 255, 254). Insofar as they propose a fundamental rethinking of conventional notions of progress and civilization (255, 259), they inaugurate a "postcolonial" historiography whose ultimate objective is to shift to Europe's outer rim the point of departure of (western) modernity.

Edward Said, who considers James's 1938 history emblematic of the intellectual *voyage in,*[2] discerns in such projects "a sign of adversarial internationalization in an age of continued imperial structures":

> No longer does the logos dwell exclusively, as it were, in London and Paris. No longer does history run unilaterally, as Hegel believed, from east to west, or from south to north, becoming more sophisticated and developed, less primitive and backward as it goes. Instead, the weapons of criticism have become part of the historical legacy of empire, in which the separations and exclusions of 'divide and conquer' are erased and surprising new configurations spring up. (Said, *Culture and Imperialism* 244–45)

As J. Michael Dash expresses it in more specific terms, "it was in Haiti that Caribbean thought first emerged as a contestation of the reductive mystification of colonialism," and it is therefore "through Haiti that we can grasp the inescapable historical nature of the other America" (*Other America* 42). Similarly, Maximilien Laroche asserts that upon "proclaiming its independence, Haiti sought to put an end to the European History of the world and begin an American History in which Amerindians and Africans would . . . make a truly *New* World, [and] set about beginning History all over again" ("Haitian Postmodernisms," 119–26). It is thus nothing short of a counter-History of the modern that is at stake for Césaire and James, and the Haitian Revolution functions as a privileged sign and site in this historiographic operation.

Both writers begin consequently by contesting precisely colonialism's "reductive mystifications," that is, the depictions of the Haitian Revolution as a "distorting mirror" of the French original (qtd. in Rémusat, *L'Habitation de Saint Domingue* lxxxi), a "general frenzy of vindictive rage that flared up in all those plantations as a result of the reckless actions of the National Convention" (Kleist, "Betrothal in San Domingo" 231), or a senseless devastation engendered by "those would-be liberal ideas with which France intoxicates itself and [which] are a poison below the tropics" (Hugo, *Bug-Jargal* 97). In James's and Césaire's retelling, the San Domingo revolution adumbrates "the poetry of the future." Like Marx's nineteenth-century revolution, Haiti is the content that goes far beyond the pseudo-universalist phrases of coeval France (Césaire, *Toussaint* 309). By reworking the metropolitan revolution in terms of their own imaginary,[3] in other words, the slaves teach revolutionary France an object lesson about the struggle for freedom (James, *Black Jacobins* 120). The fourth chapter of *Black Jacobins* is accordingly entitled "The San Domingo Masses *Begin*," and chapter 5, "And the Paris Masses *Complete*." As one of the rebels in James's eponymous 1936 tragedy adduces,[4] "The white slaves in France heard that the black slaves in San Domingo had killed their masters and taken over the houses and property. They heard that we did it and they follow us" (*C. L. R. James Reader* 74).

"There is no 'French Revolution' in the French colonies," Césaire argues concurrently; "there is rather in each French colony a specific revolution, born on the occasion of the French Revolution, linked to it, but unfolding according to its own laws and particular objectives" (*Toussaint Louverture* 22). The slaves constituted the only segment of colonial society "able to understand the Revolution in depth," he concludes (177). As Susan Buck-Morss asserts, "the black Jacobins of Saint-Domingue surpassed the metropole in actively realizing the Enlightenment goal of human liberty, seeming to give proof that the French Revolution was not simply a European phenomenon but world-historical in its implications. If we have become accustomed to different narratives [she continues], ones that place colonial events on the margins of European history, we have been seriously misled" ("Hegel and Haiti," 835–36). In the end, then, James's and Césaire's "counter-histories" seek to overturn the predictable and dominant plot of the Eurocentric narrative of emancipation. The latter relegates slavery to a premodern survival rendered obsolete and finally abolished by the emergence of two characteristic features of occidental modernity: rationalist political thought and industrial capitalism. The structure of this linear plot requires that the abolition of slavery *result from* an emancipatory struggle originating in the west.

In *The Wretched of the Earth*, Frantz Fanon identifies the univocity of the western epic of modernity as one of the inaugural and most legitimate targets of anti-colonialist violence: "The colonizer makes history. His life is an epic, an odyssey. He is the absolute beginning" (*Les damnés* 40). In contrast, the colonized masses form an "almost mineral backdrop" for "the innovative dynamism" of this Odyssean impetus (40). To borrow Edouard Glissant's terms, the colonized Other is the "flesh of the world," the material that the west needs to sublimate in order to feed its claims of universality (*Le discours antillais* 190). For Fanon, colonialism inflicts upon the colonized a state of "immobility," a stagnant time (*un temps mort*) that can be interrupted only when the latter resume their forward march and set out "to make [their own] History" (*Les damnés* 53). Glissant's correlate to this induced historical lethargy is "the mimetic drive" (*la pulsion mimétique*)—the "impossible" and "impracticable" desire to replicate metropolitan history and culture—which he posits as the chronological and ideological successor of the slaves' initial oppositional strategy: the imagined return to Africa (*le Retour*).

This "imitation obsession," whose "insidious violence" the colonized endure as a collective trauma (Glissant, *Le discours antillais* 31), later takes the form of a turn away (*le Détour*) from a thorough recognition of actual modes of colonial oppression and domination. It constitutes a praxial and epistemological "parallax" that, by occluding and displacing the Real, threatens to defer indefinitely the transformation of local counter-hegemonic movements into a full-fledged nationalist struggle (32). For, like Fanon, Glissant posits nationalism as the transcendent stage of resistance: a resolution of "impossible" antinomies that will finally overcome the "parenthetical" temporality [epochality?] induced by an "exterior" and *absolutely* overdetermining History (*Le discours* 73, 88, 161).

As my approximation of Fanon and Glissant indicates, I do not share J. Michael Dash's conviction that "Fanon's dream . . . is that of restoring the lost paradise," or that his writings reveal "a nostalgia for a prelapsarian, mythical past" (*Other America* 70). Unlike Dash, what I should like to illuminate here is not the extent to which Glissant's thought "represents a decisive break" (or a major epistemological shift) from the so-called classics of Caribbean culture and literature (151). I wish rather—and no doubt more modestly—to concentrate on the possibly less perceptible ways in which Fanon's texts, as well as Césaire's and James's, may in fact adumbrate Glissant's allegedly "new conceptual categories" (*Other America* 158).

Thus, as opposed to a "discontinuous" historical movement, in which the determinant socioeconomic transformations are governed by external factors, or, according to the terms of an-*other* history (Glissant, *Le discours antillais* 157), the historical itinerary that James and Césaire endeavor to trace re-situates the Revolution's origin in colonial space. By positing "the slave-trade and slavery [as] the economic basis of the French Revolution" (*Black Jacobins* 47), as the engine that drove the wheels of Europe's sweeping commerce and the source from whence its industry drew its sustenance (48–49), James anticipates the assertion Fanon will make about Europe's "dependency" on the colonial Third World: "Europe is literally the creation of the Third World. The riches which smother her were stolen from underdeveloped peoples" (*Les damnés* 76).

This thesis echoes Oswald de Andrade's lapidary phrase regarding Europe's intellectual dependency on the New World in the "Manifesto de Antropofagia": "Without us Europe would not even have its poor declaration of the rights of man" (14). (The politico-economic corollary to this reversal, Andrade declares in a later piece, is the "Industrial Revolution [feeding] off the vein of our precious metals" [*Estética e política* 283]). Indeed, Susan Buck-Morss has recently reformulated this claim, arguing that "the economic practice of slavery—the systematic, highly sophisticated capitalist enslavement of *non*-Europeans as a labor force in the colonies . . . came to underwrite [by the mid-eighteenth century] the entire economic system of the West" ("Hegel and Haiti" 821).

In their radical expansion of the *letter* of the Declaration of the Rights of Man (Césaire, *Toussaint Louverture* 310), in their plan "to stretch the constitutional declarations of the European governments to the limit"[5]

(James, *C. L. R. James Reader* 294), the Haitian insurrectionists arguably propel themselves *ahead* of the metropolis. Hence, James writes, "the national struggle against Bonaparte in Spain, the burning of Moscow by the Russians that fills the histories of the period, were *anticipated and excelled* by the blacks and Mulattoes of the island of San Domingo" (*Black Jacobins* 356–57; my emphasis). Paul Gilroy notes in a recent commentary of James's text that "the concentrated intensity of the slave experience is something that marked out blacks as the first truly modern people, handling ... dilemmas and difficulties which would only become the substance of everyday life in Europe a century later" (*Black Atlantic* 221).

For Gilroy, by the same token, the horror of the Middle Passage should be understood not as the contradiction but as a constitutive part of both the philosophical discourse of modernity and technological advancement. Gilroy puts it succinctly: "the time has come for the primal history of modernity to be reconstructed from the slaves' point of view" (*Black Atlantic* 55), and "for the inversion of the relationship between margin and centre as it has appeared within the master discourses of the master race" (45). It is under the sign of historiographic reversal as well that James and Césaire produce their histories. But, in a more specific sense, they share with Fanon and Glissant the sense that the crucial and radical measure of the modernity of Haiti's revolutionary struggle resides in its incipient nationalism.[6]

Césaire, paraphrasing Du Bois, opens his political biography with the assertion that "San Domingo is the first modern nation to have posed ... in all its social, economic, and racial complexity the great problem which the 20th century is laboring to resolve: the colonial problem" (*Toussaint Louverture* 21–22). Toussaint Louverture, he observes, is "the first anticolonialist leader that history has known" (189). Like the paradigmatic "new South American republics" in Benedict Anderson's classic study of nationalism, Haiti presumably foreshadows "the new states of Africa ... in the mid twentieth century" (B. Anderson, *Imagined Communities* 52). Concomitantly, James affirms that "the concluding pages [of his history, written in 1938] envisage and were intended to stimulate the coming emancipation of Africa" (*Black Jacobins* vii).

Césaire and James both propose therefore that in the months following August 22, 1791, when, at the place called Bois Caïman, they took a collective oath to exterminate the white slave owners and overrun the colony of San Domingo, the slaves gradually raise their struggle to the higher level of national resistance. The violent transformation of a slave colony into an independent nation becomes a crucial index of the modernity of the San Domingo revolution. *Nation* is in fact the proper name of "the new spirit" that James detects in the slave rising (*Black Jacobins* 154)—presumably, the more ascendant stage of "the spirit of the thing" that, as he argues, the slaves had readily gleaned from the metropolitan revolution.[7] For both writers, the crucial "historical articulation" between rebellion and national revolution is the personage of Toussaint Louverture (Césaire, *Toussaint Louverture* 299).

Amid "the vast impersonal forces at work in the crisis of San Domingo," Toussaint emerges as the decisive human factor (James, *Black Jacobins* 91). He is the "architect of the future . . . the genius who arrives to impose some order" on the flaming ruin to which the uprising had reduced the colony's prosperous North Plain (Lamming, *Pleasures of Exile* 125). Out of this chaos, he would lay "the foundations of an independent nation" (*Black Jacobins* 240). To Césaire, Toussaint is "the center of Haitian history," indeed of Caribbean history, the human vortex into which everything in San Domingo converges, and from which everything in turn irradiates: "They had bequeathed him armed bands. Out of these he had made an army. They had left him with a jacquerie. He had made of it a Revolution; out of a populace he had made a people. Out of a colony, he had made a state; better yet, a nation" (*Toussaint Louverture* 299–300).

Césaire's Toussaint bears a striking resemblance to the Romantic hero of Lamartine's 1850 drama *Toussaint Louverture*, whose stature is epitomized in a celebrated line from the play (134) spoken by a Napoleonic general in the play *Cet homme est une nation*. The sentiment is corroborated by the Lamartinian hero himself:

> You were but a herd, and I make you a nation!
> . . . .
> Let every black soul be fulfilled by my own!
> Every great thought is one single woof
> Whose myriad threads, lining up in close order,
> Respond as a single one to the skill of the weaver. (73)

Yet if Toussaint's heroism is Romantic, it is a Romanticism of the Hegelian kind.

In a well-known passage, Hegel defines the African as the prototype of "the Unhistorical, Undeveloped Spirit," lingering "on the threshold of the World's History" (*Philosophy of History* 99). Addressing the category of political constitution, he consigns the whole of sub-Saharan Africa to a sort of historical *Pre-conscious*:

> The standpoint of humanity [among this race] is mere sensuous volition with energy of will; since universal spiritual laws ... cannot be recognized here. ... The political bond can therefore not possess such a character as that free laws should unite the community. There is absolutely no bond, no restraint upon that arbitrary volition. Nothing but external force can hold the State together for a moment. A ruler stands at the head, for sensuous barbarism can only be restrained by despotic power. (*Philosophy of History* 96)

Along similar lines, and much like the Bonaparte of James's 1936 drama, the young Victor Hugo sees "the whole of the rebel forces [as] a mass of means without an end" (*Bug-Jargal* 176), as "impertinent blacks" who need to be "put in their place," (James, *C. L. R. James Reader* 91). Indeed, to the French novelist, the entire revolution appears as little more than a grotesque farce, with Toussaint presumably playing the part of an uppity "parodist" of Napoleon (*Bug-Jargal* 175n).

By contrast, the historical role of Césaire's Toussaint encompasses "the whole domain that separates the *merely thought* from concrete reality" (*Toussaint Louverture* 309). Enabling the abstract universalism of the French Revolution to become concrete, Toussaint operates as the dialectic's mediating term: "He inscribes himself and inscribes the revolt of the black slaves of San Domingo in world history" (310). He consequently places under erasure Hegel's characterization of Africa as "the land of childhood, which lying beyond the day of self-conscious history, is enveloped in the dark mantle of Night" (*Philosophy of History* 91).

In maintaining that the "simple and sober truth" Toussaint expresses "in the crude words of a broken dialect" actually "excelled ... the language and accent of Diderot, Rousseau, and Raynal, of Mirabeau, Robespierre, and Danton" (James, *Black Jacobins* 197–98), in positioning him and "the backward and ignorant mass [he led] in the forefront of the historical movement of his time," James, like Césaire, counters Hegel's dictum that "the Negro ... exhibits the natural man in his completely wild and untamed state" (*Philosophy of History* 93), and that his mind cannot "be conscious of any Universality" (95). Much more recently, Susan Buck-Morss has reiterated the same point, arguing that the constitution drafted by Toussaint Louverture in 1801 "was in advance of any such document in the world" ("Hegel and Haiti" 834).

Putatively, it is the historical agency of the Black Jacobins that at once negates and transcends these sweeping exclusions of the African from universal history. It translates the idea of the Revolution from an abstract universal into a concrete reality. The "struggle for the transformation of a formal right into a real one, a struggle for *recognition* as human beings" (Césaire, *Toussaint Louverture* 310), as Eugene Genovese affirms, enables "the passage from an Afro-American call to holy war to the universalist claims of the Rights of Man" (*From Rebellion to Revolution* 123).

The Haitian Revolution unequivocally invalidates Hegel's "banal and apologetic argument" (Buck-Morss, "Hegel and Haiti" 859) that slavery, by virtue of its institution within a State, "is itself a phase of advance from the merely isolated sensual existence—a phase of education—a mode of becoming participant in a higher morality and the culture connected with it" (Hegel, *Philosophy of History* 99). For Hegel, of course, the African has yet even to descry the faint glimmer of his dawning Spirit, let alone contemplate in a free relation the solar radiance that his own *constructed* consciousness reflects back to him. The "mentality" of Hegel's "Negroes" remains, as a matter of anthropological fact, hopelessly "sunk within itself and making no progress, and thus corresponding to the compact, differenceless mass of the African continent" (*Philosophy of Mind* 43).

Like "the original inhabitants of America" (who are "like small children," "the dullest savages," and "a vanishing, feeble race"), the Negroes must also "be regarded as a race of children" (*Philosophy of Mind* 45, 42). It is the logic of this rationalization of modern slavery and, by extension, "the implicit racism" (Buck-Morss, "Hegel and Haiti" 850) of Marx's assessment of British imperialism from the teleological standpoint of the imminent world revolution as simultaneously the best and worst thing to have befallen colonized populations, that James and Césaire strive to overturn. Their histories vie to transfigure modernity from the structure that would mitigate the horrors of slavery into the condition that slavery enables.

In this desire to undo Hegel, or at least revise him, Césaire and James echo the Brazilian *antropofagistas,* for whom the dialectical journey toward "cannibalistic" man—toward the irrevocable and irresistible entrance into History of hitherto "ahistorical peoples" (O. de Andrade *Do 'Pau-Brasil'* 189)—coincides with a Spenglerian twilight of the west, with a postscript to Hegel. This, however, does not necessarily entail the correlate advanced by J. Michael Dash that they share "an ideal of communion with a natural primordial world that was opposed to what was seen as the degenerate Western modernity" (*Other America* 62). While their ideological framework is undeniably Spenglerian and, as the following example from Alejo Carpentier will illustrate, far from uncommon in the cultural context of Latin America in the 1930s and 1940s, the specific character of the utopian vision they propose does not appear to me as self-consistent as a cursory reading would initially suggest.

González Echeverría has characterized the main character of Alejo Carpentier's "Like the Night" ("Semejante a la noche"; one of the stories in a 1944 collection entitled *Guerra del tiempo* [*The War of Time*]) not altogether unfairly as a kind of transparent narrative device. "The protagonist merely relates his own story, without reflecting upon it or taking cognizance of the obvious tour de force of which he is an object. History . . . parades behind him like a series of backdrops, without leaving their image on his text" (González Echeverría, *Alejo Carpentier* 158). In effect, the six events that compose this historical decor span over three thousand years, but if the narrator serves as a technique, it is a procedure that seeks to put to question "the linear, hierarchical vision of a single History that would run its unique course" (Glissant, *Caribbean Discourse* 66).

The story's protagonist is at the outset a young warrior from the Argolian city of Mycenae about to embark on a military expedition. The destination of the latter shifts in time and space from Troy (the simile in the story's title is borrowed from a description of Apollo's furious descent to earth in the opening book of *The Iliad*). In the second section, it is the Americas, as a Spanish fleet is about to leave Seville only a few years after Columbus's discovery of the "Indies." In the third, it is to San Domingo that a French expedition anchored off Bordeaux waits to set sail in the early decades of the seventeenth century, a period when France was initiating what would be a thirty-year struggle with Spain and Britain for possession of the colony. In the fourth, Normandy is the point of destination of an expeditionary force about to depart from an unnamed North American city (presumably New York) in order to "finish once and for all with the new Teutonic Order" (Carpentier, *Guerra del tiempo* 39).

The story's closing section returns to ancient Greece, as the dejected hero, whose martial pride had given way to a sense of impotence and nausea (*Guerra del tiempo* 41), can hardly hold back his tears after listening to a crusty old soldier's devastatingly "materialist" appraisal of the Achaean war effort: "in reality, behind the enterprise shielding itself with such lofty aims, there were many dealings that wouldn't benefit the fighters one single bit. It was mostly about selling more crockery, more fabrics . . . and opening up new trade routes to the bartering peoples of Asia, thus doing away once and for all with Trojan competition" (42).

Founded as it is on *real premises,* the veteran's cynical reading of the Trojan War recalls Marx's insistence in *The German Ideology* that the writing of history must always set out from the "material conditions" under which men live (42). It unveils the material bases of a series of pivotal stages in the history of the west: (1) the destruction of the Minoan-Mycenaean civilization and the subsequent maritime ascendance of the Achaean Greeks, (2) the discovery and conquest of the New World, (3) the incipient decline of Spain's hegemony in the Americas, and (4) the rise of the United States as a world power in the post–World War II period. This economic underside is signified in the story by the goods (wheat, olive oil, and wine) being conveyed to the warships at the end of each section. In addition, the Crusade motif, introduced—with no apparent narrative motivation—in the seventeenth-century segment located at the center of the story, reinforces this materialist underpinning.

Here the protagonist, upon coming across a barker peddling the Elixir of Orvieto in a Bordeaux market, recalls how "some time ago" (it would have been over four hundred years ago, in fact), he had been on the verge of joining "the Crusade exhorted by the Fulk of Neuilly" (*Guerra del tiempo* 37). This Fourth Crusade, launched by the French in 1200 as part of an effort to revive the old spirit of the Crusades by Pope Innocent III, "had ended up, as everyone knows, with Christians fighting against Christians" (37).

Organized ostensibly against Egypt, the expedition eventually led to the storming and capture of Constantinople in 1204, a diversion carried out under the influence of Venice in order to exact commercial concessions from the court of Cairo. Of all the previous Crusades, the fourth is thus perhaps the one that is most overtly governed by lay directives. Yet, as a whole, the Crusades—their "desire to capture souls" notwithstanding— "were [always] sustained, in part, by the capture of booty" (Abu-Lughod, *Before European Hegemony* 47). From this standpoint, their primary result was to wrench Europe out of its economic stagnation. They functioned as "the mechanism that reintegrated northwestern Europe into a world system from which she had become detached after the 'fall of Rome'" (47).

The Crusade motif returns, in the World War II section, clad in humanistic garb (that is, in the form of allusions to the impending demise of the New Teutonic Order and humanity's attendant entrance into "the long-awaited future where man would be reconciled with his fellow man." It is in this way synecdochic of the idealisms (or ideologies) that are, in the last instance, sublated by the weight of *actuality,* by what Marx will call material conditions.

In strict terms, the protagonist's historical trajectory follows the "unique course" of a hierarchical, Eurocentric History. Nevertheless, the story's denouement provides a sort of emendation to this linear historical itinerary. The west at the end of the History outlined in the narrative is not

Europe but the New World—a space that, in accordance to the Spenglerian framework informing Carpentier's early historical fiction—is about to supersede a Europe plunged into unspeakable barbarity. The point of origin of the modern "Crusade" has shifted westward. This westward shift is an outcome that, although entirely congruent with the logic of his system, Hegel, for instance, seems to have been unable, or unwilling, to envision.[8]

In *The Lost Steps,* Carpentier's narrator-protagonist provides a more harrowing and historically specific description of Europe's "end of History": "The goal of centuries moving steadily toward tolerance, kindness, mutual understanding" (96). The statement alludes to the totalitarian parody of modernity's emancipatory project, which Beethoven's Ninth Symphony comes to symbolize in the novel. On the lips of Nazi POW's (the erstwhile denizens of the death camps), Schiller's resounding verses assume an unbearable irony. The "cloudless blue of [their] Utopia" is violently rent into so many "unfulfilled promises" and "Messianic pretensions" (97). Contrasted with the "the most cold-blooded barbarism of history," the atrocities committed by the "forces of benightedness" purportedly clutching Latin America, the "Continent without History," appear "like gay pages from a novel of adventure" (95). It is the topography of barbarity and civilization—the two opposing "forces" in Latin America's epic struggle to modernize—which is here inverted.

In this nightmarish Europe, the narrator uncovers a sinister modernity, which is at the same time the inexorable epilogue to its project:

> Everything bore witness to torture, mass extermination, crematories, all set in walls spattered with blood and ordure, heaps of bones, human dentures shoveled up in the corners, [and] even worse deaths accomplished coldly by rubber-gloved hands in the neat, bright, aseptic whiteness of operating-rooms. Two paces away, a sensitive, cultivated people [went on] studying the racial glories, playing Mozart's *Eine kleine Nachtmusik,* reading Hans Christian Andersen's [*Little Mermaid*] to their children. This . . . was new, sinisterly modern. (*Lost Steps* 94)

Its idiom, a "new language" composed of "walls so shattered that they seemed the letters of an unknown alphabet" (94) is recorded with cold precision by "those who made entries in their black oilcloth-bound notebooks" (95).

In stark contrast to this lexicon of horror—the epitaph to European modernity—would putatively unfold the gigantic signs, the alphabet of the Unknown, carved in "thousands of petroglyphs [strewn across the Amazon forest] that spoke a language of animal forms, astral symbols, and mysterious designs" (145)—which, as González Echeverría argues, echoes the Romantic monism that forms "the basis of Carpentier's 'marvelous American reality'" (*Alejo Carpentier* 181):

> I raised my eyes and found myself at the foot of the gray wall with the rock carvings attributed to the demiurge who . . . triumphed over the Flood and repopulated the world. . . . Neither Deucalion, nor Noah, nor the Chaldean Unapishtim, nor the Chinese or Egyptian Noahs left their signature scrawled for the ages at the point of their arrival . . . so clearly inscribed. (*Lost Steps* 204–5)

For the narrator-protagonist, this 'marvelous' telluric script contains the promise of a new ("post-diluvian") beginning: the *other* of occidental modernity. It is a task that is doomed to fail, because, among several other reasons, it reproduces the epistemic itinerary of the very sixteenth-century exegetes whose descriptions of the jungle function as a sort of blueprint for his own journey.

The narrator of *Los pasos perdidos* seeks, as the promise and recompense for his reading and deciphering labor, the ultimate revelation of a sovereign and primitive Text. As Foucault conjectures about the presuppositions of the sixteenth-century episteme:

> It was very possible that before Babel, before the Flood, there had already existed a form of writing composed of the marks of nature itself, with the result that its characters would have had the power to act upon things directly, to attract them or repel them, to represent their properties, their virtues, and their secrets. A primitively natural writing, of which certain forms of esoteric knowledge, and the cabala first and foremost, may perhaps have preserved the scattered memory and were now attempting to retrieve its long-dormant powers. (*Order of Things* 38–39)

Yet, as Gonzàlez Echevarría has argued, *The Lost Steps* "is the quintessential Latin American story and its critical undoing"; it "dismantles the central enabling delusion of Latin American writing: the notion that in the New World a new start can be made, unfettered by history" (*Myth and Archive* 4). In spite of this destructive narratorial procedure, however, the petroglyphs question both the validity and value of the enlightenment narrative of emancipation. They serve as the reminder of the latter's utter collapse, of the imperative to wipe the slate clean and begin the work of civilization anew.

It is in a similar light that we ought to read Césaire's contention that European bourgeois humanism deems Hitler's genocidal policies an unforgivable crime precisely because he "applied to Europe colonialist procedures which until then had been reserved exclusively for the Arabs of Algeria, the coolies of India, and the blacks of Africa."⁹ As C. L. R. James insists in a 1964 essay on Lenin, despite their "faults and blunders," underdeveloped countries "represent something new in a decaying world" (*C. L. R. James Reader* 332), for the dynamic of history is now "in the opposite direction—instead of movements from Europe stimulating revolutionary developments in Africa, liberation struggles in Africa have unleashed movements of tremendous importance in Europe itself" (377–78). Just as in *The Black Jacobins* he posits the Haitian Revolution and war of independence as refutations of Hegel's consignment of Africans to the threshold of world history, here, too, James endeavors to undermine the overpowering singularity and linearity of dominant models of modernity.

Far less apocalyptically, Glissant has recently echoed this point: "poor nations, by their very eruption, had made it possible for new ideas to be born: ideas of otherness, of difference, of minority rights, of the rights of peoples" (*Poetics of Relation* 136). In James's case, though, the world-historical meaning of these "erupting" nations is derived precisely from Hegel (utilized here as the convenient proper name for a hegemonic conception of History). In the last instance, to reject Hegel seems ineluctably to buttress the foundations of his system.

In Foucault's terms, these revisions of Hegel fail in the end to escape Hegel. At best, their putative anti-Hegelianism becomes one of Hegel's "tricks directed against us, at the end of which he stands motionless, waiting for us" (Foucault, *Archaeology of Knowledge* 235). Whether, at worst, such Hegelian "returns" end up reenacting a neurotic "failure" of the dialectic, an obsessive slippage of the *Aufhebung* into a rhetorical instance of Freud's repetition-compulsion—as has been alleged of the fundamental Marxian texts "through which the history of the West has been most forcefully thematized" (Mehlman, *Revolution and Repetition* 7)—is a question I will not pursue here.

Indeed, in its peculiarly cheery (not to say "Hegelian"[10]) dismissal of the problem of human agency, this question "might be labeled [an early instance of] an easy postmodernism [that] attacks both rationality and universality through an obvious and banal relativism" (Gilroy, *Black Atlantic* 44–45). Gilroy instructs us, in fact, that "the intellectual and cultural achievements of the black Atlantic populations exist partly inside and not always against the grand narrative of Enlightenment and its operational principles" (48). Concurrently, Glissant, as we have seen, reminds us that "the West is not monolithic [and has] itself produced the variables to contradict its impressive trajectory every time" (*Poetics of Relation* 191). Broadly speaking, then, "marginal" critiques of modernity may also affirm it. Whatever psychoanalytical tinge these critical affirmations may disclose interests me far less than their historical and epistemological implications.

I should begin by putting aside any suggestion that these rewritings of western cultural and epistemological models represent something "obviously gone wrong," or that they signal both a "loss of identity and difference," an inauthentic "assimilation into the categories of the West" (Miller, *Theories of Africans* 19, 23). To formulate my critical task as a matter of striking an epistemological balance ("to reconsider with scepticism the applicability of all Western critical terms and to look to traditional . . . cultures for terms they might offer" [25]), would be to forget that the terms of this equilibrium have become decidedly vexed. The balance between local and western knowledges may well turn out to be as elusive as the end of the rainbow. This elusiveness notwithstanding, it behooves one to ask whether the intimate connection between the grand narrative of enlightenment and its "ex-centric" revisions can only lead us to the well-known Foucaultian verdict: "There is no single locus of Great Refusal, no soul of revolt, source of all rebellions, or pure law of the revolutionary. Instead there is a plurality of resistances [that] can only exist in the strategic field of power relations" (Foucault, *History of Sexuality,* 95–96). Is James's and Césaire's turn upon the modern, then, always-already a *re*turn to the point of origin it seeks to contest—a recurrence, moreover, at once determined and enabled by that contested term itself?

Like the History Césaire and James attempt to rewrite, the histories (with a small h) they posit as its negation inevitably also reveal "a necessary dependency of all destructive discourses, [and] must inhabit the structures they demolish" (Derrida, *Writing and Difference* 194). In Lyotard's terms, their reappropriations of the modern betray an Oedipal conception of rewriting that often understands itself in "the sense of remembering, as though the point were to identify crimes, sins, calamities engendered by the modern set-up—and in the end to reveal the destiny that an oracle at the beginning of modernity would have prepared and fulfilled in our history" (*Inhuman* 27). They therefore face the unavoidable risk of producing the kind of rewriting that "cannot fail to perpetuate the crime [of modernity], and perpetrate it anew instead of putting an end to it" (28).

By shifting the problem of modernity's rewriting to this familiar theoretical register, one comes face to face with an equally familiar double bind. For if the insuperable limit of both my critical discourse and the ones with which it engages is Language itself: "we have no language—no syntax and no lexicon—which are foreign to this history [of metaphysics]; we can pronounce not a single destructive proposition which has not already had to slip into the form, the logic, and the implicit postulations of precisely what it seeks to contest" (Derrida, *Writing and Difference* 280–81), then there would appear to be little left to do other than resist the naming of modernity's Other, and point cunningly to Hegel's ghost looming with quiet persistence at every bend of one's critical journey.

Yet this limit, which Paul Gilroy acknowledges as well, needs itself to be interrogated, or *rewritten*. If we assume that the political imperative for Caribbean writers is to question "modernity's claim to ground its legitimacy on the project of liberating humanity as a whole through science and technology" (Lyotard, *Inhuman* 34), then it becomes a little too facile to argue, on the one hand, that by extending the democratic revolution to a new form of subordination (Mouffe, "Hegemony" 96), Haiti anticipates contemporary (even "postmodern") political struggles and, on the other hand, to leave *unthought* the Outside or Beyond of modernity toward which such an argument gestures.

While decidedly complicit with "the history of metaphysics" whose supersession they arguably seek, Césaire and James—just like the *antropofagistas* of Brazil—may ultimately dwell "in a place that is neither within nor without this history" (Derrida, *Writing and Difference* 194). This is the indeterminate region whose contours Gayatri Spivak has sought to trace. Against the tendency to turn the struggle of the marginal in metropolitan space into the "unexamined referent of all postcoloniality," and against those "ethnicist academic agendas [that] make a fetish out of identity," Spivak posits a "postcolonial agency [that] can make visible that the basis of *all* serious ontological commitment is catachrestical, because [it is] negotiable through the information that identity is, *in the larger sense,* a text, [a postcolonial agency that] can show that the alternative to Europe's long story . . . is not only short tales (*petits réçits*) but tampering with the authority of storylines. In *all* beginning, repetition, signature" (*Outside in the Teaching Machine* 65).

The account of *antropofagia* I sketch out toward the end of chapter 1 might therefore prove just as cogent for Césaire's and James's readings of Haiti's revolution. As determined as their theoretical production undoubtedly is by the very western "magisterial texts" it attempts to displace, it may also disclose the potential to turn those texts into "our servants, as the new magisterium constructs itself in the name of the Other" (Spivak, *Critique of Postcolonial Reason* 7). What I should like to chart in what follows, then, are precisely the different topologies of that impossible "(t)exterior" (in Certeau's sense) as it emerges in a body of Caribbean literary texts in which the ideas of progress and revolution figure as pivotal references. It is the latter's strategies of eroding the mastery of Europe's grand narratives at the same time that they replicate their "master" plots that I seek to describe. My point of departure is the familiar figure of Toussaint Louverture.

The "Spirit" of Toussaint Louverture and Haiti's Passage into World History

In Césaire's best-known poetic work, *Cahier d'un retour au pays natal* (*Notebook of a Return to My Native Land*), Toussaint's figure signals the speaker's first claim to *négritude*.[11] It inaugurates a process that culminates in the triumphant affirmation of his racial and cultural identity. "Imprisoned in whiteness," locked in a "little cell" at Fort-de-Joux,[12] the "Black Consul" is evoked parenthetically and in higher-case characters: "(TOUSSAINT, TOUSSAINT LOUVERTURE)" (Césaire, *Collected Poetry* 46). His proper name is inscribed in "the sterile sea of white sand" (47)—the confining whiteness—that is putatively History's blank page: the Unhistorical space of Hegel's "Negroes," say.

It is perhaps no wonder that prior to Toussaint's name, the only other expressions to appear in capitals in the poem are liturgical: ALLELUIA, KYRIE ELEISON, and CHRISTIE ELEISON (*Collected Poetry* 41). In the colonial setting that opens the *Cahier* these phrases emblematize the paralysis (or what J. Michael Dash calls "the despairing vision of Martinique" [*Other America* 65]) induced by Catholic ideology in colonial territory: "At the peak of its ascent, joy bursts like a cloud . . . and one lives as in a dream . . . this town . . . crawls on its hands without the slightest desire to drill the sky with a stature of protest" (*Collected Poetry* 41).

As against these indexes of alienated resignation, of an ecstatic servility before the mercy of the Lord, *Toussaint* arises as the genuine emancipatory cry. Like the excruciating geography of "the archipelago arched with an anguished desire to negate itself" (47), Toussaint figures the "non-Historical" history that the speaker, after an initial "stature" of repulsion and distantiation, comes to claim as his authentic patrimony, *Ce qui est à moi* (What is mine): "Haiti where négritude rose for the first time and stated that it believed in its humanity" (47). This allusion to the San Domingo Revolution initiates the poem's turn—around Toussaint's pivotal figure—beyond History's "threshold" and into History proper.

Dash views the *Cahier* in similar terms, "as a map that releases the colonial world . . . from an imperialist vision of culture" (*Other America* 67). Nevertheless, he regards this "new way of seeing" as constraining and "reductionist," as "an almost religious vision . . . impervious to metamorphosis" and ultimately "outside of the contradictions of historical change and the plurality of contact and interaction" (68, 64, 65). Césaire's modernist (or "nativist") poetics, as Dash defines it, is "a poetics based not on diversity but invariance, [on] the rediscovery of a primordial order of things" (67). In this manner, it seems oddly reminiscent of T. S. Eliot's metaphysical conception of Tradition. The reading I elaborate in the remainder of this chapter departs significantly from this characterization of Césaire's project. To a certain extent, I propose a reading of *Cahier* that is, if not entirely at odds, at least more nuanced and less cohesive than Dash's peremptory reduction of Césaire's poetic language to "a totalizing code, a closed primordial system" (67).

In the *Cahier*, then (to resume my reading), Haiti gives transcendent meaning and continuity (or "consanguinity") to the isolated revolutionary potentialities that the experiences of slavery and colonialism produce:

monstrous putrefactions of stymied
revolts
marshes of putrid blood
trumpets absurdly muted
land red, sanguineous, *consanguineous* land. (47; my emphasis)

The parentheses around Toussaint's name, when it is evoked in capital letters on the preceding page of Césaire's book, are thus the negative image (as well as the negation) of a Historical blank. At one and the same time they cancel and duplicate a trope that is itself already doubled: "a little cell, the snow *doubles* it with white bars" (47; my emphasis).[13] The parentheses serve as the graphic index of Toussaint's break out of the epistemological dungeon to which a Eurocentric History had hitherto remitted him. They signal the *overture*[14] of Black History (or Négritude) onto the Universal—the shift from a lower to a higher case—that is, beyond the enforced *pettiness* and stagnation of colonial space-time: *le petit matin* (or "daybreak," literally: "little morning") with which the poem opens: "the hungry Antilles, pitted with smallpox, surveyed night and day by a cursed venereal sun, the inert town [of Fort-de-France, Martinique], clever at discovering the *point of disencasement,* of flight, of dodging," and a population "*detoured* from its cry of hunger, of poverty, of revolt, of hatred, this throng so strangely chattering and mute" (35; my emphasis).

To cite C. L. R. James's pithy summary of the *Cahier*'s central theme, "Africa and Africans will move towards an integrated humanity . . . no longer from external stimulus but from their own self-generated and independent being and motion" (*C. L. R. James Reader* 304). Toussaint's figure articulates the colony's immobilized spatio-temporality with global civilization. Yet this *encasement* is not only opposed to but coterminous (literally: *par-en-thetic*) with the very History that obliterates Haiti's universality. Toussaint's articulation (or mediation), in other words, is incomplete. To borrow Césaire's own expression, it is *une insuffisante synthèse*—an incompleteness that arises from his "deducing the existence of his people from an abstract universal rather than grasping their uniqueness in order to raise them to universality" (*Toussaint Louverture* 310).

In a chapter of his biography entitled "The Sacrifice," Césaire argues that in the months preceding his arrest by Napoleon's agents, Toussaint had grown increasingly aware of his alienation from the Haitian masses. He had concluded that his intimate and conflicting involvement with the principal events of the period had made him an obstacle to the union and reconciliation of the Haitian people that was indispensable for the achievement of general emancipation. Imbued with this tragic sense of his revolutionary destiny, Toussaint sacrificed his life "for the salvation of his people," therein accomplishing the most consummate of his political acts (*Toussaint Louverture* 283). Only after his death do the true dimensions of his "martyrdom" come to light, for Toussaint's sacrifice enables his parousia as the Soul of the Revolution: "It is through Toussaint Louverture that the passage to spirit is made" (309).

As Édouard Glissant's figure of the old Louverture, Napoleon's lone and moribund prisoner at Fort Joux, realizes just prior to his death, "my land needs my absence"; "I began with [the people]. They are already advancing in the coming noon; they continue *through my night,* while I remain behind to protect their passage!" (*Monsieur Toussaint* [1981] 78, 62; emphasis added). In this respect, the role Césaire assigns to Louverture resembles the one Anthropophagists ascribe to the Tupi: he is less a revolutionary hero than a synecdoche of an *Aufhebung*. By the same token, Césaire's Toussaint embodies, if only transitorily, the Zeitgeist. He is as much the instrument of "the mind or spirit of his time" and his people, as his people serve him as an instrument for the accomplishment of his deeds (Hegel, *Philosophy of Mind* 13). As I have already indicated, however, for Césaire, the circumstances of Toussaint's death represent precisely an interruption of this dialectic. It is significant, in this light, that his "passage to spirit" be figured by a nocturnal tropology in *Notebook:*

Death traces a shining circle
above this man
death stars softly above his head

death breathes, crazed, in the ripened
cane field of his arms

. . . .

death expires in a white pool of silence. (49)

Toussaint's *Aufhebung* thus remains simultaneously within and without the Hegelian text. The great Night's work of Spirit outlined in the poem indicates not just the limits of Toussaint's purported embodiment of the Zeitgeist, but the extent to which the historical work that the Haitian people will carry out supersedes his own. In the final instance, then, he serves his people as an instrument for the accomplishment of their historical destiny. The poem will thus endeavor to recuperate the *unique* and *concrete* historical content of the slave revolt, the very content that Toussaint ultimately fails both to grasp and to express. At the same time, however, Toussaint will have lived out one of the defining moments of Hegel's master/slave dialectic—that is, the sublatory moment denied the African slaves in the *Philosophy of History*: "it is only through staking one's life that freedom is won" (*Phenomenology of Mind* 114).

Yet, because Toussaint's death so radically affirms the *abstract* universality of his struggle for emancipation and recognition, his death simultaneously produces another, and greater, contradiction: the failure to attain an *actual* existence in which the freedom he strove and died for would be fully recognized. It is therefore only *at the end* of his death that his revolutionary struggle can acquire universal meaning. His death remains nonetheless an essential and ineluctable stage in Haiti's historical passage to the universal. In this sense, the silent and pleonastic (or dialectic) "expiration" of Toussaint's death echoes the parenthetical invocation of his name.

It is the negation that the enduring future legacy of his historical labor ("the ripened cane field of his arms") will affirm. For, as Césaire argues in his biography, "what resisted French power in San Domingo, its cannon fire and infantry charges [that is, Napoleon's massive military campaign to restore the island to slavery], was the *spirit* of Toussaint Louverture, the spirit forged by Toussaint Louverture" (*Toussaint Louverture* 299; my emphasis). As with Bernard Shaw's proto-nationalist Saint Joan, whose "spirit," by the admission of one of her enemies, returned after her immolation to conquer the English (*Saint Joan* 154), it was also Toussaint's "spirit which [posthumously] moved the black army" and ultimately made the struggle "hopeless for the French" (James, *Black Jacobins* 367).

In answer to the question that closes his invocation of Toussaint ("the splendor of this blood will it not burst open?" [*Collected Poetry* 49]), *Cahier*'s speaker summons a "full [and] ample voice" that will sing and *tell* the history of "this land without a stele [marker], these paths without memory" (49). The emergence of this collective "narrative voice"[15] signals the *actual* sublation of the revolution into the world-historical. Retracing the trajectory of the 1791 revolt, which, in Alejo Carpentier's words, begins with a necromantic charge "against the last trenches of the goddess Reason" (*El reino de este mundo* 81), the speaker starts out by similarly rejecting western rationalism:

Reason, I crown you evening wind.
Your name voice of order?
To me the whip's corolla

. . . .

Because we hate you
and your reason, we claim kinship
with dementia praecox with the flaming madness
of persistent cannibalism. (49)

A few lines later, claiming to "have assassinated God with my laziness / with my words with my gestures / with my obscene songs" (53), he symbolically heeds the command Bouckman issues at Bois Caïman: "Throw away the symbol of the god of the whites [the cross] who has so often caused us to weep, and listen to the voice of liberty which speaks in the hearts of us all" (James, *Black Jacobins* 87). It is, of course, under the image of this "white god" that the colonial town lies prostrate and stagnant, helpless before "the hysterical grandsuck of the sea" (39). In this initial moment, then, the speaker sets out to negate and surpass what Adorno and Horkheimer define as a "totalitarian" enlightenment, whose "logical subject [is] the burgher, in the successive forms of slaveowner, free entrepreneur, and administrator" (*Dialectic of Enlightenment* 83). More to the point, the association of Reason with the slaver's whip reiterates the inextricable connection Paul Gilroy has established between racism and rationalism ("racial terror is not merely compatible with occidental rationality but cheerfully complicit with it" [*Black Atlantic* 56]).

Immediately following his decision to "speak for" his native land ("My mouth shall be the mouth of those calamities that have no mouth, my voice the freedom of those who break down" in the dungeon [*cachot*] "of despair" [45]), the speaker concedes: "I have no right to measure life by my sooty finger span; to reduce myself to this little ellipsoidal nothing [Martinique] trembling four fingers above the [Equatorial] line" (45). To measure life by one's finger span is arguably to replicate occidental History's reduction of the human and the universal, a reduction that the speaker will subsequently negate in turn by tracing out the imprints of black labor upon the face of the world: "And I say to myself Bordeaux and Nantes and Liverpool and New York and San Francisco / not an inch of this world devoid of my *fingerprint*" (47; my emphasis).

It is as though the speaker is here duplicating Toussaint's misprision of his people's historical work. Accordingly, in the *Cahier*'s last section, the "alienated" and autobiographical interiority of the opening section's poetic voice is supplanted by the plural voice of the risen masses (the pronoun *nous* is the last capitalized word in the poem), in the collective freedom cry of which the poet has appointed himself the custodian: "And we are standing now, my country and I . . . the strength is not in us but above us, in a voice that drills the night" (Césaire, *Collected Poetry* 77).

In this way, the starry halo above Toussaint's head (48) marks the initial stage in a progressive expansion of the confines of the Fort-de-Joux dungeon—and, by antonomasia, of the inert, insular space of the colony—into the terrain of the universal. The astral circle prefigures the cosmic harmony between the revolutionary masses and the planetary (or world) revolution, the "perfect circle of the world, enclosed concordance . . . the flesh of the world's flesh[16] pulsating with the very motion of the world" (69), that embodies the Négritude reclaimed in the *Cahier*'s final segment. To appropriate the enigmatic verse from Pauline Lumumba's eulogy of her husband Patrice in Césaire's *Saison au Congo,* the circle of stars signifies "la très belle copulation des astres et du désastre" (126).

This "perfect circle of the world" reconciles in a single image the figure of Damballah, the Serpent God forming a mystical eternal wheel, and the dialectic "circle that presupposes its end as its goal, having its end also as its beginning" (Hegel, *Phenomenology of Spirit* 10). Just as the little cell where Toussaint languishes is negated in its stellar projection, the island of Martinique annuls its "insularity" as it opens out to universal history. It becomes the "non-closure island" [*île non-clôture*] (46), a site whose expunction from universality was "always-already" abrogated by its brutal insertion into the *consanguineous* geography of the Triangle: "my original geography . . . the world map made for my own use, not tinted with the arbitrary colors of scholars, but with the geometry of my spilled blood" (77). The global dimension of this diasporic experience is thus the antithesis to that *particular* European universalism whose conception of human rights Césaire brands elsewhere as "narrow and fragmentary, incomplete and biased and, all things considered, sordidly racist" (*Discourse on Colonialism* 15).

From this point, the poem will ascend to its final utopic moment: a vision of what Fanon calls the reintroduction of Third World humanity into the world (*Les damnés* 79),[17] or Césaire's somewhat roseate idea of "a new society that we must create with the help of our brother slaves, a society rich with all the productive power of modern times, warm with all the fraternity of olden days" (Césaire, *Discourse* 31). As the metaphor of the world's "perfect circle" underscores, the Third World Revolution will be literally universal: "there is room for everyone at the convocation of conquest [*au rendez-vous de la conquête*] and we know now that the sun turns around the earth lighting the parcel designated by our will alone and that every star falls from the sky to earth at our omnipotent command" (77).

Its privileged symbol is an oxymoronic "burgeoning midnight sun" (81) that sublates the "cursed venereal sun" overlooking the stagnant colonial town at the beginning of the poem (35). The image of the heavens subjugated to human will negates, in turn, the *dis-astrous* stellar cartography of colonial oppression: "At the end of [daybreak], the great *motionless* night, the stars *deader* than a caved-in balafo, / the teratical bulb of night, sprouted from our vilenesses and our renunciations" (39; my emphasis). The black sun amends the solar trajectory of the Spirit of the west. It is the *negative* of the enlightenment sun, belying the urgency "to begin everything anew . . . to re-examine the soil . . . and, why not, the sun" (Fanon, *Les damnés* 75), to begin "the only thing in the world / worth beginning: The End of the world" (Césaire, *Collected Poetry* 55).

It is from the ruins of a Europe agonizing beneath the jackboots of the "flunkies of order" (*les larbins de l'ordre*), a "Europe utterly twisted with screams . . . [a] Europe that . . . proudly overrates itself" (59); it is upon the debris of a "white world / horribly weary from its immense efforts / its stiff joints [cracking] under the hard stars" (69)—in the same Europe in whose ruins the narrator of Carpentier's *Lost Steps* deciphers the destruction of the enlightenment project—that a new humanity will rise. "For it is not true that the work of man is done . . . the work of man has only just begun" (Césaire, *Collected Poetry* 76). Like the poetic production of the Brazilian Modernistas, Césaire's *Cahier* thus professes a distinctively modernist faith in the auroral promise that the west's twilight signifies for the peoples dwelling "on the hidden face of the earth."

For Dash, this formulation reveals "an ideal of communion with a natural primordial world [opposed to] a degenerate Western modernity"

(*Other America* 62). As I have been suggesting, this analysis is itself reductive and predicated on a dichotomy that is in large measure imposed. It seems peremptorily to reject the possibility that Césaire's and Fanon's critiques of hegemonic models of modernity are not only "inside" these western discourses but ultimately enabled and sustained by them. Dash's provocative interpretation of the *Cahier*'s closing image, the corollary of the new (or *revolutionary*) humanism I briefly discuss above, is governed by a similar kind of exegetical "finalism."[18]

In the poem's last lines, the speaker promises to fish "the malevolent tongue of the night"—"in its motionless verrition [immobile verrition]"—from "the great black hole where a moon ago I wanted to drown" (85). Eshelman and Smith, doubtless the most accomplished translators of Césaire's difficult poem, conjecture that the neologism *verrition* may have been coined from the Latin verb *verri* ("to sweep, to scrape a surface, or to scan"). *Verrition* could therefore describe the sweeping motion (or motionlessness) of the night's "malevolent tongue." It would, as Dash asserts, derive its central meaning from "the persistent dream of beginning again . . . the importance of invention" (*Other America* 64). Yet in a characteristic move, Dash then proceeds to "localize" and restrict the semantic range not just of the term but of the *Cahier*'s final metaphor. "The malevolent tongue of night" is hence "clearly" a reference "to the eruption of Mont Pelé, which in 1902 destroyed the town of Saint Pierre," to the cataclysmic event that, for Césaire, embodies the possibility of a "new Caribbean beginning" (64). This "new order" is then promptly located outside of (or in a site "uncontaminated by") history; what "the obscure newness of this invented word" consequently registers is a "magical retrieval of purity" (64).

In my own reading, I should like to associate—perhaps catachrestically—verrition with revolution (in both the planetary and social senses). Not only is this variation on a conventional sidereal trope an image of poetic writing itself (*la nuit en son immobile verrition*), but it condenses the crucial negations that have set the poem *in motion*. To begin with, the motionless nocturnal "revolution" recapitulates the revolving midnight sun (that is, the dark side of Reason, or the shadow cast by and on the enlightenment). It negates the latter's pseudo-universalism by instantiating the incompletion of the work of humanism.

On one side, the oxymoronic *immobile verrition* fuses (or immobilizes) the plurality of black voices (described as "quicksanded" and "forgotten" in the poem's first section [37]) with the poetic writing that seeks to give expression to it. In this regard, the "verrition" points to a *revolutionary* poetics, that is, the synthesis between the motionlessness of script and the political praxis it aspires to elicit. On the other side, the phrase preserves the colonial lethargy that opens the poem ("in this *inert* town, this desolate throng *under the sun,* not connected with anything that is expressed, asserted, released in the broad daylight" [37]), raising it to a higher dialectical stage (*une immobile* verrition) that simultaneously contains and supersedes that initial inertia. Indeed, "the great black hole" is the final destination of "the lustral ship"—a dialectical fusion of "the fierce [pre-Columbian] pirogue" [71] and the liberated "slave ship [cracking] everywhere" (79)—piloted by the risen "nigger scum" (*négraille*) (81) at the end of the poem.

This "black hole" represents the "one sea" that remains to be crossed (81):

> no the unequal sun is not enough for me
> coil, wind, around my new growth
> . . . .
> bind me with your vast arms to the luminous clay
> bind my black vibration to the very navel of the world
> . . . .
> then, strangling me with your lasso of stars
> rise,
> Dove
> rise. (85)

The Dove, the "sky licker" (85) whose sweeping ascent is repeated and transcended in the malevolent tongue's verrition, harks back to "the owl," which the poet anoints his "beautiful inquisitive angel" (83)—a probable allusion to the aspect of the Vodoun soul called the *ti-bon-ange* (little angel): "one's aura, and the source of all personality, character and willpower" (Davis, *Serpent and the Rainbow* 181). The owl, which must await a final contrapuntal crossing of the sea before it can hoot, merges Vodoun and speculative reason. Its invocation at the end of the *Cahier* stands in contrast to the "the stagnant air, unbroken by the brightness of a single bird" (*sans une trouée d'oiseau clair*) (41), which is one of the several images of the colonial town's exclusion from History in the poem's opening section. Unlike its Hegelian counterpart, however, Césaire's owl will wing its flight not at dusk but at midnight. In this way, the poem snakes back to its beginning either (or both) like the mystical "black serpent that cinches the sky" (81) or Hegel's circular dialectic.

It would be a little too easy to dismiss the *Cahier*'s apparently naive prophetic tone, as does J. Michael Dash, for example, who sees it (no doubt correctly) as representative of "a heroic, modernist practice" (*Other America* 163). For all its familiar thematization of the emergent and the new, however, Césaire's poem also puts into question the validity of a Eurocentric History. Thus, the poem's final moment is plainly marked as Utopian. The emancipatory time toward which it gestures is yet to come. It is a projection into a future whose fixity is indicated by the closing invocation of a revolutionary *firmament*. This, in turn, removes the revolution from history and reinserts it into textuality. The *temps à venir* would thus be the incomplete symphony (*la synthèse*) of which Toussaint is still only the overture: *une insuffisante synthèse*.

As Césaire maintains at the end of his biography, however, his dialectical insufficiency notwithstanding, Louverture gives the decisive thrust to the history of Haiti: "That is why [he] well deserves the name which his present-day compatriots give him: *le Précurseur* [the Forerunner]" (*Toussaint Louverture* 310). In the end, then, the place of Césaire's Toussaint is analogous to the one Sartre assigns *négritude* in his memorable definition of the concept:

> *Négritude* appears as the minor term [*le temps faible*] of a dialectical progression. The theoretical and practical assertion of the white man's supremacy is the thesis; the position of *négritude* as an antithetical value is the moment of negativity. But this negative moment is not sufficient [*n'as pas de suffisance*] by itself, and the Blacks who use it know this very well; they know that it is intended to prepare the synthesis or realization of the human in a society without races. Thus *négritude* contains the seeds of its own destruction [*est pour se détruire*], it is a *passage* and not an outcome [*aboutissement*], a means and not an ultimate end. ("L'Orphée noir," xli; my emphasis)

"Born of Evil and pregnant with a future Good," Négritude lives "like a woman who is born to die and who senses her own death even in the richest moments of her life" (xliii). The "tragic beauty" with which *she* adorns herself seems to be that of Césaire's Toussaint as well. In this way, what Dash regards as one of "the more arresting ambiguities of Césaire's poetic vision"—that is, "the fact that the clarifying fire of the Césairean volcano would eventually make negritude itself an obscurantist and obsolete ideology" (*Other America* 136)—is, in fact, not an ambiguity but a dialectical (or "logical") necessity.

In a well-known rejoinder to *L'Orphée noir*, Fanon argues that the upshot of Sartre's dialectical reading of Black Consciousness is an effacement or, what amounts to the same thing, an overdetermination of *négritude*'s agency and historicity, of the perplexity and unpredictability of its historical becoming:

> When I read that page, I felt that I had been robbed of my last chance. . . . It is not I who make a meaning for myself, but it is the meaning that was already there, pre-existing, waiting for me. . . . The dialectic that brings necessity into the foundation of my freedom drives me out of myself . . . I am not a potentiality of something. I am wholly what I am. I do not have to look for the universal. . . . My consciousness [does not hold itself out as] a lack. It *is*. (*Black Skin, White Masks* 133, 134, 135)

As Fanon intimates here, in his reading of the *négritude* movement, Sartre seems to lose sight of his considerably more Hegelian account of Jewish identification—one of the philosophical points of departure of Fanon's own essay—where the "authentic Jew," faced with a malignant anti-Semitism, abandons the "myth of universal man" and fully embraces his own historical and cultural specificity (Sartre, *Réflexions sur la question juive* 166). He "makes himself Jewish" (*se fait juif*) and thereby eludes not only the reach of the anti-Semitic slur but also representation *tout court* (167). For if the revindicatory claim of what Sartre calls *un racisme anti-raciste* also allegedly follows the trajectory of the master/slave dialectic, if in effect it initiates "the passage to universal self-consciousness" (Hegel, *Philosophy of Mind* 175), then it should mark 'the beginning of wisdom.'

It is the slave, in other terms, who must move *ahead* of the master in the dialectical progression to universal self-consciousness. As a self-proclaimed representative of "the master race," Sartre therefore makes a fundamental error—in effect, he undercuts the "inner logic" of the dialectic altogether—when he arrogates to himself the task of naming the content of this "third stage." Not only should the latter's definition remain necessarily open, but since, in Hegelian terms, this "identitarian" struggle simultaneously "forms the *beginning* of true human freedom" (175), the master's appropriation of the dialectic's "defining" moment can only constitute a step backward into "egotistic individuality": an interruption of the forward march to "true" universality. In this sense, Sartre repeats Hegel's own contradictory postulates regarding the historical potentiality of the African, that is, what Susan Buck-Morss calls his "retreat from [the] revolutionary radicalism" he supposedly evinces in *The Phenomenolgy of Spirit* ("Hegel and Haiti" 858).

According to the very dictates of speculative reason (as formulated in Hegel's *Phenomenology of Mind*), the slave should embody modern subjectivity and stand at the forefront, not the threshold, of History (as Hegel will later propose in *The Philosophy of History*). As I argue, the arbitrariness—and indeed the banal racism—of this fundamental misreading of the master/slave dialectic represents a characteristic sign of the enduring Eurocentrism that Césaire, Fanon, and James all attempt, in their own way, to expose and undercut. No wonder, then, that James has called Sartre's "explanation of what he conceives Négritude to mean . . . a disaster" (*Black Jacobins* 401n). Yet it was Sartre's pronouncement of the movement's death "on the very day of its birth" (Adotevi, *Négritude et négrologues* 75) that set down the terms of the polemic (surrounding the meaning and efficacy of *négritude* both as a movement and a concept), a polemic that was to seethe in Africa's post-independence period.

Wole Soyinka's sweeping dismissal of the movement as wholly dependent on European aesthetics and epistemology may well be the most frequently cited salvo. Commenting on Sartre's assessment of the movement and Fanon's response to it, Soyinka concludes:

> Negritude stayed within a pre-set system of Eurocentric intellectual analysis both of man and society and tried to re-define the African and his society in those externalized terms. . . . The autumn of the flowers of evil had, through a shared tradition of excessive self-regarding, become confused with the spring of the African rebirth . . . [Negritude] accepted the consequences that befall the junior relation in all dialectical progressions. [And Negritudinists] tried to constrict the protean universalism of the African experience into the obverse monothetical appendage (Sartre calls it anti-thesis, naturally) of a particularised, unprovable and even irrelevant European criterion. (*Myth, Literature* 136, 138)

Whatever the merits of Soyinka's assertions about the irrelevance, undemonstrability, and provincialism of Hegelian thought, one should note that to consign the dialectic to the fixity and conceptual poverty of a "European criterion" is to be unmindful of its subtlety and complexity. That Sartre, Fanon, and Césaire all attempt to understand *négritude* in dialectical terms should not determine a priori its total dependence upon and reduction to European philosophical or ideological systems (Soyinka does not appear to distinguish between the two). As I indicate above, to relegate the movement to a "junior relation" is to reproduce Hegel's own misreading of the African subject's role in the making of modernity. It is, in effect, to contravene the logic of dialectical progressions, which stipulates the African's "seniority."

In part, however, the tenor of Soyinka's critique coincides with that of the critical onslaughts upon what Césaire, in a 1973 interview, called "an

159 The Shadow Cast by the Enlightenment

ideology founded on negritude" (Depestre, *Pour la révolution* 144). It was from this discourse of "authenticity" that Césaire, as originator of the neologism, strove to dissociate himself:

> When a (let us say) literary theory is placed at the service of a political program, I believe it becomes infinitely despicable. . . . I refuse to consider myself, in the name of *négritude,* the brother of Mr. François Duvalier, to mention only the dead, or of several other sinister characters who make my hair stand on end. . . . Therefore, I do not reject *négritude,* but I do regard it with an extremely critical eye. . . . Moreover, my conception of *négritude* isn't biological, but cultural and historical. . . . I think it ill-advised to deem black blood an absolute and to consider the whole of history as the development across time of a black substance which would predate history. . . . If one does that, one lapses into a reverse racism [*un gobinisme renversé,* a term that one cannot help but juxtapose with Sartre's shibboleth concerning *négritude*'s "anti-racist racism"]. And that seems serious to me. Philosophically it is unsupportable. (144)

Thus, the philosophical undemonstrability that Soyinka ascribes to *négritude* in toto is here attributed to one of its particular ideological strands. Critical as he is of Sartre's dialectical 'death sentence,' Fanon insists concomitantly on the necessity to supersede the moment of cultural transvaluation:

> It was not the black world that laid down my course of conduct. My black skin is not the wrapping of specific values. . . . My life should not be devoted to drawing up the balance sheet of Negro values. . . . I do not want to exalt the past at the expense of my present and of my future. . . . I [commit] myself to fighting for all my life and with all my strength so that never again would a people on earth be subjugated. . . . The Negro is not. Any more than the white man. Both must turn their backs on the inhuman voices which were those of their respective ancestors in order that authentic communication be possible. (*Black Skin* 226–31)

In the famous "National Culture" chapter in *The Wretched of the Earth,* Fanon characterizes *négritude*'s "unconditional affirmation of African culture" as crucial to the elimination of certain stigmas and prejudices, but also as ultimately "irresponsible," leading to a political and epistemological "blind alley' (*Les damnés de la terre* 159–61). Just like Césaire's Toussaint, then, *négritude* is at once a failure and an achievement.

It is literally a *movement,* a passage into a higher stage, which derives its historical meaning precisely from what it *lacks,* from its *negativity.* The fallacy (or political irresponsibility) to which Fanon and Césaire (and, in a different vein, Soyinka) refer involves the unexacting transformation of this dialectical negativity into a fixed positive value: the ethical and onto-epistemological foundation of an authentic Black Consciousness.

The defense and illustration of *négritude* as a set of specific attributes and values is the task selected by the movement's other "father," Léopold Senghor, whom the Cameroonian philosopher Marcien Towa describes as *négritude*'s "principal vulgarizer" (*Léopold Sédar Senghor*, 99). According to Towa, Senghor's central aim is to posit the African subject's biological specificity and then deduce from it his conduct and culture (104). In Senghor's perspective, modern technology becomes the biologically hereditary "racial privilege" of whites, just as blacks' "biological constitution" renders them forever incapable of competing with Europeans in the domain of reason and science (107). The Senghorian term for this mental predisposition is "ethnocharacterology." It draws a sharp contrast between European and African "mentalities":

> Whereas a great number of Europeans and Americans, namely the French and the Anglo-Saxons, think with their heads, by means of concepts and schemata logically linked with each other, Mediterraneans and Africans, specifically Arabs and Blacks, think with their souls—I would even say: their heart, in the sense of *thumos*—by means of analogic images, formed intuitively in the manner of the feeling-thinking subject. As Leo Frobenius writes, "in [African] civilization . . . *sensitivity is thought [la sensibilité est pensée]*." (Senghor, *Les fondements de l'africanité* 55; emphasis in the original)

"The African is as it were shut up inside his black skin. He lives in primordial night. He does not begin by distinguishing himself from the object. . . . He does not analyze it . . . he *feels* it" (Senghor, *Prose and Poetry* 29–30).

Like Hegel's Negroes, Senghor's Africans remain "beyond the day of self-conscious history . . . enveloped in the dark mantle of Night" (Hegel, *Philosophy of History* 91). By contrast, European reason "is discursive, logical, instrumental chrematistic" (Senghor, *Prose and Poetry* 99). The solution to this cultural (and indeed, ontological) dichotomy is our old friend *métissage culturel*, which for Senghor constitutes the ideal of a *civilisation de l'universel* (*La poésie de l'action* 85): "the civilization of the universal cannot be universal except by being a dynamic synthesis of all the cultural values of all civilizations. It will be monstrous unless it is seasoned with the salt of négritude" (Senghor, *Prose and Poetry* 98).

It is a similar fusion of feeling and reason that informs the closing lines of Senghor's "New York," where the northern metropolis is entreated to "let black blood flow into your blood / That it may rub the rust from your steel joints, like an oil of life, / That it may give to your bridges the bend of buttocks and the suppleness of creepers" (Moore and Beier, *Penguin Book of Modern African Poetry* 237). Let it be said in passing that the contrast between this banal image of First and Third World "cooperation" and Césaire's militant linkage of Africa's emergence into an integrated humanity with the senescence and the disintegration of the "white world" could scarcely be starker.

Like José Vasconcelos and the Brazilian adherents of his "cosmic race" ideal, Senegal's poet laureate construes this cultural mixture in aesthetic, even eugenic terms, as "the synthesis of the reconciled beauties of every race" (qtd. in Towa, *Léopold Sédar Senghor* 109). "In order to blossom and flower," Senghor reiterates, one must "open oneself out to other continents, to other races, to other nations. . . . In short in order to come together one must be. But in order *to be more* [être plus], one must open oneself to the Other" (*Poésie de l'action* 92). As Towa remarks, the African's position in this rendezvous of races and cultures cannot but be a subordinate one. While the European continues to conduct this great civilizational symphony, the African, Towa jokes, is relegated to the rhythm section (*Senghor* 113).

To coin the Sartrean metaphor, the black race is imbued with the "tragic beauty" of a woman born to die, who senses her own death even in the richest moments of her life. It is somehow appropriate, then, that for Senghor, the symbol of black Africa should be the Queen of Sheba, the privileged agent of the "Mediterranean miracle" of cultural (and biological) miscegenation (*Poésie de l'action* 153). In an ode entitled "On the Appeal from the Race of Sheba," Senghor enjoins the biblical Black Mother to "salute in the red evening of your age / THE BRIGHT DAWN OF A NEW DAY," the utopian time and place where, to the strains of "the universal *Marseillaise* . . . we are all together, different colours. . . . Different features . . . and languages" (*Prose and Poetry* 127, 126).

Towa's conclusion is devastating: what Senghor calls 'négritude' is a "rigorously racist theory" (*Senghor* 104); its "emplotment" coincides almost word for word with colonial racism (115). More specifically, however, Senghorian *négritude* is neocolonialism's quasi-official ideology: "the mortar of the prison house where colonialism intends to confine us, and which we [Africans] must therefore tear down" (Towa, *Essai sur la problématique philosophique*, 47). Similarly, for Ousmane Sembene, *négritude* is "the debility of African man," the "great defect of our time" that, "instead of fostering the subjection of nature by science, upholds oppression and engenders venality, nepotism, intrigue, and all those weaknesses with which we try to conceal the base instincts of man."[19] In the caustic verdict of Stanislas Adotevi, "*négritude* as a whole is a eunuch's desire, a mobile sterility" (*Négritude et négrologues* 82). It is the expression of a repressed "politics of domination which no longer dares to speak its name. [It] is neocolonialism's current discourse . . . the *black* way of being *white*" (207).

As these scathing critiques of Senghorian *négritude* demonstrate, it is not because he has produced a literature that is finally a rewriting of Hegel that Senghor has "obviously gone wrong," as Christopher Miller would have it (*Theories of Africans* 19), but rather because he replicates a common "Eurocentric" misreading of Hegel—because he negates what appeared to be, at least in the dawn of African independences, the imminent fulfillment of Africa's revolutionary promise, and subjects this *modern* revolutionary potential to a "particularised, unprovable and even irrelevant" notion of modernity. In this specific way, the *négritude* polemic repeats the terms of the debate between *verde-amarelistas* and Antropofagistas over the content of an authentic (and radical) Brazilian identity. As with the modern Anthropophagus, the definition of that for which Toussaint "sacrifices himself" will arguably determine the extent to which emergent cultures and societies will breach with that prescriptive and ethnocentric idea of the modern.

If then, in Césaire's and James's treatments of the hero, the phantasmic third instance for which Toussaint sacrifices himself still carries a familiar German name (*Aufhebung*), to posit its putative *parousia* in the world as a necessarily "wrong" or "thoughtless" reiteration of Eurocentric epistemological models is to miss the disruptive potential that such adductions to the plot of Europe's long story can harbor. Although western discourses are doubtless reproduced, they are rewritten *with a difference*. And even if this difference is produced in the spirit of a contribution to the enlightenment tradition, that difference—that addition—subscribes to the logic of supplementarity. It finally returns to call radically into question the authority of that emancipatory tradition.

Whatever name we end up assigning to this questioning (postmodernity, postcoloniality . . .) seems far less significant than the crucial fact that it emerges from the margins. Thus, for the Martinican poet, if the revolution he set in motion is to find its "true content," the impossible symbiosis for which Toussaint yearned must be transcended. Likewise, C. L. R. James designates Toussaint's "negative side" as his hamartia: "a total miscalculation of the constituent events" (*Black Jacobins* 291). According to James, Toussaint fails because he attempts "the impossible" (291), an impossibility that bears more than a passing resemblance to that which Senghor defines as the ideal of a *civilisation de l'universel.*

As Toussaint's French secretary foretells in Édouard Glissant's *Monsieur Toussaint,* Louverture "has only one flaw . . . and it is by means of this flaw that we will destroy him: he believes in order and prosperity" (42). Imagining revolutionary France to be "the highest stage of social existence," and recognizing the "practical necessity" of the French connection to Haiti "in its long and difficult climb to civilisation," James argues, Toussaint pursues a policy of protection and appeasement of the whites that, never having been thoroughly explained to the masses, leaves them in "a state of stupor" (*Black Jacobins* 289, 286). "He ignored the black laborers, bewildered them at the very moment that he needed them most, and to bewilder the masses is to strike the deadliest of all blows to the revolution" (287). This James regards as Toussaint's tragic flaw, his double failure: a "failure of enlightenment, not of darkness" (288). As Edward Said observes, Toussaint's internalization of "the literal truth of the universalist sentiments propounded by the European Enlightenment . . . his willingness to trust European declarations, to see them as literal intentions rather than class and history-determined remarks of interests and groups [reveal] his sincerity and also his latent flaw" (*Culture and Imperialism* 246).

The remainder of James's argument shows, however, that Toussaint's tragic "insufficiency," the *impossibility* of his political practice, is fundamentally a question of time. It is simultaneously to aspire "too much for the time" and to "lag behind events" (*Black Jacobins* 291, 321), at once to arrive too late and begin too soon, to live out the paradox of the future (*post*) anterior (*modo*). For Maximilien Laroche, this is Haiti's paradox as well: "in relation to the historical evolution of those nations which dominate today's world, Haiti is situated in the paradoxical position of being in an "after" (post-), which is, at the same time, a "before" (pre-)" ("Haitian Postmodernisms" 119).

To read Toussaint's dilemma according to this now commonplace dichotomy is not merely a matter of extending to *post*-modernity James's and Gilroy's reorientation of modernity's origins. It is, more importantly, to suggest that Toussaint's "failure" does not, in fact, mark the minor moment in a dialectic whose staging ground has shifted to the planet's "hidden face." Rather, it points to the impossible or aporetic double time of 'underdevelopment.' As we shall see in the next chapter, this is the aporia that defines the representation of post-independence Haiti in several exemplary Caribbean literary texts.

6 The Marvelous Royalty of Henri Christophe's Kingdom

Cultural Difference and the Temporality of Underdevelopment

> It was like entering the atmosphere of another age, because the air was thinner in the rubble pits of the vast lair of power, and the silence was more ancient, and things were hard to see in the decrepit light . . . and there we saw him . . . older than all old men and old animals on land and sea, and he was stretched out on the floor, face down, his right arm bent under his head as a pillow, as he had slept night after night of his ever so long life of a solitary despot.
> —Gabriel García Márquez, *Autumn of the Patriarch*

AIMÉ CÉSAIRE'S *La tragédie du roi Christophe* (*The Tragedy of King Christophe*) chronicles the reign of Henri Christophe, the former general in Toussaint's army who founded a monarchy in the northern part of the island after the assassination of Dessalines (Haiti's first president) in 1806. The play traces Christophe's *tragic* and *fallacious* institution of what could be called a developmentalist double bind as Haiti's national goal: "The [Haitian] people must seek, desire, accomplish something *impossible!* Against Fate, against History, against Nature . . . the first step out of chaos, an assault by the sky upon the altar of the sun, a monument which places on its feet a people who were forced to live on their knees, the annulment of the slave ship."[1] What "the first Monarch crowned in the New World" (*La tragédie* 39) is describing here is the Citadel La Ferrière, his fortress above the clouds, in whose "poetic ruins" Alejo Carpentier first glimpsed a synecdoche of America's "marvelous real."[2]

In Césaire's play, La Ferrière represents an insuperable contradiction in Christophe's political program. Thus, a structure whose prodigious construction is made possible only by the brutal and wholesale conscription of the population's labor is paradoxically decreed a symbol of "the freedom of an entire people" (*La tragédie* 62–63). A fortress allegedly intended as the last line of defense against the desperate onslaughts of a royal and pro-slavery Europe is erected under the aegis of a New World monarchy that is either the ancien régime's derisory "caricature" (47), or a "perfect black replica of the best that old Europe has done in the matter of royal courts" (31). La Ferrière figures the paradox that the Haitian State has become under Henri Christophe. The Citadel appears to epitomize a grateful emulation of the Christian State. It is the model of "the repeating island," in Édouard Glissant's sense of an impossible and impracticable mimetic drive to replicate metropolitan history and culture, to dwell in a "parenthetical" temporality *absolutely* overdetermined by the dynamics of an external History.

One of the crucial indexes of this historical overdermination is the itinerary of development that Christophe lays out:

> I ask too much of men, but not enough of Blacks! . . . All men have the same rights [but] some have more duties than others. That's where the inequality lies. An inequality in what is demanded of us. . . . [Have] all men . . . experienced deportation, the slave trade, slavery, the collective lowering to the status of beasts . . . received that vast insult, the all-denying sputum upon their bodies, their faces[?] Only we, Blacks! . . . [We are] *at the lowest bottom of the pit . . . it is from there that we long for fresh air, for light, for the sun.* And if we want to climb out of it . . . we must ask more of Blacks than of anyone else. . . . It is an ascent the likes of which has never been seen. (*Tragédie* 59; my emphasis)

In this apparent gloss of Hegel on the African's exception from universal humanism, Christophe clearly presumes himself to be personally hailed by the prevailing European discourses of progress and modernity. In articulating the ethical duty to educate (black) mankind, his program of development replies explicitly to the enlightenment's political and philosophical *demand*.[3]

Thus, Christophe sees in the State "something thanks to which this people of deportees roots itself, burgeons, blossoms, pouring out upon the face of the world . . . something which, by force if need be [au besoin par la force], requires them to . . . exceed themselves" (23). For Christophe, the Ideal State is already in place in Europe, a continent that, as Hegel claims, "exhibits more or less the development and realization of freedom unimpeded by the caprice of a despot" (*Philosophy of Mind* 45). It is a reflection of the metropolitan sun that must be traced out in outline from the bottom of Haiti's temporal "pit." And it is Christophe who converts himself into the solipsistic embodiment of this political Ideal.

Like García Márquez's Rabelaisian autocrat, he alone is the Fatherland (*El otoño del patriarca* 70), the patriarch of Haiti's big family (*La tragédie* 39). He is the only man existing in time allowed to coincide with man as Idea, as Schiller might have put it, the "external force" that alone can hold Hegel's "Negro-State" together, the despotic ruler single-handedly restraining its "sensuous barbarism" (*Philosophy of History* 96). But, like Toussaint, his former commander-in-chief whom he betrayed to the French, he is also a Precursor of sorts. As a "trivial, pitiful puppet" (*La tragédie* 43), he foreshadows those Ubu-esque "Fathers of the Motherland, as this kind of character is called in the Caribbean" (15)—one of the "sinister characters who make [Césaire's] hair stand on end," "the crowned [kings] of Latin American barbarism," to borrow James's description of Duvalier (*Black Jacobins* 409)—who routinely anoint themselves the Zeitgeist's Instruments and, in turn, instrumentalize their peoples in the name of the Zeitgeist.

"The people must be raised to civilization" is one of Christophe's recurrent proclamations in *La tragédie* (53). Christophe's political program could therefore prefigure the "despicable" politics of authenticity—grounded on biological conceptions of *négritude*—enacted by the likes of Papa Doc Duvalier and Zaire's Mobutu. His Citadel would be the analogue to Senghor's epidermal Castle, immuring a black specificity conceived in absolute terms, what Marcien Towa designates an ideological prison house. Having arrogated to himself the hero's right to found a state, Christophe is at once the individual become the nation—"ennobled to the stature of man as Idea," and "the ideal man suppressing empirical man . . . the State annulling individuals" (Schiller, *Aesthetic Education of Man*, 19). In this sense, La Ferrière negates not the slave ship but the "great promise" that Toussaint's revolution had laid "open to Blacks the world over" (*La tragédie* 43). It serves as both the emblem and the avatar of the repressive Fortress State that was to become the bane of the Antilles.

As I have already intimated, though, it is in a European political construct that Christophe finds the blueprint for his single-minded project of raising Haiti to universality, of effecting its transition from a mass of transplanted slaves into a nation-state—a process that Hegel designates "the realization of the Idea" in political form (*Philosophy of Right*, 218). It is in western terms as well that one must understand Christophe's pressing need to coax a smile of recognition from "the face of the world": "The whole world is watching us, citizens, and people think black men are lacking in dignity. A king, a court, a kingdom, that's what we must show them if we want to be respected" (*La tragédie* 28).

The dilemma Christophe faces, then, is as tragic and foundational as Toussaint's. But, unlike his former commander-in-chief, Christophe attempts no expansion or revision of occidental rationalism. He seeks rather to integrate his people, *au besoin par la force,* into a universal history whose particular terms and destination he accepts unquestioningly. If his rationale for erecting a state structure seems ostensibly to contradict the banally racist designation of "Negro" consciousness as unhistorical, it ends up ratifying a reductive (and Eurocentric) reading of the Haitian state as a grateful adoption of Christianity, as an improving instinct to imitate superior European political models.

To quote one of Christophe's courtiers, "sometimes History can only pass through one route. And everyone follows it" (80). That route runs of course from east to west, and by selecting it, Christophe will revive the "charming paradox [of] serving freedom by means of servitude" (*La tragédie* 80), of nominating his slave regime as a historically necessary "phase of advance . . . a phase of education" (Hegel, *Philosophy of History* 99). He thereby reproduces exactly the "pseudo-universalism" whose limits Toussaint and his Black Jacobins strove to surmount.

It is appropriate in this regard that the first command issued by the play's master of ceremonies is "to start the rehearsal" (*commencer la répétition*) (30).[4] The stage directions for the scene indicate appositely that the court proceedings should be acted out as "a sort of farcical and clumsy general rehearsal" (*répétition*) (35). As Christophe's secretary, the baron Vastey, cynically remarks, the script for this repetitive farce is the idea of development itself: "Have you noticed whom Europe sent us when we requested the help of the International Technical Assistance agency? Not an engineer. Not a soldier. Not a teacher. But a master of ceremonies! That's what civilization is . . . form! The forming of man! . . . The form, the matrix from which being, substance, man himself rises. . . . The void, but a void that is prodigious, generative, plasmatic" (32).

Vastey adds that only Christophe, "with his marvelous potter's hands kneading Haïtian clay" (32), has the instinctive ability to discern, or to feel, "the line snaking its way into the future, the form" (32). As if to confirm the baron's judgment of his political-aesthetic potential, Christophe will later declare to his secretary that "human material is itself to be recast. How? I don't know. We will try it out in . . . our little workshop! The smallest section of the universe can become immense if the hand is mighty and the will unflinching" (50–51).

On the face of it, Christophe's despotism repeats the terms of Toussaint's military dictatorship: "Toussaint made himself into a whole cabinet like a fascist dictator" (James, *Black Jacobins* 159). Both regimes are hence *formless* in the Kantian sense: "Every form of government which is not representative is, properly speaking, without form" (Kant, *On History,* 96). The distance between Christophe's despotic "formalism" and the radical social transformation directed by Toussaint is considerable, however:

> Behind [Toussaint's] despotism the new order was vastly different from the old ... for the revolution had created a new race of men.... The potentialities in the chaos began to be shaped and soldered by his powerful personality, and thenceforth it is impossible to say where the social forces end and the impress of his personality begins. (*Black Jacobins* 242, 249)

If, despite or perhaps because of Toussaint's iron-fisted rule, historical action and movement are arguably the catalysts in his radical transformation of Haitian society, Christophe's transformation appears, in contradistinction, to be determined by his will alone. Toussaint's former general thus treats the human "clay" he attempts to mold with the same violence and contempt that Schiller's artisan (potter?) shows for the shapeless mass he sets out to form. Insofar as his actions "come closest to artistic creation because they ... are driven by an irresistible ... urge to impose their stamp on historical evolution" (Ogan, "Faszination und Gewalt," 17), Christophe prefigures another fateful gloss of Schiller's *Staatskünstler:* Goebbels's *Führer.* His rule thus expresses "the triumph of repressive equality" (Hoekheimer and Adorno, *Dialectic of Enlightenment* 13), the implacable excision of the incommensurable, the totalitarian reduction of the heterogeneous to a single form: the One. And *form,* as we have seen, is a key element in this process.

Form is nonetheless a polyvalent notion in this play. Possibly recapitulating the Platonic *nous, form,* first of all, outlines a future that, to paraphrase Octavio Paz, is already happening "over there" and is still nothing in Christophe's simulacral kingdom. It is a hollow in time, the elusive shadow that Europe's past will always project upon the confining walls of Haiti's present, the "not-yet" and the "elsewhere" defining the temporality of underdevelopment. *Form* also represents the Hegelian mold whose absence reduces Haiti's autonomy to a mere *formality.* It is what Haiti lacks (a State, a Republic, a Civilization ...) and the lack that is Haiti (*le vide générateur*).

The end toward which Christophe, the artisan of black humanity, shapes his human material is itself a void therefore—a blank slate that at once coincides with and exceeds modernity's stereotypical desire to wipe out everything that comes before it in order to begin anew. For—as I suggest in my discussion of Ricardo's *Martim Cererê* and Bopp's *Cobra Norato* in chapter 2—the modern wish to forget the past is rendered meaningless, pleonastic, when transposed to a site whose past is relegated by the very discourses of European modernity to the Unhistorical, to what, by definition, can neither be forgotten nor remembered. As Christophe seems to acknowledge, modernization, in this sense, cannot but constitute *quelque chose d'impossible,* something negated by both the nature and the logic of the very model of modernity he is seeking to impose on his island kingdom. It is a double negative: the destruction of a historical blank (the African *un*-History) for the sake of a historical blank (a future that will inescapably remain Europe's past).

For Christophe, Haitian history must unfold like Melquíades' encoded parchments before the eyes of the last Buendía in García Márquez's *One Hundred Years of Solitude.* In it he will also willy-nilly decode the very "instant that he was living, deciphering it as he lived it, prophesying himself in the act of deciphering the last page of the parchments, as if he were looking into a speaking mirror" (422). Like José Arcadio Buendía's brilliant yet belated discovery that "the earth is as round as an orange," his idea of progress will be forever untimely: "a theory that [will always] already [have] been proved in practice" elsewhere (5).

Suspended between a "not yet" and an "already," progress by its very logic is legible only as the numinous afterimage radiating from events. Unlike Kant's "historical sign," which demonstrates "the disposition and capacity of the human race to be the cause of its own advance toward the better" (*On History* 142–43), what lies behind historical phenomena in Christophe's Haiti is not an image of universal emancipation but civilization's detritus, its waste products. Like Macondo, Haiti appears destined to be thrown "into the corner where [places] that have stopped being of any service to creation are kept" (García Márquez, *Leafstorm* 93), "wiped out by the wind and exiled from the memory of men" (*One Hundred Years* 422).

Nevertheless, at the very end of his life, Christophe makes one final, pusillanimous attempt to reverse the cruel fate to which his political helmsmanship has driven his tragic kingdom. Even though, for the duration of his rule, Christophe sought apparently to fulfill the Christian promise borne by the patronymic he shares with Haiti's "discoverer,"[5] in the final moments of his life he reclaims African culture as his ultimate ontological truth.

In Carpentier's *Kingdom of This World,* Christophe reaches this epiphanic conclusion as he resignedly surveys the burning of his plantations, of his dairies and his cane fields, and witnesses with dread the historical return heralded by the revenant "drums of Bouckman, the drums of the Grand Alliances, all the drums of Voodoo": "Henri Christophe, the reformer, had attempted to ignore Voodoo, molding with whiplash a caste of Catholic gentlemen. Now he realized that the real traitors to his cause that night were [the saints], and the Evangelists whose books he had ordered kissed each time the oath of loyalty was sworn" (*Kingdom* 147–49).

Before expiring, Césaire's Christophe also loses faith in Europe's model of development, belatedly recognizing its ineluctable in-completion: "Africa! Help me to return, carry me like an old infant in your arms and . . . Strip me of all these clothes. . . . Of my nobles, my nobility, my scepter, my crown. And cleanse me! Oh cleanse me of . . . my kingdom" (*La tragédie* 147). In this manner, at the moment of his death and the dissolution of his reign, Christophe, like James's Toussaint, inhabits a kind of post-enlightenment.

Christophe's final realization of the historical and cultural simulacrality of his Europeanized kingdom resonates uncannily with a recent and influential account of the postmodern condition. Hence, at the end of this life, he appears to recognize in the parodic kingdom he has fashioned an "original historical situation in which [he and his people] are condemned to seek History by way of . . . simulacra of [a] history, which itself remains forever out of reach" (Jameson, *Postmodernism* 25).

To be sure, the complex techno-scientific processes that are the object of Jameson's analysis have as yet no equivalent in the Haiti of Henry Christophe. Still, the dilemma he defines as the apprehension of "present reality and . . . present history with the spell and distance of a glossy mirage" appears also to define Christophe's kingdom in the play. The local collapse of history inaugurated by his farcical instance anticipates the global a-historicity whose genre of choice, according to Jameson, is the pastiche, and which he famously defines as "blank parody, a statue with blind eyeballs" (*Postmodernism* 17). It is to a comparable level of banal and inconsequential mimicry, a similar historical blind alley, Césaire's play suggests, that Christophe's uncritical and wholesale subjection of his reign to the paralogism of development ultimately relegates his kingdom.

In Carpentier's *Kingdom of This World*, the final absorption of the ruler's cadaver into "the entrails" of the fortress of La Ferrière serves as a fitting epitaph to the elaborate "blank parody" that is his State. As "the mortar finally closed over the eyes of Henri Christophe, [he] would never know the corruption of the flesh, flesh fused with the very stuff of the fortress, inscribed in its architecture, integrated with its body bristling with flying buttresses" (155–56). He is literally converted into a "statue with blind eyeballs," an individual symbolically petrified into the unviable political mold into which he has sought to confine his country.

Even in this *form*, however, Christophe remains, as I mention above, the metonym of what Carpentier names, in the original preface to the novel, *lo real maravilloso* (the marvelous real). "My first inkling of the marvelous real [as Carpentier's canonical phrase goes] came to me when, near the end of 1943, I was lucky enough to visit Henri Christophe's kingdom" (Carpentier, "Marvelous Real" 84). *Lo real maravilloso* is for the Cuban novelist the index of Latin America's cultural and historical authenticity: "we were already *original*, in the right and true sense of the term, long before the concept of *originality* was offered to us as a goal" (Carpentier, *Tientos y diferencias* 133). "The presence and vitality of this marvelous real was not the unique privilege of Haiti," Carpentier concludes just as famously, "but the heritage of all of America. . . . After all, what is the entire history of America if not a chronicle of the marvelous real?" ("Marvelous Real" 87, 88).

The notion of the marvelous real, as González Echeverría defines it with admirable succinctness, involves an effort to isolate "something which would be exclusively Latin American . . . buried beneath the surface of [its] consciousness, where . . . Europe is only a vague memory of a future still to come" (*Alejo Carpentier* 123). As J. Michael Dash argues, "marvelous realism [is] one of the most valiant attempts to ground otherness in New World space"; it represents yet another variant of "the need to establish a separate and unique American identity" (*Other America* 88).

Few notions have been more fiercely debated and more thoroughly examined in Latin American cultural discourse than Carpentier's ambivalent and inchoate theory. To retrace the history of these debates is obviously well beyond the scope of my analysis. In what follows, I therefore remain within the narrow parameters of my study and limit myself to gauging whether the main assumption upon which Carpentier's master concept rests ("that the marvelous exists only in America") does indeed disclose "a spurious European perspective, since it is only from the other side that alterity and difference may be discovered—the same seen from within is homogenous, smooth, without edges" (González Echeverría, *Alejo Carpentier* 128).

As is the case with Senghor and the Modernistas of Brazil, for Carpentier, Latin America's distinction "from all the other histories of the world" derives from the fundamental fact that "American soil was the stage for the most sensational ethnic encounter ever registered in the annals of our planet ... the most awesome [miscegenation (*mestizaje*)] which has ever been contemplated" (*Tientos y diferencias* 133). This fusion of antipodal ethnicities and previously unknown cultural and historical experiences produces a magical, syncretic world that exhibits "in a raw, living, already formed state ... everything that the surrealists made up" (156). The genealogy of this idea that the uniqueness of American culture stems from the continent's singular ethnic composition has also been painstakingly explored before. To some extent, it relates to the notions of "racial democracy" discussed in the first three chapters of this book.

Like Fernández Retamar, Carpentier borrows and amplifies José Martí's concept of *mestizaje*, regarding it as "a case unique to *the entire planet* ... not an accident but rather the essence, the central line" (Fernández Retamar, *Caliban* 4). *Mestizaje* represents the paradigmatic expression of a culture born of revolution, "of our multisecular rejection of all colonialisms," a culture, moreover, that, though produced by a synthesis, "does not limit itself in the least to a mere repetition of the elements that formed it" (38, 37).

As Amaryll Chanady asserts, Carpentier seeks to challenge "the dominant [western] historiographic paradigm ... and [replace] it with one that does not correspond to what is traditionally regarded as truth" ("Territorialization of the Imaginary" 138). In broad terms, then, what Carpentier deems marvelous in Christophe's kingdom (and in America as a whole), is its unrepeatability: the *difference* in its adaptation of borrowed cultural and political models, which the novel's Christophe discovers only too late.

The Cuban novelist's identification of the baroque as the defining feature of Latin American art and culture is also reminiscent of Oswald de Andrade's conceptions of cultural originality (reviewed in chapter 1). González Echeverría has correctly cautioned the reader of Carpentier's critical essays about their recapitulatory character, referring to the novelist's "attempt to blend positions fifteen years apart in the amalgam of the longer version of 'De lo real maravilloso,'" for instance (*Alejo Carpentier* 222).

The concept of the baroque replaces the "marvelous real" in Carpentier's thought. In so doing, González Echeverría avers, Carpentier faces an insurmountable contradiction between *lo real maravilloso*'s emphasis on originality and the definition of the baroque as the product of multiple traditions. This contradictoriness is retained in Carpentier's formulation of the concept. Thus, citing Eugene d'Ors, Carpentier construes the baroque as "a *spirit* rather than a *historical style*," as "a kind of creative impulse that recurs cyclically throughout history in artistic forms" ("Baroque and the Marvelous Real" 95, 90). The baroque would then constitute something akin to the Spirit of the marvelous real: "Why is Latin America the chosen territory of the baroque? Because all symbiosis, all *mestizaje,* engenders the baroque" (100).

Both a *human constant* and a spirit of artistic prodigality and proliferation that compensates for a perdurable *horror vacui,* the baroque abolishes the pastiche. While it suggests, as Dash argues, "a poetics of infinite translation: no text or word . . . is [anything] but the representation of things that have already been represented" (*Other America* 94), Carpentier's baroque transcends blind and neutral imitation: "Absurd is he who tries to erect today, in 1975, a gothic cathedral by copying the best models. It would be a useless *absurd pastiche,* bearing no relation to anything whatsoever" ("Baroque" 93; my emphasis). On the other hand, the baroque spirit "can reappear at any moment and does, in fact, reappear in many of the creations of today's most modern architects" (95).

The baroque, in brief, is the sign of an eternally recurrent, or properly *modal,* modernity: "the baroque *always* projects forward and tends, in fact, to a phase of expansion at the culminating moment of a civilization, or when a new social order is about to be born" ("Baroque" 98). To apprehend this sense of the baroque is necessarily to think through the paradox of a cyclical, or *constant,* modernity.

This is exactly the inner contradictoriness that, according to Djelal Kadir, discloses the rhetoricity, the ficticiousness (and factitiousness) of Carpentier's *real maravilloso:*

> Far from the achievement of a 'unified syncretism,' the cultural multiplicity, which Carpentier assumed to be the foundation of a 'marvelous reality' and its syncretism proves to be an uncontrolled polysemy, a baroque heterotopia whose weave . . . cannot synthesize its variability into transcendent unity. . . . If there is anything 'marvelous' in this, it is the marvel of fabrication, of a baroque process infused with the prodigious energy of multifarious American circumstances which intensify eccentric proliferation. (*Questing Fictions* 101, 102)

For Kadir, what marks the impossibility of Carpentier's project is thus 'reality' itself. To posit the marvelous—"oxymoronically"—as a Real, as the autonomous historical content, which it would be the obligation of an authentic Latin American literature to express ("Our duty is to reveal this [baroque] world" [Carpentier, *Tientos y diferencias* 190]), is to lapse into a basic error. Given the propinquity of the baroque to de-authorize "all privileged programs and centeredness" (Kadir, *Questing Fictions* 90), Carpentier's attempt to construct a baroque reality cannot but redound in failure.

This failure is predicated on a marvelous *royal* (to pun on the ambiguity in the Spanish original): the arbitrary decree of a prior and exterior referent, "in the manner of dynastic or serial succession" (Kadir, *Questing Fictions* 93), upon an unruly and always recalcitrant (that is to say, baroque) textuality. Carpentier's mistake, in other words, is at once to impute "to *history* a transcendental status . . . an independent status (akin to Hegel's 'spirit of history') *outside* the text" and to presume "an anterior ontological presence" (92, 93). In the end, what this failure demonstrates, Kadir affirms, is that "literature is literature and there can be nothing outside literature where literature is concerned" (94).

Not only does this familiar formalist retort to the question of literature's referentiality foreclose any serious inquiry into the problem of representation, but to conclude a critique of Carpentier's "mimetic theory" by evoking the stereotype of autotelism ends up eliding the ineluctable historicity of this very definition of literature.[6] His professed anti-transcendentalism notwithstanding, Kadir cannot claim to distinguish a rhetorical (or aesthetic) truth from a referential fallacy without appealing to a transcendental signifier. In invoking Literature as the locus of a stable and apparently eternal (yet nontranscendental?) truth, Kadir ends up resurrecting an *episteme* that, as Foucault observes in the *Order of Things*, was already on the wane during the historical baroque.

In addition, by contradictorily evoking the contextual at the end of the chapter, Kadir seems poised finally to search for the truth (or proof) of his method outside the text. Carpentier's "predicament," he remarks, "is essentially no different from the one which Baroque sensibility . . . had to confront . . . within the context of the late 16th and most of the 17th centuries" (*Questing Fictions* 104). Oddly enough, the inescapable slippage of 'reality' into a subversive and exuberant tropology (the irreducible rhetorical domain that had heretofore served as the truth authorizing Kadir's hermeneutics) is now placed under the aegis of a contextual imperative: that is, the predicament that "a Baroque sensibility *had* to confront."

Nevertheless, *context* is still reduced to a trope: an analogy (an American dilemma "no different from" a previous European one). Kadir's context seems as self-enclosed and tautological as his idea of literature: it is now as it was then because it cannot but always-already be like this. It is a reiterated reflex, whose auto-referential determination inevitably serves as a subterfuge for a demiurgic first cause (a creative principle or artistic genius), a spirit, in sum. For Carpentier's 'spirit of history' Kadir substitutes a literary spirit and hence allows a specter to continue haunting his deconstruction of a purportedly naive historicism. Like Capentier's, his baroque is a spirit—a spirit of "ex-centricity" and subversiveness or, as the late novelist would have put it, a spirit of revolution.

One key distinction, of course, is that Kadir, who cites as one of the foundations for his argument the de Manian proposition I discuss in chapter 1 ("the bases of historical knowledge are not empirical facts but written texts, even if these texts masquerade in the guise of wars and revolutions" [*Blindness and Insight* 165]), insists upon the insuperable rhetoricity of any revolution. But there is another more significant difference. If, for Carpentier, the American baroque is the local instantiation of a human constant that emerges in response to (or concomitantly with) radical social changes and historical transformations, for Kadir it appears to be the de-contextualized repetition of a presumably conjunctural aesthetic. It reproduces, without a context, a European historical style (which emerged by some unexplained [historical?] necessity in "the late 16th and most of the 17th centuries"). As a result, it becomes another fitting (aesthetic) expression of the "mimetic" temporality of underdevelopment, of the 'magical-realist' curse of reliving forever the morning of the Discovery.

Ironically, Kadir himself evinces here precisely that "equivocal historical pertinacity" that elsewhere he identifies in "Eurocentric discourse": "Emergent cultures are emerging from a Eurocentered colonial past into a Eurocentered paradigm of cultural advancement: the other is othered into/unto us; we exclude it as other . . . to include it, teleologically and prospectively, into our sameness" (Kadir, *Other Writing* 29). What thus remains unaddressed and unaccounted for in the enforced return of the [European] Same (of a "predicament . . . essentially no different from the one which Baroque sensibility . . . had to confront . . . within [another] context") is precisely what Carpentier's troublesome concept seeks to reckon with: "the difference that is characteristic of Latin American cultural production" (Alonso, *Burden of Modernity* 48).

It is toward a delineation of this difference that I now proceed. González Echeverría shrewdly observes that the key distinction between Carpentier's baroque (as "a new conceit" to designate "that which is particularly Latin American") and his earlier notion of a 'marvelous real' rests upon a kind of ironic self-reflexivity: "a writing that purports to name for the first time even while it is conscious of naming for the second time, of being a renaming" (*Alejo Carpentier* 224). This observation provides a crucial point of departure for my analysis below. Needless to say, I attempt concomitantly to undercut García Canclini's dismissal of *lo real maravilloso* as a 'paradigm' "that lazily wants to explain us by the 'marvelously real' or a Latin

American surrealism," which fails entirely to account for "our hybrid cultures" (*Hybrid Cultures* 6). Whatever else may be imputed to the polemical 'marvelous real,' intellectual sloth is the least of its faults, I would submit.

Carpentier insists that one of the major indexes of Latin America's specificity is "the virginity of the landscape" ("Marvelous Real" 88). He identifies as a defining feature of America's baroque "the unruly complexities of its nature and vegetation . . . the telluric pulse of the phenomena that we still feel" ("Baroque" 105). In this he anticipates Glissant's suggestion that in Caribbean literature "the relationship with the land . . . becomes so fundamental that landscape in the work stops being merely decorative or supportive and emerges as a full character. . . . The individual, the community, the land are inextricable in the process of creating history" (*sont indissociables dans l'épisode constitutif de leur histoire*) (*Caribbean Discourse* 105–6). More recently, the Martinican writer has proposed that the expansion and relativization of conceptions of Nature form "the very basis of the baroque tendency" (*Poetics of Relation* 79).

As it becomes naturalized both as an art form and "a way of living the unity-diversity of the world," the baroque is prolonged and resignified in "the unstable mode of Relation"[7]; "in this full-sense, the 'historical' baroque prefigured . . . present-day upheavals of the world" (*Poetics of Relation* 79). Glissant's insight sets the stage for a more nuanced reading of what González Echevarría terms "the complicity of history and nature" in *El reino de este mundo,* a reading that can now question the "symphonic concordance, in the style of Romantic or Renaissance poetry, between events and nature" that putatively governs the novel's plot (*Alejo Carpentier* 136).

Nature—true to one of its privileged figurations in the novel as Damballah, the Serpent God—and like that mystical eternal wheel itself, constitutes both the point of departure and destination of a pleonastic quest for origins and originality in *El reino*. It "rules history and the disposition of the story," as González Echevarría puts it (*Alejo Carpentier* 137). Nature is the primal script, "the telluric pulse" that seems to determine the marvelous motions of Haiti's history. It is significant, therefore, that the novel opens with Mackandal's poison rebellion, which Carpentier designates elsewhere as "one the first authentic revolutions of the New World" ("Baroque" 105), a revolt that is symbolically rooted in the slaves' deep-seated belief in Mackandal's lycanthropic powers. In contrast with the enlightenment ideal of a mastered nature, Mackandal's revolution is grounded on his intimate and mystical acquaintance with "the secret life of strange species given to disguise, confusion and camouflage" (*Kingdom* 23). It is sustained by his power not only to mirror but to fuse himself with the natural world. It is Mackandal, as González Echeverría notes, who summons up Nature.

In this respect, "the subterranean advance of death" (*la subterránea marcha de la muerte*) (*El reino de este mundo* 29) that *el mandinga* unleashes is not solely the harbinger of Bouckman's "great uprising" (*Kingdom of This World* 42). Insofar as it is sanctioned by chthonic powers, Mackandal's "authentic revolution" also expresses the complicity between history and nature that allegedly "pervades the whole story" (*Alejo Carpentier* 136). As depicted in Carpentier's *Kingdom,* a similar primordial force seems to occasion the rout of Napoleon's troops a decade later under Dessalines's command, following the death in a French dungeon of the purportedly "assimilationist" Toussaint. Like Mackandal's underground revolt, Dessalines's campaign falls under the sway of Ogun, the Master of the Swords: "Now the Great Loas smiled upon the Negroes' arms. Victory went to those who had warrior gods to invoke. Ogun Badagri guided the cold steel charges against the last redoubts of the Goddess Reason" (*Kingdom* 103).

To borrow Wole Soyinka's *bon mot,* Ogun is "elder brother to Dyonisus" (*Collected Plays* 1: 235). According to the Nigerian author, the Yoruba god combines "the Dyonisian, Appollonian and Promethean principles"; he is the essence of destruction and creativity, the representative of a "revolutionary" Nature (Soyinka, *Myth, Literature, and the African World* 26). The symbolic function that the Leader of the Chorus of Slaves assigns to Dyonisus in Soyinka's rewriting of Euripides' *Bacchae* could thus easily refer to Ogun as well:

> Welcome the new god!
> . . . .
> Slaves, helots, the near and distant dispossessed!
> This master race . . .
> have met their match. Nature has joined forces with us.
> Let them reckon now, not with . . .
> a new remorseless order, forces
> Unpredictable as molten fire in mountain wombs.
> (Soyinka, *Collected Plays* 1: 240)

Soyinka's portrayal of Ogun as "the embodiment of a challenge, the Promethean instinct in man, constantly at the service of society for its full self-realisation" (*Myth* 30), echoes the Luso-African writer Pepetela's invocation of the same deity, in his novel of Angola's armed struggle for independence, as "the African Prometheus": a manifestation of man's self-affirmation in defiance of the gods (Pepetela, *Mayombe* 71). To Soyinka, Ogun is "not merely the god of war but the god of revolution in the most contemporary context—and this is not merely in Africa, but in the Americas to where his worship has spread" (*Myth* 54n). Ogun, Soyinka continues, is also the "Lord of the Road," the deity who embodies the knowledge-seeking instinct; the god of passages and prophetic wisdom, who "harnessed the resources of science to hack [his way] through primordial chaos for the gods' reunion with man" (27).

In a similar manner, Carpentier's Ogun embodies the slaves' desire to return, to undo the Middle Passage by bridging the gap between this side of the Atlantic and the sublime yonder. For, as Stuart Hall writes, "*Africa* is the name of the missing term, the great aporia . . . at the center of [Caribbean] cultural identity" ("Cultural Identity and Diaspora" 112). Africa, in this sense, alludes to "the prehistory of Afro-America or New World Africa—to be strictly distinguished from the named contemporary continent"; its meaning resides in "the undeconstructible experience of the impossible" (Spivak, *Critique of Postcolonial Reason* 430). In Carpentier's representation of Haiti's struggle for independence, the imaginary plenitude of Vodoun cosmogony seeks not only to restore a "natural truth" but also to register the originality of that identitarian search. Even Christophe's final attempt to return to Africa becomes a measure of this authenticity: the embodiment of a truth that the language of the masters could never hope to grasp.

Yet the monarch's posthumous *inscription* into the very architecture of the Citadel, like Toussaint's fatal detention in a metropolitan dungeon, contrasts sharply with Mackandal's magical persistence in the kingdom of this world, with his tenacious survival in the oral history of the slaves, despite the masters' efforts to contain him. The lesson that the spectacle of his *auto da fé* is intended to impart to the gathered slaves ("this time *the letter* would be inscribed with fire, not blood" [*El reino* 40; my emphasis]) is thus literally swept by the wind, negated by his "terrible" defiance in the face of execution, and the slaves' unswerving faith in the ability of the Mighty Powers from the Other Shore to outwit the whites: "Mackandal moved the stump of his arm . . . in a threatening gesture which was none the less terrible for being partial, howling unknown spells and violently thrusting his torso forward. The bonds fell off and the body of the Negro rose in the air, flying overhead, until it plunged into the black waves of the sea of slaves. A single cry filled the square: 'Mackandal sauvé!'" (*Kingdom* 51–52).

179 The Marvelous Royalty of Henri Christophe's Kingdom

Not surprisingly, the slaves' triumphant exuberance in the aftermath of Mackandal's immolation befuddles the plantation owners, who can regard it only as confirmation of the same familiar racist stereotypes (the basis for "a number of philosophical considerations on the inequality of the human races," as a sign of "the Negroes' lack of feeling at the torture of one of their own" (52–53). The incommensurability between the slaves' natural world and the culture of the masters is therefore nearly absolute at this point. The essence of the former is irrevocably beyond the grasp of the latter's understanding.

This cultural and linguistic struggle undergoes a subtler variation in Capentier's second major novel, as González Echeverría has observed as well. In *The Lost Steps,* it reemerges as the antinomy between a modern lexicon of genocidal horror and the Utopian promise contained in the petroglyphs' enigmatic inscriptions. In its earlier incarnation in *Kingdom,* the opposition seems to replicate the contrast drawn by Rousseau in *The Essay on the Origin of Languages* between the technicity and exactitude of scriptural languages and the force and passion of oral ones. It resonates with Rousseau's chary distinction "between what is original and what is artificial in the actual nature of man" (*Social Contract* 44).

In this narrow sense, "the heavy signs drawn in charcoal" (*Kingdom* 30), Mackandal's ciphered chronicle of his elemental revolt, would exemplify what Rousseau considers the most primitive mode of writing, a pictorial representation of objects that corresponds to the savage stage of humanity (*Origin of Language* 17). To the same "primitive" order would belong "the favorable auspices" (*los signos propicios*) (66) that signal the outbreak of Bouckman's war against the whites. In the end, however, the world of the insurrectionary slaves has little in common with the enlightenment notion of a primordial "state of childhood." The notion that Ti Noël, the novel's protagonist, has of monarchy, for instance, is as radically concrete as his fellow slaves' idea of revolution:

> In Africa the king was warrior [riding "with lances in hand at the head of (his) hordes"], hunter, judge, and priest; his precious seed distended hundreds of bellies with a mighty strain of heroes. In France, in Spain, the king sent his generals to fight in his stead; he was incompetent to decide legal problems, he allowed himself to be scolded by any trumpery friar. And . . . the best he could do was engender some puling prince who could not bring down a deer without the help of stalkers. (*Kingdom* 14)

The model of kingship that Ti Noël evokes here (and that he has received from Mackandal) appears to come straight out of the Mande oral epic of

Sunjata Keita, the semi-legendary founder of the Mali empire, conflated in the novel with "the fierce [fifteenth-century monarch Kankan] Musa, founder of the invincible empire of the Mandingues" (*Kingdom* 13). (Mackandal's Mandeka origins are, of course, pertinent in this context). The near identification of "the concept denoting political superiority [and] the concept denoting superiority of soul" carries a decidedly Nietzschean inflection (*Genealogy of Morals* 31). What particularly interests Carpentier in the San Domingo revolt, then, seems to be the slaves' purported attempt to obliterate the master's "inauthentic" symbolic order.

By the same token, as Ti Noël's juxtaposition of African and European monarchic ideals indicates, Carpentier's narrative seeks to probe the revolutionary potentiality already prefigured in the paradox of an alleged master race subjected to the rule of a "slave morality." It is as though the slaves seek to incinerate the master's signs, replacing them with a primordial language drawn "from the very breast of nature": "The horde had set out for the Cap, leaving behind fires that had a name when one searched the base of the pillars of smoke that curved upward to the sky" (*Kingdom* 75).

As an event, the burning of the plantations appears to escape representation, to resist "being mastered symbolically" (Dash, *Other America* 93). It is "something which [the] imagination could only compare with a storm over some brimstone lake of hell" (Bell, *All Souls' Rising* 180). If this all-consuming conflagration, punctuated, in the words of Faulkner's Colonel Sutpen, by a "rank sweet rich smell as if . . . the thousand secret dark years which had created the hatred and the implacability, had intensified the smell of the [burning] sugar" (*Absalom! Absalom!* 310), is not exactly *la fin du monde*—as a contemporaneous plantation owner would have it, it does nevertheless bring something violently to an end.

By setting everything aflame, the slaves effectively extract themselves and the space of the colony from the circuit of global exchange. Their destruction literally and figuratively burns them out of circulation, negating their commodity status and reducing to ashes both the product of their labor and the socioeconomic apparatus that their enslavement enables and sustains. At one and the same time, they destroy both the base and the superstructure.

Significantly, upon Ti Noël's return from Cuba, his master's old plantation has been reduced to "fragments of wall which looked like the thick broken letters of an alphabet" (*Kingdom* 112). During his final stroll through the royal palace, as his plantations are in turn going up in flames, Henri Christophe beholds, in a "fulminating" glare, "the chapel filled with images that had turned their backs on him, of symbols [*signos*] which had gone over to the enemy" (149). As we have seen, after his recognition of the occident's symbolic and epistemological betrayal, Christophe embraces once again the gods of Africa. As the insurrectionists' drums approach and "the fire lighted up the mirrors of the Palace," it becomes "impossible to tell which were flames and which reflections. All the mirrors of Sans Souci were simultaneously ablaze" (149–50).

It is as if the very principle of mimesis is set on fire here: not only the bedrock of Christophe's simulacral marvelous royalty but also the instrumentality of the sign system. Ultimately, it is the enlightenment—"the last redoubts of the Goddess Reason" (*Kingdom* 103)—that is burned up in a violent *dialectical* conflagration. It is its torch of reason that is "redundantly" set ablaze. Appropriately enough, among the sundry objects Ti Noël pillages from the royal palace stand "three volumes of the *Grande Encyclopédie* on which he was in the habit of sitting to eat sugar cane" (170). Hence, the historical period covered in *Kingdom of this World* (from Mackandal's uprising in the 1750s to the early years of the so-called Mulatto Republic that comes to power after Christophe's suicide in 1820) is crowned with the return of a despotism of Reason, for which Christophe's reign operates as a kind of bridgehead.

"This endless return of chains . . . which the more resigned began to accept as proof of the uselessness of all revolt" (*Kingdom* 177–78) is heralded by the arrogant Surveyors [*los Agrimensores*]: the advance guard of the "between-the-tides aristocracy [*aristocracia entre dos aguas*] . . . which was now taking over the old plantations, with their privileges and rank" (177). With the Surveyors, who move about "insolently measuring everything and writing things in their books with thick carpenter's pencils" (175), comes a rationalistic scriptural economy whose ruthless exactitude contrasts sharply with Mackandal's cabalistic "heavy signs drawn in charcoal" (30). (Mackandal is, in fact, evoked in the following paragraph as the Seer who had failed to foresee this "postcolonial" return of forced labor [176–77]).

Just as crucial to the novelistic elaboration of the "cultural struggle" I have been outlining here is the fact that Ti Noël's sojourn in Santiago de Cuba coincides with the period of Toussaint's ascendancy. This geographical displacement of the novel's action operates a kind of diegetic "bracketing" of a stage in the San Domingo revolution that, from the old slave's "Africanist" standpoint, can only be judged as inauthentic. Thus, in contradistinction to Toussaint's strict prohibition of Vodoun—precisely the practice that plantation owners fear as the slaves' "secret religion that upheld and united them in their revolts" (*Kingdom* 78–79)—in opposition to the reestablishment of an alien Catholic symbology that Christophe repudiates in his final hour, the baroque ebullience of the Santiago Cathedral holds for Ti Noël "an attraction, a power of seduction in presence, symbols, attributes, and signs similar to those of the altars of the *houmforts* consecrated to Damballah, the Snake god. Besides, St. James [Santiago] is Ogun Faï, marshal of the storms, under whose spell Bouckman's men had risen" (86). This affinity underscores the hybrid cultural location of Santiago.

The Cuban variant of Christianity traces a Utopian trajectory in the cultural and social composition of Latin America. It is oriented toward the future fusion of the culture of the slaves and that of the masters, the transcendence of the antinomy between the rational and the natural. This resembles the syncretistic ideal that Soyinka detects in Ogun's "promiscuous [co-]existence with Roman Catholic saints [and] 20th-century technological and revolutionary expressionism [in] Cuba, Brazil, and much of the Caribbean" (*Myth, Literature* 1). Indeed, the Nigerian playwright's adaptation of Euripides' *Bacchae* could well be read as an attempt to restore both to Ancient Greece (the Thebes so central to Attic tragedy) and to Christianity the Asian "features" that a narrowly ethnocentric metaphysical tradition has consistently sought to efface.

The play thus reverses the conventional (Eurocentric) interpretation of the dream of Cadmus's sister Europa, re-affirming instead Asia's claim that she owns the maiden (continent), that she is the one who gave birth to her and is therefore Europe's cultural matrix. Soyinka's Dyonisus (Ogun's younger brother [*Collected Plays* 1: 234]) consequently reminds the rabidly ethnocentric Pentheus (when the latter arrogantly proclaims that, unlike the barbarians, "Greece has a culture" [269]) that he has "seen among your so-called / Barbarian slaves, natives of lands whose cultures / Beggar yours" (269). The same Dyonisus, just before dispatching Pentheus to his gruesome fate, to be sacrificed for "a new [hybrid] order," presents him, as one of two visions of this hybrid or "Dyonisian future," with the miracle at the wedding of Canaan, performed by a Christ-figure wearing the "ambiguous thorn-ivy-crown of Dyonisos" (287).

In this way, then, the play registers "an attitude of philosophic accommodation [that] is constantly demonstrated in the attributes accorded to most African deities, attributes which deny the existence of impurities or 'foreign' matter, in the gods' digestive system" (*Myth, Literature* 54). It is this almost *antropofagista* absorption of exogenous material and experiences into "the lore of the tribe," Carpentier's novel suggests, that Toussaint's allegedly uncritical acceptance of France's cultural and epistemological primacy negates. In light of the novel's syncretistic cultural argument, then, Toussaint's supposed "Eurocentrism" would constitute a plausible ground for his conspicuous absence from the novel.[8]

It is now possible to suggest a different reading of Carpentier's focus on "the virginity of [America's] landscape" ("Marvelous Real" 88), with its "telluric pulse" ("Baroque" 105). As I have tried to indicate in the foregoing analysis, *Kingdom of This World* does not quite establish a Romantic "confluence or parallel between the nature of the New World and its history," as González Echevarría asserts (*Los pasos perdidos* 35; my translation). Rather, Nature in the novel operates as a trope for what is ultimately unpresentable: the irreducible difference in the Caribbean replications of western culture and discourses. Carpentier's uses of nature break with "Romantic" tropology insofar as they aim precisely at severing the correspondence Hegel imposes between the Negro's dormant mentality ("sunk within itself") and "the compact, differenceless mass of the African continent" (*Philosophy of Mind* 43).

In Carpentier's *Kingdom,* the slaves' association with the natural world, instead of signifying their immersion in a blighted state of mental childhood, a state of fugitive and inconstant ideas, marks their assumption into world-history—a universal history, moreover, whose "absolute end" is Africa rather than Europe. A brief comparison between the elaboration of this historical argument through natural imagery in *Kingdom of This World* and the representation of the Amazon jungle in *The Lost Steps* may serve to illustrate the point I am attempting to make here.

In the later novel, the narrator, upon reaching the threshold of the Amazon, is "amazed [at] the inexhaustible mimetism [*el inacabable mimetismo*] of virgin nature. Everything here seemed something else, thus creating a world of appearances that concealed reality, casting doubts on many truths" (165). Yet, despite this vertiginous repeatability, despite the incessant "deceit, subterfuge, duplicity . . . disguise, stratagem, artifice [*juego de aparencias*], metamorphosis" (*Lost Steps* 166), this "hidden nation, [this] map in code, [this] vast vegetable kingdom [*país*]" (126) finally manages to draw the evanescent outline of "a new world," made up of "shapes that were those of matter in which [a] form was beginning to delineate itself" (Carpentier, *Los pasos perdidos* 229).

In the last instance, it is a similar unrepeatable trace that Christophe's kingdom, as a synecdoche of the continent, and notwithstanding its apparent lack of originality, retains as well. Like the "surprising seashells," in whose "wonderfully precise [*la maravillosa precisión*] conical architecture, of masses in equilibrium, of tangible arabesques," Esteban, the protagonist of *Explosion in a Cathedral* (*El siglo de las luces*), perceives the "intimation" (or *intuition*) of "all the baroquisms to come" (Carpentier, *Explosion* 180), Haiti, for Carpentier, adumbrates the baroque poetry of Latin America's "marvelous" future.

The unrepeatable signature of these "immense telluric baroques" (Carpentier, *Lost Steps* 126) inscribes itself symbolically upon the *mestizo* features of Latin America's history: "Here [in "this Caribbean Mediterranean"], after long being scattered, the descendants of the lost tribes had met again, to mingle their accents and their lineaments, to produce new strains, mixing and commixing, degenerating and regenerating. . . . in an interminable proliferation of new profiles, new accents and proportions" (*Explosion in a Cathedral* 183). And: "Several races had met in this woman: Indian in the hair and cheekbones, Mediterranean in brow and nose, Negro in the heavy shoulders and the breadth of hips. . . . There was no question but that this living sum of races had an aristocracy of her own" (*esa viviente suma de razas tenía raza*) (*Lost Steps* 81).

Similarly, for Guyana's Wilson Harris, it as though this untranslatable "duplicity" of the word *raza* (race), of this racial sum and summa, is converted precisely into the sign of America's difference: "What was clear was the necessity to penetrate, replay, reinterpret, and not succumb to, formulae of static evolution: to respond to the true, multiple voices—familiar, unfamiliar, native, alien—that run in one's mixed inheritance, mixed blood" (*Carnival Trilogy* 403). As Edouard Glissant stresses, this "practice of [Caribbean] *métissage*" does not participate in "some vague [Senghorian] humanism," whereby one would savor the pleasure of "melting into the other" (*se fondre dans l'autre*). Rather, *métissage* relates to each other (*met en Relation*), "on an equal basis, and for the first time ever known to us, histories which we now know to be convergent. . . . It orients itself toward a [relational] future [and] seeks to recapture the memory of those effaced histories" (*Le discours antillais* 462).

Both Carpentier's notion of *lo real maravilloso* and Harris's metaphor of the carnival ("a reinterpretation of the great masks of legend and history, the progressions, digressions, reversals of great myth" as well as "a repetition of familiar texts become however strangely cross-cultural" [*Carnival Trilogy* 372, 204]) seek therefore to define an "inappropriate" or supplementary replication of the European Same. The Latin American baroque, like the Antillean carnivalesque, would thus set in motion "an infinite chain, ineluctably multiplying the supplementary mediations that produce the sense of the very thing they defer: the mirage of the thing itself, of immediate presence" (Derrida, *Of Grammatology* 157).

In this specific sense, then, both "the inexhaustible mimetism," which Carpentier seems to posit as Latin America's "cultural logic," and the "displacement of time-frames [that] break a one-track commitment to history," which Harris construes in a similar vein and places under the sign of Carnival (*Carnival Trilogy* 325), could be said to anticipate Homi Bhabha's definition of mimicry and hybridity as properly *postcolonial* oppositional practices:

> Mimicry is . . . the sign of the inappropriate . . . a difference or recalcitrance which coheres the dominant strategic function of colonial power, intensifies surveillance, and poses an immanent threat to both 'normalized' knowledges and disciplinary powers. . . . The paranoid threat from the hybrid is finally uncontainable because it breaks down the symmetry and duality of self/other, inside/outside. In the productivity of power, the boundaries of authority—its reality effects—are always besieged by 'the other scene.' (*Location of Culture* 86, 116)

In this sense, Carpentier's "marvelous real" adumbrates Bhabha's political gloss of Derrida's notion of supplementarity: "postcolonial space is now 'supplementary' to the metropolitan centre; it stands in a subaltern, adjunct relation that doesn't aggrandize the *presence* of the West but redraws its frontiers in the menacing, agonistic boundary of cultural difference that never quite adds up" (*Location* 168).

It is in the light of this incessant and "inappropriate" play of substitutions that we should read the portentous eruption of a tropical storm at the end of *Kingdom of This World*: "Toward the Cap the sky was dark with the smoke of fires as on the night when all the conch shells of the hills and coast had sung together. The old man hurled his declaration of war against the new masters, ordering his [imaginary] subjects to march in battle array against the insolent works of the mulattoes in power" (185). The storm recalled here is, of course, that of August 1791. For Carpentier, the hurricane constitutes another of the privileged (natural) tropes of America's difference: "our continent is a continent of hurricanes (the first American word to have become part of universal language, seized on by the sailors of the Discovery, was *hurricane*), a continent of cyclones, earthquakes, tidal waves, floods, which impose a redoubtable rhythm, due to their periodicity, upon an almost untamed nature, a nature still largely subjected to its primordial upheavals" (Carpentier, *Ensayos* 29).

This "meteorological" pulse operates in the manner of Carpentier's baroque, for its incidence in his fiction also signifies "the culminating moment of a civilization . . . a new social order . . . about to be born"

("Baroque and Latin America" 98). Just as the word *hurricane* is America's contribution to the global lexicon, the hurricane in *The Kingdom of This World* serves as a trope for the continent's ascension to the world-historical. This rhetorical link is by no means unique to Carpentier. "I hear the storm," Césaire declares in a similar spirit in the *Discourse on Colonialism*.

In "Le verbe marronner," that same stormy August night emerges as a metaphor of the birth of Haitian nationalism: "I recall / the insane song of Bouckman delivering [Haiti] / with the forceps of the storm" (Césaire, *Collected Poetry* 369). The hurricane also figures the transformed poetic persona at the end of the *Notebook:* "coil, wind, around my new growth" (83). Not surprisingly, however, Césaire's most sustained elaboration of this image is reserved for his adaptation of Shakespeare's *Tempest*.

In the prologue of Césaire's play, a group of European travelers strives to gain "the Cyclopean eye" of the storm (*Tempest* 3), in what could be called a characteristic Odyssean gambit. This may be a figural allusion to what Fanon calls the colonizer's "epic," or what Horkheimer and Adorno regard as Odysseus's embodiment of "the principle of capitalist economy . . . of the traveler's justification of his enrichment at the expense of the aboriginal savage" (*Dialectic of Enlightenment* 61–62). In both *Tempests,* this inaugural storm turns out to have been "brewed up" by Prospero's redoubtable technological power (Césaire, *Tempest* 11). In Césaire's adaptation, however, Caliban's "liberation struggle" ultimately negates Prospero's ersatz storm.

Significantly, then, Caliban launches his revolt with a contrapuntal invocation of Shango, the Vodoun god of rain (*Tempest* 59) and by proclaiming an alliance with the island's fauna against Prospero, "the hereditary and common enemy": "How can any animal—any natural animal, if I may put it that way—go against me on the day I'm setting forth to conquer Prospero! Unimaginable! Prospero is Anti-Nature! And I say, down with Anti-Nature!" (58). By the end of the play, an "aged and weary" Prospero, his gestures "jerky and automatic," can only feebly intone his promise to "protect civilization" in the face of an inexorable natural encroachment upon his dominion: "Odd, but for some time now we seem to be overrun with opossums. Peccaries, wild boar. . . . It's as though the jungle was laying siege to the cave" (75).

What Caliban appears at one and the same time to be recuperating and redefining is, to borrow Peter Hulme's words, "the link between barbarity and hurricanes" (*Colonial Encounters* 99). Referring specifically to sixteenth-century English travel narratives, Hulme argues that "the hurricane is an attribute of native savagery, a fact confirmed by its tendency of attacking precisely . . . the marks of civility . . . [the term 'hurricane'] ultimately displaced words from an established Mediterranean discourse that were clearly thought inadequate to designate phenomena that were alien and hostile to European interests" (99–100).

It is in this context of "native resistance" that Caliban's invocation of Shango ought to be read as well. As with the other Caribbean revisions of Hegel I examine above, the condition of possibility of Caliban's overturn of the master is precisely the master's order of knowledge:

> I'll impale you! And on a stake that you've sharpened yourself! You'll have impaled yourself! Prospero, you're a [grand illusionist]: deception [is your strong suit]. And you lied to me so much, about the world, about yourself, that you've ended up by imposing on me an image of myself: underdeveloped . . . incompetent, that's how you made me see myself! And I loathe that image . . . and it's false! But I know you. . . . And I also know myself! And I know that one day my bare fist . . . will be enough to crush your world. The old world is falling apart! (*Tempest* 71)

Caliban's lucid recognition here of the contingency of the relation between the master's tools and the master's power gainsays the "genealogical" link between race and civilization upheld by a kind of bourgeois humanism at the end of which Césaire invariably finds Hitler (*Discourse on Colonialism* 14–17).

One of the *loci classici* of this type of cultural Arianism, which Césaire in the *Discourse* illustrates by quoting from Ernest Renan's *Réforme intellectuelle et morale,* is the final act of Renan's own *Caliban* ("a sequel to *The Tempest*"), an allegory of the rise of the Third Republic from the ashes of the Paris Commune. Before the spectacle of Caliban's ascension to Prospero's "rightful" seat of power ("Caliban, c'est le peuple" [*Caliban* 82]), the chorus leader proclaims:

> All civilization is the work of the aristocracy. . . . It is [the aristocracy] that has disciplined the inferior races either by subjecting them to the harshest treatment or by terrorizing them with superstitious creeds. The inferior races, such as the emancipated Negro [*nègre*], begin by displaying a monstrous ingratitude toward their civilizers. When they succeed in freeing themselves of their yoke, they call them tyrants, exploiters, impostors. (Renan, *Caliban* 85; my translation)

As I have indicated in a previous discussion of Hegel, this lordly refusal to recognize the legitimacy of the bondsman's struggle for freedom reproduces a familiar impasse in the "master narrative" of emancipation. Césaire stages this paradox in the second scene of *A Tempest,* where Prospero re-creates for Miranda the circumstances leading up to his exile from Milan. In exactly the same terms that Renan uses in his *mise-en-scène* of Prospero's judgment in the name of Caliban (or, "the people"), and in the terms that in turn resonate with those of the sentence pronounced by the Inquisition on Galileo,[9] Prospero is condemned for the kind of enlightened or speculative thinking that he will later refuse Caliban ("The world is decidedly upside down. We've seen everything now: Caliban a dialectician!" [*Une tempête* 87; my translation]).

In this manner, Prospero's self-ascribed "civilizing mission" becomes, to borrow the phrase of Brecht's Galileo, "a progress away from mankind" (*wird . . . ein Fortshreiten von der Menschheiten weg sein*) (*Life of Galileo* 108). Nonetheless, in marked contrast to the German playwright's anachronistic hero, Césaire's Prospero never acknowledges his betrayal to the cause of human progress. Prospero, too, squanders "a unique opportunity . . . to lighten the burden of human existence . . . to use [his scientific] knowledge for the benefit of the people, instead of handing [that] knowledge to those in power for them to use, fail to use, misuse—whatever suited their objectives" (108–9).

It is Prospero's racist rejection of Caliban's capacity for "self-conscious" reflection that Caliban's struggle negates in turn, just as Césaire's "postcolonial" revision of Shakespeare's tragicomedy attempts to undo the logic of Renan's sequel. Thus, the felicitous "Romantic" confluence between Bouckman's uprising and the tempest is seized upon as the "countersign" of Hegel's reduction of "Negro consciousness" to a vegetative dormancy. The *natural* that both Césaire and Carpentier posit, like that of the Brazilian *antropofagistas,* is not so much an original state as a speculative result: an *Aufhebung* that aims, in part, at annulling Hegelian logic itself. With Carpentier's detour through a Nietzschean genealogy of ethical and cultural values, the negation of Hegel's speculative rationalism becomes at the same time a "transvaluation" of his Eurocentric notion of the historical. In the space of the imaginary, at least, a hybrid America—not Europe—has become "the end of History."

Hence, the final pages of Carpentier's *Kingdom* seek to undo Hegel's claim that "the mind of the African remains shut up within itself, feels no urge to be free and endures without resistance universal slavery" (*Philosophy of Mind* 46). In an unequivocal reply to this weighty cultural judgment, Ti Noël is presented, in a moment of anagnorisis, as reaching the dialectical-materialist conclusion that the history of humankind is summed up in its effort to make the abstract universal concrete:

> The old man ... had a supremely lucid moment. [H]e glimpsed once more the heroes who had revealed to him the power and the fullness of his African forebearers, making him believe in the possible germinations the future held. ... Now he understood that a man ... suffers and hopes and toils for people he will never know, and who, in turn, will suffer and hope and toil for others who will not be happy either, for man always seeks a happiness far beyond that which is meted out to him. ... For this reason ... *man finds his greatness, his fullest measure, only in the Kingdom of this World.* (*Kingdom* 184–85; my emphasis)

Ti Noël's postscript to Hegel recapitulates Kant's rationale for presupposing a natural plan for the accomplishment "here on earth" of the emancipation of the human race: "What is the good of esteeming the majesty and wisdom of Creation in the realm of brute nature ... if that part of the great stage of supreme wisdom which contains the purpose of all the others—the history of mankind—must remain an unceasing reproach to it? If we are forced to turn our eyes from it in disgust, doubting that we can ever find a perfectly rational purpose on it and hoping for that only *in another world*?" (Kant, *On History* 25; my emphasis).

Ti Noël succeeds in translating from Heaven to "this world" the topos of his u-topian Kingdom. His commitment to the future, his consciousness of the necessity to subordinate his own being and time to "the crosscultural humanities of the future" (Harris, *Carnival Trilogy* 258), to borrow Wilson Harris's phrase, echoes the tragic sense of historical destiny Césaire ascribes to the dying Toussaint. The promise of a redemptive *micrological* beginning, of the "little Christmas" (*petit Noël*) that his name encloses, is transposed into historical space and time, a "concrete" *beyond*. It is an Idea of emancipation ("man always seeks a happiness far beyond that which is meted out to him") that is at once universal (i.e., *worldly*) and humanist.

In this respect, Ti Noël repeats the transition from the Christian conception of the universal, "the triune God who contains difference within himself," to a notion of the "concrete universal," the desire for "the development and realization of freedom unimpeded by the caprice of a despot" (Hegel, *Philosophy of Mind* 45–46). In other words, by transcending the immediacy and *actuality* of his own individual existence, by projecting his own destiny beyond the confines of his own temporality, Ti Noël performs precisely the intellectual labor that Hegel defines as proper to Europeans and "alien to other races" (46).

It is, fittingly enough, an *auspice* that announces Ti Noël's supersession of his individual consciousness, his "passage into Spirit": "a wet vulture who turns every death to his own benefit and who sat with outspread wings, drying himself in the sun, a cross of feathers which finally folded itself up and flew off into the thick shade of Bois Caiman" (*Kingdom* 186). Although the vulture's symbolic function is unmistakable, the precise nature of its symbolism remains an open question. For instance, this counterpart to the parrot/narrator winging its way to Lisbon at the end of Andrade's *Macunaíma* could certainly be read as portending the return of Nietzsche's amoral "birds of prey" (in Carpentier's contrapuntal gloss of Nietzsche's *Herrenrasse*), or the destruction of "western metaphysics" (through a "self-overcoming" [Selbstaufhebung]) that Nietzsche foretells at the end of his *Genealogy of Morals*.

In a similar vein, the vulture's "cross of feathers" could signify an "eccentric" negation of, or addendum to, Hegel's Absolute Spirit taking flight at dusk, the Spirit of the occident whose dialectical "Calvary" closes *The Phenomenology of Spirit*. Indeed, an "auspicial" reading of the vulture's flight is what the narrator of *The Lost Steps* proposes: "this omnipresence of the bird, which spread the sign of the wing over the terrors of the jungle, brought to my mind the transcendence and plurality of the Bird in the mythologies of this world" (268).

This sentence serves as the introduction to a series of specific examples, ranging from "the Bird-Spirit of the Eskimos" to the winged heads of Tierra del Fuego, illustrating the predominance of the Bird in American cosmogonies. The crucial argument, then, is not merely that "the sign of the wing" carries a teleological valence, but that it is the privileged sign of non-occidental thought. For Carpentier, the Bird is thus a metaphor of a distinctly nonwestern idea of the future.

It is also the sign of the wing that extends over Césaire's inquiry into the future of the African revolution in *Une saison au Congo*. Patrice Lumumba, the hero of Césaire's historical drama, accuses the future dictator Mokutu of destroying in one fell swoop Africa's "promise and affirmation of life": "the great rainbow bird which graces the ceiling of one hundred and fifty million men" (Césaire, *Une saison* 92). The rainbow bird symbolizes the *telos* of Lumumba's emancipatory discourse.

Lumumba, who earlier in the play defines his political aspiration as a desire to be "a beautiful bird, a herald to the world that the Kongo is born to us" (29), stakes not only a *continental* claim to freedom, but a universal one: "Je parle et je rends l'Afrique à elle-même! Je parle, et je rends l'Afrique *au monde*!" (Césaire, *Une saison* 105; my emphasis). At the end of *Une saison,* in a gesture that is consistent with the terms of both Toussaint's and Ti Noël's "passage into spirit," Lumumba chooses "the bronze remixture" [*la remige mordorée*] where the ibis dwells, the span and soaring [*élan et empan*] of the bird, as his own sign "to usher in the new times [*les temps neufs*]" (104).

For the ghostly narrator of Wilson Harris's *Palace of the Peacock*, the "starred peacock"—"instantly transported to know and to hug to himself his true invisible otherness and opposition" (Harris, *Guyana Quartet* 116)—signifies an *Aufhebung* of the Carib that resonates with that of Oswald de Andrade's Anthropophagus. By the same token, the protagonist of Harris's *Infinite Rehearsal* discovers in "The Ecstasy of the Wing and the Ecstasy of the Serpent . . . the source of all philosophy . . . a measure of creative rehearsal, incompletion" (Harris, *Carnival Trilogy* 178–79). Just as in *Kingdom*, then, the wing in flight is a trope (an *auspice*) of utopia, not simply a figure of "the future's miraculous community of souls born of the divisions of the past" (407) but of a "distrust of futures that come upon us before one knows the choices one is making, before one knows one's potential age, one's deepest age, one's cross-cultural heritage and body of wisdom to come abreast of the tools that may damn or save (one cannot say) the human race" (218).

The Haitian Revolution—as the greatest in a long series of slave rebellions in the New World—constitutes, in this sense, a paradigmatic attempt to parent a local future, a future for which there is as yet no phrase, indeed for which the enlightenment's phrases will always have come too late, will always dwell in a kind of *post*. As a character in Carpentier's *Explosion in a Cathedral* wryly remarks, referring to the Decree of the Abolition of Slavery (of February 4, 1794): "All the French Revolution has achieved in America is to legalise the Great Escape [*el gran marronaje*] which has been going on since the 16th-century. The blacks didn't wait for you, they've proclaimed themselves free a countless number of times" (231). It is the vexed relationship between 1789 and Latin America's struggle for political emancipation that informs the central plot of this novel that occupies me in the next and last chapter of the book.

7 "Something New in a Decaying World"

Alejo Carpentier's *El siglo de las luces*, or, The Signs of Progress on the Margins of History

> The powers and creativeness which the leaders of the underdeveloped countries have so signally shown, spring from the fact that they represent something new in the world, the rejection of the role on which a dominant civilisation for centuries had built itself, and without which it sinks itself deeper and deeper into moral and political decay.
> —C. L. R. James, "Lenin and the Problem," *C. L. R. James Reader*

> Poor nations, by their very eruption, had made it possible for new ideas to be born: ideas of otherness, of difference, of minority rights, or the rights of peoples. These ideas, however, seemed only to dust the surface of the swirling magma.
> —Édouard Glissant, *Poetics of Relation*

GONZÁLEZ ECHEVERRÍA, who considers Carpentier's *El siglo de las luces* (1962) (*Explosion in a Cathedral*) "one of the most penetrating studies of the transition from the Enlightenment to Romanticism in Spanish America" (*Los pasos perdidos* 36), insists that this seemingly conventional historical novel offers "a radical revision of the historical process portrayed in *The Kingdom of This World*" (*Alejo Carpentier* 232).[1] Beneath its ostensibly traditional narrative armature, the same critic continues, the novel hides "a radical experiment with history and the narrative" (226). González's shrewd assessment sets the exegetical ground for my own reading of *El siglo*'s subtle exploration and profound interrogation of the notion of modernity.

Critics of the novel usually make the important point that the two decades covered in *El siglo*, 1789 to 1809, lay the economic and political foundation for "the strange marriage of new forms of European revolutionary thought with familiar forms of European sovereignty in the colonies"

(Handley, *Postslavery Literatures* 118). As González Echeverría remarks, this period overlaps with the one depicted in *Kingdom of This World*. *El siglo*'s protagonists (the son, daughter, and nephew of a wealthy Spanish-born retailer whose death precedes the novel's action), belong to a similar social class—the emerging Cuban mercantile bourgeoisie—as the Haitian *haute bourgeoisie* portrayed in *El reino*. This clearly symbolic death of the patriarch, or "of the old ways," as González would have it (*Alejo Carpentier* 228), suggests another crucial synchrony between the history of the family whose evolution the novel traces and the social history that constitutes its backdrop. One of the key ways in which *Explosion in a Cathedral* "revises" its predecessor, however, is self-consciously to place the Haitian Revolution beyond its narrative scope.

The August storm that across the Windward Passage is greeted by the unisonous chant of the "conch shells of the hills and coast" (*Kingdom* 185) —*Kingdom*'s privileged historical referent—is presented in *Cathedral* from the limited and (literally) confined viewpoint of three Creole adolescents. It has now been consigned to the edges of the novelistic action, reverberating faintly within the walls of an old colonial manor, besieged "by the unusualness [*lo insólito*] of a situation which disorganised the normal order of things and established a chaos in the rooms"; it is reduced to a *domestic* "scene of the cataclysm" (*Explosion* 60).

This "vast [manorial] disorder" is further condensed into an image of the sexual awakening of one of the adolescent protagonists. For the aptly named Sofia ("a name which defined the woman who bore it as possessing a 'smiling wisdom' [*gay saber*]"), this sexual upheaval outweighs "in importance the collapse of walls, the destruction of belfries, the foundering of ships—she had been *desired*" (*Explosion* 254, 60). It surpasses even her disturbing sense that she stands "on the threshold of an epoch of change" (47). The promise of epochal change thus seems to be "fulfilled" only at the personal level: "the play-time of adolescence had come to an end . . . opening the doors of an unknown world for her" (58). Sofia initiates a 'sentimental education' that, in narrative terms, takes the place of Haiti's coetaneous entrance into world-history.

What *El reino* treats as its referent (the difference in Haiti's putative repetition of Europe's long story of emancipation) has now been pushed beyond the limits of narrative discourse. I postpone for now an inquiry into the consequences and meanings of this narratorial "marginalization" of the Haitian Revolution and look instead at the alternate itineraries of its narration. One of the most significant of these is the final Caribbean voyage presented in the novel.

On the last leg of a clandestine journey to Cayenne, where she expects to be reunited with Victor Hugues, the man she regards as her first and true love, Sofía makes the epiphanic discovery that her voyage's destination was, from the beginning, announced in her name: "She was amazed that her name should have occurred like that, in the Captain's stupid remark. It was too extraordinary a coincidence not to be read as an omen, a warning, a premonition. A wonderful destiny awaited her. The future had been beckoning to her secretly ever since a certain night when a Will had made itself felt by thundering on the door of the house" (307). Sofía's tutor in this process—the subject of this unbending Will—is, of course, Hugues himself, a Port-au-Prince trader who also becomes the herald of the revolution, or at least the fulcrum of its discursive proliferation, in the novel. In this sense, Sofía's journey to French Guiana is Victor's final seduction—a sexual conquest that follows on the heels of a rhetorical one.

It is, in effect, Victor's "muddled" and incendiary speech that, in *Cathedral*'s first chapter, initiates the political awakening of Sofía's cousin Esteban: "The terms *liberty, happiness, equality, human dignity* . . . recurred continually in this reckless exposition, and were used to prove the imminence of a great conflagration [*un Gran Incendio*], which to-night Esteban accepted as a necessary purification, as an Apocalypse which he longed to witness as soon as possible, so that he might start his life as a man in a new world" (70). Esteban, for whom Victor personifies the revolution itself and symbolizes a social transformation and renewal that seem finally within reach at the end of the long eighteenth century (as Carpentier himself has asserted), flings himself through the "door" that Hugues "opens out" for him (*El siglo de las luces* 49).

What the remainder of Esteban's narrative will chart out—in an apparently strict adherence to the bildungsroman's generic requirements—is the road leading to a moment of recognition that is nearly the complete obverse of Ti Noël's moment of lucidity. Esteban sinks into a profound disillusionment upon discovering the irremediable chasm between his own Idea of this purifying and apocalyptic Event and the concrete circumstances that present themselves as the embodiment and fulfillment of that Idea. A similar disappointment awaits Sofía at the end of her flight to Victor. The seeds of this disillusion are in a sense already contained in the very structure of the revolutionary feeling that Esteban experiences before embarking on his own odyssey. As Carpentier himself suggests, this disillusionment is prefigured in the particularity of the Idea of the Revolution imparted to him.

This conceptual narrowness is first indicated by the relegation of Haiti —indisputably the most significant "reverberation" of the French Revolution in the New World—to the novel's "outer rim"—a marginalization reiterated at the diegetic level when Hugues travels to the site of this "gigantic conflagration" [*un incendio gigantesco*], the place that the novel names anachronistically as Haiti (82). Having received news of the slave uprising in the Plaine du Nord, and seized with anxiety about the fate of his San Domingo business, Victor travels to Port-au-Prince, where he lands soon after a mulatto uprising. Confronted with an event of whose historical significance his mulatto friend Ogé (another historical character) is never in doubt ("It coincided too closely with other events, of universal import [*alcance universal*], to be merely a revolt of black incendiaries and violators of women" [*Explosion* 82]), Hugues is peculiarly blind to the "universal reach" of what he witnesses:

> With his back to a city which seemed to be boasting of having buried its past beneath a mountain of ashes, [Victor] became more French than ever, now that he could speak French to Frenchmen, and learn the latest news from his country. This was interesting, unusual [*insólitas*], extraordinary. . . . 'And there I was haggling over contraband silk, when things like this were happening in the world,' said Victor, raising his hands to his head. 'Over there they are witnessing the birth of a new humanity.' (89–90)

Before the destruction of the very social order he rails unceasingly against, Hugues the universal humanist turns oddly ethnocentric, "more French than ever." The only upheaval he can identify is his own: "His life . . . was suspended between a past which had been destroyed and a future it was impossible to foresee" (87).

Confronted with the slaves' radical expansion of the referent of the Declaration of the Rights of Man, with the violent "birth" of their humanity, their great historical rupture, Hugues can detect only History's *European* point of origin and destination. His narrow perspective on the events unfolding before his very eyes repeats and reinforces the earlier narrative superposition of the particular upon the universal, of the personal upon the societal. To put it in other terms, Victor's perspectival shift in the face of the San Domingo insurgency (which precedes the transposition of the novel's action to Europe) parallels *Cathedral*'s "marginalization" of what in *Kingdom* was the central narrative project.

To a certain extent, the opposition between western discourses of rationalism and an authentic revolutionary idiom that structures *Kingdom*'s plot informs this episode as well. But in *Cathedral* that sphere is shunted to the "far corners" of the narrative. It surfaces only in a contrapuntal grammatical form, as the insistent question that, as George Handley astutely remarks, pervades the entire novel: "With what language, with what value system, can we identify the Caribbean difference Haiti embodies?" (*Postslavery Narratives* 120). It emerges as a trace whose diaphanous contours can barely be deduced from its rhetorical negatives—which are the sole images that the narrative now hazards to present: "For two days they *talked* of nothing but revolutions.... To *talk* of revolutions, to *imagine* revolutions, to *place oneself mentally* in the midst of a revolution, is in some small degree to become master of the world. Those who *talk* of revolutions find themselves driven to making them" (*Cathedral* 71; my emphasis).

It is both the truth and the lie of this conjectured coincidence between the word and the world (theory and praxis) that the novel will proceed to limn. In chapter 5, for example, a revolution-weary (and thoroughly Gallicized) Esteban will propose as the cause for the revolution's failure precisely this tropological excess, this redoubling of its prophecies and allegorizations: "This time the Revolution has failed. Perhaps the next will be the real one.... We must beware of too much fine talk, of Better Worlds created by words. Our Age is succumbing to a surfeit of words" (*Cathedral* 261).

The epigraph to this section of the novel ironically confirms the inadequateness of discourse to its revolutionary example or the "gulf between ideals and praxis" (González Echeverría, *Alejo Carpentier* 237): *No hay que dar voces* ("One must not call out"; literally: "one must not give voice [to it]"). The phrase is taken from a collection of Goya's etchings about the Spanish war of independence, *Los desastres de la guerra* (*The Disasters of War*), selected titles of which occasionally serve as section headings in *El siglo de las luces*.

As González Echeverría notes, these pervasive allusions to Goya indicate a "corrosive, parodic impulse" (*Alejo Carpentier* 256). The caption in question here describes one of about eighteen sketches from a period (1811–12) when the population of French-occupied Madrid was facing mass starvation. Its imperative is presumably directed at the destitute figures in the foreground (and issued by the fashionable French personages silhouetted in the far background). An improper—and admittedly "literal" —reading of the phrase would deem it a commentary on the specific nature of the historical situation represented. In this latter sense, it would suggest a limit-experience that no discourse could hope to encompass, or a "fluid, open-ended and repetitive" Caribbean space that "resists being mastered symbolically" (Dash, *Other America* 93).

In contrast, Victor Hugues, who is often depicted as discoursing "without respite" (*sin tregua*) (311), proceeds, as a matter of course, to clad the event in blustery and exorbitant oratory. He exemplifies, in this manner, that characteristically western garrulity that Oswald de Andrade disparages in a famous *boutade*: *O homem europeu falou demais* (*Estética e política* 285) (European man has talked too much). The logorrhea Oswald satirizes here resembles the rhetorical compulsion that seizes Carpentier's Columbus before those "crazy [Caribbean] islands, floating, sleepwalking, having little to do with [*ajenas a*] the maps and texts that had nourished [him]" (*Harp and the Shadow* 86): "I had to describe that new land. But when I tried to do so, I was halted by the perplexity of one who tried to name things totally different from what is known . . . and I was not another Adam, chosen by Christ to name the things of the world. I could make up words, certainly; but the word would not reveal the thing, if the thing were not already known" (86).

Not surprisingly, Hugues himself makes a fundamental distinction between his own project of conversion and Columbus's: "For the first time a fleet is advancing towards America without bearing crosses aloft. Columbus' ships had them painted on their sails. They were the symbol of the servitude about to be imposed on the men of the New World in the name of a Redeemer. . . . [We] are going there . . . to abolish privilege and to establish equality" (*Explosion* 125). Nevertheless, it is precisely the proximity between the figurative force of Columbus's invention of the Indies and that of the emancipatory discourses disseminated by Hugues that is underscored by Esteban's recollection of the archipelago's transformation "into an immense stained-glass window" of hagiographic toponyms by Renaissance explorers during the final stage of his return voyage from what he melodramatically calls his life "amongst [French] barbarians" (*Cathedral* 245, 248).

Indeed, Hugues's emancipatory project belongs to a "philanthropist" tradition that, as George Lamming's allegorical novel *Natives of My Person* tries to demonstrate, is indissoluble from the history and logic of conquest. In Lamming's novel, a mysterious ship commandant seeks to atone for the ravages of European occupation in a fictional New World island by undertaking an "enterprise that would start life afresh [in] virgin lands" and "build in a soil that is new and freely chosen such an order as might be the pride and example for excellence for [Europe] herself"—an order that putatively expresses a colonial "ambition in reverse" (112–13, 10–11).

Not surprisingly, however, both the generic constraints of the commandant's travel narrative (moving outward from a European center) and the authoritative terms of his Utopia will render this new order ineluctably rhetorical. Hugues's revolution succumbs under an analogous "excess of writing" (*Natives* 133). It dissolves into a "vision of ink" (133). Ultimately, then, the conquering impetus of Hugues's rationalistic discourse duplicates that of the very evangelical obscurantism it seeks to displace.

Were one to posit, for example, the axis of the crucifix, that is, the meeting point between the two crossbeams (the enigmatic synecdoche of the Gospel inscribed on the fluttering canvas of Columbus's sails), as the figure for the coincidence between the Word and the World—a sign/referent correlation that is the crux of both the Christian and the enlightenment projects of conversion—then this correspondence, like the dialogue that Esteban, upon a visit to a hospital in French Guiana, intuits between "the stark geometry of [a] black wooden cross and the [sea], the fluid immensity of the universal womb," this correspondence could only be located "outside of time and place" (*fuera de toda contingencia y lugar*) (*Explosion* 222). It could happen only within discursive space, as the intersection between the Sign and a referent produced by writing itself. As González Echeverría writes regarding Carpentier's notion of the baroque, "the text [is] an evasive gesture that points to itself as a beginning that never was" (*Alejo Carpentier* 224).

Upon his return to Cuba from revolutionary France, Esteban will duplicate discursively Hugues's turn away from Haiti's "repetition" of the French Revolution. "The *ideas* which he had left behind had now caught up with him, in an environment where everything seemed organised to neutralise them. The people who were pitying the lot of the slaves to-day had bought fresh negroes to work on their haciendas yesterday. . . . Forty years too late, people were reading books in favour of revolution which that revolution itself, impelled into unforeseen channels, had made [out of date]" (*había desactualizado*) (*Explosion* 274).

Esteban's translation of the gap between revolutionary ideals and praxis into a developmental narrative, into the specifically Caribbean emergence of "a shadow configuration of what once prevailed in the First World" (Perry Anderson "Modernity and Revolution" 329), ultimately reasserts what, from Hugues' standpoint, for instance, might be called the *properly* European origin of emancipatory thought. By thus reducing the Antillean reverberations of 1789 to a familiar paradigm of imitation, Esteban loses sight precisely of the irreducible "supplementarity" of such "marginal" reiterations, of the cultural and historical difference toward which Carpentier's fiction insistently gestures. In the discourses collected in the novel, though, this difference is alternately transcoded into an eschatological desire and a belated echo of Europe's past. It is relegated to the order of a political sublime: the dehiscence (or point of suspension) between an eternal future tense and an alien preterit.

It is out of a similarly remote and unfamiliar past that a ship whose "cargo" of slaves had thrown its Spanish crew overboard, looking "so antiquated and unusual . . . that it seemed to have sailed out of another century—a boat manned by men who still believed that the Atlantic ended in a Sea of Darkness" (*Explosion* 185) seems to arrive as well. This complex episode, perhaps inspired in part by the scene of Oroonoko's capture in Aphra Behn's eponymous novella, illustrates with singular force Carpentier's deliberate problematization of history.

The appearance of the ancient slave ship in *El siglo,* a possible echo of the liberated slaver piloted by the risen *négraille* invoked at the end of Césaire's *Cahier,* is prefigured in the novel's previous section by the emergence of "a fish from another epoch" that surges forth to break the "great silence foreshadowing an Event" (*Explosion* 178), "for what might perhaps be only the second time since the astrolabe was brought into these seas" (179). At first glance, this employment of natural imagery to hint at "all the [social and historical] baroquisms to come" (180) is reminiscent of the metaphorizations of the primordial or original temporality of the Haitian revolution in *El reino de este mundo.* But in this scene, the metaphor's tenor is sundered from its vehicle. As a result, the figure never fully constitutes itself. The slave trader's anachronism, for instance, turns out to be double-edged. It pertains just as much to the mutineers as to the enlightenment idea of emancipation that Victor Hugues had been commissioned to carry across the Atlantic. It is nonetheless on the strength of that idea that the mutinied slaves place themselves under the protection of the French: "All along the African coast they knew that the [French] Republic had abolished slavery in its American colonies, and that the negroes there were now free citizens" (186).

Notwithstanding France's democratic tenets, the French captain determines to sell "the shipload of blacks" (188) in one of the Dutch islands. When Esteban, appalled at this duplicity, invokes the Decree of the Abolition of Slavery, the captain, by way of justification, alludes to a prerevolutionary slave-trading ship, "owned by a philosophe and friend of Jean Jacques" (189), which was called *Le Contrat Social.* The cruel irony of the slave ship's name reproduces (or "literalizes") Rousseau's inexplicable omission of the Africans in his impassioned condemnation of enslavement and oppression all over the world.

As Susan Buck-Morss affirms, "he declared all men equal and saw private property as the source of inequality, but he never put two and two together to discuss French slavery for economic profit as central to arguments of both equality and property" ("Hegel and Haiti" 831). This, of course, is a contradiction that is familiar, one might even say constitutive of European enlightenment discourses. In order to drive home his point, the Captain—whose anecdote obviously invites a similar ironic reading of the ship he commands, *L'Ami du peuple*—shows Esteban a letter, signed and sealed by the revolution's commissar in Guadeloupe (Victor Hugues), authorizing the sale of captured slaves in Dutch ports.

The double-think indicated in the commissar's letter resonates with a momentous—and equally contradictory—epistolary instance in the history of the Americas: an early-sixteenth-century missive to Emperor Charles V by a famous Dominican friar, whom one of *Explosion*'s characters will later brand "one of the worst criminals in history" (233). In the opening sentence of his *Historia universal de la infamia,* Borges sardonically sums up the "crime" alluded to here: "In 1517 Father Bartolomé de las Casas felt very sorry for the Indians who exhausted themselves to death in the laboring hells of the Antillean gold mines, and he advised Emperor Charles the fifth to ship in blacks who might exhaust themselves to death in the laboring hells of the Antillean gold mines" (17).

In effect, the revolutionary squadron, for which *L'Ami du peuple* serves as an unofficial flagship, "resurrected" not only "the traditions of the corsairs of old" (189), but those of the Spanish conquest itself: "The old India Companies, with their coffers and jewel cases, were being revived here in this remote extremity of the Caribbean Sea" (197). Leaving aside the vexed question of the alleged role of the Apostle of the Indies in introducing the slave traffic to the Antilles, I should like merely to mention that the eighteenth-century reproduction of this antinomy between the principles of humanism and those of capital severely undermines the progressivist claim advanced by the heralds of the French Revolution in the Caribbean. These European "liberators" end up replicating exactly the contradictoriness of an older (Catholic) emancipatory discourse—the very "false universalism" in fact that Hugues, as a good deist, wishes radically to distinguish from the one he professes.

Here, too, as in the opposition between "Totemic Man" and "Theological Man," between "pre-historic" Caribs and sixteenth-century conquistadors, evoked in a later section of the novel, "two irreconcilable historical periods [confront] one another" (244). But in the slave trader episode, the temporal rift is more incommensurable. As a result of their endeavor to inscribe their "barbaric" mutiny into the emancipatory narrative of the French Republic—putatively the highest expression of civilization and freedom at the time—the slaves have the humanity for which they struggled summarily negated. They are restored to their "non-historical" status as commodities, forced—precisely by those who have imported to the Antilles a metropolitan "idea of freedom"—to follow in the opposite direction the historical itinerary charted by the Haitian insurgents.

Hence, the time of the mutinied slaves' anachronistic struggle projects itself well beyond the "temporality of excess" (174) (*una temporalidad desaforada*) of their would-be liberators. The purported pastness of their mutiny has been transposed, by the end of the episode, into a future whose "necessity" the revolutionaries have yet even to conceive, let alone desire. At the same time, by seeking to insert their own strife into a European temporality, and thus effectively negating their own agency, the mutinied slaves now come face to face with a dilemma that, according to Fanon, the "Antillean Negro" will confront after the 1848 abolition of slavery. "The upheaval reached the Negroes from without. The black man was acted upon. Values that had not been created by his actions, values that had not been born of the systolic tide of his blood, danced in a hued whirl round him" (*Black Skin* 220).

Glissant discusses this impasse in similar terms: "The 'liberation' of the slaves created another trauma, which comes from the trap of citizenship granted; that is, conceded; that is, imposed" [*Caribbean Discourse* 161]). Bereft of the option to struggle *actively* for their freedom, "the former slaves," Fanon continues, never experience a decisive and "historically necessary" challenge to their humanity. They remain frozen in a *reactional* stance, mired in *ressentiment*.

If then, on the one hand the novel proposes to chart the concrete historical *results* of France's revolutionary discourses in the Caribbean, that is, the odd coupling between emerging European emancipatory discourses and old forms of European domination (hence the epigraph from *The Zohar*: *Las palabras no caen en el vacío* [words do not fall into a vacuum]), on the other hand, and specifically in episodes such as that of the liberated slave ship, it intimates that the relationship between such discourses and historical events, or *actuality*, is fraught with contradictions and interruptions.

It is the paradoxical motility of the revolution's idioms, in fact, that Carpentier seeks to convey by dint of a series of strategic descriptions of the painting referenced in the novel's English title. To Carpentier, this undated baroque oil painting attributed to Monsù Desiderio (1593–c. 1644), "an unknown Neapolitan master" (*Explosion* 19), "symbolizes the commotion produced by the French Revolution" (*El siglo de las luces* 47). In the novel, the picture is described as "the terrible suspense of [a] silent earthquake, [a] silent cataclysm, [an] illustration of the end of Time, hanging there within reach of their hands" [*Explosion* 19).

Explosion in the Cathedral is a *tela* ("painting") with a *telos,* in other (punning) terms. It is at one and the same time the harbinger of revolutions to come and the reduction of their promise to plastic reproducibility. Asked by Sofia how he can stand to look at it, Esteban replies, "It's so I get used to it" (*Es para irme acostumbrando*) (*El siglo de las luces* 21), "without knowing why, but with that automatic insistence which can lead us to repeat an inferior pun that makes no one laugh, for year after year whenever the circumstances recur" (*Explosion* 19). Like Esteban's stock response to it, the picture punningly reiterates the imminence of an epoch of change. It performs an iterative epochality (or bracketing) of the great event: "[Sofia] was exasperated by the checked motion, the everlasting fall which never fell, of the broken, scattered columns in the 'Explosion in a Cathedral'" (48).

The rupture figured by the painting is in this sense not so much outside of time as conjugated in the future anterior—at once *not yet* and *already.* Like the closing lines of Césaire's *Cahier,* it figures a paradoxical immobilization of historical change. Yet, unlike the last movement of Césaire's poem, the future liberation it portends has already sunk into the (European) past; it has already been reduced to a text. It is as though the painting serves as a reminder that, to quote Peter Weiss's Jacques Roux, "the revolution / which burns up everything / in blinding brightness / will only last as long as a lightning flash" (*Persecution and Assassination* 46).

It is, of course, in the nature of representations—especially baroque representations—always to emerge either before or after this elusive revolutionary "now," never to coincide with it. And it is the painting's asymptotic effect that Esteban, dazzled "by the extraordinary proximity of events," experiences in revolutionary Paris: "One seemed to be in the midst of a gigantic allegory of a revolution rather than a revolution itself, a metaphorical revolution, a revolution which had been made elsewhere, which revolved on a hidden axis" (*Explosion* 95). *Explosion in a Cathedral,* then, operates as the figure for a process of codification that makes the revolution possible while simultaneously leading to its ineluctable failure, its institutionalization, or integration into the state.

At the same time, one is tempted to read what Esteban names as the revolution's *elsewhere* and *hidden axis* as the very plantation economy and slave labor regime that the San Domingo insurgents had just set ablaze in the preceding chapter. In any event, Esteban's inability to live out the historicity of the revolution at once reverts and reverberates with Victor Hugues's own historical myopia before the "extraordinary proximity" of the San Domingo rebellion. Both instances reproduce the troublesome slippage of the revolution's present into its figural re-presentation, into the impossible yet inevitable framing of its futural openness. As González Echeverría observes, "what allegory reveals [in *Explosion*] is an emptying process, by means of which each [emblem] can only attain meaning by alluding to something else" (*Alejo Carpentier* 255). In the last instance, it is the *exterior* of these protean and agonistic figurations of the modern revolution that the novel seeks simultaneously to invoke and preserve outside of its narrative frames.

Upon his return to Cuba, Esteban suddenly stops, "stirred to the very depths," in front of the painting: "In it were prefigured, so to speak, so many of the events he had experienced that he felt bewildered by the multiplicity of interpretations to which this prophetic, anti-plastic, un-painterly [*ajeno a todas temáticas pictóricas*] canvas . . . lent itself" (*Explosion* 253). At the end of chapter 5, this interpretive lure gives way to that harrowing sense of fatality that also comes over the last Buendía, as he feverishly deciphers the end of his own bloodline unfolding in Melquíades's manuscript: "Even the stones I'm going to break now were present in this picture" (296). Disheartened and defeated, Esteban tears a gash in the canvas.

He sunders the painting's delicate balance between the left aisle's colonnades shattering into fragments in midair and the right aisle's row of columns standing, like the apse at its center, "momentarily" and eternally intact. The juncture of the "before" and the "after" of the explosion—the plastic seizure of the cataclysmic *instant*—is now irreparably split; the explosive *now* placed forever beyond the pale of representation. No longer is the painting the prophecy of a rupture, but the rupture of prophecy.

The novel's ensuing plot sequence certainly seems to confirm the sense that Esteban's gesture writes the revolution's epitaph. Arrested for sedition, he will make his second passage across the Atlantic as a political prisoner of the Spanish Crown. And the following chapter, which relates Sofia's reunion with Victor in Cayenne, chronicles the slow and ignominious death of the ideal of 1789 in the colonies: "This time the Revolution has failed. Perhaps the next will be the real one' (*Explosion* 261).

It is nonetheless the Eurocentric notion of history implicit in Esteban's reading of the "failure" of the revolution that will be surreptitiously displaced in the remainder of the novel. In *Explosion*'s penultimate chapter, Victor Hugues, now an agent of the Consulate in Cayenne, organizes "a merciless punitive expedition against the encampments of runaway slaves [*los palenques cimarrones*] which were multiplying too rapidly in the jungle" in the aftermath of Napoleon's revocation of the Decree of Abolition (328). The campaign ends in complete disaster.

Hugues, who had earlier set out to "conquer Nature here," "to make [mankind's] puny presence felt in an expanse of green reaching from Ocean to Ocean like an image of eternity" (325), admits to having failed calamitously in both endeavors. "It's not war," he declares upon his return from the ill-fated expedition, "you can fight men, you can't fight trees" (330). And one of his officers adduces: "Fire a canon in the jungle and all that happens is that an avalanche of rotting leaves falls on your head" (330). As Glissant remarks, "the forest of the maroon was . . . the first obstacle [that] the slave opposed to the *transparency* of the planter. There is no clear path, no *way forward* in this density" (*pas de chemin évident, pas de ligne dans ce touffu*) (*Caribbean Discourse* 83).

The ex-centric historical trajectory signified by the maroons' alleged association with the natural world (often presented as a given in *Kingdom of This World*) is registered only negatively in *Explosion*, framed by the restricted optic of European Others. From the interstices of the novel's central plotline, the maroons' phantasmal and "primitive" (or "pre-historical") lineaments return to foretell a future that projects itself beyond and outside the plot of the European enlightenment's long story.

The incommensurability between two similarly divergent meanings and indeed experiences of history—one linear and archival, the other mnemonic and mythic, is a central and recurrent problem in Édouard Glissant's literary production. In his 1964 novel *Le quatrième siècle,* this opposition is played out in a decades-long debate (centered on disparate conceptions of the past and the nature of historical change) carried out between an old seer, or *quimboiseur,* and his young western-educated interlocutor, Mathieu Béluse.

In his historical play, *Monsieur Toussaint* (1961), it takes the form of a vacillation between two aporetic temporalities, embodied on the one hand by the "rationalist" Toussaint and on the other by the maroons' "raging refusal" (*Fourth Century* 234) (*rage de refus* [*Le quatrième siècle* 231]) of the plantation regime: two "vectors of time [*rayonnements du temps*] . . . like two days following one after the other logically without ever meeting all around the earth" (Glissant, *Monsieur Toussaint* [1981] 96). As Mackandal reminds Toussaint:

> Before they even knew the word revolution, we were already running in the forest. . . . We the maroons . . . We were building our republic! . . . Freedom cannot be taught! It has no date of beginning! Freedom has grown in the forest since the arrival of the first slave ship. . . . The time which carried [Toussaint] forward is different from the one [we] live in . . . [Toussaint] left the free road on the heights and groveled on the [colonial] road [*la (route) coloniale*] . . . he thinks San Domingo belonged to the Republic, not the Republic in San Domingo. (*Monsieur Toussaint* [1981] 36–37, 51, 55)

In his final hour, Toussaint appears to heed the warning the Dead deliver about the imperious univocity of the enlightenment's lexicon of freedom: "Let your history [*histoire*] sleep amidst fire and chaos. . . . Fear the word that *throws light* on [*éclaircit*] what is obscure! In the end you will be left with those words in your hand, like a dead serpent" (41). Yet, as the play closes, Toussaint's ghost is unable to make the final "passage into spirit," to sail from the New World to Africa, and bind his own time with Mackandal's. He is doomed to flit indecisively along a hyphen connecting/severing the time of a contrapuntal fulfillment of the enlightenment's oracle and the "counter-historicity" of the maroons.

Glissant defines this equivocation between the idea of modernity as the fulfillment of the Other's prophecy and the insistent remembrance of a past that is (according to a rationalist conception of history) "not yet historical" as both the peculiar condition of the Antilles and the imperative of Caribbean writing:

> The past, to which we were subjected, which has not yet emerged as history for us, is, however, [harrowingly] present [*nous tourmente*]. The duty of the writer is to explore this [torment,] to ['reveal'] it [in] a continuous fashion in the immediate present. This exploration is therefore related neither to a schematic chronology nor to a nostalgic lament. It leads to the identification of a painful notion of time and its full projection forward into the future, without the help of those plateaus [segments] in time from which the West has benefited, without the help of that collective density that is the primary value of an ancestral cultural heartland. This is what I call *a prophetic vision of the past*. (*Caribbean Discourse* 63–64)

Monsieur Toussaint's treatment of the heterodox and polyphonic narratives of the Haitian revolution discloses exactly such a prophetic vision, as well as the sense that the modernity Toussaint labors so strenuously to reproduce in Haiti is inextricably linked with the horror of slavery. "Nous naissons à la souffrance. C'est notre modernité," Glissant asserts (*Le discours antillais* 409).

In general terms, then, Glissant's project involves tampering with the authority of a linear and hierarchical History and inverting "the relationship between margin and centre as it has appeared within the master discourses of the master race," that is, reconstructing "the primal history of modernity . . . from the slaves' point of view" (Gilroy, *Black Atlantic* 45, 55):

> It is not because . . . African or American peoples have 'entered into History' that one can conclude today that . . . a hierarchical conception of the 'march of History' is no longer relevant. Reality [*les faits*] has, for example, forced Marxist thought to concede that it is not in the most technically advanced countries, nor in the most organized proletariat, that the revolution will *first* [triumph]. (Glissant, *Caribbean Discourse* 63)

From this revised perspective, to lag behind the irresistible course of History with a capital H is at one and the same time to be *ahead* of it, to adumbrate, in praxis, the latter's obsolescence.

In *Explosion in a Cathedral,* the image that most prominently registers this reversal is the preamble's guillotine. Carpentier's description of the "grim apparatus" erected in the bows of a ship sailing west to the island of Guadeloupe recalls Victor Hugo's account of the guillotine's sinister arrival on the scene of his novel about the Vendée rebellion: "a silhouette made of straight and hard lines, looking like a Hebrew letter or one of those Egyptian hieroglyphics that were part of the alphabet of ancient mystery" (*Quatrevingt-treize* 474). For Hugo, "la guillotine, c'était la révolution"; it signifies the "redoubtable straight line" (475, 153), the weighing, measuring and regulation of man that sums up the Convention's stark Utopian ideal.

In *Explosion,* on the other hand, the guillotine outlines the novel's prologue "like a doorway opening onto an immense sky" (*Explosion* 7). "The door-guillotine is the dynamic mediator between formlessness and fixity"; like the painting *Explosion in a Cathedral,* it figures the text itself, "its constitution at an unstable point where past and future are one for an instant" (González Echeverría, *Alejo Carpentier* 253). The door-guillotine thus emblematizes a narrative portal: "the threshold of an epoch of change" (*Explosion* 47), as well as the sequence of figurative doors about to open for Sofía and Esteban. At the same time, it operates as the synecdoche for a kind of totalitarian enlightenment. In this latter sense, it may represent the latest of several circumscribing "futures" that have journeyed westward across the Atlantic since Columbus's landfall in the archipelago.

Thus, when Esteban rebukes Victor for bringing "that" across the Atlantic, citing with mordant irony a medieval Spanish proverb (*la letra con sangre entra* [the word must be worked in with blood]), the future commissar of Guadeloupe replies sententiously:

> That and the printing-press are the most essential things we've got on board.... For the first time a fleet is advancing towards America without bearing crosses aloft. Columbus' ships had them painted on their sails. They were the symbol of the servitude about to be imposed on the men of the New World in the name of a Redeemer.... He turned round suddenly and pointed to the decree [of the Abolition of Slavery]. We, the cross-less, the redeemer-less, the god-less, are going there . . . to abolish privilege and to establish equality. (*Explosion* 125)

Like Hugo's Gauvain, who discerns, beneath the "Hebraic" starkness of the Jacobin Republic's "barbaric scaffolding," a lustral—"Egyptian"—"temple of civilization" taking shape (*Quatrevingt-treize* 466), Hugues posits the revolution's spiritual "work" (*l'oeuvre invisible et sublime* 406) as the repudiation of appraisals of the Convention as a "suicidal vengeance" (Dickens, *Tale of Two Cities* 295) or as "the most horrid, atrocious, and afflicting spectacle that perhaps ever was exhibited to the pity and indignation of mankind" (Burke, *Reflections on the Revolution* 58).

Nonetheless, *Explosion*'s prologue suggests a far more intricate and contradictory relationship between discourse and event than the one reflected in this familiar exchange between Jacobin apologies and Tory indictments of revolutionary terror. For, as I have been arguing, Carpentier, like the other Caribbean writers I have treated in this and previous chapters—and indeed Brazil's *antropofagistas*—ultimately aims at undermining "the concept of a linear and hierarchical History." In contrast to *Kingdom of This World,* which seeks to narrativize the sites and signs of the insurgent slaves' reversals and undoings of this authoritative History, *Explosion in a Cathedral* suspends its diegesis on the brink of the untranscendable chasm between the temporality of the European enlightenment and that of its Antillean Others.

Only beyond and outside the discursive tradition figured by the novel's preambular image, the frame guillotine, in other words, will these contrapuntal histories unfold. Although his reading of this image differs from mine, González Echeverría's keen observation about the guillotine's figural function is apposite here: it "appears as a frame left standing after the demolition of a house, or before its construction" (*Alejo Carpentier*

252). As a closer look at *Explosion*'s epilogue should make clear, whenever it confronts the perplexity and undecidability of such liminal "experiences," Carpentier's narrative invariably folds back into its diegetic frames.

The epilogue reintroduces the narrative point of view that opens the novel. Sofia's elder brother Carlos (one of the original trio of adolescents), who has remained for most of the novel on the margins of the action, travels to French-occupied Madrid in search of his vanished sister and cousin. As a result of his laborious efforts to reconstruct their final days, "a story [*historia*] began to constitute itself out of scraps, full of gaps and unfinished paragraphs, like an ancient chronicle that has been partly restored by re-assembling the scattered fragments" (*Explosion* 343).

It is at the moment that Sofia and Esteban plunge into "the human tide" (*la marejada humana*) (347) rising up "in rebellion against their masters" (348), against Napoleon's invading troops, on May 2, 1808, that the narrative "begins to disappear into thin air" (*se va esfumando*), to borrow Carpentier's own metaphor (*El siglo* 50):

> The entire population of Madrid had poured into the streets, in an impromptu uprising as devastating as it was unexpected, without having been incited by printed propaganda or rhetorical speeches [*artificios de oratoria*]. Eloquence was confined to gestures . . . to universal enthusiasm [*la universalidad del furor*] . . . Sofia left the window: 'Let's go down there!' she cried, snatching down swords and daggers from the collection on the wall. Esteban tried to restrain her: . . . 'Who are you going to fight for?' 'For the people who've run into the streets,' cried Sofia. . . . And Esteban saw her leave the house, impetuous and excited [*enardecida*, "filled with enthusiasm"] . . . with an energy he had never seen before. . . . Arming himself with a shot-gun, he flew downstairs. That was all that was known. . . . No further trace of them or of their final resting place was ever found [*nadie supo más de sus huellas ni del paradero de sus carnes*]. (347–48)

Even in a first reading, the difference between the dissolution of these "two individual existences . . . into a tumultuous and bloody totality" (*un Todo*) (346) and the comparable *convulsión colectiva* (*El siglo* 412) that is the French Revolution seems most readily perceptible in terms of the relationship between discourse and event.

In contrast to the French Revolution, which is repeatedly heralded in the novel by a redoubling of discourses and oracular pronouncements, the May 2nd rebellion erupts spontaneously and without a script. The narrative void into which Sofia and Esteban slide, along with "the entire population of Madrid," is in a sense doubled by the uncanny silence that precedes the uprising itself: the total absence of propaganda and "oratorical artifice," an almost hieratical reduction of rhetoric to gesture.

Although the Madrid insurgency will also ultimately fail, although it will be savagely put down "in a night of slaughter, of grim mass executions, of exterminations," its failure will certainly not be attributable to verbal excess, to "too much fine talk, [to] Better Worlds created by words" (*Explosion* 348, 261). And if Madrid's popular uprising would seem to be the final validation of the novel's epigraph: the words of the French Revolution do not fall into a void—indeed, in Carpentier's gloss, they continue to grow and fructify even after the revolution's "death" under Thermidorian reaction (*El siglo* 53)—this "validation" also paradoxically negates those very discourses.

The historical analogon to this paradox is the indeterminate social and political character of the Spanish "counter-revolution" itself. While it is true that "Spain's war of independence set off the Latin American wars of independence and the birth of the new republics" (González Echeverría, *Alejo Carpentier* 231), where to plot this troubling event along an axis of occidental progress becomes a particularly troubling question.

For instance, the Madrid insurgency eventually gives rise to the peasant movement that introduces "the military tactic which in [the twentieth] century has become completely identified with revolutionary warfare, the guerrilla" (Hobsbawm, *Age of Revolution* 107). Yet, as Hobsbawm observes, this tactic, which was to play such a central role in Latin America's future liberation struggles, was at the turn of the nineteenth century almost always placed at the service of a "militant church-and-king conservatism"; it was a sign of "backwardness," "the almost exclusive preserve of the anti-French side" (107).

From a colonial standpoint, Napoleon's conquest of Iberia temporarily severs Spain's American possessions from the metropolis, thus contributing substantially to the first wave of liberation movements that were to be renewed and carried to successful completion about a decade later under the three liberators. The Creole liberation of Spanish America, which arguably looms on the historical horizon as one of the watershed results of May 2, 1808, would itself have an ambivalent place in such a long story of emancipation. It is both a stage of development and a retrocession.

From the imperial ruler's standpoint, the emergence of the new Latin American republics seems cut from the same cloth as the Haitian insurrection. From the Haitian rebels' point of view, however, it reproduces and reaffirms the ethnocentric restriction of the lexicon of liberation. Creole liberation negates Haiti's promise of a "concrete universalism," the emancipatory desire that Ti Noël expresses at the end of *The Kingdom of This World*.

In short, from its inception and straight through and including its brutal suppression and ambiguous "results," May 2nd remains a disarticulated collective resistance, a mode of purposeless praxis, lacking both the strategic linkages and the process of codification that would enable it to expand into a full-fledged revolution. One would therefore be hard pressed to decipher the Idea it presumably sets out to realize or embody.[2] Only through a superior intellectual effort, a supreme illusion, could one translate this spontaneous uprising into a sign of progress in a philosophy of history. As a political event, May 2nd is on the order of the sublime. And like the sublime, what "determines" it is its indeterminacy, its formlessness, precisely the impetuosity and excitement, the *enthusiasm* that appears to overtake Sofía in her final hour.

"L'enthousiasme est un mode extrême du sublime," Lyotard writes in his seminal reading of Kant's "political critique" (*Le différend* 239). For Kant, enthusiasm constitutes the historical sign that points to the human disposition to progress, "to advance toward the better." Faced with the unbearable and brute immediacy, with the undecidability of revolutionary events (which "may succeed or miscarry ... may be filled with misery and atrocities to the point that a sensible man, were he boldly to hope to execute [them] successfully the second time, would never resolve to make the experiment at such cost"), a distant observer will nevertheless experience an empathetic feeling, Kant writes, "a wishful participation [*eine Teilnehmung dem Wunsche nach*] that borders on enthusiasm" (*On History* 144).

Since the very expression of this sympathy "is fraught with danger," Kant continues, it can therefore "have no other cause than a moral predisposition in the human race" (*On History* 144). Esteban, to follow a character analysis proposed by Carpentier himself (*El siglo de las luces* 48), reveals himself unable, until perhaps his final reluctant plunge into Madrid's insurgent popular tide, to face the sublime feeling aroused by the irreconcilable gap between his preconceived Idea of the revolution and the historical situations that present themselves as the concretization of that Idea. Sofía, on the other hand, embodies a kind of political sublimity: a revolutionary praxis, which, again, according to Carpentier (*El siglo* 50), is incommensurable with her time.

In this specific sense, she does indeed "embody a new force ushered in by the new century" (González Echeverría, *Alejo Carpentier* 230). Her revolutionary enthusiasm constitutes a sign of human progress that in her own epoch can never be experienced, or that can be presented only *negatively.* Sofia, in full concordance with the etymology of her proper name, is herself a figure for an emancipatory future, for a "wisdom" as yet unpresentable and unreachable. But the progress she signifies is no mere iteration of the one Kant presupposes.

One key difference resides in the fact that her participation in the insurrectionist "game," though fraught with mortal danger, is neither "disinterested" nor "universal" (Kant, *On History* 143). Hers is not a "wishful" *Teilnehmung,* but a participation in *the act.* It is praxis in the Marxian sense, one is tempted to add, though in its disarticulation from revolutionary doctrine, in its untheorized spontaneity, it is also fundamentally un-Marxian. For, as Lenin notes, "the 'spontaneous element', in essence, represents nothing more nor less than consciousness in an *embryonic form* . . . the primitive . . . awakening of consciousness. . . . [It is] more in the nature of outbursts of desperation and vengeance than of *struggle*" (*What Is to Be Done?* 31).

A more crucial distinction between the "progress" that Sofia's revolutionary ardor portends and the one predicted by Kant lies in the fact that, albeit primitive and dormant from Lenin's doctrinaire perspective, Sofia's enthusiasm ultimately points beyond Kantian sublimity, possibly to what Lyotard calls "a new type of sublime, more paradoxical still than that of enthusiasm":

> a sublime in which we would feel not only the irremediable gap between the Idea and what presents itself to 'realize' that Idea, but also the gap between the various families of phrases and their respective legitimate presentations . . . the Idea that this purpose consists in the formation and free exploration of Ideas in the *plural.* ("Sign of History" 409)

The inchoate and archaic *crónica* Carlos painstakingly compiles out of scraps and scattered fragments thus surfaces against a single line of "progress," and along with it emerge all the eccentric, phantasmal, and "primitive" histories (of Caribs, maroons, and mutinied slaves . . .) tucked away in the margins of the novel.

Like these narrational "excrescences," Carlos's chronicle overruns the perimeter of "the unified field" of "a History with a capital H." It is an unrealizable reconstruction, whose empty spaces—the narrative counterparts to the gash Esteban tears in the painting's canvas before he is led off to a Ceuta *presidio*—are at once an index of "primitivism" and of futurity. They signal precisely the temporal undecidability that underpins Carpentier's use of titles from Goya's etchings of the Spanish war of independence as epigraphs to several sections of his novel.

This procedure generates an inverted chronological sequence whereby captions referring to a series of incidents from the ruthless quelling of the Madrid uprising by Napoleon's "revolutionary" army are pressed into service as legends for events that, in a few instances, occurred as long as two decades prior to Napoleon's invasion of Iberia. One explanation that readily presents itself for this series of intended anachronisms is the formal one. Such anachronisms suggest "the density of the historical field encompassed by the text," a history that is narrated "from a perspective that is already the future of that history [and thus] integrates the past and the future in a single line" (González Echeverría, *Alejo Carpentier* 236).

Section 11, for example, relating Victor Hugues's arrival in Port-au-Prince at the height of the slave uprising in the Plaine du Nord, carries as its epigraph (¿*Qué alboroto es éste?* [What commotion is this?]). This is the title of an etching depicting a vulpine hussar in the process of confiscating property from a Spanish family whose members are presented in the foreground in anguished postures. Dispossession is the obvious and superficial referential connection between Goya's etching and a section in which Hugues comes upon his burned-out bakery and in the end surrenders himself to an odd "emancipating feeling of possessing nothing, of being left without property, without any furniture, a single contract or a book" (*Explosion* 86–87).

Otherwise the link between sign and referent is at best a strained one, and not just because the quest for a "signified," once transposed to the novel's textual field, must inevitably slide along a chain of signifiers. In the novelistic environment, Goya's question evidently acquires a markedly distinct inflection. Not only does the "original" meaning of *alboroto* (disturbance) need to be extended to include revolt or upheaval, but the theme of dispossession, to say nothing of the problem of property, carries a decidedly different meaning in the Haitian context. This new signification does not arise from a one-to-one correlation between title and image, in this case, but is rather generated by the movement from one signifier to another (between what have now become epigraphs and new "referents" that are themselves but "effects" produced by a set of interlinked signifiers).

The only section with which Goya's epigraph coincides chronologically is the last one: Carlos's fragmented and unfinished reconstruction of Sofía and Esteban's last moments: *Así sucedió* (It happened this way). Nonetheless, the etching that it entitles represents the plundering of a church by French troops—an image that has little direct bearing on the action of the epilogue. In addition, given the inchoateness of Carlos's *historia*, the phrase's epideictic pretension is evidently undone in the text.

It is, of course, a similar irony that defines Carpentier's *El siglo de las luces* as a whole—a narrative belonging to that most aporetic of genres: a *historical* novel. It is as though the gap between the narrative discourse and the "histories" it has sought to present becomes as conspicuous as the patched-up tear on the canvas of *Explosion in a Cathedral*. There is, moreover, a semantic reciprocity between the novel's first and last epigraphs that redoubles the autotelism already mentioned above.

The last epigraph repeats the first with a slight adverbial and tense difference: *Siempre sucede* (It always happens) heads the section in which Victor Hugues is introduced. On the one hand what lies between the *always* of the first and the *already* of the last is the yawning abyss that separates the Idea of the Revolution from that which presents itself as the realization of that Idea. The novel's final allusion to the eponymous painting indicates precisely this impossible suture between Idea and presentation, between discourse and example: "When the last door had closed, the picture of the 'Explosion in a Cathedral,' which had been left behind— perhaps deliberately left behind—ceased to have any subject [effacing itself (*borrándose*), becoming a mere shadow]" (349).

On the other hand, between the epigraphs' two *tenses* opens up a fissure that structures the relationship between the epigraphs and the diegetic material that they purportedly illuminate, between the painting and the Idea of the Revolution. This gulf has its counterpart in the incompatibility between the discourses of the French Revolution and the struggles for liberation that the narrative of History tends to transcribe in minor key. These are the "minor" events that surface recalcitrantly on the margins of *Cathedral*. These heteroclite shards, dispersed like so many etiolated remnants throughout the novel, come back in its edges, in its hollows and its rifts, to disturb the seamless order of the historical trajectory that ostensibly governs the novel's central plot.

Conclusion

IN GENERAL and schematic terms, my main concern throughout this study has been to relocate the emergence of postcoloniality (defined broadly as both "agency" and a specific mode of cultural and discursive resistance to dominant discourses of modernity) in New World avant-garde movements, that is, precisely within those modernisms that have been traditionally designated as peripheral and imitative. My hypothesis is thus essentially an adaptation and expansion of the claims advanced in distinct forms by C. L. R. James, Aimé Césaire, and Oswald de Andrade.[1]

Like Andrade, Césaire, and James, I, too, have argued in the foregoing chapters that Europe's foundational discourses of modernity are enabled and sustained by the very ("native") peoples and cultures that such discourses have consistently relegated to the margins (or indeed excised from) the "experience" of the modern. On the face of it, then, my critical project has amounted to a reversal: an effort to disclose the derivative or "dependent" character of a particular hegemonic (that is, European) model of modernity supposedly—and always imperfectly—"copied" in Brazil and the Caribbean, for example.

While this kind of inversion of margin and center has undeniably framed the structure of my analyses throughout this book, I have concomitantly endeavored to push my critical approach beyond a mere overturning of established hierarchical categories. I have, in other words, pointedly avoided suggesting that the literary and cultural production under study here was postmodern or postcolonial *avant la lettre*.

My proposition that Brazilian and Caribbean avant-gardes "adumbrate" several of the concerns broadly associated with postcoloniality nowadays has therefore not been made in the spirit of compensation for an actual or perceived lack (of development, intellectual sophistication, etc.). Rather, it reflects my abiding conviction that the "great narrative" of development that the west's "magisterial texts" compose in broad outline has been irrevocably transformed after the early twentieth century, when that enduring story begins to be appropriated and resignified "in the name of the Other," and when its plot begins to be interrogated, fragmented, and "adulterated" from the "margins."

In my estimation, then, these "marginal" repetitions of the signs of modernity and modernism affect a fundamental rethinking and reformulation of the modern. Hence, if it is certainly possible, as several of my preceding readings amply demonstrate, to encounter examples of literature and historiography in the Caribbean and Brazil that are predicated on organicist or nativist conceptions of culture as well as on a wholesale acceptance of transcendental categories of subjectivity, it is in the end reductive to ascribe such "monologism" to the whole of Caribbean or Brazilian avant-gardes.

Just as overly simple, I believe, is the suggestion that recent poetic and theoretical production from the Americas constitutes a decisive epistemological rupture with these earlier movements and concerns. I have stressed, in fact, that—far from following a more or less unbroken line from foundationalism, or a belated romantic predilection for origins and plenitude, in the early twentieth century to a "postmodern" (and salutary) recognition of New World cultural "experience" as relational and rhizomorphic— New World theory and poetics from the modernist epoch instead betray subjacent and significant continuities with its "postmodernist" counterparts. The processes of cultural exchange between the metropolis and "the periphery," from their inception, have been characterized by indeterminacy, interruption, and perplexity, in other words.

As I intimate above, one could argue persuasively that the emergence of a universal subject in European philosophical discourses is not only inextricably connected to but in effect conditioned in the last instance by the latter's erasure of the "native." It is this link (or structural "dependency") as well as this "erasure" that, as I have sought to show, both *négritude* and *antropofagia* attempt not only to reveal but, more crucially, to undo. In this specific sense, both movements anticipate the purported postcolonial project to "provincialize the west."

However inchoately and contradictorily, the modernist texts I have examined here succeed in altering our understanding and construction of the modern and in producing what could be termed an incipient "counter-discourse" of modernity. At the same time, the plurivocality and radical perspectivism associated with the oppositional strategies they employ need to be considered as coterminous to a relative extent not just with contemporary "postcolonial" discourses but also with metropolitan ones—whose heteroglossic, open-ended, and at times self-contradictory dimension no study of peripheral modernities can afford to neglect, I would insist.

Nevertheless, one of the regrettable and unintended consequences of the particular nature and scope of my study has been the notable absence of women writers. Although this absence in large measure reflects the fact that the literary movements I have analyzed were almost completely male-dominated, it does at least indicate the extent to which these texts, while tampering with the authority of some of the west's more perdurable narratives, are also firmly inscribed in patriarchal structures of thought that often remain unquestioned and unchallenged.

By the same token, I would emphasize that to make good this "lack" in my project would not necessarily be a simple matter of adding a few representative figures. Not only have female writers "played a vital role [in] the emergence of a [New World] postmodernity," as J. Michael Dash points out (*Other America* 108), but they have brought radical changes to it, changes, moreover, that are at least as complex and crucial as those that the "peripheral" modernisms I analyze above have produced in hegemonic conceptions of the modern. It is in this sense that literature by women ought to be considered. Indeed, this kind of thoroughgoing consideration would constitute a fundamental companion to the present study.

Notes

Introduction

1. I am referring here to Dipesh Chakrabarty's description of an 'oppositional' (and properly *post*-colonial) historiographic project: "the understanding that 'we' all do 'European' history with our different and often non-European archives opens up the possibility of a politics and project of alliance between the dominant metropolitan histories and the subaltern peripheral pasts. Let us call this the project of *provincializing* 'Europe,' the 'Europe' that modern imperialism and (third-world) nationalism have, by their collaborative venture and violence, made universal" ("Postcoloniality" 240–41; my emphasis).

2. As Lyotard himself has noted, this "grand narrative of the decline of grand narratives" dates back at least to Hesiod and Plato "and follows the narrative of emancipation like a shadow" (*Postmodern Explained* 29).

3. I make this argument especially in the third and last chapter of *A Nostalgia of Stone for the Indefinite Sea*.

4. This "desire" is encapsulated in the famous shibboleth from Oswald de Andrade's 1928 "Manifesto Antropófago": "I am only interested in what is not mine" ("Só me interessa o que não é meu").

5. My translation; Paz, *El laberinto de soledad* 244.

1. Lapses in Taste

1. I am obviously referring to Roger Shattuck's popular account of the French avant-garde: *The Banquet Years*.

2. Oswald de Andrade, "Schema ao Tristão de Athayde" 3. These phrases are not Oswald's but Raul Bopp's, from a letter to Jurandyr Manfredini (an "Anthropophagist" from Cuiritiba), which Oswald quotes in its entirety in one of his columns from the *Revista*.

3. "Futurism" was the term commonly used by Brazil's aesthetic "rebels" before the more generic term *modernista* replaced it following the Week of Modern Art.

4. Compare this to Marinetti's rejection of Latin syntax in the "Technical Manifesto of Futurist Literature" (1912): "The Latin sentence that has served us

so far was a pretentious gesture with which a pretentious and myopic intelligence endeavored to tame the multiform and mysterious life of matter. The Latin sentence was therefore stillborn" (my translation; in *Futurisme* 110).

5. "À la fin tu es las de ce monde ancien. . . . Tu en as assez de vivre dans l'antiquité grecque et romaine" (Apollinaire, *Alcools, suivi de le bestiaire* 7).

6. "The persistence of the anciens régimes, and the academicism concomitant with them, provided a critical range of cultural values *against which* the insurgent forms of art could measure themselves but also *in terms of which* they could partly articulate themselves. Without the common adversary of official academicism, the wide range of new aesthetic practices have little or no unity: their tension with established or consecrated canons is constitutive of their definition as such" ("Modernity and Revolution" 325).

7. "That idol, black eyes and yellow mop of hair, without [parents] or court . . . his domain, insolent azure and green, runs along beaches," etc. (Rimbaud, *Oeuvres Complètes* 457 [Cette idole, yeux noirs et crin jaune, sans parents ni cour . . . son domaine, azur et verdure insolents, court sur des plages].

8. Mennotti del Picchia was the cofounder, with Cassiano Ricardo and Plínio Salgado, of the 1926 *Verde Amarelo* (Green and Yellow, i.e., the colors of Brazil's national flag) movement.

9. Menotti del Picchia, *República dos Estados Unidos do Brasil* 119. This stanza seems to gloss Marlow's [or Conrad's] famous childhood recollection: "when I was a little chap I had a passion for maps. I would look for hours at South America, or Africa, or Australia, and lose myself in the glories of exploration. At that time there were many blank spaces on the earth, and when I saw one that looked particularly inviting on a map (but they all looked that) I would put my finger on it and say, When I grow up I will go there" (Conrad, *Heart of Darkness* 22). In "Geography and Some Explorers," Conrad recounts a similar episode as an autobiographic reminiscence: "One day, putting my finger on a spot in the very middle of the then white heart of Africa, I declared that some day I would go there" (Conrad, *Last Essays* 16). In the same essay, he describes how his boyish homage to the European explorers of East Africa's Great Lakes: "It consisted in entering laboriously in pencil the outline of [Lake] Tanganyika on my beloved old atlas, which, having been published in 1852, knew nothing, of course, of the Great Lakes. The heart of its Africa was white and big. . . . Thus I would imagine myself stepping in the very footprints of geographical discovery" (14).

10. The sentiment expressed here echoes Marinetti's celebration of technology in the "Futurism Manifesto": "we will sing of the nightly fervor of arsenals and shipyards blazing with violent electric moons; greedy railway stations that devour smoke-plumed serpents; factories hung on clouds by the crooked lines of their smoke; bridges that stride rivers like giant gymnasts, flashing in the sun with a glitter of knives" (in *Futurisme* 87). In *La raza cósmica,* José Vasconcelos describes with similar enthusiasm the industrial potential of Brazil: "the industrial flowering of São Paulo, and the industry of contemporary Brazil as a whole, are nothing

more than the beginning of a manufacturing power greater than any that history has ever seen. . . . What England did on a small scale, Brazil will do on a grand scale. And since Brazil is not an island but a continental culture, it will encompass the planet more effectively and will lay the foundation for an empire greater than any that has ever existed" (*La raza cósmica* 79; my translation).

11. Salgado, "O Significado da Anta" 288. The resonance with Marinetti's first Manifesto is unmistakable: "Let them come therefore, the good arsonists with charred fingers! . . . Here they are! Here they are! . . . Go on, set fire to the library shelves! Divert the course of canals and flood the museum vaults!" (Marinetti, "Fondation et manifeste du futurisme" 88).

12. *Nhengaçú* is a Tupi word meaning literally "long talk" or "speech."

13. If one accepts José de Alencar's derivation of "Tapuia," this sense of flight is contained in the etymology of the word itself. According to the nineteenth-century novelist, "Tapuia" is a compound term signifying "enemy or barbarian." Its specific meaning is "those who fled the village," from the combination of *taba* ("village") and *puyr* ("to flee") (Alencar, *Iracema* 57n).

14. The term *bandeirante* is derived from *bandeira* (literally "flag"), the name given to the expeditions. The principles according to which these explorations were organized harked back to the late medieval and sixteenth-century *bandeira*, an army group of 250 men with an insignia of its own (also called *bandeira*). The double meaning of *bandeira* obviously comes into play in the choice of *verde-amarelo* (the colors of the national flag) as the movement's name.

15. In an April 1920 chronicle for *Correio Paulistano*, Paulo Menotti del Picchia provides an early and stark formulation of this thesis: "Nothing appreciable has been bequeathed to us by the race vanquished by the invasion of cosmopolitanism, absent a few high-sounding names of snakes, rivers and cities. . . . Not much, as we can see" (*O Gedeão do modernismo* 103). Less than a year later, in a column entitled "Matemos Peri!" (Let us kill Peri!), Menotti reiterates the point, calling for the "death" of the protagonist of José de Alencar's Romantic classic *The Guarani*, a hero "borrowed from Chateaubrîand, and therefore a genuine Frenchman" (*O Gedeão* 194): "I never believed in the real existence of the Indians. . . . The only notice I have of them, from ethnographic treatises and museum documents, makes me think of them as vague legends of primates, Anthropopithecine, megatherians, and other crepuscular things. . . . Peri was a naked and tawny stain upon our national dignity" (194). "Peri symbolizes the superstition of the past; he is the centenarian voice of vigilant misoneism, bleaching the fiber of our daring revelatory of new horizons and new conquests. . . . Let us give to Brazil . . . its appearance of a modern, pioneering people, of creators and thinkers, free and original, a chrysalis emerging from its cocoon for the great flight into space and light. For that reason, the *surge et ambula* of the new miracle is summed up in this symbolic and prophetic formula: Let us kill Peri!" (196–97).

16. In an early chronicle, Menotti del Picchia makes this historical continuity explicit: "We are the continuation of that overflowing life which the caravels of

Columbus and Cabral brought to the American soil" (*O Gedeão do modernismo* 104).

17. O. de Andrade, *Pau Brasil* 83. I must express my gratitude to the anonymous evaluator of this book for her or his suggestions regarding the most appropriate translation of Mário's ironic phrase.

18. O. de Andrade, *Do 'Pau-Brasil'* 14. Oswald's "Manifesto Antropófago" has been translated into English by Leslie Bary ("Oswald de Andrade's 'Cannibalist Manifesto'"). I have elected not to use the terms "cannibal" and "cannibalism" as translations of *antropófago* and *antropofagia,* first because of the former's derivation from *Carib,* as well as the colonialist myths and misprisions that have, since Columbus's coinage, defined it. (For an excellent discussion of the origin and uses of the word *cannibal,* see Hulme, *Colonial Encounters* 13–43.) Second, I have sought to maintain the "ethnographic" specificity of the Anthropophagists' effort to recuperate the metaphysics of the Tupis' ritual practice of anthropophagy. This specificity is lost, I believe, in the ideologically charged (and referentially empty) signifier "cannibal." Although I have consulted Bary's translation, unless otherwise indicated, all translations from the Portuguese are my own.

19. In the initial stages of his militancy in the Communist Party of Brazil (PCB), which he joined in 1931, Oswald renounced his Anthropophagist period. After his rupture with the party in 1945, and indeed during the years immediately preceding it, he returned to Anthropophagy—now converted and expanded into a full-blown philosophical conception of the world—in what Benedito Nunes calls a process of philosophical conversion and critical opposition to Marxist theses (O. de Andrade, *Do 'Pau-Brasil'* xvi–xvii).

20. I do not consider it germane to the argument I am developing here to go into a detailed discussion of the influence that different philosophies and schools of thought (which include, but are not limited to, Kierkegaard, Proudhon, Bachofen, Spengler, Max Weber, and Ortega y Gasset) exerted on Oswald's theory of Anthrophagy—a task that Benedito Nunes performs magisterially.

21. "We want the *Caraíba* Revolution. Greater than the French Revolution. The unification of every effective revolt *oriented towards man.* . . . The golden age announced by America" (O. de Andrade, *Do 'Pau-Brasil'* 14; my emphasis).

22. This rejection of 'idealism' may be a reaction against Marinetti's famous eulogy of the hygienics of war and of "beautiful Ideas that kill" in the first Futurist Manifesto: "Nous voulons glorifier la guerre—seule hygiène du monde—le militarisme, le patriotisme, le geste destructeur des anarchistes, *les belles Idées qui tuent,* et le mépris de la femme" (Marinetti, *Futurisme* 87; my emphasis).

23. I.e., Brazil, or "the land of palm trees" (from the combination of the Tupi-Guarani word for palm tree [Pindob] and *rama* [land or region]).

24. For James, as for Hegel, the "abstract universal is "man—in his simple quality of man—[whose] infinite value abolishes, *ipso facto,* all particularity attaching to birth or country" (*C. L. R. James Reader* 163).

25. "The power of the spirit to appropriate what is foreign to it is revealed in

a strong inclination to assimilate the new to the old . . . according to the degree of its power to appropriate, its 'digestive power' ['Verdauungskraft'], to speak in a metaphor—and indeed 'the spirit' is more like a stomach than anything else" (Nietzsche, *Beyond Good and Evil* 160–61).

26. This (self-)insertion of conquerors and travelers into the pantheon of savage deities is, of course, a common *topos*. Anthony Pagden surmises that such 'primitive' reactions "may be attributed not so much to fear of Spanish and Portuguese technology—by which neither the Indians nor the Africans seem to have been unduly impressed—but to the mere fact that the Europeans were outsiders, strangers—and very strange strangers at that" (*Fall of Natural Man* 17).

27. Léry, glossing a passage in which Francisco López de Gómara describes the wonderment of the natives of Hispaniola at the Spaniards' ability to communicate "in silence," that is, through writing (*Historia general de las Indias* ch. 34), reports that the Tupinambá among whom he lived regard his reading his notes back to them as a sorcery and a marvel (Léry, *Histoire d'un voyage* 231–32). Thevet's interpreter deceptively informs his Tupi hosts that the books in the abbot's possession were a gift from the moon and the stars, and that the Frenchman was therefore a friend of *Tupã*, the Tupi "god of thunder" (19). Staden's captors refer to a tome he carries (presumably the Bible) as a sheaf of "thunder hides" [*Donnerhäute*] that endow him with sacred powers and the skill to summon up windstorms.

28. "We must listen to naked man" (O. de Andrade, *Estética e política* 285); "we can only attend to the orecular world . . . The World undated. Uninitialed. . . . Down with the truths of missionary peoples. . . . Down with the clothed and oppressive reality recorded by Freud" (O. de Andrade, *Do 'Pau-Brasil'* 15, 16, 17, 19). The word *roteiro* (itinerary) is repeated seven times in a single *a linea* of the "Manifesto antropófago" (15). *Roteiro* (sailing chart) was also one of the most common genres among early-sixteenth-century Portuguese writings on the New World.

29. "We are a dessert country" probably occurs for the first time in a manifesto entitled "Ordem e Progresso" (Order and Progress, the national motto inscribed in Brazil's flag), published in *O homem do povo* (The Man of the People), the Communist periodical edited by Oswald and Patrícia Galvão: "Here [in Brazil] foreign capital has strangely distorted the economy. It turned a country which possesses the greatest iron reserves and the highest hydraulic potential into a dessert country. Coffee, sugar, tobacco and bananas" (in Schwartz, *Vanguardas* 254).

30. O. de Andrade, *Dentes de dragão* 124. For Oswald, Brazil's process of industrialization also constitutes an imposition: "getting Ford-ed" [*forder-se*], as he punningly puts it (*Dicionário de Bolso* 90). The pun, reminiscent of Ubu's "scandalous" opening exclamation ("Merdre"), is untranslatable. It hinges on the close similarity between the verb Oswald "derives" from the proper noun Ford [*forder*] and the verb *foder* (to fuck). The phrase appears in a posthumously published "pocket dictionary" of aphoristic definitions of major intellectual figures. The entry for Ford reads, in its entirety, "Creator and experimenter of the neologism 'forder-se' ['to get Ford-ed'], which means 'to get it in the head or in any other

place due either to excess or lack of initiative. We, for example, are 'Ford-ed' [estamos "fordidos"]" (90).

31. Mário de Andrade, for example, alludes to Modernismo's close ties with São Paulo's "traditional [coffee] aristocracy," the sponsors of a "salon movement" that generated the "greatest intellectual orgy that the country's artistic history has ever registered" ("O movimento modernista" 236, 238). Toward the end of his Marxist phase, Oswald refers similarly to the movement's "fertilizing material causes drawn from industrialized São Paulo" and to "its class compromises with the bourgeois golden period of the first rise in coffee prices" (*Ponta de Lança* 95). Raul Bopp also links *modernismo* with "a small cultured élite . . . a rural semi-nobility [that] blossomed with the support of coffee" (*Movimentos modernistas* 16). On the other hand, another *modernista*, Cassiano Ricardo, in a 1972 retrospective of the movement, makes a clear distinction between the so-called populism of his own brand of nationalist modernism, between *verde-amarelismo*'s "contact with the street and the people," and the high-society allegiances of the "salonists" (*Invenção de Orfeu* 5). Oswald makes an analogous claim for Anthropophagy: "we abandoned the salons and became the tramps [*os vira-latas*] of modernism" (*Ponta de Lança* 97). The question Roberto Schwarz raises becomes cogent in this respect: "How can one not notice that the subject of Anthropophagy —which is, in this sense, similar to that of nationalism—is the Brazilian in general, with no class specification?" (*Misplaced Ideas* 9). We have, in fact, already come across this erasure of class specificity in Oswald's conflation of settlers and slaves (*Estética e política* 283) in a fragment quoted above. Schwarz makes the same critique of "the third world aesthetic" that seems especially to inform Oswald's "A Crise da Filosofia messiânica": "the Third World mystique covers up class conflicts and gives a naive, though violent view of conflicts between nations, and above all of their interdependence" (*Misplaced Ideas* 174).

32. The coincidence between the Anthropophagist return to the textual legacy of the conquest and its turn away from the civilization brought in the caravels, the simultaneity of its defense of "natural man" and its acclamation of the Baroque as the "Utopian style" (O. de Andrade, *Do 'Pau-Brasil'* 223, 227), would appear to support Anderson's claim. In a reassessment of Anthropophagy, Haroldo de Campos also contends somewhat contradictorily that the Baroque "deconstructs the logocentrism we inherited from the West. . . . It is an anti-tradition which passes through the gaps of traditional historiography, which filters through its breaks, which edges through its fissures [based] on the recognition of certain marginal paths or patterns alongside the preferred course of normative historiography" ("Rule of Anthropophagy" 49–50).

2. In the Land of the Great Serpent

1. In a well-known letter to Alceu de Amoroso Lima (May 1928), written as the galleys of *Macunaíma* were being set, Mário de Andrade claims to "regret" the unhappy coincidence between the publication of his text and the appearance

of "Osvaldo's [sic] manifesto" and to deplore the fact that, although written in six days in December 1926 and "corrected and amended in January of 1927," the book will still "appear entirely anthrophagic" (M. de Andrade, *Macunaíma* 400).

2. Raul Bopp incorporates elements of this legend into one of his short poems ("Princípio"). The same legend lends the plot structure to Cassiano Ricardo's *Martim Cererê* (1928), another *modernista* epic, and is included as one of the episodes of Mário de Andrade's *Macunaíma*.

3. The custom of acquiring the names of enemies is recorded in the earliest European accounts of Brazil. Staden reports that a Tupi warrior will receive "so viele Namen als er Feinde getötet hat" (*Zwei Reisen* 129) (as many names as the number of enemies he has killed), and Thevet concurs: "tout autant d'ennemis que chacun d'eux a occis en bataille tout autant de noms peult-il porter, et tant plus le nombre en est grand, ils en sont plus louez et reverez de leurs compaignons, comme ayans vengé la mort de plusieurs de leurs parens, que les ennemis avoient massacrez et mangez avant" (*Les français en Amérique* 54) (as many enemies as each one of them has slain in battle so many names can he bear, and the greater the number, the more they are praised and revered for it by their companions for having thus revenged the death of several of their relatives, whom the enemy had killed and eaten before).

4. Both González Echevarría and Doris Sommer attempt, in different ways, to undo this allegorical interpretation, the former by reclaiming what he terms the modernity of the novel, that is, the extent to which it "invalidates the message contained on the doctrinal level and offers a critical view of literature itself" (*Voice of the Masters* 56), the latter by exposing the limitations or aporetic suspensions of the narrative of patriarchal legitimation (*Foundational Fictions* 287–89). In my brief references to Gallegos's novels, on the other hand, I seek only to illustrate the proliferation of the "ideologeme" of development or civilization in the literature of the period.

5. It is difficult not to see in this line an echo of Oswald's call for a "synthesis" between "the forest and the school" in the "Manifesto Pau Brasil": "We have a dual and ever present foundation—the forest and the school. The credulous and dualist race and geometry, we fed on algebra and chemistry right after the nursing bottle and anise tea. A mixture of 'rock-a-by-baby' [dorme nenê que o bicho vem pegá] and algebraic equations" (*Do 'Pau-Brasil'* 9).

6. *Serpente* was the name of a vessel built in Rio de Janeiro that participated in the combined Spanish-Portuguese campaign against the Guarani Indians known as the Guaraní War (1753–56). It is described in an eighteenth-century Portuguese epic of the war as "the painted Serpent, work and labor of the new world" (Gama, *O Uruguay* 44).

7. Alencar's protagonist translates his name for Iracema as "warrior's son." As the author explains in a note, he derives this meaning from the name's Latin origin and its provenance from Mars (*Marte* in Portuguese) (Alencar, *Iracema* 19n).

8. Oswald de Andrade, for example, brands it "a grotesque caricature of a *chanson de geste*" (*Estética e política* 244). For Menotti del Picchia, Rita Durão's poem exemplifies an "Arcadian academicism" (*O Gedeão do modernismo* 196). In a poem dedicated to Raul Bopp and Oswald de Andrade, a contributor to the *Revista de Antropofagia* derides it for its inauthentic representation of Brazil's *sertão* (Lima, "Santa Rita Durão" 6).

9. The poem's protagonist has a historical counterpart whose Christian name was Diogo Álvares. He was reportedly involved in several polygamous relationships with Amerindian women, having left a copious miscegenated progeny (Pereira, *Fontes do Caramuru* 11–12). A 1532 "Diary" of a Portuguese voyage of exploration along the Brazilian coast records that the expedition's commanders received valuable information about the contested province's interior from "a Portuguese man," presumably Álvares, "who had lived for twenty two years" among the savages, and whom the fleet met in present-day Bahia de Todos os Santos on March 13, 1531 (Lopes de Sousa, *Diário da navegação* 47). Not surprisingly, Durão's Caramurú is strictly and exemplarily monogamous.

10. Belém is also the district of Lisbon, on the right bank of the Tagus (the present site of the Baroque Tower of Belém), from which Africa- and Indies-bound vessels departed throughout the fifteenth and sixteenth centuries.

11. In this also he echoes Vasconcelos: "The world of the future will belong to whoever conquers the Amazonian region.... It is therefore crucial that the Amazon remain Brazilian.... With all the resources of such a region ... the synthesis race will be able to consolidate itself culturally. Close to the great river, Universopolis will rise up, and from there the crusades will depart, the fleets and airplane squadrons which will spread the good news." (Vasconcelos, *La raza cósmica* 32).

12. Referring to the "interminable wanderings of the ancient *paulistas*," or São Paulo–based *bandeirantes,* Saint-Hilaire declares, in a phrase that Ellis uses as the epigraph for his *Raça de gigantes*: "On est saisi d'une sorte de stupéfaction, on serait tenté de croire que ces hommes appartenaient à *une race de géants*" (my emphasis; Saint-Hilaire, *Viagem à província de São Paulo* 27). For Oswald de Andrade, to call the *bandeirantes* a "race of giants" is to lapse into one of "the high-sounding bits of nonsense upon which inept teachers and feeble writers thrive" (*Do 'Pau-Brasil'* 178). The historical legacy of the *bandeiras,* he continues, is arguable. Their territorial gains notwithstanding, they "also carried out one of the greatest destructive campaigns in American history" (178).

13. In his memoirs, Menotti, who describes Brecheret as completely lacking in a humanistic education and thoroughly ignorant of "our history" (*A longa viagem* 118), claims to have suggested the theme of the monument to the young sculptor: "I described for the artist ... those deeds which surpassed Jason's circumnavigation and provided the Fatherland with an epic unequaled by the Homeric poems. We need not engender myths to give to [the account of] our national dawn ... heroes [who were] more awe-inspiring than the imaginary Greek heroes. ... I believe it was my rather Latin, emphatic eloquence, punctuated with gestures

illustrating the daring of the heroes' incursions into the back lands' thickets that gave Brecheret the inspiration for that violent ascending line which makes up the architectural greatness of the monument" (119).

14. The line is a direct quote from the one of the most famous and quoted lines from the first decade of Camões's epic poem, *Os Lusíadas*.

15. "Está formada esta prouíncia à maneira de hua harpa" (Magalhães de Gândavo, *Historia da prouíncia* 8) (This province is shaped in the likeness of a harp).

16. This list of racial labels provides an indication of Brazil's complex racial hierarchy. A *cafuzo* is the offspring of an African and an Amerindian; *caboclo* generally applies to a (white and Amerindian) "half-breed," but could also refer to any mixed race person ("mulatto") with straight hair; a *bujamé* is the child of the union between a mixed race (white and African) man and an African woman.

17. "My heroes are not the winners of battles who opened new chapters in History: Julius Caesar, Hannibal, Napoleon, etc. but rather men who confronted unknown worlds, such as our own *bandeirantes*" ('Bopp passado a limpo' 36n).

18. "The history of Penetration" (O. de Andrade, *Do 'Pau-Brasil'* 14) or "geographic extension" (Bopp, *Movimentos modernistas* 82).

19. Since *Jacy* literally means "our mother," it could also refer to the Motherland, to "the innocent spirit of the infant land . . . throwing a bit of illusion" into the hearts of the urban crowd amongst whom the poet respectfully removes his hat, paying homage to the beloved "star-sign" [*letreiro de estrêlas*] (Ricardo, *Poesias completas* 202).

20. *Marco Zero* is also the title of perhaps the best known of Oswald's social realist novels.

21. "Café-Expresso" is the second poem in the penultimate section of Ricardo's epic—the last section being the *envoi*. The sequence of poems in this "urban" section is as follows: "The Skyscraper Poem," "Café-Expresso," "The Hour of the Future," "The Immigrant's Daughter," "Girl Drinking Coffee," and "Geographic Song." The title of this section alludes to the cities and coffee plantations as "the living traces" left by the *bandeirantes*, whose deeds of geographic exploration the previous section commemorates.

22. In the fourth poem of *Martim*'s penultimate (or urban) section ("The Immigrant's Daughter"), a second substitution takes place, as "the blond daughter of the immigrant" now becomes the object of the poet's desire.

23. González Echevarría, qtd. in Carpentier, *Los pasos perdidos* 46.

24. "On one scaly trunk, a trunk of ochre streaked with pale green, there would become visible, when the waters settled, the Sign carved on its bark with the point of a knife some three spans above the level of the waters" (Carpentier, *Lost Steps* 278). I should add that I find J. Michael Dash's assertion that "the V suggests the French *vie*, which indicates the ecstatic discovery of life in its natural form as well as the rebirth of the composer's creative energies" (*Other America* 84–85) intriguing, but ultimately unconvincing.

3. God in the Machine

1. Unless otherwise indicated, all citations of the novel are from the 1988 edition.

2. The "traditional" character of this transformation of heroes into stars is mentioned by Mário in a 1927 letter to the poet Manuel Bandeira (*Macunaíma* [1988] 397). It is a motif that André Thevet, for example, describes in some detail in his Cosmographie universelle (*Les français en Amérique* 57–58).

3. This probable satirical reference to the Herculean progenitors of the 'race of giants' will be discussed below.

4. The bull named Espácio (*boi-Espácio*) is sung in a very old popular romance from Brazil's Northeast. The name also resonates appropriately with the word *espaço* (space).

5. Macunaíma is as "black as pitch" (*preto retinto*), a son of the "Tapanhuma" tribe (a Tupi term meaning "dark-skinned," which was extended, in the sixteenth century, to designate fugitive slaves); he is born "in the [dark] depths of the virgin forest" in the midst of an immense silence and descends from "the Fear of the Night" (5) (No fundo do mato virgem nasceu Macunaíma, herói de nossa gente. Era preto retinto e filho do medo da noite).

6. Although it would be well beyond the scope of my analysis in this chapter, it would nevertheless be of great interest—especially in light of the discussion of Modernismo's politics of "racial" and national identity—to juxtapose the radical alteration of Macunaíma's ethnicity with the process that Sergio Miceli defines as the "Brazilian [cultural] elite's" "negotiation" of its public (that is, plastic and photographic) images. Thus, for example, Mário de Andrade—who, according to Miceli, had by his own admission been largely unsuccessful in 'negotiating' the inclusion of certain personal traits (or "qualities") that he wished to be brought out in Lasar Segall's famous 1927 portrait of the writer—finds in the portrait executed in 1935 by the "official painter" Portinari, whose friendship he had assiduously cultivated during the four years prior to the painting's execution, "the visual response to [his] expectations . . . in the matter of plastic representation" (Miceli, *Imagens negociadas* 83). In contrast, Segall, "as a good complicated Russian and a good mystical Jew," had, in Mário's own words, captured "what was perverse in [him], what was unattractively sensual" (*feiamente sensual*) (90). Miceli adduces that Segall's portrait produces a kind of "disclosure of all the traits that belied Mário's "worldly and sexual [or homosexual] inclinations which he did not feel ready or able to acknowledge publicly" (90).

7. According to Koch-Grünberg, Macunaíma is derived from a combination of the word "Máku" = evil and the augmentative suffix "ima" = very or great (qtd. in M. de Andrade, *Macunaíma* (1978) 333). Nevertheless, in nineteenth-century Amerindian translations of the Bible, and as a result of an 1868 (mis)translation of the name by an English missionary as "invisible Being, all goodness and greatness" (333), Macunaíma became the very name of God—a

common enough mistake, as the first European missionaries' use of the term *Tupã* (thunder) to designate the Christian god indicates. The actual meaning of the name is probably "great liar."

8. Or *uiara:* the enchantress of Tupi mythology and the likely Amerindian source of the *mãe-d'água* figure.

9. That is, in Heidegger's terms, "ordered to stand by, to be immediately at hand, indeed to stand there just so that [they] may be on call for a further ordering," (*Question Concerning Technology* 17).

10. In this respect, I would disagree with Jean Franco's proposition that the novel contains "a vision of an integrated and modern Brazil whose distinctive form of civilization and culture would not be a mere regional folk-culture" (*Modern Culture* 98).

11. The largest and most famous of these was the *quilombo* of Palmares in the then captaincy of Alagoas, a 20,000-strong "Negro State" destroyed in 1694 by a *bandeirante* expedition under the leadership of Domingos Jorge Velho.

4. Cannibal Allegories

1. As the director explains in a 1995 interview, government support for independent Brazilian films was generated by a tax on profits of companies that distributed foreign films in Brazil (Sadlier, *Nelson Pereira dos Santos* 131).

2. These conflicting versions of the same mutiny actually figure at the center of a polemic between Léry and Thevet. Léry, who repeatedly questions the accuracy and "good faith" of Thevet's account of the Fort Coligny episode, spends most of the rather long preface to the second edition of his *Histoire* trying to disprove the cosmographer's version of events. As Darlene Sadlier reminds us in her recent study of Pereira dos Santos, this ironic opening sequence includes a number of visual and auditory clues that reinforce its newsreel idiom. The off-screen voice, for example, was an actual newsreel announcer. The Mozart French horn concerto playing in the background was likewise the popular soundtrack for the short newsreel "Atualidades francesas" (French current events) shown in Brazilian movie theaters in the 1960s (Sadlier, *Nelson Pereira dos Santos* 61–62). Sadlier's assertion that the scene (and, indeed, the film as a whole) "suggests that the historical archive is as riven by conflict as contemporary politics, and it makes clear that the country's past and present-day realities are not distinct" (59) resonates with my own reading.

3. It is perhaps relevant in this context that the film that is said to have launched the Cinema Novo movement in 1963, *Os cafajestes* (The Hustlers) by Ruy Guerra, counts among its most "scandalous" innovations the first representation of full frontal nudity in Brazilian cinema. Guerra's film was consequently banned ten days after its screening. The police commissioner who issued the decree branded the film as "immoral, filthy, and repugnant," as well as an apology of rape, kidnapping, licentiousness, the use of narcotics, and other crimes against Christian morals and behavior (Johnson, *Cinema Novo x 5* 94).

4. Jodelle, *Oeuvres complètes* 1: 124. Since the historical events upon which the film is based take place around 1557, this represents undoubtedly an intentional anachronism.

5. The texts cited include the royal cosmographer André Thevet's *Cosmographie universelle* (1575), his Huguenot rival Jean de Léry's *Histoire d'un voyage faict en Brésil* (1578), Hans Staden's narrative, the letters of the Jesuit missionaries José de Anchieta and António Nóbrega (two of Brazil's mythic founding fathers), the *História* of Brazil (1576) by Magalhães Gândavo, a 1587 treatise by the plantation owner Gabriel Soares de Sousa, and, finally, a 1560 letter to the Portuguese king by Mem de Sá, the third governor of Brazil.

6. Private conversation with the author.

5. The Shadow Cast by the Enlightenment

In the second epigraph Carlyle refers to Quashee (feminine: Quasheba), which, like Sambo, was a stereotypical name for Africans that "derived from the Twi day-name for Sunday and hence [was] given to boys born on Sunday. . . . Carlyle may also be punning on quashee, meaning squash, pumpkin" (Carlyle, *Nigger Question,* 12n). Carlyle's derisive term "pumpkin" for the watermelons, cantaloupes, or any tropical fruit resembling a pumpkin, such as breadfruit, mango, or papaya, in which blacks allegedly kept "their beautiful muzzles [buried] up to the ears . . . imbibing sweet pulps and juices" (4).

1. The thesis that James and Césaire adumbrate here, that in several respects industrial development in Europe depended on colonial processes, has been perhaps too narrowly associated with the so-called Caribbean school of history. In recent years, however, it has seen some significant reformulations in western historiography. Fernand Braudel remarks, for example, that "in Brazil, and in the islands of the tropical belt of Spanish America" the sugar mills "were in fact manufactories, concentrations of labour, of hydraulic or animal power" (*Wheels of Commerce* 302). J. M. Blaut, on the other hand, extending James's proposition regarding the slave regime in Santo Domingo, argues that Europeans "found it possible to advance the capitalist industrial production system—large-scale, organized, semi-mechanized—to its highest level, for that era, *mainly* in the plantation system, using slave labor" (*Colonizer's Model* 204; emphasis in the original).

2. "An especially interesting variety of hybrid cultural work" produced by anti-imperialist writers from the peripheries who have immigrated to the metropolis (*Culture and Imperialism* 244).

3. According to James, from the perspective of the San Domingo slaves, "the white slaves in France had risen, and killed their masters, and were now enjoying the fruits of the earth. It was gravely inaccurate in fact, but they had caught the spirit of the thing" (*Black Jacobins* 81).

4. This drama was originally called *Toussaint L'Ouverture* but was subsequently revised under the title of *Black Jacobins*.

5. I am quoting out of context James's characterization of the Ghanaian struggle for political independence.

6. After participating, along with Frantz Fanon, in Césaire's successful election campaign of 1945, Glissant was to move away from the politics and poetics of Négritude. Not only would he elaborate an idea of identity based on the space and history of the Caribbean rather than race, but in direct contrast to Césaire's political collaboration with the French metropolis, he was to militate (with Guadeloupe's Paul Niger) for the independence of France's Overseas Departments of Martinique, Guadeloupe, and Guyane. It is not my intent to gloss over these crucial political differences, even though a detailed account of these differences would be well outside the purview of this chapter. As I point out above, here I wish merely to outline in broad strokes the features that their "counter-histories" have in common.

7. The slaves "had heard of the revolutions and had construed it in their own image: the white slaves in France had risen, and killed their masters, and were now enjoying the fruits of the earth. It was gravely inaccurate in fact, but they had caught the spirit of the thing" (James, *Black Jacobins* 81).

8. As Hegel writes in *Philosophy of Mind*, "It must be said that America has a younger appearance than the Old World and in its historical development is inferior to the latter" (41).

9. *Discourse on Colonialism* 14. Césaire's denouncement of colonialism as *la négation pure et simple de la civilisation*, as "the machine for crushing, for grinding, for degrading peoples" (60), as well as Fanon's insistence that "colonialism is not a thinking machine, nor a body endowed with reason, [but] violence in its state of nature" (*Les damnés* 47) should be read in the same vein.

10. I am thinking rather specifically of Hegel's "banal and apologetic" exclusion of Africa from History.

11. As James himself reminds us, Césaire's seminal text was published in Paris a year before *Black Jacobins* appeared in London (*Black Jacobins* 402). In the years since the inaugural enunciation of the term *négritude* in this very text, a notable polemic has developed around this contentious and multivalent term. Since this is not yet the time to pursue this debate, I borrow, as a convenient starting point, Benita Parry's elegant and succinct definition: "Négritude is not a recovery of a pre-existent state, but a textually invented history, an identity effected through figurative operations, and a tropological construction of blackness as a sign of the colonised condition and its refusal" (Parry, "Resistance Theory/Theorising Resistance" 93–94).

12. Fort-de-Joux is the prison situated in the Jura range where Toussaint died on April 7, 1803, just as "his comrades in arms, ignorant of his fate, were drafting the declaration of Independence" (James, *Black Jacobins* 365).

13. Here is how the verse reads in the original French: "Une petite cellule, la neige la double de barreaux blancs" (Césaire, *Collected Poetry* 46). In keeping with

the sequence of my analysis, I have chosen to translate *doubler* literally as "double" as opposed to adopting the translator's rendition of the same verb as "to line."

14. "Overture" is, of course, the literal meaning of Toussaint's assumed last name. According to James, the name originates from an exclamation by a French commissioner of San Domingo at the news of yet another victory by the black general: "This man makes an opening everywhere." James further speculates that the slaves may have called him L'Ouverture from the gap in his teeth (*Black Jacobins* 126n). Whatever the origins of this nom de guerre, both James and Césaire interpret the transformation of Toussaint Bréda (the surname taken from the plantation where he was a slave) into Toussaint Louverture as a crucial moment in the general's revolutionary career (*Black Jacobins* 126; Césaire, *Toussaint Louverture* 189). The "written proof" of this radical change is Toussaint's famous call to arms of August 29, 1793 (cited by the two writers): "Frères et amis, Je suis Toussaint Louverture, mon nom c'est peut-être fait connaître jusqu'à vous. J'ai entrepris la vengeance. Je veux que la liberté et égalité règnent à Saint-Domingue. Je travaille à les faire exister. Unissez-vous à nous" (*Toussaint Louverture* 191; James, *Black Jacobins* 125).

15. Here, again, by affirming the *collective* nature of this poetic voice, I am proposing a reading that diverges considerably from that of Dash, who alludes to "Césaire's demiurgic poet [who] holds the key to knowledge," and believes that the Martinican poet projects an "idea of the author as the fountainhead of truth . . . [and] an authoritative self presiding over a totalized vision" (*Other America* 80, 73).

16. *Chair du monde,* it will be recalled, was exactly Edouard Glissant's metaphor for the colonized Other.

17. In this regard, too, I must own up to my complicity in producing what J. Michael Dash has designated "a sanitized version of Fanon," since, as my comments should attest, I fundamentally disagree with his proposition that "Fanon's dream, like Césaire's, is that of restoring the lost paradise. In his euphoric insistence on the ideal of the nation reborn, Fanon is conceptualizing the behavior and culture of the group outside of historical contact and individual idiosyncracies" (*Other America* 70).

18. *Vers un nouvel humanisme* is one of the first phrases of Fanon's *Peaux noires, masques blancs* (25).

19. Sembène, *Money-Order* 6. Sembène's Léon Mignane, the patriarchal African philosopher and head of state, the founder of the idea (or ideology) of Authénégraficanitus in the political roman à clef *Le dernier de l'Empire* (The Last of the Empire), is a thinly veiled parody of Senghor.

6. The Marvelous Royalty of Henri Christophe's Kingdom

1. Césaire, *La tragédie du roi Christophe* 62–63; my emphasis. Unless otherwise indicated, all translations of Césaire's *La tragédie du roi Christophe* are my own.

2. "My first inkling of the marvellous real [*lo real maravilloso*] came to me

when, near the end of 1943, I was lucky enough to visit Henri Christophe's kingdom—such poetic ruins, Sans-Souci [the royal palace] and the bulk of the Citadel of La Ferrière, imposingly intact in spite of lightening and earthquakes" (Carpentier, "Marvelous Real in America" 84).

3. "But who will offer me . . . something that will educate, no, that will *edify* the people" (*La tragédie* 61).

4. The master of ceremonies is described with intentional anachronism as "a White assigned by TESCO (Technical, Educational, Scientific Cooperation Organization [In American English in the original]) as a technical aide to underdeveloped regions" (*La tragédie* 30n).

5. I.e., *Christum Ferens,* "the bearer of Christ."

6. See, for example, Todorov: "the literary text does not enter into a referential relationship with the 'world,' as sentences of everyday speech often do; it is not 'representative' of anything but itself" (*Fantastic* 10).

7. "A mode of [cultural] encounter . . . linked not to a creation of the world but to the conscious and contradictory experience of contacts among cultures" (Glissant, *Poetics of Relation* 33, 144).

8. A character named Toussaint shows up once in the novel at the height of Mackandal's poison rebellion, never to be mentioned again: "Toussaint, el ebanista, había tallado unos reyes magos, en madera, demasiado grandes para el conjunto, que nunca acabaran de colocarse, sobre todo a causa de las terribles córneas blancas de Baltasar—particularmente realzado a pincel—, que parecían emerger de la noche del ébano con tremebundas acusaciones de ahogado" (Carpentier, *El reino de este mundo* 35). (Toussaint, the cabinet maker, had carved the Three Wise Men in wood, but they were too big for the Nativity, and in the end were not set up, mainly because of the terrible whites of Balthasar's eyes, which had been painted with special care, and gave the impression of emerging from a night of ebony with the terrible reproach of a drowned man [*Kingdom of This World* 45]). But since this Toussaint is a contemporary of Mackandal (Louverture, who was around forty-five at the time of Bouckman's rising, would have been a mere child in 1757), since he is a cabinetmaker at the Lenormand de Mézy plantation rather than a coachman for the *habitation* Bréda, it is unlikely that he shares anything except his Christian name with the revolutionary hero. On the other hand, Carpentier's Toussaint might have had as his source one of the characters from Alfred Jarry's *Ubu Cuckolded,* Memnon, Dawn's legendary son. There was a colossal statue of Memnon near Thebes in Egypt that the rays of the rising sun had the power to make sing. In his first appearance in the play (act 3, scene 3), Memnon plays a prelude on his flute "since dawn is breaking" (Jarry, *Ubu Plays* 92) and sings the following song: "Je fus pendant longtemps ouvrier ébéniste / Dans la ru' du Champ-d'Mars, d'la paroiss' de Toussaints; / Mon épouse exerçait la profession d'modiste" (Jarry, *Tout Ubu* 227) (A cabinetmaker was I for many a long year, / Rue du Champs de Mars in All Saints' Parish; / My dear wife was a dressmaker" [*Ubu Plays* 92]).

9. "La très Sainte Inquisition pour l'intégrité de la foi et la poursuite de la perversité hérétique, agissant par délégation spéciale du Saint-Siège apostolique, informée des erreurs que tu professes, insinues et publies contre Dieu et la Création" (Renan, *Caliban* 79; Césaire, *Une tempête* 21) ("The very Holy Inquisition for the perservation and integrity of the Faith and the pursuit of heretical perversion, acting through the special powers entrusted to it by the Holy Apostolic See, informed of the errors you profess, insinuate and publish against God and his Creation" [*Tempest* 10]).

7. "Something New in a Decaying World"

1. As González Echeverría writes in reference to the novel's "apparently anachronistic form": "So traditional is *Explosion in a Cathedral* in its outward form that a critic has called it 'a challenge to the modern novel,' in the sense that it seems to spurn the experimental nature of modern narrative in favor of a dated historical and realistic design" (*Alejo Carpentier* 226).

2. As my commentary indicates, I do not concur with George Handley's suggestion that Carpentier's representation of 'the people' "is haunted by a kind of romance": "'The people' seem to stand outside the deeply historical contingencies that otherwise act profoundly on the individual characters Carpentier does choose to represent.... In this Marxist recourse to mythologizing the folk, history threatens to collapse back into ideological thinking" (*Postslavery Narratives* 129–30).

Conclusion

1. For James, in fact, the argument extends to the economic and social structures that ground the modern "experience."

Bibliography

Abu-Lughod, Janet. *Before European Hegemony: The World System, A.D. 1250–1350*. Oxford: Oxford University Press, 1989.
Adotevi, Stanislas Spero K. *Négritude et négrologues*. Paris: Union Générale d'Éditions, 1972.
Ahmad, Aijaz. *In Theory: Classes, Nations, Literatures*. London: Verso, 1992. Originally published in *Social Text* 17 (Fall 1987): 73–101.
Alencar, José. *Iracema*. São Paulo: Editora Ática, 1992.
"Algumas notas sobre o que já se tem escrito em torno da nova descida antropofágica na nossa literatura." *Revista de Antropofagia* 2, no. 4 (April 7, 1929). Reprint, São Paulo: Companhia Lithographica Ypiranga, 1976.
Alonso, Carlos J. *The Burden of Modernity: The Rhetoric of Cultural Discourse in Latin America*. New York: Oxford University Press, 1998.
Althusser, Louis, and Etienne Balibar. *Reading Capital*. Trans. Ben Brewster. London: Verso, 1986.
Anderson, Benedict. *Imagined Communities: Reflections on the Origin and Spread of Nationalism*. Rev. and extended ed. London: Verso, 1991.
Anderson, Perry. "Modernity and Revolution." In *Marxism and the Interpretation of Cultures,* ed. Cary Nelson and Lawrence Grossberg. Urbana: University of Illinois Press, 1988, 317–38.
Andrade, Joaquim Pedro de. "Cannibalism and Self-Cannibalism." In *Brazilian Cinema,* ed. Randal Johnson and Robert Stam. Austin: University of Texas Press, 1988.
———. "Criticism and Self-Criticism." In *Brazilian Cinema,* ed. Randal Johnson and Robert Stam.
———. *Macunaíma*. Filmes do Serro, Grupo Filmes, Condor Filmes, 1969.
Andrade, Mário de. "De São Paulo." *Ilustração Brasileira,* Nov. 1920. Reprinted in *Brasil: 1° Tempo Modernista—1917/29 (documentação),* ed. Marta Rossetti Batista, Telê Ancona Lopez, and Yone Soares de Lima, 56–58. São Paulo: Instituto de Estudos Brasileiros, 1972.
———. *Ensaio sôbre a música brasileira*. [São Paulo:] Livraria Martins Editora, 1972.

———. *Macunaíma: O herói sem nenhum caráter*. Ed. Telê Porto Ancona Lopez. Rio de Janeiro: Livros Técnicos e Científicos Editora, 1978.

———. *Macunaíma: O herói sem nenhum caráter*. Rev. ed. Ed. Telê Porto Ancona Lopez. Rio de Janeiro: Livros Técnicos e Científicos Editora, 1988.

———. "O movimento modernista." *Aspectos da Literatura Brasileira*. São Paulo: Livraria Martins Editora, n.d.: 231–55.

———. "Oswald de Andrade." *Revista do Brasil* [105] (Sept. 1924). Reprinted in *Brasil: 1° Tempo Modernista—1917/29 (documentação)*, ed. Marta Rossetti Batista, Telê Ancona Lopez, Yone Soares de Lima, 219–25. São Paulo: Instituto de Estudos Brasileiros, 1972.

———. "Oswald de Andrade: Pau Brasil sans pareil, Paris, 1925." Reprinted in *Brasil: 1° Tempo Modernista—1917/29 (documentação)*, ed. Marta Rossetti Batista, Telê Ancona Lopez, Yone Soares de Lima, 225–32. São Paulo: Instituto de Estudos Brasileiros, 1972.

Andrade, Oswald de. *Dentes de dragão: Entrevistas*. Ed. Maria Eugenia Boaventura. São Paulo: Editora Globo, 1990.

———. *Dicionário de Bolso*. Ed. Maria Eugenia Boaventura. São Paulo: Editora Globo, 1990.

———. *Do 'Pau-Brasil' à antropofagia e ás utopias*. Vol. 6 of *Obras completas*, ed. Benedito Nunes. Rio de Janeiro: Civilização Brasileira, 1972.

———. *Estética e política*. Ed. Maria Eugenia Boaventura. São Paulo: Editora Globo, 1991.

———. "Moquém." *Revista de Antropofagia* 2, no. 5 (April 14, 1929): 6. Reprint, São Paulo: Companhia Lithographica Ypiranga, 1976.

———. "Oswald de Andrade's 'Cannibalist Manifesto.'" Trans. Leslie Bary. *Latin American Literary Review* 19 (July–December 1991): 35–47.

———. *Pau Brasil: Poesias reunidas*. Vol. 7 of *Obras Completas*, ed. Benedito Nunes. Rio de Janeiro: Civilização Brasileira, 1972.

———. *Ponta de lança: Polémica*. Vol. 5 of *Obras Completas*, ed. Benedito Nunes. Rio de Janeiro: Civilização Brasileira, 1971.

———. "Schema ao Tristão de Athayde." *Revista de Antropofagia* 1, no. 5 (Sept. 1928): 3. Reprint, São Paulo: Companhia Lithographica Ypiranga, 1976.

———. "Uma adesão que não nos interessa." *Revista de Antropofagia* 2, no. 10 (June 6, 1929): 10. Reprint, São Paulo: Companhia Lithographica Ypiranga, 1976.

Apollinaire. *Alcools, suivi de Le Bestiaire et de Vitam impendere amori*. Paris: Gallimard, 1980.

Appiah, Kwame Anthony. *In My Father's House: Africa and the Philosophy of Culture*. Oxford: Oxford University Press, 1992.

Aranha, Graça. *Obra completa*. Ed. Afrânio Coutinho. Rio de Janeiro: Instituto Nacional do Livro, 1969.

Averbuck, Lígia Morrone. *Cobra Norato e a Revolução Caraíba*. Rio de Janeiro: José Olympio Editora, 1985.

Bell, Madison Smartt. *All Souls' Rising*. New York: Penguin Books, 1996.

Benítez Rojo, Antonio. *La isla que se repite: El Caribe y la perspectiva posmoderna.* Hanover, N.H.: Ediciones del Norte, 1989.
Benjamin, Walter. *Illuminations: Essays and Reflections.* Ed. Hannah Arendt, trans. Harry Zohn. New York: Schocken Books, 1968.
Berman, Marshall. *All That Is Solid Melts into Air: The Experience of Modernity.* New York: Penguin Books, 1988.
Bernardet, Jean-Claude. *Trajetória crítica.* São Paulo: Polis, 1978.
Bhabha, Homi. *The Location of Culture.* New York: Routledge, 1992.
Blaut, J. M. *The Colonizer's Model of the World: Geographical Diffusionism and Eurocentric History.* New York: Guilford Press, 1993.
Boal, Augusto. *Theater of the Oppressed.* Trans. Charles A. and Maria-Odilia Leal McBride. New York: Urizen Books, 1979.
Bopp, Raul. *'Bopp passado a limpo' por ele mesmo (Considerações em torno de uma crítica, publicada em páginas literárias do 'Estado de São Paulo e do 'Correio do Povo,' de Porto Alegre).* Rio de Janeiro: Gráfica Tupy, 1977.
——. *Cobra Norato.* Rio de Janeiro: José Olympio Editora, 1994.
——. *Cobra Norato e outros poemas.* Rio de Janeiro: Livraria São José, 1956.
——. *Movimentos modernistas no Brasil, 1922–1928.* Rio de Janeiro: Livraria São José. 1966.
——. *Putirum (poesias e coisas de folclore).* Rio de Janeiro: Editora Leitura, [1969].
——. *Samburá (Notas de viagens & saldos literários).* Brasília: Editora Brasília, [1973].
——. *Vida e morte da antropofagia.* Rio de Janeiro: Civilização Brasileira, 1977.
Borges, Jorge Luis. *Collected Fictions.* Trans. Andrew Hurley. New York: Penguin Books, 1998.
——. *Historia universal de la infamia.* Madrid: Alianza Editorial, 1971.
Braudel, Fernand. *The Perspective of the World.* Vol. 3 of *Civilization and Capitalism (15th–18th Century).* Trans. Siân Reynolds. New York: HarperCollins, 1985.
——. *The Structures of Everyday Life.* Vol. 1 of *Civilization and Capitalism (15th–18th Century).* Trans. Siân Reynolds. New York: Harper & Row, 1981.
——. *The Wheels of Commerce.* Vol. 2 of *Civilization and Capitalism (15th–18th Century).* Trans. Siân Reynolds. New York: Harper & Row, 1982.
Brecheret, Victor. "Monumento das Bandeiras." *Papel e Tinta* 1, no. 3 (July 1920). Reprint in *Brasil: 1° Tempo Modernista—1917/29 (documentação),* ed. Marta Rossetti Batista, Telê Ancona Lopez, and Yone Soares de Lima, 54–56. São Paulo: Instituto de Estudos Brasileiros, 1972.
Brecht, Bertolt. *Brecht on Theatre: The Development of an Aesthetic.* Ed. and trans. John Willett. New York, Hill and Wang, 1964.
——. *Man Equals Man and the Elephant Calf.* Ed. John Willet and Ralph Manheim, trans. Gerhard Nellhaus. New York: Arcade, 2000.

———. *Leben des Galilei*. Berlin: Suhrkamp Verlag, 1963.
———. *Life of Galileo*. Trans. John Willet. Ed. John Willet and Ralph Manheim. New York: Arcade, 1994.
Breton, André. *Manifestes du surréalisme*. Paris: Gallimard, 1981.
Buck-Morss, Susan. "Hegel and Haiti." *Critical Inquiry* 26:4 (Summer 2000): 821–65.
Burke, Edmund. *Reflections on the Revolution in France*. Ed. J. G. A. Pocock. Indianapolis: Hackett, 1987.
Campos, Álvaro de. *Poesias de Álvaro de Campos*. Vol. 2 of *Obras Completas de Fernando Pessoa*. Lisbon: Edições Ática, 1980.
Campos, Haroldo de. *Morfologia do Macunaíma*. [São Paulo:] Editora Perspectiva, [1973].
———. "The Rule of Anthropophagy: Europe under the Sign of Devoration." Trans. Maria Tai Wolff. *Latin American Literary Review* 14 (January–June 1986): 42–60.
Carlyle, Thomas. *The Nigger Question*. John Stuart Mill. *The Negro Question*. Ed. Eugene R. August. New York, Appleton-Century-Crofts, 1971.
Carpentier, Alejo. *El arpa y la sombra*. Mexico City: Siglo Veintiuno Editores, 1979.
———. "The Baroque and the Marvelous Real." *Magical Realism: Theory, History, Community*. Ed. Lois Parkinson Zamora and Wendy B. Faris. Durham: Duke University Press, 1995.
———. *Ensayos*. México, D.F.: Siglo Veintiuno Editores, 1990.
———. *Explosion in a Cathedral*. Trans. John Sturrock. New York: Farrar, Straus and Giroux, 1989.
———. *Guerra del tiempo: Tres relatos y una novela*. México: Compañía General de Ediciones, 1968.
———. *The Kingdom of This World*. Trans. Harriet de Onís. New York: Noonday Press, 1989.
———. *The Lost Steps*. Trans. Harriet de Onís. New York: Farrar, Straus and Giroux, 1989.
———. "On the Marvelous Real in America." In *Magical Realism: Theory, History, Community*, ed. Lois Parkinson Zamora and Wendy B. Faris. Durham: Duke University Press, 1995.
———. *Los pasos perdidos*. Ed. Roberto González Echeverría. Madrid: Cátedra, 1985.
———. *El reino de este mundo*. Santiago de Chile: Editorial Universitaria, 1969.
———. *El siglo de las luces*. Ed. Ambrosio Formet. Madrid: Cátedra, 1983.
———. *Tientos y diferencias*. Montevideo: Arca, 1967.
Castillo-Durante, Daniel. "From Postmodernity to the Rubbish Heap: Latin America and Its Cultural Practices." In *Latin American Postmodernisms*, ed. Richard A. Young. Amsterdam: Editions Rodopi, 1994.
Certeau, Michel de. *Heterologies: Discourse on the Other*. Trans. Brian Massumi. Minneapolis: University of Minnesota Press, 1986.

———. *The Writing of History.* Trans. Tom Conley. New York: Columbia University Press, 1988.
Césaire, Aimé. *Collected Poetry.* Trans. and ed. Clayton Eshleman and Annette Smith. Berkeley: University of California Press, 1983.
———. *Discourse on Colonialism.* Trans. Joan Pinkham. New York: Monthly Review Press, 1972.
———. *Une saison au Congo.* Paris: Éditions du Seuil, 1966.
———. *Une tempête, d'après "La tempête" de Shakespeare: Adaptation pour un théâtre nègre.* Paris: Éditions du Seuil, 1969.
———. *A Tempest.* Trans. Richard Miller. Ubu Repertory Theater publications. New York: G. Borchardt, 1985.
———. *Toussaint Louverture: La révolution française et le problème colonial.* Rev. ed. Paris: Présence Africaine, 1962.
———. *La tragédie du roi Christophe.* Paris: Présence Africaine, 1970.
Chakrabarty, Dipesh. "Postcoloniality and the Artifice of History: Who Speaks for 'Indian' Pasts." In *Contemporary Postcolonial Theory: A Reader,* ed. Padmini Mongia. London: Arnold, 1996.
Chanady, Amaryll. "The Territorialization of the Imaginary in Latin America: Self-Affirmation and Resistance to Metropolitan Paradigms." In *Magical Realism: Theory, History, Community,* ed. Lois Parkinson Zamora and Wendy B. Faris. Durham: Duke University Press, 1995.
Colón, Cristóbal. *Los cuatro viajes: Testamento.* Ed. Consuelo Varela. Madrid: Alianza Editorial, 1986.
Conrad, Joseph, *Heart of Darkness (with The Congo Diary).* Ed. Robert Hampson. New York: Penguin Books, 1995.
———. *Last Essays.* Garden City, N.Y.: Doubleday, Page, 1926.
Costa, Oswaldo. "Revisão necessária." *Revista de Antropofagia* 2, no. 1 (March 7, 1929): 6. Reprint, São Paulo: Companhia Lithographica Ypiranga, 1976.
Dash, J. Michael. *The Other America: Caribbean Literature in a New World Context.* Charlottesville: University Press of Virginia, 1998.
Davis, Wade. *The Serpent and the Rainbow.* New York: Warner Books, 1987.
de Man, Paul. *Allegories of Reading: Figural Language in Rousseau, Rilke, and Proust.* New Haven, Conn.: Yale University Press, 1979.
———. *Blindness and Insight.* Minneapolis: University of Minnesota Press, 1983.
Depestre, René. *Pour la révolution, pour la poésie.* Montréal: Leméac, 1974.
Derrida, Jaques. *Of Grammatology.* Trans. Gayatri Chakravorty Spivak. Corrected ed. Baltimore: Johns Hopkins University Press, 1997.
———. "Signature Event Context." *Margins of Philosophy,* 307–30. Trans. Alan Bass. Chicago: University of Chicago Press, 1982.
———. *Specters of Marx: The State of the Debt, the Work of Mourning, and the New International.* Trans. Peggy Kamuf. New York: Routledge, 1994.
———. *Writing and Difference.* Trans. Alan Bass. Chicago: University of Chicago Press, 1978.

De Toro, Alfonso. "The Epistemological Foundations of the Contemporary Condition: Latin America in Dialogue with Postmodernity and Postcoloniality." In *Latin American Postmodernisms,* ed. Richard A. Young, 29–51. Amsterdam: Editions Rodopi, 1994.

Dickens, Charles. *A Tale of Two Cities.* New York: Bantam Books, 1983.

Dirlik, Arlif. "The Postcolonial Aura: Third World Criticism in the Age of Global Capitalism." *Critical Inquiry* 20 (Winter 1994): 328–56.

Durão, José de Santa Rita. *O Caramurú.* In *Épicos Brasileiros,* ed. F. A. de Varnhagen, 69–383. Lisbon: Imprensa Nacional, 1845. Originally published 1781.

Ellis, Alfredo. *A Madrugada paulista: Lendas de Piratininga.* São Paulo: Liga Confederacionista, 1934.

———. *Raça de gigantes: A civilisação no planalto paulista.* São Paulo: Editorial Helios, 1926.

Fanon, Frantz. *Black Skin, White Masks.* Trans. Charles Lam Markmann. New York: Grove Weidenfeld, 1991.

———. *Les damnés de la terre.* Paris: François Maspéro, 1961.

———. *Peau noire, masques blancs.* Preface and postface by Francis Jeanson. Paris: Éditions du Seuil, 1965.

Faulkner, William. *Absalom! Absalom!* New York: Vintage Books, 1972.

———. *Go Down, Moses.* New York: Vintage Books, 1990.

Fernández Retamar, Roberto. *Caliban and Other Essays.* Trans. Edward Baker, foreword by Fredric Jameson. Minneapolis: University of Minnesota Press, 1989.

Flaubert, Gustave. *Trois contes: Un coeur simple; Légende de Saint Julien Hospitalier, Hérodias.* Paris: Garnier Frères, 1969.

Foucault, Michel. *The Archaeology of Knowledge.* Trans. A. M. Sheridan Smith. New York: Harper & Row, 1976.

———. *The History of Sexuality.* Vol. 1: *An Introduction.* Trans. Robert Hurley. New York: Vintage Books, 1990.

———. *The Order of Things: An Archaeology of the Human Sciences.* Trans. Alan Sheridan. New York: Vintage Books, 1973.

Franco, Jean. *The Modern Culture of Latin America: Society and the Artist.* New York: Frederick A. Praeger, 1967.

Freire, Paulo. *Pedagogy of Hope: Reliving Pedagogy of the Oppressed.* Trans. Robert R. Barr. New York: Continuum, 1995.

Freud, Sigmund. *The Ego and the Id.* Trans. Joan Riviere. Ed. James Strachey. New York: W. W. Norton, 1989.

———. *The Interpretation of Dreams.* Trans. and ed. James Strachey. New York: Avon Books, 1965.

———. *Totem and Taboo: Some Points of Agreements between the Mental Lives of Neurotics and Savages.* Trans. and ed. James Strachey. New York: W. W. Norton, 1989.

Freyre, Gilberto. *Casa Grande e Senzala (Formação da família brasileira sob o regimen de economia patriarchal).* Rio de Janeiro: Schmidt, 1936.

Gallegos, Rómulo. *Canaima*. Ed. Charles Minguet. Madrid: Collección Archivos, 1991.

———. *Doña Bárbara*. Mexico City: Espasa Calpe Mexicana, 1989.

Gama, José Basílio. *O Uruguay*. In *Épicos Brasileiros*, ed. F. A. de Varnhagen, 5–68. Lisbon: Imprensa Nacional, 1845.

García Canclini, Nestor. *Hybrid Cultures: Strategies for Entering and Leaving Modernity*. Trans. Christopher L. Chiappari and Silvia L. López. Minneapolis: University of Minnesota Press, 1995.

García Márquez, Gabriel. *Autumn of the Patriarch*. Trans. Gregory Rabassa. New York: Harper & Row, 1991.

———. *La Hojarasca*. Buenos Aires: Sudamericana, 1990.

———. *Leafstorm and Other Stories*. Trans. Gregory Rabassa. New York: Harper & Row, 1979.

———. *One Hundred Years of Solitude*. Trans. Gregory Rabassa. New York: Perennial Classics, 1998.

———. *El Otoño del patriarca*. Buenos Aires: Editorial Sudamericana, 1975.

Genovese, Eugene D. *From Rebellion to Revolution: Afro-American Slave Revolts in the Making of the Modern World*. New York: Vintage Books, 1981.

Gilroy, Paul. *The Black Atlantic: Modernity and Double Consciousness*. Cambridge, Mass.: Harvard University Press, 1994.

Glissant, Édouard. *Caribbean Discourse: Selected Essays*. Trans. J. Michael Dash. Charlottesville: University Press of Virginia, 1989.

———. *Le discours antillais*. Paris: Seuil, 1983.

———. *The Fourth Century*. Trans. Betsy Wing. Lincoln: University of Nebraska Press, 2001.

———. *Monsieur Toussaint*. Paris: Editions du Seuil, 1961.

———. *Monsieur Toussaint*. Trans. Joseph G. Foster and Barbara A. Franklin. Washington, D.C.: Three Continents Press, 1981.

———. *Poetics of Relation*. Trans. Betsy Wing. Ann Arbor: University of Michigan Press, 2000.

———. *Le quatrième siècle*. Paris: Éditions Seuil, 1964.

González Echevarría, Roberto. *Alejo Carpentier: The Pilgrim at Home*. Ithaca: Cornell University Press, 1977.

———. *Myth and Archive: A Theory of Latin American Narrative*. Durham, N.C.: Duke University Press, 1998.

———. *The Voice of the Masters: Writing and Authority in Modern Latin American Literature*. Austin: University of Texas Press, 1988.

Guerra, Ruy. "Popular Cinema and the State." *Brazilian Cinema*. Ed. Randall Johnson and Robert Stam, 101–3. Austin: University of Texas Press, 1988.

Hall, Stuart. "Cultural Identity and Diaspora." In *Contemporary Postcolonial Theory: A Reader*, ed. Padmini Mongia. London: Arnold, 1996.

Handley, George B. *Postslavery Narratives in the Americas: Family Portraits in Black and White*. Charlottesville: University Press of Virginia, 2000.

Harris, Wilson. *The Carnival Trilogy*. London: Faber and Faber, 1985.
———. *The Guyana Quartet*. London: Faber and Faber, 1994.
Hegel, G. W. F. *The Phenomenology of Mind*. Trans. A. V. Miller. Ed. J. N. Findlay. Oxford: Oxford University Press, 1977.
———. *The Philosophy of Mind*. Trans. A. V. Miller. Oxford: Clarendon Press, 1971.
———. *The Philosophy of History*. Trans. J. Sibree. New York: Dover, 1956.
———. *The Philosophy of Right*. Trans. T. M. Knox. Oxford: Clarendon Press, 1965.
Heidegger, Martin. *The Question Concerning Technology and Other Essays*. Trans. William Lovitt. New York: Harper & Row, 1977.
Hobsbawm, Eric. *The Age of Revolution*. New York: Vintage Books, 1996.
Horkheimer, Max, and Theodor Adorno. *Dialectic of Enlightenment*. Trans. John Cumming. New York: Continuum, 1986.
Hugo, Victor. *Bug-Jargal*. Paris: Alphonse Lemerre, 1912.
———. *Quatrevingt-treize*. Ed. Yves Gohin. Paris: Gallimard, 1979.
Hulme, Peter. *Colonial Encounters: Europe and the Native Caribbbean, 1492–1797*. London: Methuen, 1986.
James, C. L. R. *The Black Jacobins: Toussaint L'Ouverture and the San Domingo Revolution*. 2nd ed. New York: Vintage Books, 1989.
———. *The C. L. R. James Reader*. Ed. Anna Grimshaw. Oxford: Blackwell, 1992.
———. *The Future in the Present: Selected Writings*. Westport, Conn.: L. Hill, 1977.
Jameson, Fredric. "Beyond the Cave: Demystifying the Ideology of Modernism." *The Ideology of Theory: Essays 1971–1986*. Vol. 2: *The Syntax of History*. Minneapolis: University of Minnesota Press, 1988.
———. "Modernism and Imperialism." *Nationalism, Colonialism and Literature*. Minneapolis: University of Minnesota Press, 1990.
———. "Modernism and Its Repressed; Or, Robbe-Grillet as Anti-Colonialist." *The Ideology of Theory: Essays, 1971–1986*. Vol. 1: *Situations of Theory*. Minneapolis: University of Minnesota Press, 1988.
———. *Postmodernism; or, The Cultural Logic of Late Capitalism*. Durham, N.C.: Duke University Press, 1991.
———. "Third World Literature in the Era of Multinational Capitalism." *Social Text* 15 (Fall 1986): 65–88.
Jarry, Alfred. *Oeuvres complètes*. Ed. Henru Bordillon. Paris: Gallimard, 1987.
———. *Tout Ubu: Avec leurs prolégomènes et paralipomènes*. Ed. Maurice Saillet. Paris: Le Livre de Poche, 1963.
———. *The Ubu Plays*. Trans. Cyril Connoly and Simon Watson Taylor. New York: Grove Press, 1969.
Jodelle, Étienne. *Oeuvres complètes*. Ed. Enea Balmas. 2 vols. Paris: Gallimard, 1965–68.

Johnson, Randall. *Cinema Novo x 5: Masters of Contemporary Brazilian Film.* Austin: University of Texas Press, 1984.

Kadir, Djelal. *The Other Writing: Postcolonial Essays in Latin America's Writing Culture.* West Lafayette, Ind.: Purdue University Press, 1993.

———. *Questing Fictions: Latin America's Family Romance.* Minneapolis: University of Minnesota Press, 1986.

Kant, Immanuel. *Critique of Judgment.* Trans. J. H. Bernard. London: Collier Macmillan, 1951.

———. *Critique of Practical Reason.* Ed. and trans. Lewis White Beck. New York: Macmillan Publishing Company, 1993.

———. *On History.* Ed. Lewis White Beck. Trans. Lewis White Beck, Robert E. Anchor, and Emil L. Fackenheim. New York: Macmillan, 1963.

Kleist, Heinrich von. "The Betrothal in San Domingo." *The Marquise of O and Other Stories.* Trans. Martin Greenberg. Preface by Thomas Mann. London: Faber and Faber, 1963.

Lamartine, Alphonse de. *Toussaint Louverture: Poëme dramatique.* Paris, 1889.

Lamming, George. *Natives of My Person.* Ann Arbor: University of Michigan Press, 1992.

———. *The Pleasures of Exile.* London: Allison & Busby, 1984.

Laroche, Maximilien. "Haitian Postmodernisms." In *Latin American Postmodernisms,* ed. Richard Young, 119–26. Amsterdam: Editions Rodopi, 1997.

Larsen, Neil. "Postmodernism and Imperialism: Theory and Politics in Latin America." In *The Postmodernism Debate in Latin America,* ed. John Beverly, Jose Oviedo, and Michael Aronna. Durham, N.C.: Duke University Press, 1995.

Lenin, Vladimir Ilich. *What Is to Be Done? Burning Questions of Our Movement.* Trans. J. Fineberg and G. Hanna. Ed. V. J. Jerome. New York: International, 1969.

Léry, Jean de. *Histoire d'un voyage fait en la terre du Brésil.* Ed. Jean-Claude Morisot. Geneva: Librairie Droz, 1975.

———. *History of a Voyage to the Land of Brazil, Otherwise called America.* Trans. Janet Whatley. Berkeley: University of California Press, 1992.

Lévi-Strauss, Claude. *Tristes tropiques.* Paris: Librairie Plon, 1955.

———. *Tristes Tropiques.* Trans. John and Doreen Weightman. New York: Penguin Books, 1992.

Lima, Jorge. "Santa Rita Durão." *Revista de Antropofagia* 2, no. 1 (March 7, 1929): 6. Reprint, São Paulo: Cia, 1976. Lithographica Ypiranga.

Lobato, Monteiro. *Urupês.* Vol. 1 of *Obras completas de Monteiro Lobato.* São Paulo: Editora Brasiliense, 1961.

Lopes de Sousa, Pêro. *Diário da navegação de Pêro Lopes de Sousa (1530–1532).* Ed. Jorge Morais-Barbosa. Lisbon: Agência Geral do Ultramar, 1968.

López de Gómara, Francisco. *Historia general de las Indias.* Lima: Comisión Nacional del V Centenario del Descubrimiento de America—Encuentro de dos Mundos, 1993.

Lyotard, Jean-François. *The Differend: Phrases in a Dispute.* Trans. George Van Den Abbeele. Minneapolis: University of Minnesota Press, 1988.

———. *Le différend.* Paris: Les Éditions de Minuit, 1983.

———. *The Inhuman: Reflections on Time.* Trans. Geoffrey Bennington and Rachel Bowlby. Stanford, Calif.: Stanford University Press, 1991.

———. *Instructions païennes.* Paris: Galilée, 1977.

———. *The Postmodern Condition: A Report on Knowledge.* Trans. Geoff Bennington and Brian Massumi. Foreword by Fredric Jameson. Minneapolis: University of Minnesota Press, 1984.

———. *The Postmodern Explained: Correspondence, 1982–1985.* Trans. Don Barry et al. Ed. Julian Pefanis and Morgan Thomas. Minneapolis: University of Minnesota Press, 1992.

———. *Rudiments païens: Genre dissertatif.* Paris: Union Générale d'Éditions, 1977.

———. "The Sign of History." *The Lyotard Reader.* Ed. Andrew Benjamin. Oxford: Blackwell, 1989.

Lyotard, Jean-François, and Jean-Loup Thébaud. *Just Gaming.* Trans. Wlad Godzich. Minneapolis: University of Minnesota Press, 1985.

Macherey, Pierre. *Pour une théorie de la production littéraire.* Paris: François Maspéro, 1966.

Madureira, Luís. *A Nostalgia of Stone for the Indefinite Sea: Empire, Nation and Revolution in Portuguese and Lusophone African Fiction.* Lewiston, N.Y.: Edwin Mellen Press, forthcoming.

Magalhães de Gândavo, Pêro. *Historia da prouíncia de Sacta Cruz a que vulgarmente chamamos Brasil* (facsimile of 1576 ed.). In *Histories of Brazil.* ed. John B. Stetson Jr. New York: Cortes Society, 1922.

Mallarmé, Stéphane. *Oeuvres.* Ed. Yves-Alain Favre. Paris: Éditions Garnier, 1985.

Marinetti, F. T. "Fondation et manifeste du futurisme." In *Futurisme: Manifestes, Proclamations, Documents,* ed. Giovanni Lista. Lausanne: Editions l'Age d'Homme, 1973.

Marx, Karl. *A Contribution to the Critique of Political Economy.* Ed. Maurice Dobb. New York: International Publishers, 1981.

———. *The Eighteenth Brumaire of Louis Napoleon.* New York: International Publishers, 1984.

Marx, Karl, and Frederick Engels. *The German Ideology (Part One).* Ed. C. J. Arthur. New York: International, 1984.

Mehlman, Jeffrey. *Revolution and Repetition: Marx / Hugo / Balzac.* Berkeley: University of California Press, 1977.

Menotti del Picchia, Paulo. *Juca Mulato: Poemas.* São Paulo: Livraria Martins Editora, 1960: 21–85.

———. *A longa viagem (2a etapa: 1918–1930).* São Paulo: Livraria Martins Editora, 1972.

———. *O Gedeão do modernismo: 1920–22.* Ed. Yoshie Sakiyama Barreirinhas. São Paulo: Civilização Brasileira, 1983.

———. *República dos Estados Unidos do Brasil: Poesias (1907–1946).* São Paulo: Livraria Martins Editora, 1958.

Miceli, Sergio. *Imagens negociadas: Retratos da elite brasileira (1920–40).* São Paulo: Companhia das Letras, 1996.

Miller, Christopher. *Theories of Africans: Francophone Literature and Anthropology in Africa.* Chicago: University of Chicago Press, 1990.

Montaigne, Michel. *Les essais.* 3 vols. Ed. Pierre Villey. Paris: Quadrige, Presses Universitaires de France, 1988.

Moore, Gerald, and Ulli Beier. *The Penguin Book of Modern African Poetry.* Harmondsworth: Penguin Books, 1998.

Mouffe, Chantal. "Hegemony and New Political Subjects: Toward a New Concept of Democracy." In *Marxism and the Interpretation of Culture,* ed. Cary Nelson and Lawrence Grossberg. Urbana: University of Illinois Press, 1988: 89–104.

———. "Radical Democracy: Modern or Postmodern?" Ed. Andrew Ross. *Universal Abandon? The Politics of Postmodernism.* Minneapolis: University of Minnesota Press, 1988: 31–45.

Mudimbe, V. Y. *The Idea of Africa.* Bloomington: Indiana University Press, 1994.

Nietzsche, Friedrich. *Beyond Good and Evil: Prelude to a Philosophy of the Future.* Trans. R. J. Hollingdale. New York: Penguin Books, 1990.

———. *The Birth of Tragedy (Out of the Spirit of Music).* Trans. Shaun Whiteside. Ed. Michael Tanner. New York: Penguin Books, 1993.

———. *Die Geburt der Tragödie oder Griechentum und Pessimismus.* In *Werke in Drei Bänden,* vol. 1, ed. Karl Schlechta. Munich: Carl Hanser Verlag, 1960.

———. *Jenseits von Gut und Böse: Zur Genealogie der Moral (1886–1887).* Ed. Giorgio Colli and Mazzino Montinari. In *Nietzsche Werke,* vol. 2, section 6. Berlin: Walter de Gruyter, 1968.

———. *On the Genealogy of Morals and Ecce Homo.* Trans. Walter Kaufmann and R. J. Hollingdale. Ed. Walter Kaufmann. New York: Vintage Books, 1967.

———. "On the Uses and Disadvantages of History for Life." *Untimely Meditations.* Trans. R. J. Hollingdale. Cambridge: Cambridge University Press, 1983.

———. "Vom Nutzen und Nachteil der Historie für das Leben." *Unzeitgemäße Betrachtungen.* In *Werke in Drei Bänden,* vol. 1. Ed. Karl Schlechta. Munich: Carl Hanser Verlag, 1960.

———. *Will to Power.* Trans. Walter Kaufmann and R. J. Hollingdale. Ed. Walter Kaufmann. New York: Vintage Books, 1968.

Ogan, Bernd. "Faszination und Gewalt—Ein Überblick." *Faszination und Gewalt: Zur polititischen Ästhetic des Nationalsozialismus.* Ed. Bernd Ogan and Wolfgang W. Weiß. Nuremberg, 1992.

Ortiz, Fernando. *Contrapunteo cubano del tabaco y azúcar: Advertencia de sus*

contrastes agrarios, económicos, históricos y socials, su etnografía y su transculturación. Ed. Enrico Mario Santí. Madrid: Ediciones Cátedra, 2002.
Ortiz, Renato. *A moderna cultura brasileira.* São Paulo: Editora Brasiliense, 1988.
Pagden, Anthony. *The Fall of Natural Man: The American Indian and the Origins of Comparative Ethnology.* Cambridge: Cambridge University Press, 1982.
Parry, Benita. "Resistance Theory/Theorising Resistance, or Two Cheers for Nativism." In *Contemporary Postcolonial Theory: A Reader,* ed. Padmini Mongia. London: Arnold, 1996.
Paz, Octavio. *El laberinto de soledad: Postdata, vuelta a el laberinto de la soledad.* Mexico City: Fondo de Cultura Económica, 1993.
Peña, Richard. *"How Tasty Was My Little Frenchman."* In *Brazilian Cinema,* ed. Randal Johnson and Robert Stam, 191–99. New York: Columbia University Press, 1995.
Pepetela. *Mayombe.* São Paulo: Editora Ática, 1982.
Pereira, Carlos de Assis. *Fontes do Caramuru de Santa Rita Durão.* São Paulo: Emprêsa Gráfica da Revista dos Tribunais, 1971.
Rama, Angel. *La ciudad letrada.* Hanover, N.H.: Ediciones del Norte, 1984.
———. *La crítica de la cultura en América Latina.* Ed. Saúl Sosnowski and Tomás Eloy Martínez. Barcelona: Biblioteca Ayacucho, 1985.
———. *Transculturación narrativa en América Latina.* Mexico City: Siglo XXI Editores, 1982.
Ramos, José Mário Ortiz. *Cinema, estado e lutas culturais (anos 50, 60, 70).* Rio de Janeiro: Paz e Terra, 1983.
Ramos, Julio. *Desencuentros de la modernidad en América Latina: Literatura y política en el siglo XIX.* Mexico City: Fondo de Cultura Económica, 1989.
Rémusat, Charles. *L'habitation de Saint Domingue; ou, L'insurrection.* Ed. J. R. Derré. Paris: CNRS, 1977.
Renan, Ernest. *Caliban, suite de la tempête.* Ed. Colin Smith. Manchester: Manchester University Press, 1954.
———. *Qu'est-ce qu'une nation? Et autres essays politiques.* Ed. Joël Roman. Paris: Presses Pocket, 1992.
Ricardo, Cassiano. *22 e a poesia de hoje.* N.p.: Ministério da Educação e Cultura, 1964.
———. *Invenção de Orfeu (e outros pequenos estudos sobre poesia).* São Paulo: Conselho Estadual de Cultura, 1974.
———. *Marcha para Oeste (A influência da 'Bandeira' na formação política do Brasil).* 2 vols. Rio de Janeiro: Livraria José Olympio Editora, 1970.
———. *"Martim Cererê:* Biografia e documentário do livro." In *Cassiano Ricardo,* ed. Sonia Brayner, 99–106. Brasília: Civilização Brasileira, 1979.
———. *Poesias completas.* Rio de Janeiro: Livraria José Olympio Editora, 1957.
Richard, Nelly. "Cultural Peripheries: Latin America and Postmodernist Decentering." In *The Postmodernism Debate in Latin America,* ed. John Beverley, Michael Arona, and José Oviedo. Durham, N.C.: Duke University Press, 1995.

Rimbaud, Arthur. *Collected Poems*. Ed. and trans. Oliver Bernard. London: Penguin Books, 1962.

———. *Oeuvres complètes*. Ed. Pierre Brunel. Varese, Italy: Librarie Générale Française, 1999.

Rincón, Carlos. "The Peripheral Center of Postmodernism: On Borges, García Márquez and Alterity." In *The Postmodernism Debate in Latin America*, ed. John Beverley, Michael Arona, and José Oviedo. Durham, N.C.: Duke University Press, 1995.

Rivera, José Eustacio. *La vorágine*. Santiago: Editora Zig-Zag, 1953.

Rocha, Glauber. *Revisão crítica do cinema brasileiro*. Rio de Janeiro: Editora Civilizacão Brasileira, 1963.

Rousseau, Jean-Jacques. *On the Origin of Language*. Trans. John H. Moran and Alexander Gode. Chicago: University of Chicago Press, 1986.

———. *The Social Contract and Discourses*. Trans. G. D. H. Cole. Ed. J. H. Brumfitt and John C. Hall. London: Dent, 1973.

Sadlier, Darlene J. *Nelson Pereira dos Santos*. Urbana: University of Illinois Press, 2003.

Said, Edward W. *Culture and Imperialism*. New York: Vintage Books, 1994.

Saint-Hilaire, Auguste. *Viagem à província de São Paulo*. Trans. Regina Regis Junqueira. Ed. Mário Guimarães Ferri. São Paulo: Editora da Universidade de São Paulo, 1976.

Salgado, Plínio. *Despertemos a nação!* Rio de Janeiro: Livraria José Olympio Editora, 1935.

———. "A Língua Tupy." *Revista de Antropofagia* 1, no. 1 (May 1928). Reprint, São Paulo: Companhia Lithographica Ypiranga, 1976.

Salgado, Plínio. "O Significado da Anta." *Festa*, Jan. 1, 1928. Reprint, *Brasil: 1E Tempo Modernista—1917/29 (documentação)*, ed. Marta Rossetti Batista, Telê Ancona Lopez, and Yone Soares de Lima. São Paulo: Instituto de Estudos Brasileiros, 1972.

Salgado, Plínio, Paulo Menotti del Picchia, and Cassiano Ricardo. "Nhengaçú verde amarelo (Manifesto do verde-amarelismo ou da Escola da Anta)." In *Vanguarda Européia e Modernismo Brasileiro (Apresentação crítica dos principais manifestos, prefácios e conferências vanguardistas, de 1857 até hoje)*, ed. Gilberto Mendonça Teles, 233–39. Petrópolis, Brazil: Editora Vozes, 1972.

Santos, Nelson Pereira dos. *Como era gostoso o meu francês* (How Tasty Was My Little Frenchman). Nelson Pereira dos Santos, K. C. Eckstein, L. C. Barreto Produções Cinematográficas, César Thedim, 1972.

Sartre, Jean-Paul. "L'orphée noir." *Anthologie de la nouvelle poésie nègre et malagache de langue française*. Paris: Presses Universitaires de France, 1948.

———. *Réflexions sur la question juive*. Paris: Gallimard, 1954. Schiller, Friedrich. *On the Aesthetic Education of Man, in a series of Letters*. Trans. Reginald Snell. New Haven, Conn.: Yale University Press, 1954.

Schwartz, Jorge, ed. *Vanguardas Latino-Americanas: Polêmicas, manifestos e textos críticos*. São Paulo: Iluminuras, 1995.

Schwarz, Roberto. *A Master on the Periphery of Capitalism*. Trans. John Gledson. Durham, N.C.: Duke University Press, 2001.

———. *Misplaced Ideas: Essays on Brazilian Culture*. Ed. and trans. John Gledson. London: Verso, 1992.

Sembène, Ousmane. *The Money-Order, with White Genesis*. Trans. Clive Wake. London: Heinemann, 1972.

Senghor, Léopold Sédar. *Les fondements de l'africanité; ou, Négritude et arabité*. Paris: Présence Africaine, 1967.

———. *La poésie de l'action: Conversations avec Mohamed Aziza*. Paris: Stock, 1980.

———. *Prose and Poetry*. Ed. and trans. John Reed and Clive Wake. London: Heinemann, 1976.

Shattuck, Roger. *The Banquet Years: The Origins of the Avant-Garde in France, 1885 to World War I*. New York: Vintage Books, 1955. Rev. ed., 1968.

Shaw, George Bernard. *Saint Joan: A Chronicle Play in Six Scenes and an Epilogue*. New York: Penguin Classics, 1946.

Sommer, Doris. *Foundational Fictions: The National Romances of Latin America*. Berkeley: University of California Press, 1993.

Soyinka, Wole. *Collected Plays*. 2 vols. London, New York: Oxford University Press, 1973.

———. *Myth, Literature, and the African World*. Cambridge: Cambridge University Press, 1978.

Spivak, Gayatri Chakravorty. *Critique of Postcolonial Reason: Toward a History of the Vanishing Present*. Cambridge, Mass.: Harvard University Press, 1999.

———. *Outside in the Teaching Machine*. New York: Routledge, 1993.

Staden, Hans. *Zwei Reisen nach Brasilien, 1548–1555*. Ed. Karl Fouquet. Marburg an der Lahn: Trautvetter & Fisher, 1963.

Stephanson, Anders. "Regarding Postmodernism—A Conversation with Fredric Jameson." In *Universal Abandon? The Politics of Postmodernism*, ed. Andrew Ross, 3–30. Minneapolis: University of Minneapolis Press, 1988.

Thevet, André. *Les français en Amérique pendant la deuxième moitié du XVIe siècle: Le Brésil et les Brésiliens*. Ed. Suzanne Lussagnet. Paris: Presses Universitaires de France, 1953.

Todorov, Tzvetan. *The Fantastic: A Structural Approach to a Literary Genre*. Trans. Richard Howard. Foreword by Robert Scholes. Ithaca, N.Y.: Cornell University Press, 1975.

Towa, Marcien. *Essai sur la problématique philosophique dans l'Afrique actuelle*. Yaoundé, Cameroun: Editions CLE, 1971.

———. *Léopold Sédar Senghor: Négritude ou servitude?* Yaoundé, Cameroun: Editions CLE, 1971.

Tucker, Robert C., ed. *The Marx-Engels Reader*. New York: W. W. Norton, 1978.

Vasconcelos, José. *La raza cósmica: Misión de la raza iberoamericana*. México City: Asociación Nacional de Libreros, 1983.
Vespucci, Amerigo. *Letters from a New World*. Trans. David Jacobson. Ed. Luciano Formisano. New York: Marsilio, 1992.
Weiss, Peter. *The Persecution and Assassination of Jean-Paul Marat as Performed by the Inmates of the Asylum of Charenton under the Direction of the Marquis de Sade*. Trans. Geoffrey Skelton. New York: Atheneum, 1966.
———. *Die Verfolgung und Ermordung Jean Paul Marats, dargestellt durch die Schauspielgruppe des Hospizes zu Charenton unter Anteitung des Herrn de Sade: Drama in 2 Akten*. Frankfurt a. M.: Suhrkamp, 1967.
White, Erdmute Wenzel. *Les années vingt au Brésil: Le modernisme et l'avant-garde internationale*. Paris: Éditions Hispaniques, 1972.
Williams, Raymond. *The Country and the City*. New York: Oxford University Press, 1973.
———. *The Politics of Modernism: Against the New Conformists*. Ed. Tony Pinkney. London: Verso, 1989.
Xavier, Ismail. *Alegorias do subdesenvolvimento: Cinema novo, tropicalismo, cinema marginal*. São Paulo: Editora Brasiliense, 1993.

Index

Abu-Lughod, Janet, *Before European Hegemony,* 141
Academia Brasileira de Letras, 25
Adorno, Theodor, *Dialectic of Enlightenment* (with Horkheimer), 151, 168, 186
Adotevi, Stanislas, *Négritude et négrologues,* 158, 162
Ahmad, Aijaz, *In Theory,* 7
Alencar, José, 35, 59, 219n13, 219n15, 223n7; *Iracema,* 59, 219n13, 223n7; *O Guarani,* 35, 219n15
Alonso, Carlos, 3, 4–5, 47; *The Burden of Modernity,* 3, 5, 47, 175
Althusser, Louis, *Reading Capital* (with Balibar), 42
Álvares, Diogo, 224n9
Amaral, Tarsila do, 21, 22
Amazon, the, 14, 15, 29, 52–58, 69, 71, 75, 82–84, 102, 119
Anchieta, Father José de, 65, 73, 74, 228n5
Anderson, Benedict, 136; *Imagined Communities,* 137
Anderson, Perry, 2, 26, 36, 41, 42, 45, 47; "Modernity and Revolution," 2, 45, 47, 198, 218n6
Andrade, Joaquim Pedro de, 16–17, 111–13, 122; "Cannibalism and Self-Cannibalism," 117, 123; "Criticism and Self-Criticism," 122; *Macunaíma,* 16–17, 111–22, 130
Andrade, Mário de, 15, 24, 25, 26, 28, 34, 52, 85–110, 113, 116, 122, 129, 222n31, 223n2; *Ensaio sôbre a música brasileira,* 88, 91; *Macunaíma,* 15–16, 34, 52, 85–110, 111, 116, 118, 119, 121, 122, 190, 223n2; "O Movimento Modernista," 24, 25, 26, 27–28, 122, 222n31; "Oswald de Andrade," 28
Andrade, Oswald de, 1, 13, 14, 21, 23–24, 27, 29, 34–44, 52, 53, 57, 60, 63, 71, 73, 78, 79, 87, 112–13, 114, 119, 135, 172, 191, 197, 214, 222n32, 224n8, 224n12; "A crise da filosofia messiânica," 36–38, 119, 222n31; *Dentes de Dragão,* 221n30; *Dicionário de Bolso,* 221n30; *Estética e política,* 27–28, 35, 38, 39, 41, 43, 52, 60, 62, 114, 128, 135, 197, 222n31, 224n8; "Manifesto antropófago," 1, 13, 22, 35–38, 42, 43, 50, 52, 72, 73–74, 91, 118, 120, 123, 126, 127, 135, 221n28; "Manifesto da poesia pau-brasil," 27, 28, 57, 69, 223n5; *Marco Zero,* 71n20; *Poesia Pau-Brasil,* 27–28, 29, 43, 88; *Ponta de Lança,* 71, 222n31
Anta school, 30, 91
Anthropophagy. See *antropofagia*
antropofagia, 13, 14, 16–17, 18, 21–23, 24, 26, 33, 34–51, 52, 56–57, 72, 73, 74, 75, 87, 91–92, 93, 95, 112–13, 114, 118, 121, 126, 127–28, 129, 139, 146, 149, 162, 182, 188, 191, 207, 215
Appiah, Kwame Anthony, *In My Father's House,* 8
Appolinaire, "Zone," 26
Aranha, Graça, 25
Arawak, 31
Arco e Flexa, 72–73
Aristotle, 101
Athayde, Tristão de, 87–88, 104
avant-garde, 42, 45, 122; in America, 2; in Brazil, 25, 28, 119, 214, 215; in the Caribbean, 6, 214, 215; in Europe, 25

Averbuck, Lígia, 53, 57, 84; *Cobra Norato e a Revolução Caraíba*, 53

Bakhtin, Mikhail, 113
Balibar, Etienne, 42
Bandeira, Manuel, 226n2
bandeirantes, 15, 31–32, 61–71, 76–77, 79, 98, 99, 102, 119
Barthes, Roland, 88
Bary, Leslie, 220n18
Behn, Aphra, 199
Bell, Madison Smartt, *All Souls' Rising*, 180
Benítez Rojo, Antonio, *The Repeating Island* (*La isla que se repite*), 2
Benjamin, Walter, 220n18; *Illuminations*, 109
Berman, Marshall, *All That Is Solid Melts into Air*, 2, 44
Bernardet, Jean-Claude, *Trajetória crítica*, 123
Bhabha, Homi, 2, 8, 9, 11, 12, 50, 107–10, 185; *Location of Culture* (Bhabha), 2, 8, 11, 50, 107–10, 185
Blaut, J. M., *The Colonizer's Model of the World*, 228n1
Boal, Augusto, *Theater of the Oppressed*, 123
Bopp, Raul, 14, 15, 18, 22, 23, 29, 30, 34, 43, 52–61, 68–69, 105, 119, 222n31; 'Bopp passado a limpo,' 225n17; *Cobra Norato*, 14, 15, 52–61, 66, 68–69, 71–76, 80–81, 84–85, 99, 102, 117, 169; *Movimentos modernistas no Brasil*, 22, 34, 43, 52, 53, 57, 69, 71, 84, 85, 93, 102, 112–13, 222n31, 225n18; *Putirum*, 58, 60–61; *Samburá*, 56, 58, 71; *Vida e Morte da Antropofagia*, 22, 34, 53
Borges, Jorge Luis, 3, 87, 200; *Ficciones*, 87; *Historia universal de la infamia*, 200
Braudel, Fernand, 32, 61, 62, 65, 84; *The Perspective of the World*, 62, 65, 84; *The Structures of Everyday Life*, 32, 61; *The Wheels of Commerce*, 228n1
Brecheret, Victor, 62–63, 77, 102; "Monumento das Bandeiras," 63, 77, 102, 119
Brecht, Bertolt, 92, 116, 117, 123, 128; *Brecht on Theatre*, 128; *Life of Galileo* (*Leben des Galilei*), 188; *Man Equals Man*, 92; *Mother Courage*, 116

Breton, André, *Manifestes du surréalisme*, 53
Buck-Morss, Susan, 133, 135, 138, 200; "Hegel and Haiti," 133–34, 135, 138, 139, 157, 200
Burke, Edmund, *Reflections on the Revolution*, 207

Cabral, Pedro Álvares, 29, 34, 86
Calvin, John, 126
Caminha, Pêro Vaz de, 129
Camões, Luís Vaz de, 59, 60, 64, 66; *Os Lusíadas*, 59, 60, 66, 225n14
Campos, Álvaro de (Fernando Pessoa), "Ode Triunfal," 100
Campos, Haroldo, 88, 222n32; *Morfologia do Macunaíma*, 88, 89, 90, 103; "The Rule of Anthropophagy," 222n32
cannibalism. See *antropofagia*
Cannibal Modernities, 1, 13
Carlos, Roberto, 121
Carlyle, Thomas, 131; *The Nigger Question*, 131
Carpentier, Alejo, 15, 19–20, 31, 43, 65, 81, 139, 188; *El arpa y la lira* (*The Harp and the Shadow*), 197; "The Baroque and the Marvelous Real," 172–73, 176, 183, 186; *Ensayos*, 185; *La guerra del tiempo*, 140; "Marvelous Real in America," 164, 171, 176, 230–31n2; *Los pasos perdidos* (*Lost Steps*), 15, 81–84, 142–43, 153, 179, 183–84, 190, 192; *El reino de este mundo* (*The Kingdom of This World*), 19, 151, 169–170, 176–83, 185, 188–90, 192, 193, 195, 204, 207, 210; "Semejante a la noche," 140–42; *El siglo de las luces* (*Explosion in a Cathedral*), 19–20, 31, 43, 183–84, 191, 192–204, 206–13; *Tientos y diferencias*, 171–72, 173
Castillo-Durante, Daniel, "From Postmodernity to the Rubbish Heap," 4, 37
Cendrars, Blaise, 21, 49
Certeau, Michel de, 28, 39, 40, 129; *Heterologies*, 91, 93, 96; *The Writing of History*, 28, 39, 40, 129
Césaire, Aimé, 5, 6, 17–19, 46, 132–39, 143, 145, 146, 158–59, 162, 186, 214; *Cahier d'un retour au pays natal*, 18, 46, 147–56, 186, 199, 202; *Discourse on Colonialism*, 143–44, 153, 186, 187; *Une saison au Congo*, 152, 190–91;

Une tempête, 67, 186–88; *Toussaint Louverture,* 17, 132–39, 149, 150, 156, 230n14; *La tragédie du roi Christophe,* 18–19, 164–70
Chakrabarty, Dipesh, 217n1 (intro.)
Chanady, Amaryll, "The Territorialization of the Imaginary in Latin America," 172
Christophe, Henri, 18
Cinema Novo, 111–12, 122, 123–25, 227n3
Columbus, Christopher, 29, 34, 93
Communist Party, of Brazil. *See* Partido Comunista do Brasil
Conrad, Joseph, 54, 60, 218n9; *Heart of Darkness,* 60; *Last Essays,* 218n9
Costa, Oswaldo, 25, 34

Dash, J. Michael, 4, 5–6, 81, 135, 139, 147, 153–54, 156, 171, 173, 197, 216, 225n24; *The Other America,* 4, 5–6, 81, 133, 135, 139, 147–48, 153–54, 156, 171, 173, 180, 197, 216, 230n15, 230n17
Davis, Wade, *The Serpent and the Rainbow,* 155
de Man, Paul, 26, 41–42, 47, 90; *Allegories of Reading,* 41; *Blindness and Insight,* 26, 41–42, 90, 175
Depestre, René, *Pour la révolution, pour la poésie,* 159
Derrida, Jacques, 1, 2, 6, 9, 12, 13, 82; *Of Grammatology,* 13, 82, 85, 94, 95, 184; "Signature Event Context," 1; *Specters of Marx,* 9; *Writing and Difference* (Derrida), 2, 145–46
Desiderio, Monsù, 202
de Toro, Alfonso, "The Epistemological Foundations of the Contemporary Condition," 3
Diário de São Paulo, 22
Dickens, Charles, *A Tale of Two Cities,* 207
Dirlik, Arlif, 8, 9, 12; "The Postcolonial Aura," 8, 9
D'Ors, Eugene, 172
Du Bois, W. E. B., 136
Durão, José de Santa Rita, 59; *O Caramurú,* 59–60, 62, 129

Eliot, T. S., 148
Ellis, Alfredo, 61, 62, 65, 66, 67, 68, 105; *A Madrugada Paulista,* 61, 73; *Raça de Gigantes,* 61, 66, 68, 105, 106

Eshleman, Clayton, 155
Euripides, 177

Fanon, Frantz, 46, 135, 136, 158, 186; *Les damnés de la terre* (*The Wretched of the Earth*), 46, 134, 135, 153, 159, 229n9; *Peau noire, masques blancs* (*Black Skin, White Masks*), 156–57, 159, 201, 230n18
Faulkner, William, 34; *Absalom! Absalom!* 180; *Go Down, Moses,* 34
Fernández Retámar, Roberto, 1, 5, 172; *Calibán,* 1, 174
Flaubert, Gustave, 95; *Trois contes,* 95–96
Foucault, Michel, 83, 143; *The Archaeology of Knowledge,* 144; *The History of Sexuality,* 145; *The Order of Things,* 83, 143, 173
Franco, Jean, 25, 26, 28, 52, 53, 56, 70, 81; *The Modern Culture of Latin America,* 25, 26, 28, 52, 56, 70, 81, 110, 227n10
Freire, Paulo, 23; *Pedagogy of Hope,* 23
Freud, Sigmund, 36–37, 38, 84; *The Ego and the Id,* 84; *The Interpretation of Dreams,* 84; *Totem and Taboo,* 37
Freyre, Gilberto, 59; *Casa Grande e Senzala,* 59, 62
Frobenius, Leo, 160
Fuentes, Carlos, 55
futurism, 23, 24, 100, 217–18n4, 218n10, 220n22

Gallegos, Rómulo, 14, 54–55, 56, 66; *Canaima,* 14, 54–55, 56, 102; *Doña Bárbara,* 54, 56, 66
Galvão, Patrícia, 24, 221n29
Gama, José Basílio, *O Uruguay,* 223n6
García Canclini, Nestor, *Hybrid Cultures,* 3, 50, 175–76
García Márquez, Gabriel, 74; *Cien años de soledad* (*One Hundred Years of Solitude*), 169; *La Hojarasca* (*Leafstorm*), 75, 169, 203; *El Otoño del patriarca* (*Autumn of the Patriarch*), 120, 164, 166
Genovese, Eugene, *From Rebellion to Revolution,* 139
Gilroy, Paul, 3, 13, 17, 50, 136, 144, 146, 163; *The Black Atlantic,* 3, 13, 17, 50, 136, 144, 151, 206

Glissant, Édouard, 4, 5, 6, 19, 46, 47–48, 131, 134–35, 136, 144, 149, 165, 230n16; *Caribbean Discourse (Le discours antillais)*, 4, 6, 46, 131, 134–35, 140, 176, 184, 201, 204, 205–6; *Monsieur Toussaint*, 149, 163, 204–5; *Poetics of Relation*, 4, 5, 48, 144, 176, 192; *Le quatrième siècle (The Fourth Century)*, 204
Goebbels, Josef, 168
González Echevarría, Roberto, 54, 56, 81, 94, 140, 142–43, 171, 172, 175, 176–77, 179, 183, 192, 225n23; *Alejo Carpentier*, 81–82, 83, 140, 142–43, 171, 172, 176–77, 192–93, 196, 198, 203, 206, 207–8, 209, 210, 212; *Myth and Archive*, 143; *The Voice of the Masters*, 54, 56
Goya, Francisco de, 196, 211; *Los desastres de la guerra*, 196, 212–13
Guerra, Ruy, 124; *Os Cafajestes*, 227n3; "Popular Cinema and the State," 111, 124

Habitation de Saint Domingue, L' (Rémusat), 133
Hall, Stuart, "Cultural Identity and Diaspora," 178
Handley, George, 196; *Postslavery Narratives in the Americas*, 192–93, 196, 232n2
Harris, Wilson, 19, 184, 185, 189; *The Carnival Trilogy*, 184, 191; *The Guyana Quartet*, 191; *Infinite Rehearsal*, 191; *Palace of the Peacock*, 191
Hegel, G. W. F., 7, 14, 36, 43, 132, 142, 144, 174, 187, 188, 189; concept of history, 17, 19, 42, 50; dialectic, or *Aufhebung*, 36, 57, 92, 95, 109, 118, 144, 149, 162, 188, 191; master-slave allegory, 7, 150, 157, 158; *The Phenomenology of Mind*, 150, 152, 157, 189, 190; *The Philosophy of History*, 43, 137–38, 139, 158, 160, 166, 167; *The Philosophy of Mind*, 43, 139, 149, 157, 165, 188, 229n8; *The Philosophy of Right*, 166; subjectivity, 10–11, 157–58, 183
Heidegger, Martin, 100; *The Question Concerning Technology*, 100, 101, 227n9
Hobsbawm, Eric, *The Age of Revolution*, 209

Homem do Povo, 24, 221n29
Horkheimer, Max, *Dialectic of Enlightenment* (with Adorno), 151, 168, 186
Howards End (Forster), 76
"How Tasty Was My Little Frenchman" (Peña), 126
Hugo, Victor, 138; *Bug-Jargal*, 133, 138; *Quatrevingt-treize*, 206, 207
Hulme, Peter, 31, 186–87, 220n18; *Colonial Encounters*, 31, 186–87

Integralista movement, 30

Jakobson, Roman, 89
James, C. L. R., 17–18, 38, 46, 132–39, 145, 146, 148, 162, 192, 214; *The Black Jacobins*, 17, 131, 132–39, 150, 151, 158, 162–63, 166, 168, 229nn11–12, 230n14; *The Future in the Present*, 132
Jameson, Fredric, 7, 9–11, 12, 48–49, 76, 114; "Beyond the Cave," 48; "Modernism and Imperialism," 49, 76, 90–91; "Modernism and Its Repressed," 48; *Postmodernism*, 7, 8, 9–11, 114, 170; "Third World Literature in the Era of Multinational Capitalism," 7–8
Jarry, Alfred, 89, 99, 116; *Ubu*, 116, 231n8
Jodelle, Étienne, 126–27, 128

Kadir, Djelal, 173; *The Other Writing*, 175; *Questing Fictions*, 173–75
Kant, Immanuel, 56, 96–97, 98, 189; *Critique of Judgment*, 56; *Critique of Practical Reason*, 96–97; *On History*, 168, 169, 189, 210, 211
Kleist, Heinrich von, "The Betrothal in San Domingo," 133
Koch-Grünberg, Theodor, 86, 87, 106, 226n7; *Vom Roraima zum Orinoco*, 87
Kubitschek, Juscelino, 69

Laclau, Ernesto, 108
Lamartine, Alphonse de, *Toussaint Louverture*, 137
Lamming, George: *Natives of My Person*, 197–98; *The Pleasures of Exile*, 137
Laroche, Maximilien, "Haitian Postmodernisms," 133, 163
Larsen, Neil, "Postmodernism and Imperialism," 9
Las Casas, Bartolomé de, 200

Index

Leite Criôlo, 68, 70
Lenin, Vladimir, *What Is to Be Done?* 211
Léry, Jean de, 28, 221n27, 227n2; *Histoire d'un voyage fait en la terre du Brésil*, 28, 125, 221n27, 228n5
Lévi-Strauss, Claude, 21, 31, 45, 78, 82; *Tristes Tropiques*, 21, 31, 45, 78, 111
Lima, Jorge, 224n8
Lobato, Monteiro, 71, 101; *Urupês*, 71, 101, 102
Lopes de Sousa, Pêro, *Diário da Navegação*, 224n9
López de Gómara, Francisco, *Historia General de las Indias*, 221n27
Louverture, Toussaint, 17, 18, 131, 132–39, 149, 150, 151, 156, 158, 162–63, 166, 168, 178, 181, 182–83, 205
Luso-Brazilian studies, 14
Lyotard, Jean-François, 48, 49, 57, 102–3, 106, 109, 110; *The Differend*, 102–3, 109, 210; *The Inhuman*, 85, 100, 145, 146; *Instructions païennes*, 94, 96; *Just Gaming*, 106; *The Postmodern Condition*, 57; *The Postmodern Explained*, 49; *Rudiments païens*, 94, 96, 125; "The Sign of History," 211

Machado de Assis, Joaquim, 1, 6, 50; *Posthumous Memoirs of Brás Cubas* (*Memórias póstumas de Brás Cubas*), 1
Macherey, Pierre, 48, 49, 91; *Pour une théorie de la production littéraire*, 48, 91
Mackandal, 176, 177–79, 180, 231n8
Magalhães de Gândavo, Pêro, *Historia da prouíncia de Sacta Cruz*, 225n15, 228n5
Mallarmé, Stéphane, 89–90, 94
Marinetti, F. T., 217–18n4, 219n11, 220n22
Martí, José, 172
Marx, Karl, 12, 36, 38, 44, 47, 141; *A Contribution to the Critique of Political Economy*, 38; *The Eighteenth Brumaire of Louis Napoleon*, 12, 47; *The German Ideology*, 141
Marxism, 8, 9, 11, 121
Mehlman, Jeffrey, *Revolution and Repetition*, 144
Menotti del Picchia, Paulo, 24, 29, 55, 63, 64, 67, 72, 219n15, 219–20n16, 224n8; *Juca Mulato*, 67–68; *A Longa Viagem*, 224–25n13; *O Gedeão do Modernismo*, 24, 63, 66, 219n15, 219–20n16, 224n8;

República dos Estados Unidos do Brasil, 29, 55, 64, 68, 70–71, 73, 88, 98, 99–100, 102, 104, 105, 121
Meyer, Augusto, 87, 88, 91, 102
Miceli, Sergio, *Imagens Negociadas*, 226n6
Miller, Christopher, *Theories of Africans*, 145, 162
modernism, 22, 23, 44–50; in Brazil, 4, 5, 14–16, 18, 21, 22–35, 40, 44, 52, 55, 56, 67–68, 72, 79, 82, 86–87, 88, 91, 95, 96, 98, 101, 102, 112, 115, 118, 119, 121, 122–23, 128, 130, 153, 171, 215, 216; in the Caribbean, 4, 5; in Europe, 13, 25; in Latin America, 13, 25; "peripheral," 1, 6, 23; poetics of, 6; nonwestern, 2
modernismo. *See* modernity: discourses of, in Brazil
modernity: discourses of, 2, 11, 18, 23, 44–50, 78, 110, 162; —, in Brazil, 11, 15, 16, 80, 111, 112, 115, 136, 142, 144, 146, 165, 168, 169, 173, 192, 205, 215, 216; —, in the Caribbean, 11, 17, 136, 137; critiques of, 17, 18, 162; —, as *grand récit*, 2, 11, 18, 23; history of, 3, 13, 50; —, in Latin America, 3, 4, 5, 216; —, in the west, 1, 134, 139, 143
modernization: in Brazil, 11, 14, 15, 16, 24, 85, 111, 123; in the Caribbean, 19, 169; in Latin America, 19; unequal, 2
Montaigne, Michel, 41, 91, 93, 96, 125
Moraes, Raimundo, 87
More, Thomas, 41
Mouffe, Chantal, 108, 146
Mudimbe, V. Y., *The Idea of Africa*, 132

négritude, 6, 18, 156–62, 215, 229n11
"Nhengaçú Verde Amarelo" (Salgado et al.), 30, 32, 33, 63–64, 65, 91, 104
Nietzsche, Friedrich, 26, 33, 34, 35–36, 38, 39, 41, 107, 188; *Beyond Good and Evil*, 35, 38, 39, 97–98; *The Birth of Tragedy*, 32–33, 38; *On the Genealogy of Morals*, 38, 180, 190; "On the Uses and Disadvantages of History," 26, 107; *Will to Power*, 33, 34, 35–36, 39, 96, 98
Niger, Paul, 229n6
Nóbrega, António, 228n5
Nunes, Benedito, 36

Ogan, Bernd, "Faszination und Gewalt," 168

254 Index

Orfeu, 100
Ortiz, Fernando, 2; *Contrapunteo cubano del tabaco y azúcar,* 3
Ortiz, Renato, 29, 44, 45, 46, 47; *A moderna cultura brasileira,* 29, 44, 45, 46, 115, 122

Palmares, 227n11
Parry, Benita, "Resistance Theory/Theorising Resistance," 229n11
Partido Comunista do Brasil, 24, 220n19
Passarinho, Jarbas, 124
Paz, Octavio, 15, 45, 78, 81, 115, 168; *El laberinto de soledad,* 45, 46, 78, 81
Pepetela, 177–78; *Mayombe,* 178
Pereira, Carlos de Assis, *Fontes do Caramuru,* 224n9
Plato, 22, 35, 168; *Ion,* 86
Plume, La, 99
Politics (Aristotle), 101
Portinari, 226n6
postcoloniality, 3, 8, 9, 17, 146, 162; as agency, 7; Brazilian experience of, 7, 214; and Latin America, 7, 12
postcolonial studies, 7, 8, 11, 12, 14
postmodernism, 9–11, 49, 125, 162, 214, 215; as aesthetic, 9; as condition, 8, 108; as epoch, 3, 5, 50; in the "periphery," 4–5; poetics of, 6, 50; subjectivity, 8
poststructuralism, 8
Prado, Paulo, 27

Rama, Angel, 2, 23, 25, 26, 33, 64; *La ciudad letrada,* 26; *La crítica de la Cultura en América Latina,* 3; *Transculturación narrativa en América Latina,* 3, 25, 33
Ramalho, João, 73
Ramos, José Ortiz, 124; *Cinema, estado e lutas,* 112, 116, 123, 124, 125
Ramos, Julio, *Desencuentros de la modernidad,* 2
Renan, Ernest, 107; *Caliban,* 187, 188; *Qu'est-ce qu'une nation?* 107; *Reforme intellectuelle et morale,* 187
Revista de antropofagia, 22, 25, 34, 35, 36, 52, 224n8
Ricardo, Cassiano, 14, 15, 18, 29, 59, 61, 62, 63–68, 70, 71, 72, 74, 100, 104, 105–6, 222n31, 223n2; *22 e a poesia de hoje,* 63, 70, 73; *Invenção de Orfeu,* 222n31; *Marcha para Oeste,* 59, 61, 62, 64, 66, 67, 68, 69–70, 74, 76, 77, 78, 104, 105–6, 119; *Martim Cererê,* 14, 15, 29–30, 62, 63–68, 70, 73, 76–81, 88, 99, 103, 104, 169, 223n2
Richard, Nelly, "Cultural Peripheries," 4
Rimbaud, Arthur, 25, 26, 90; *Illuminations,* 25, 26–27
Rincón, Carlos, "The Peripheral Center of Postmodernism," 3
Rivera, José Eustacio, *La Vorágine,* 14, 54
Rocha, Glauber, 121, 123, 128; *Revisão crítica do cinema brasileiro,* 123, 125
Rousseau, Jean-Jacques, 179, 199–200; *On the Origin of Language,* 179; *The Social Contract,* 179, 199

Sá, Mem de, 129, 228n5
Sadlier, Darlene, 227n2; *Nelson Pereira dos Santos,* 227nn1–2
Said, Edward, *Culture and Imperialism,* 132, 163
Saint-Hilaire, Auguste, 61, 66, 224n12
Salgado, Plínio, 30, 31, 32–33, 64; *Despertemos a Nação!* 30, 31, 32–33, 91, 95, 104
Santos, Nelson Pereira dos, 16–17, 125; *Como era gostoso o meu francês,* 16–17, 125–30
Sartre, Jean-Paul, 158; "L'Orphée noir," 156; *Réflexions sur la question juive,* 157
Schiller, Friedrich, *On the Aesthetic Education of Man,* 166
Schwartz, Jorge, 23, 24, 25, 26, 30, 68; *Vanguardas Latino-Americanas,* 23, 24, 25, 26, 30, 68, 71, 72
Schwarz, Roberto, 6, 23, 44, 47, 50, 112, 222n31; *A Master on the Periphery of Capitalism,* 6, 50; *Misplaced Ideas,* 23, 44, 122, 222n31
Segall, Lasar, 226n6
Semana de Arte Moderna, 23, 25
Sembène, Ousmane, 161–62; *Le dernier de l'empire* (The Last of the Empire), 230n19; *Le mandat* (The Money-Order), 161–62
Senghor, Léopold Sédar, 18, 160, 162, 171; *Les Fondements de l'africanité,* 160; "New York," 160–61; "On the Appeal from the Race of Sheba," 161; *La poésie de l'action,* 160, 161; *Prose and poetry,* 160

Sertões, Os (Cunha), 62
Shakespeare, William, *The Tempest*, 67, 186
Shattuck, Roger, 217n1 (chap. 1)
Shaw, Bernard, *Saint Joan*, 150
Smith, Annette, 155
Sommer, Doris, *Foundational Fictions*, 35, 39, 55, 56, 59
Sousa, Gabriel Soares de, 228n5
Soyinka, Wole, 160, 177, 182; *The Bacchae*, 177, 182; *Myth, Literature, and the African World*, 158, 177, 178, 182
Spivak, Gayatri, 7, 12–13, 50–51; *Critique of Postcolonial Reason*, 7, 12, 13, 50–51, 146, 178; *Outside in the Teaching Machine*, 7, 13, 146
Staden, Hans, 21, 22, 125, 126, 223n3, 228n5
Stephanson, Anders, "Regarding Postmodernism," 8
subaltern, the, 10, 12, 13; and agency, 11; and women, 12

Tapuia, 30, 32, 62, 65
Thevet, André, 40, 125, 129, 223n3, 226n2, 227n2, 228n5
Todorov, Tzvetan, *The Fantastic*, 231n6
Towa, Marcien, 160, 161; *Essai sur la problématique philosophique*, 161; *Léopold Sédar Senghor*, 160, 161
transculturación, 2
transculturation, 2–3, 5, 64

Tupi, 13, 14, 22, 30, 31–33, 35, 39, 43, 54, 62, 63, 65, 91, 93, 104, 127, 129, 130, 149; cosmogony, 29–30, 52, 53, 59, 64, 76, 88, 94, 118, 226–27n7; language, 30, 226n4; migration, 31
Tupinambá, 125, 128
Tupiniquin, 129

Vargas, Getúlio, 24
Vasconcelos, José, 31, 33, 161, 218–19n10, 224n11; *La raza cósmica*, 31, 33, 224n11
Velho, Domingos Jorge, 227n11
verde-amarelismo, 14, 18, 30, 31, 33, 35, 62, 64, 69, 72, 73, 75, 91, 95, 104, 162
Vespucci, Amerigo, 39, 52, 129; *Letters from a New World*, 52, 93
Vieira, António, 36
Villa-Lobos, Heitor, 113, 116, 120
Villegagnon, 126

Walcott, Derek, 5, 6
Weiss, Peter, *Marat/Sade*, 202
White, Erdmute Wenzel, 21; *Les années vingt au Brésil*, 21
Williams, Raymond, 24, 25, 26, 34, 41, 44, 45, 46, 47; *The Country and the City*, 45, 46; *The Politics of Modernism*, 24, 25, 26, 34, 42, 44–45, 47, 74

Xavier, Ismail, *Alegorias do subdesenvolvimento*, 112, 116, 120, 124

NEW WORLD STUDIES

Vera M. Kutzinski, *Sugar's Secrets: Race and the Erotics of Cuban Nationalism*

Richard D. E. Burton and Fred Reno, editors, *French and West Indian: Martinique, Guadeloupe, and French Guiana Today*

A. James Arnold, editor, *Monsters, Tricksters, and Sacred Cows: Animal Tales and American Identities*

J. Michael Dash, *The Other America: Caribbean Literature in a New World Context*

Isabel Alvarez Borland, *Cuban-American Literature of Exile: From Person to Persona*

Belinda J. Edmondson, editor, *Caribbean Romances: The Politics of Regional Representation*

Steven V. Hunsaker, *Autobiography and National Identity in the Americas*

Celia M. Britton, *Edouard Glissant and Postcolonial Theory: Strategies of Language and Resistance*

Mary Peabody Mann, *Juanita: A Romance of Real Life in Cuba Fifty Years Ago*, Edited and with an introduction by Patricia M. Ard

George B. Handley, *Postslavery Literatures in the Americas: Family Portraits in Black and White*

Faith Smith, *Creole Recitations: John Jacob Thomas and Colonial Formation in the Late Nineteenth-Century Caribbean*

Ian Gregory Strachan, *Paradise and Plantation: Tourism and Culture in the Anglophone Caribbean*

Nick Nesbitt, *Voicing Memory: History and Subjectivity in French Caribbean Literature*

Charles W. Pollard, *New World Modernisms: T. S. Eliot, Derek Walcott, and Kamau Brathwaite*

Carine M. Mardorossian, *Reclaiming Difference: Caribbean Women Rewrite Postcolonialism*

Luís Madureira, *Cannibal Modernities: Postcoloniality and the Avant-garde in Caribbean and Brazilian Literature*